All of Me

All of Me

My Extraordinary Life

BARBARA WINDSOR

and Robin McGibbon

HEADLINE

First published in 2000
by HEADLINE BOOK PUBLISHING

10 9 8 7 6 5 4 3 2 1

British Library Cataloguing in Publication Data

Windsor, Barbara, 1937–
   All of me: my extraordinary life
   1. Windsor, Barbara, 1937– 2. Television actors and actresses
   – Great Britain – Biography 3. Motion picture actors and
   actresses – Great Britain – Biography
   I. Title
   791.4′5′028′092

ISBN 0 7472 7007 4

Typeset by Palimpsest Book Production Limited,
Polmont, Stirlingshire

Printed and bound in Great Britain by
Clays Ltd, St Ives plc

HEADLINE BOOK PUBLISHING
A division of Hodder Headline
338 Euston Road
London NW1 3BH

www.headline.co.uk
www.hodderheadline.com

To Mummy, whose love I now feel is always with me

To Scott, whose love I know is always with me

And to the Great British Public, whose love has always kept me going

Acknowledgements

To write about a lifetime and a career which spans over fifty years involves much memory-searching. It would be impossible to list everyone who has helped me. They know who they are and how much I appreciate their support. Many of them are part of my life story and are therefore mentioned in the book but in addition there are the theatres, the archivists, the press, the television and other media companies who have provided confirmation of facts concerning my professional life – to each and every one I offer a genuine, heartfelt thank you. Finally, special thanks go to everyone at my publishers Headline, who have been wonderfully encouraging and supportive throughout the writing of this book.

It is 19 July 2000 and here I am, Barbara Ann Deeks, in a chauffeur-driven limousine on my way to Buckingham Palace to collect my MBE from the Queen. Never in my wildest dreams did I think that this day would come. My only wish is that my mother could have been here with me, but I'm sure she's watching somewhere. In this extraordinary, topsy-turvy life of mine it seems incredible that I have reached this pinnacle in my career; not only will I be meeting Her Majesty this morning, but in the afternoon I will be representing my country in a parade in honour of the Queen Mother's 100th birthday. It is all so far removed from my childhood in the East End of London and I can't help thinking back to the early days when it all began ...

Barbara x

1

As a kid, I longed to be on the sunny side of the street; it sounded a great place, because my daddy was always so happy when he was singing about it. But I never found my way there until I discovered that performing could chase the gloom away and give me something to smile about.

Our home in north London was filled with tension and I was caught between two parents who didn't love each other. My father, John Deeks, was a good-looking, fair-haired, happy-go-lucky cockney who had come back from the war in 1945 with a smile and a whistle but little ambition. My mother, born Rose Ellis, was petite, with a cute figure and thick, auburn hair. She wanted more than she had and worked hard to try to get it. Daddy was keen to make the best of everything; Mummy was quick to find fault, and nothing ever seemed good enough for her.

Rosie had been smitten by John, her second cousin, before the war. Eighteen months her junior, he was a handsome barrow boy with a jack-the-lad personality and cheeky wit. She had married him in 1935, against the wishes of her family, who felt he wasn't the right man for her. The war hardened Mummy and, in the austere aftermath, I think she realised that she had made a mistake; that she wanted more than good looks, an impish smile and a nice line in patter.

On my own with my dad, I felt warm and safe and wanted, but Mummy was unpredictable, I was never quite sure what to expect. There were times when the three of us got on together, of course there were – like when we went to the pictures or a show in the West End – but, in the main, it was a case of two's company, three's a crowd. Mummy admitted that when I was born, in the London Hospital, Whitechapel, on 6 August 1937, she'd been hoping for a boy, and that she didn't like the fine, fair hair I'd inherited from my father. She would spend hours dressing it with bows or making me little hats to compensate for its lack of body.

She named me Barbara Ann Deeks. Before war was declared in 1939, the three of us lived in Shoreditch, but Mummy always thought she was more north London than East End, and when Daddy was called up, she seized the chance to move in with her mum and dad and other relatives in Stoke Newington. It was from there that, as a five-year-old, I waved goodbye to Daddy as he marched off to war and out of our lives for nearly three years. All the time Mummy and me were together in those wartime years, everything was OK: there was no hint of the frustration and anger that would later mar her enjoyment of life and make mine a misery.

With us in that small house in Yoakley Road were Mummy's sister Dolly and her husband, Charlie Windsor, and son, Kenny, and Uncle Ronnie, Mummy's youngest brother. Auntie Dolly looked after me while Mummy worked as a dressmaker in the West End. She was very strict, but although I was quite a handful I liked that, because I always knew where I was with her.

Although it sounds as if we were packed in like sardines, we were all one big, happy family. As Hitler's Luftwaffe pounded London with wave after wave of attack, many kids were evacuated to East Anglia, the West Country and the north of England, but Mummy resisted sending me away until one of my friends, a little girl called Margaret, was hit by flying shrapnel and killed. Margaret used to sit on a wall waiting for me and Auntie Dolly, who took us to school – St Mary's Infants' round the corner in Lordship Road. One morning we found the wall where Margaret sat reduced to a pile of rubble, and no Margaret. That was enough for my mother: the next thing I knew was leaving Euston for Blackpool with a number pinned to my coat and a warning from Mummy: 'Remember – don't go off with any strange men.'

I was not yet six, and so tiny that I was put at the end of the line as we all waited at Blackpool Station to get on a coach. Suddenly a lady grabbed my hand and put me in a car with a man behind the wheel. I thought it was wonderful, a treat, but, as it turned out, I would have been better off on the coach. All the other kids were allocated homes in which two or more of them stayed together, but somehow I slipped through the net and was taken to a house in Norbreck on my own. The couple who lived there told me they were married, but I sensed something was wrong: Mummy had always told me I was a wily, nosy little girl who earwigged grown-ups' conversations and heard things I shouldn't. I knew my instinct was right when the couple insisted I undressed in front of them and then, when I went to bed, the man came into my room and tried to touch me. I said: 'Mummy said I mustn't be left on my own with a man. You must come in with your wife.' After that I used to push furniture against the door, and when he tried to get in I'd screech and scream and go red in the face like my daddy. Most nights I'd cry myself to sleep, I was so frightened and miserable. I was missing Mummy dreadfully and wrote her three letters begging to be allowed to come home. Rather than revealing my fears, I complained that the planes flew too low over Blackpool and that the people all talked funny. She thought I was just trying to get attention.

God knows what would have happened to me if Mary North, a little girl I made friends with at Norbreck Primary School who lived a few doors away, had not heard me screaming and crying in my bedroom and told her mother. Mrs North alerted the authorities, who discovered that the 'married' couple were really brother and sister and were breaking the law by claiming money for looking after me. The last I saw of them was when they were taken away by the police in a Black Maria.

Luckily for me, Florence North and her husband, Ernest, offered to take me in, and soon the homesickness had vanished and I was enjoying the most wonderful life amid seaside and countryside I had never imagined existed. I still liked playing in the street, though, and must have been a bit of a tearaway, because Auntie Florence was moved to write a letter to Mummy saying she couldn't do anything with me; all I did after school was gobble down my tea as fast as possible and dash out again. Auntie Florence's proposed solution to the problem would nurture a talent no one knew I had, and spark an interest that would govern the course of my life. 'If you agree,' she wrote to Mummy, 'I intend sending Barbara to dancing school with Mary. It will occupy her mind.'

Mummy had no objection, so off I went with Mary to Norbreck Dancing School. At first I wasn't particularly keen on the idea, but once I started, I took to dancing and singing, Auntie Florence told Mummy, 'like a duck to water', and at the end of our first little concert I'd done so well I was chosen to present the dance teacher with a box of chocolates.

I was in Blackpool nearly a year, but sadly, my time there was abruptly cut short, amid something of a scandal. And it was all my doing, I'm sorry to say. One day Auntie Florence picked us up from dancing school, along with another little girl who lived in the opposite direction from our usual route home. As we left her at her house, I ran ahead, just as the headlights of a bus lit up a couple kissing passionately in a bus shelter. I was amazed to see that the man was someone I knew and started laughing. 'Hello, Uncle Ernest,' I said. I turned to Auntie Florence, who had by then caught me up, and said: 'Look, Auntie Florence, there's Uncle Ernest.' I saw the awful look on her face, then looked back to find Uncle Ernest and the woman equally horrified. I knew something was appallingly wrong. When we got home, Mary and I were sent to bed immediately. I was so shocked by the whole thing that as I walked out of the dining room, I fell into a dead faint.

I felt so, so guilty. I blamed myself for causing what was obviously a big upset between Auntie Florence and Uncle Ernest. I was not yet seven, but old enough to know that if I hadn't seen him, or at least hadn't said anything, Auntie Florence would have been none the wiser about his romance. It would not be the last time I'd blame myself for causing a marital rift. In the circumstances Auntie Florence thought it best if I went back to London. The next weekend I arrived at Euston with a note from her for Mummy. I doubt it mentioned the bus-stop kiss, but she did say: 'Barbara is only a little thing, but she means a lot to us.'

Oh, yes, and something else – a comment from the dancing school teacher: 'Barbara is a born show-off who loves to perform.'

I returned from Blackpool, a month before my seventh birthday – just as a mass evacuation of kids from London was underway, prompted by a new German threat: the 'doodlebug', a pilotless, jet-propelled aircraft which flew at low altitude carrying a ton of high explosives and blew up on impact when it ran out of fuel. All the time you could hear the planes you knew you were safe, but the moment the engine cut out, you knew it was going to crash somewhere near. We'd all be in the front room at Yoakley Road and my grandad, Charlie Ellis, would shout: 'Keep going, you bugger, keep going!' We had an Anderson shelter in the garden, but if we didn't have time to get to it, we'd dive under the table. Everyone else was scared witless, but, being too young to appreciate the danger, my cousin Kenny and I found it terribly exciting. We'd just jump on top of everyone else and Mummy would be trying to pull me down to the bottom of the pile of people for safety.

In fact, all in all it was a very happy time. I loved school. In Blackpool, with much smaller class sizes and no bombs to disrupt lessons, the standard had been higher, and back in London I found I was far ahead of my classmates at my new school, Church Street Primary, which made learning all the more enjoyable. And thankfully, Mummy took my new-found love of performing seriously. She made inquiries about dance schools in Stoke Newington and discovered one called Madame Behenna and her Juvenile Jollities, which held classes in the town hall two nights a week. Madame Behenna, a large, plump lady, very grand and very intimidating, enunciated all her instructions in a booming, theatrical voice. She charged 1s 6d for the Monday ballet and character dance class and 1s for the tap class on a Thursday. Mummy told me she would do extra work at the factory to make sure she and Daddy could afford to send me. I looked forward to those Monday and Thursday nights, as much as I looked forward to school.

My joy at being home turned to heartbreak, however, when my dear Auntie Dolly contracted an infection after eating contaminated ice-cream at the Larkswood Swimming Pool and died. Her death cast a terrible, dark shadow over the house, and particularly over Auntie Dolly's sweet husband, Charlie. In line with routine procedure when dealing with such a sudden death, he was called to the police station and interviewed. He came out a changed man. 'It's like they've accused me of killing Dolly,' he said to Mummy. He aged dramatically almost overnight and, tragically, never recovered, eventually ending up in a mental hospital.

In 1945, Mummy and I moved to a prefab in Bouverie Road. What a change! At last I had my own bedroom, and there was a toilet inside the house, not in the garden. Mummy kept telling me that the war was coming to an end and that Daddy would be home soon. I couldn't wait.

That May, everyone was saying that the war *was* over, but my father didn't come home. In the cruel way children do, the other kids, whose fathers were back safe and sound, laughed at me and told me he wouldn't, not ever, because he had been shot and killed by the Germans. I'd inherited Daddy's quick temper and would lash out, yelling: 'No he hasn't, no he hasn't. He *is* coming home.' But spring turned to summer, and then to autumn and winter, and still he didn't appear.

Then, one week before Christmas, I was playing hopscotch outside the prefab when I heard someone coming down the road, whistling, and the metallic click of steel-tipped boots on the pavement. I just knew it was Daddy.

I ran out, leaped into his arms and hugged and kissed him. I couldn't wait to tell everyone, and I was going round knocking on doors, shouting: 'My dad's home, my dad's home!' With the war over for so many months, some of the kids didn't believe me, so later I gave them some of the mint chocolates Daddy had bought overseas, and that convinced them. It meant nothing to me that my dad had been in Egypt with the 8th Army, in one of the last regiments to come home. All that mattered now was that he was safe and well and back with us.

I'd idolised him when he'd gone away in 1943, and I idolised him now. He was everything a little girl could want in a father. He was very attentive, and keen to explain things to me and to help me with my homework. He was strict – he wouldn't let me get away with much – but was fun, too. We giggled a lot together, much to Mummy's annoyance. We had the same raucous laugh and she hated it. She thought it vulgar and, in me, most unladylike. 'What on earth are you two giggling about?' she'd say, and we would try to tell her, but she never got whatever the joke was, and neither did we really, because half the time we didn't know ourselves. It was just an expression of the enviable, indefinable bond some fathers and daughters share. He was always up for larking around, and when some music came on the radio he'd grab me and dance me round the room, singing. He loved cracking jokes, too, and would often slip into the American slang he'd picked up in the army. It couldn't have been easy for him, coming back from the horrors of combat and trying to pick up the pieces of his life, but, with me, at least, he did a brilliant job, instilling in me a zest for life and a sunny outlook, as well as a lot of confidence and self-belief.

With my mother, however, he was something else entirely.

It was all about respect. And I'm afraid Mummy had little for my dad. She wanted him to aim high in life, but he, I'm sure, was just grateful to be home from the war in one piece and didn't really care what he did for a living. He went for interviews at the gas or electricity board, or whatever, but never got anywhere because he would lose his temper with the interviewers. The downside of his personality was a very short fuse, and he could go into one very quickly. He'd come home in a foul mood, and say: 'Some bit of a girl asked me what I'd been doing for the past few years and I told her, "Bloody fighting for the likes of you, that's what."'

Mummy could imagine the scene and would be embarrassed. She'd say: 'You're never going to get a job with that chip on your shoulder.' In the end, she got him one herself, as a trolley-bus conductor. She applied on his behalf, then went to London Transport with some excuse as to why Daddy couldn't be there himself, and they were so desperate for conductors that he got the job without having to see anybody. As an eight-year-old daddy's girl, I thought he looked wonderful in his uniform and I was so proud of him.

That hot temper was always getting Daddy into trouble, and the war, it seemed, was always responsible. Far from heeding the words of his favourite song, 'On the Sunny Side of the Street', and leaving his worries on the doorstep, he would bring them in with him. One day he stormed home from work early, effing and blinding and slamming doors and cupboards, and both Mummy and I knew that something worse than usual had happened. Dad wouldn't say what it was, but we learned from his bus driver, Bert, later that afternoon that Daddy had got into a row with someone who went on to accuse him of being anti-Jewish. Instead of holding out his hand and saying, 'Don't be silly, mate,' Daddy lost his rag, screaming the now familiar retort, 'Are you bloody joking? I gave up years of my life fighting for you lot!' He got so wound up that he abandoned the trolley-bus and all its passengers and caught another one home. He caused an enormous hold-up which stretched the entire length of Kingsland Road and took hours to clear. But when the red mist came down, he didn't give a monkey's about anyone or anything.

He explained to me what the war had been about, so when I saw a little Jewish boy, David Fuchs, who wore glasses, being bullied at school, I knew I had to do something. As he went to drink his milk at breaktime, two older, bigger boys pushed him and he fell and cracked his lip. Glaring at him, on the ground, they sneered: 'You dirty, rotten, stinking Jew. Why should you be given milk?' I rushed up and kicked and shoved the two older boys, shouting: 'My dad fought in the war to help them out.' I was called in front of our teacher, Mr Lugg, but only got a telling off. Whenever I was naughty, I never got the cane like other kids, only lines to write out. I think the teachers thought I was too little to be caned. I got into lots of scraps over Jews. I thought if Daddy had fought for them, obviously I had to as well.

I don't know if it was due to all the talk about Jews, but I was drawn to the area on the other side of the cemetery, where Daddy's bus stopped, because lots of Jews lived there; the Jewish Sector, we called it, and I found it fascinating, particularly the hypnotic chanting at sundown on Fridays as they prepared for their sabbath. It was all slightly theatrical, and I loved it.

Not that it was only Jews I stood up for: I'd go in to bat for any underdog I thought was getting the rough end of it. Once I got into a dust-up with a girl who lived in a neighbouring prefab over a plastic rain hat I wanted to lend to another girl.

'Don't give it to her, she's got nits,' my neighbour said.

'You shouldn't say that,' I told her. 'It's not nice.'

'She's got nits because she comes from a big family,' she went on. And for some reason that made me see red, and I waded in and whacked her. She ran off down the road, shouting: 'Yeah, and you like Jews and your mother dyes her hair and earns ten pounds a week.' I chased her, caught her and whacked her again for that. It was the Jews, more than the other things, that upset me.

Sussing that the girl would whinge to her mother that I'd bashed her up, I immediately told Mummy what had happened and why. Sure enough, her mother came bowling up the long path to our prefab and had a right go about me, but Mummy was brilliant. 'Your daughter could only have learned what she said within the four walls of her house, so I suggest you leave here immediately,' she said. The woman did, and her daughter and I never spoke to each other again.

Afterwards, Mummy sat me down and explained that it was all about jealousy. 'I'm not a housewife like most other women, Babs,' she said. 'I go to work because I want us to have things we wouldn't be able to afford if I didn't. This causes jealousy, and jealousy is very destructive.'

That was the good thing about both Mummy and Daddy: they treated me more like a little adult than as a child. In many ways, Mummy was an example of a new generation of women, and very much ahead of her time. In those days it was not the done thing for women to go out to work unless they absolutely had to, and unusual for them to have only one child. During the war, they had filled the jobs left by the men away fighting, and although this marked the start of changing attitudes, by and large they returned to a more traditional role in peacetime. Not Mummy: she was a skilled couturier, and she had always worked, and she carried on working throughout her life.

On a Saturday Mummy would take me to Joe Lyon's in Stoke Newington for a milk and dash as a reward for helping her with the shopping at the Co-Op. I loved Saturdays with Mummy – provided we didn't go out until I'd listened to the omnibus edition of *Dick Barton, Special Agent*, the radio series which enthralled most kids at that time.

The downside of having both parents working was that I was often left on my own. I loved it when Daddy was on an early shift, because he'd be back when I got home from school. If he was on late, he'd leave around 3 p.m. and I'd come home to an empty house, which was horrible. Of course, Nanny and Grandad Ellis were round the corner, but my cousin Kenny would be off with his mates, and I wanted to play with children my own age. At a loss to know what to do until Mummy came home after six, I'd go knocking on doors asking if so-and-so could come out to play. Often no one could.

Mummy and Daddy did try their hardest to make life interesting for me. One or the other took me to the pictures twice a week, once on a Sunday afternoon and once in the week. When I was left to amuse myself I created a make-believe world in my bedroom, letting my vivid imagination run wild with images I'd seen on the screen at the pictures. I would dress up and sing in front of the mirror, pretending I was a famous, glamorous film star, usually Betty Grable, who I'd seen in *The Dolly Sisters*, a Hollywood musical, with Mummy at the Odeon, Dalston. As an eight-year-old, I had no idea that this petite, lovely-looking blonde with shapely legs was Hollywood's top earner and the highest-paid woman in America. To me, she was just a sweet-natured, pretty lady who sang and danced like nobody I'd ever seen; who was everything I'd like to be. On the bus home, Mummy and I argued about who was prettiest, Betty or June Haver, who played her sister. Mummy thought June, but I wouldn't have it: Betty was the best by far, I insisted. The movie itself, about two Hungarian sisters touring America in vaudeville, had a big effect on me, too. As yet I had no dreams of going on the stage, but there was something warm and cosy about living out of suitcases while performing in out-of-the-way places that I found appealing; romantic, if you like.

Betty Grable was in all the movie magazines and there was one classic picture of her, in a one-piece swimsuit, looking over her right shoulder, that was everywhere. I would stare at it in my bedroom, then stand in front of the mirror, imitate the pose and go into one of the song and dance routines I'd seen in the movie. Betty's talent was one thing, but her look was another: I wanted so much to be like her.

When I wasn't trying to be Betty, I would comb my nine hairs and a nit over one eye, wishing I had lovely thick tresses like Mummy, and stare dreamily into the mirror pretending I was Veronica Lake, another American actress, with a sultry look, whose blonde hair fell over one eye in a unique peek-a-boo style. My childish fantasies staved off the loneliness and boredom until Mummy came home.

As an only child himself, Daddy knew about loneliness. One day he announced that he was concerned about strangers wandering about the cemetery of a convent that backed on to our garden, and suggested we got a dog. We borrowed books from the library and discussed which breed we should have. Mummy insisted she would allow only a small one, so when Daddy and I came back from the RSPCA kennel with a huge Alsatian called Tess, she freaked out and told us to take her back. I'd fallen in love with Tess on sight, so I fought for a literal underdog this time. I went on hunger strike for two days and refused to leave the dog's side, and eventually Mummy relented. Now I looked forward to getting home from school because I knew Tess would be waiting for me.

As well as my outings to the pictures with Mummy or Daddy, I also went on my own on Saturday afternoons. There was hardly any new film I didn't see – and I don't mean just harmless musicals suitable for children like *The Dolly Sisters*. If there was an 'A' film showing, which meant a child had to be accompanied by an adult, I'd hang around until I saw someone who looked friendly and ask them to take me in. Trusting in those days, or what! It didn't matter that those movies went over my head. To me, at eight, it was all just magical. I'd sit in the dark, gazing up at the huge screen, enraptured, not bothered in the slightest if I didn't understand the story.

Neither Mummy nor Daddy worried about what films I saw. Dad was always drumming into me the need to look after my teeth, and he would take me on an extra trip to the pictures if I behaved myself at the dentist's. When I boasted about this to one of my schoolteachers, she asked what we'd seen.

'*Duel in the Sun*,' I said, proudly.

This 1946 movie, starring Jennifer Jones, Joseph Cotten and Gregory Peck, was not only sexually explicit for its time but also featured a gory shoot-out.

The teacher was appalled. 'A young girl like you shouldn't be seeing a film like that.'

'Oh, Mummy and Daddy take me to all the pictures,' I said. 'They even took me to see *The Outlaw*.' You should have seen her face. That was the famous Western in which Jane Russell's plunging neckline caused a six-year censorship row.

For an extra special treat, either Mummy or Daddy, and sometimes both, would take me to the West End to see a show, and that would set my young heart pounding. The stage seemed so exciting, and the girls so glamorous in their glittering costumes. I'd sit there transfixed, lost in my fantasy world, thinking, 'I'd love to be up there.'

Like Mummy, I loved the West End: there was a vibrancy you could almost feel as you walked about the place. But there were theatres in the East End, too, and every so often, on a Friday, we'd go, with all the relatives, to see variety shows at Hackney Empire or Finsbury Park Empire and Grandad Ellis would tell me about all the great music hall stars he'd seen. Little Marie Lloyd was his favourite and he reckoned I reminded him of her. Grandad's adoration for the East End's most famous variety performer made a deep impression on me and, after I was shown a picture of her and saw how her teeth protruded, I was always sticking mine out to try to look like her.

Grandad Charlie was a lovely character, he'd been a bit of a local celebrity himself, singing and telling jokes in local pubs and drinking clubs as the 'Singing Waiter'. He was one of those popular and endearing people who was loved by everyone, adults, kids and teenagers alike. Whenever he was performing in a pub my cousins Kenny and Roy and their friends would all turn up to watch him. Grandad liked a drink and when he came home from the docks, where he worked as a teaboy, he was often tiddly from the high-proof alcohol that came off the boats. He'd travel home on the 649 bus and get off at the bottom of Church Street around 4 p.m., just as we were coming out of school. Most times he would be singing and dancing and Mummy, of course, was highly embarrassed. She told me to ignore him if I saw him like that, but I'd hang around waiting for him on purpose, because he thought the world of me, and I loved him. And I knew he'd always give me a few pennies to get a jam doughnut or some sherbet lemons from the shops opposite the school.

His wife, Nanny Eliza, was a tiny, sweet-natured lady. She'd had four daughters and had always wanted a son. She gave birth to three, all of whom she named Charlie, and all of whom died. When her fourth son was born she'd named him Ronnie instead, and, thankfully, he survived.

It was only a matter of time before my parents' different personalities and prorities in life led to a serious rift between them. My dad felt a woman's place was at home, and he could not understand why my mother wanted to work. And she couldn't understand why he didn't want to better himself. They began to argue, over money at first, but soon the least little thing could start them off. What Mummy wore, for example. She was very fashion-conscious, obviously influenced by working in the West End, and would set off every morning in colourful clothes that suited her auburn hair and showed off her shapely legs and figure. Daddy, on the other hand, preferred to see her, in the daytime, at least, in flat brogues and tweed suits buttoned up high. There was a bit of the prude in him, I suppose.

One day Mummy came home with a pair of emerald green high-heeled shoes she thought would go well with a beautiful beige gabardine suit she had made herself for VE day. Daddy didn't like them at all and went into one, screaming and shouting that they were too flashy. A few weeks later, she put on a brightly coloured blouse she had just bought and he went spare over that, too. It was as if he resented her buying smart clothes with the money she had worked hard for.

However, he didn't object to her getting all dolled up for a Saturday night at the pub, usually the Axe in Bethnal Green, with the whole family. I loved those nights. What made them extra special for me was when everyone came back to Yoakley Road after the pub for a 'Dutch auction'. We had an old, upright piano, and everyone had to sing a song, or do a turn – even Mummy. Daddy had a lovely voice, and would sing 'On the Sunny Side of the Street', or 'How Yer Gonna Keep 'Em Down on the Farm', and, of course, I didn't have to be asked twice to get up and do a number or three.

I didn't see so much of my paternal grandparents because Mummy didn't approve of them. They represented for her everything she didn't like about the East End. Grandad Deeks, who was a docker, had a horrendous temper after a few drinks, and Nanny Deeks, a cleaner, though very sweet, was short and overweight. We nicknamed her Fat Nanny. Once a month, Daddy would take me to their home, in Flower and Dean Street, opposite Petticoat Lane, and we would go to the local pub. What Mummy objected to was them leaving me outside with a lemonade and some crisps while they were drinking inside. When she and Daddy went to a pub with her parents, she would make sure it had an upstairs room where I could play with other children.

Mummy enjoyed the family Saturday nights in the pub but sometimes when Daddy went to the pub at lunchtime on a Sunday, she gave him a hard time. Perhaps she felt she worked as hard as he did and resented being left at home while he was out enjoying himself, or maybe it was the working-class tradition of going drinking before your Sunday dinner that she objected to. It was probably a bit of both. Whatever the reason, all the time he was out, I would sense her getting more and more worked up and I'd tug at her dress and ask her not to start a row when Daddy came home. But she couldn't help herself. He would arrive, perhaps a little tipsy but always happy, always giggling, and Mummy would be in the kitchen, tight-lipped and frosty. If he went over and tried to kiss her while she drained the potatoes or whatever, she'd shrink from him. 'You smell of booze,' she'd say, making a face. If he was quiet, that would be wrong, too. 'Yes, yes, dinner's coming up,' she'd say, almost as if she was goading him into retaliating so that she could have a go at him. More often than not, he didn't disappoint her. 'What's wrong with you, Rosie?' he'd say. 'What's the matter? Just because I went out for a drink?'

Well aware of Daddy's temper, I'd beg Mummy to ignore him. But being part of a new generation of women who weren't prepared to sit back and be walked over, she'd lip him back. He'd say something else, and soon they were off. He'd start pushing her around and knocking her about and sometimes he'd even chuck the Sunday lunch in the garden. I'd be screaming, 'Don't, don't, don't!' but it was useless, because Daddy could never walk away from a row.

I dreaded those Sundays as much as Mummy did, but I never felt the scream-ups were Daddy's fault. It wasn't as if he rolled in drunk and spoiling for a fight. On the contrary, he was in a happy mood after a good time at the pub and was just looking for a bit of fun, but that didn't suit Mummy. Mind you, Daddy could have bitten his lip, ignored her and let her stew in her own juice, but that short fuse always seemed to spark an over-reaction. Once he went to the bedroom, his face red with fury, grabbed the fur coat and the emerald green shoes Mummy treasured, opened the back door and threw them out in the mud, screaming abuse at her. Mummy pleaded, 'John, John, the neighbours,' but he retorted: 'Fuck the neighbours,' and went to the garden fence and yelled: 'Are you all watching? Are you all listening?'

If the rows started at night, I would lie in bed thinking of ways to stop them. On a visit to London Zoo I'd been terrified of the snakes, so I'd scream out that there were snakes in my bed in the hope that it would distract Mummy or Daddy from what they were arguing about and one of them would come in to me. It was a ploy I used often, and sometimes it worked.

The arguments were all very East End, everything Mummy hated, and she would feel so bitterly ashamed. She was always worried about what people thought of her. That's why she kept the net curtains of the prefab pristine and regularly dyed them different colours. She wanted the inside of the house looking nice, but it had to be seen to be smart and impressive from the outside as well.

Thanks to the time I spent at school in Blackpool, I was so ahead of the game at school that my teachers allowed me to sit my Eleven-Plus exam a year early, and I went on to achieve the highest mark in north London. My parents were absolutely thrilled.

I had a choice of three grammar schools, and although we weren't Catholic, Mummy favoured Our Lady's Convent in Stamford Hill. When I went for my interview, I was sold on it, too. I was really taken with all the beautiful-looking nuns walking around in their dramatic, black, long, flowing habits. Soon after starting there, a month after my eleventh birthday in 1948, I was swanning round in the kitchen with a tea-towel wrapped round my head and my hands together in an attitude of prayer declaring that I wanted to be a nun when I grew up.

That fad soon passed, though, and Mummy and Daddy started talking seriously about what I should do when I left the convent. I didn't consider the stage as a possible career, even though I was now having extra tap lessons on Thursdays at Madame Behenna's as well as coaching from a tap expert in Tottenham once a month.

Being able to both sing and dance, I had become something of a star turn at Madame Behenna's. Unlike other kids, I never suffered from stagefright: confidence oozed out of me and I was always eager to get out on that little town hall stage and show what I could do. We performed in two charity competitions a year in and around London, and I had no trace of nerves in those, either. In fact, when I was in the wings waiting to go on, I'd have one foot on the stage because I was busting a gut to get on. When I was called, I'd almost fling myself out. Rather than just singing one song or dancing one number, I would perform a little act, singing and dancing to a medley of fast and slow songs, to show how versatile I was. And I was successful, too: I won all sorts of medals and certificates. I came first only once, however. The rest of the time I nearly always came second.

In one competition, sponsored by Sunshine Homes for the Blind at the YMCA in Tottenham Court Road, a stranger took great exception to me not getting first place and made her feelings loudly known to the judges. I had sung a selection of Al Jolson numbers, in contrast to the winner, who sang a sickly-sweet song in a very posh voice, and this woman felt there had been a bit of snobbery in the voting.

'It's a disgrace,' she called out. 'It's not right. The little blonde girl should be first.' She came over to us later and told Mummy: 'Your girl didn't get first because of where you come from.' To me and Mummy, though, coming second was still a big deal.

It was when I was about twelve, and a talent scout named Brian Mickey, who had recently discovered the young Morecambe and Wise, came to watch one of our charity concerts at Stoke Newington Town Hall that everything changed. Mr Mickey thought I might be suitable for a pantomime at Wimbledon Theatre.

'That little girl who sang "Good, Good, Good",' he said to Madame Behenna after the show. 'I'd like to meet her mother.'

'My Barbara, go on the stage?' Mummy said indignantly when she was introduced to Mr Mickey. 'I'll have you know she's going to be a foreign language telephonist.'

It was the first I'd heard of this particular ambition, but there you go. Anyway, it took all Brian Mickey's powers of persuasion to talk Mummy into it, but eventually she gave in and agreed to take me to the Wimbledon Theatre the next Saturday to audition for the Eleanor Beam Babes, a child dancing troupe.

I assumed that the audition would be held in a small room, but we were directed to the stage door. I'd never seen a stage door before; I didn't even know such a thing existed. Someone came and led me down some stairs, all very dark, and we walked along a corridor and through a door. And then I wasn't in a room at all, but on the stage. All those years soaking up the enchantment of the theatre on the other side of the footlights had been magical, but standing on the stage that Saturday afternoon was exhilarating. It just took my breath away.

I sang 'On the Sunny Side of the Street' and did a tap routine and some acrobatics. Then some other kids came on to the stage and formed a pyramid with me on the top. When it was over everyone said 'Well done' and asked me where I'd learned to sing and dance. Suddenly I felt special and wanted, and a part of what I'd watched and loved since I was small. I was so, so happy because everyone seemed so pleased with me. When I saw Mummy afterwards, she said that when I'd come out on to that stage it was as if someone had waved a magic wand and transformed me into a totally different person.

I passed the audition and was told that rehearsals would start in early December prior to a two-week run. I would need time off from school, but Mummy didn't see that as a problem as school work always tailed off towards Christmas. On the bus home, I was so thrilled, so pleased with myself. I couldn't wait for Monday to come round so that I could tell my friends.

The song that made Daddy so happy had, it seemed, been good for me, too. Life was indeed sweet, on the sunny side of the street.

2

THE REVEREND MOTHER SOON WIPED THE SMILE OFF MY FACE. She refused to give me time off school for the panto, and I was so heartbroken that my attitude to school changed overnight. I'd always been a bit disruptive, but now I started taking a pride in doing what I shouldn't and became a real rebel. We were supposed to wear our hats outside school, but I deliberately didn't; we weren't supposed to eat sweets or cakes in the street, but I did – in fact I scoffed the biggest jam doughnuts I could buy. And I found any excuse not to do my homework. Every Friday at assembly we were asked to put up our hands if we were guilty of any such misdemeanours, and I took great pleasure in putting mine into the air at every opportunity. I started getting so many bad marks that Mummy was called in and told that the girl who had been such a conscientious, hard-working scholar had suddenly become the worst-behaved child in the school. What had got into me, they wanted to know. But Mummy could not tell them because she had no idea. Neither did I, really, at the time. I didn't consciously set out to be loud and rebellious or to let my work slide, but it was the only way I had, I suppose, of venting my anger and disappointment at being stopped from doing something I'd set my heart on.

Once, as a punishment, I had to learn Puck's speech from *A Midsummer Night's Dream* overnight and recite it at morning assembly. I got through it faultlessly and went back to my seat tingling with excitement as the whole school applauded. That gave me intense satisfaction, because I'd wanted to prove to everyone I could do something difficult if I put my mind to it.

Mummy and Daddy told me they had been warned that I had to pull my socks up. I loved it at that convent and did not want to leave. I managed to improve my behaviour thanks to a sixth-form pupil named Peggy, who made me realise that in being naughty, I was not only letting myself down, but other pupils, too. Each week our house, Lourdes, and the three other houses were awarded points for exemplary school work and good conduct and, at the end of term, the one with the highest number of points was awarded a cup. Peggy sat me down and explained that my bad behaviour was ruining our chances of winning the prestigious trophy.

So I began to knuckle down and show that I could be a good girl again. I came top in my form's weekly exam, and for the next couple of terms had no occasion to hold up my hand to any misdemeanours. But in spite of my good intentions it didn't last. The desire to go on the stage never left me and – out of frustration, I suppose – I became so disruptive that, during the 1950 summer term, Mummy was again summoned to see the Reverend Mother, who had by now identified the problem. I had become a different child since not being allowed to do the pantomime, she said. If the stage was what I wanted, then perhaps that was an avenue my mother should explore.

A few days later, Mummy phoned Eleanor Beam, who suggested she contacted one of two theatrical schools which provided academic education as well as stage training. One was the Italia Conti in Soho, the other Aida Foster's in Golders Green. Soho was more convenient from Stoke Newington, but Mummy wouldn't have dreamed of sending me to an area where prostitutes plied their trade on every corner. So she rang Aida Foster's for an appointment and was asked to take me to the school for an audition the following Saturday morning. She did the best she could with my hair on the Friday night, spreading some green jelly stuff over it until it was stiff and setting it in pin curls. 'Let's pray it's not raining tomorrow,' she said.

We had to take three buses to get to Golders Green, but I didn't care and neither, I think, did Mummy: we were both far too excited at the prospect of finding a school that would encourage my wish to go on the stage and give me a decent education at the same time.

We walked through the school gates into a different world, a world in which, or so it seemed from photographs on the walls, every girl looked like a Hollywood beauty, and some of them, such as Elizabeth Taylor and Jean Simmons, actually were. No sooner had Mummy proudly displayed my certificates and silver and bronze medals than Aida Foster dragged us back into the real world. All my achievements counted for nothing here, she said: they were OK for a local dancing school that cost 1s 6d on a Monday and 1s on a Thursday, but this was a school that trained girls for a professional stage career, and it was filled with beauties blessed with talent to match their stunning looks. If that brought Mummy down to earth, I didn't notice, because it all went completely over my head. I was so flash I believed I was God's gift to the theatre; I thought showbiz was waiting for me. And I was not in the least nervous about auditioning. I could not wait to prove that I was every bit as talented as the girls in the photographs. I was not fazed even when we were taken to the biggest rehearsal room I'd ever seen, with mirrors on all sides, and asked what I wanted to perform. With a confidence belying my years, I went into my staple, 'On the Sunny Side of the Street', with all the well-rehearsed gestures and expressions, and followed up with 'Are You From Dixie?' I did some tap dancing, which I was good at, and a bit of ballet, which I wasn't. Then I had to do a character dance and recite a poem. Afterwards Mummy and I were taken back to Aida's office, where we waited, looking at the photographs of all those pretty girls who were nothing like me, while Aida, her daughter Anita, and the woman – known to pupils as Miss Pat – who ran the school for them, discussed my audition among themselves. Studying those film star faces with their creamy complexions, framed by long ringlets and little Peter Pan collars and bows, I saw myself for the first time for what I was: short and fat, with the split fringe in my fine hair emphasising my full, round, dimpled face. It was not a nice feeling.

After what seemed like for ever, Aida, Anita and Miss Pat came into the office. Aida looked at my mother and said: 'Well, Mrs Deeks, your daughter isn't the usual little lady we have coming through our doors. She's different. But we all think she's got something. We don't know what it is, but she has *something*. And we would be prepared to take her next term.'

Aida then talked about how much it was all going to cost. I would need two pairs of block-top and one pair of soft ballet shoes; one maroon and one blue leotard; cardigan and tights; blue and white shorts; white sweater and shoes for tap, and a dress and shoes for ballroom dancing, as well as a uniform for afternoons, when I would do school work. Being not yet thirteen, and very immature for my age, I did not understand the enormity of the financial commitment. All I knew was that I desperately wanted to go to Aida Foster's. I knew I could do it, that I'd be OK. On the way home, Mummy told me that she would do more piecework to earn enough extra money to send me for one term to see how I did. I was so, so happy. Now, on the three buses back to Stoke Newington, I forgot all about those film star faces in Aida's office. Talent was what counted, not looks. Hadn't I been the one everyone wanted to see perform at Madame Behenna's? I'd be the same success at Aida Foster's, I was sure of that.

*   *   *

On the September morning I was to start at Aida Foster's the butterflies were flying around my tummy as I put on my new maroon and pale blue uniform. I was nervous, but excited, too, as I walked to the bottom of Bouverie Road to catch the 106 bus to Finsbury Park. Having no idea what to expect at school, I lost myself in thought as the second, smaller bus, the 210, left the heavily built-up areas behind and climbed to the green fields of Allington and the picturesque village of Highgate. I found myself thinking of Dick Whittington, who had passed through there on his way to the City of London; then, as the bus dropped down to Hampstead, past the famous Spaniard's Inn, I daydreamed about another Dick – the legendary highwayman, Dick Turpin. The lovely long journey made me forget what first-day nerves I had, but by the time I reached Golders Green Hippodrome and stepped on to the third bus, which would take me along Finchley Road to Aida Foster's, the butterflies were waking up again.

And then I saw the tall girls, with pretty faces and long hair, getting out of big, shiny cars, and I knew I had arrived at a place where I had every reason to be nervous.

At my previous schools, I'd always seemed to end up in charge and other kids had followed me. But I was the only girl starting at Aida Foster's that autumn term, and no one knew me. I wandered around, not knowing where I was going, much less what I was going to do when I got there. There seemed to be a few working-class girls, but the majority were from wealthy backgrounds, and if it was not their daddy who drove them to school in the Rolls-Royce, it was the chauffeur. That morning, all Mummy's ambitions to get out of the East End came back to me: mingling among those elegant girls with the frightfully posh accents I'd heard only on radio or in films, I felt insignificant and common. And, if I'm honest, I felt inferior, too.

To make matters worse, that morning's lessons included pointe ballet, in which we had to balance on the ends of our toes on blocked shoes. Girls who were willowy and light found this painful, but for a fairy elephant like me, it was excruciating, and when the class was over, I had tears in my eyes. Whether they were for my battered toes or bruised ego, I can't be sure. As if my confidence were not low enough, one of the girls, Patricia Wilson, was told I looked like her, and I heard her snort by way of reply: 'Don't insult me.'

It was a relief to start singing and dancing lessons; at least I would come into my own then. But even these came as a shock: suddenly I realised that, no matter how good I thought I was, there were other girls with far more talent than I had. At Madame Behenna's I'd been the little star; here I was a nobody, and my pride was hurt.

Mummy had packed me some lunch, and on that miserable Monday morning, even this proved to be a mistake that made me feel silly. Seeing me take my sandwiches out of my satchel, one of girls said, snootily, 'We don't have sandwiches – we go out to eat.' I had no idea what she was talking about. I did not know what 'going out to eat' was. Patricia Wilson, bless her, came over to me and apologised for having been so rude about me earlier. 'I didn't mean it,' she said. 'Why don't you come out with the rest of us?' I appreciated the gesture, but turned it down, preferring to eat on my own in the state of mind I was in.

After lunch we all went across the road to another part of the school for lessons. And it was there, thankfully, that my superior education rescued me from what would otherwise have been the unhappiest day of my life. In the classroom, I was streets ahead. I quickly realised that the other girls might have been better looking, might have had longer hair and legs and have come from wealthier backgrounds, but their parents had clearly put stage training ahead of academic education.

Outshining those budding stars in one area at least lifted my self-esteem and I went home that afternoon feeling a little better about myself than I had at lunchtime. But deep down, I was afraid of what was in store for me: at Aida Foster's I was just a tiny cog in a huge wheel. What, I wondered, would I have to do to get myself noticed above all those glamour girls with their fashionable looks and accents?

For the next three months, I was desperately unhappy. I'm sure the girls did not set out to intimidate me or make me feel awkward, but that's what happened. Not only did they speak better than me, they had more money, too: they had plenty to enjoy themselves 'eating out', while most of what Mummy gave me went on bus fares, and if I did have any left over, it was only sixpence or so. And when it came to auditions for film or stage parts, I was never picked: producers and casting directors wanted pretty, long-legged girls with peaches-and-cream complexions and plums in their mouths, and that wasn't me. I was little and plump, with an accent more Mile End than Mayfair. Invariably, they would echo what Aida had said at my audition. 'She has got *something*, but we don't know what it is.'

Not surprisingly, I started looking forward more and more to the afternoon lessons, the only classes where I felt I had some worth. I was so far ahead of everyone else that when our teacher, Mrs Clarke, was not available on a couple of days, I was chosen to sit at the front of the class and tell everyone else what to do. I only had to set them compositions to write, but I felt great. I had a vivid imagination, so coming up with ideas was no problem and it was little wonder that before long some of the girls were asking me to help them with their homework.

The whole point of going to Aida Foster's, however, was to learn my craft better and, as Christmas approached, I became more and more despondent. I badly needed an audition to show off my vivacious, perky personality, but there was no call, it seemed, for a tiny, fat song-and-dance kid. However, just when it seemed that Christmas 1950 was going to be a miserable one for me, Aida did something that lifted my spirits, made me feel proud and gave me hope for the future. She called me into her office and said: 'I know how unhappy you are, Barbara. And I know how much you want to perform on stage. So I've decided to give you a part in my annual pantomime at Golders Green Hippodrome.' I left her office walking on air. Being chosen for the pantomime was a great honour, and I could barely wait for rehearsals to start.

That panto was one occasion when being so tiny paid off: I was put at the end of the chorus line, and consequently given a speaking part. It was only a four-word sentence – 'Here comes the Baron!' – but it meant the world to me, and I yelled it out with gusto twice a day for six weeks. And I was being paid £3 a week for it. I loved being in the panto but my happiness was clouded by the discovery of something I didn't understand, but certainly didn't like: some of the girls at Aida Foster's were not only wealthy but snobs as well.

I was thrilled one night when my father came to see the panto straight from work. I was always proud that my daddy was a bus conductor and thought nothing of him wearing his uniform to the theatre. But at the next evening's performance, I heard one or two of the girls backstage laughing and making snide cracks. One of them said: 'Can you believe it? A bus conductor! How awful. How could he come in his uniform? You'd think he'd be ashamed.'

I rushed into the dressing room and went bananas, chucking a big tin of Leichner theatrical face powder all over them. The woman chaperoning us shouted: 'Barbara Deeks! Stop it!'

'Did you hear what they said about my father?' I asked her.

But she just kept yelling, 'Stop it. BARBARA DEEKS, STOP IT!'

Then she bawled at me: 'You know, I knew you were going to be trouble.'

So I grabbed another tin of powder and threw it all over her hair.

Aida called me into her office and tore me off a strip. 'You must behave like a young lady at all times,' she told me.

I persevered at Aida Foster's, with the help of what I earned in the panto, and, discovering that not all my schoolmates were rich or posh, settled in and made friends. But still, in spite of my hard work and Aida's support, I never seemed to get the chance to show what I could do. I just couldn't get my foot far enough in the door to open it.

One morning in 1952, a couple of months before my fifteenth birthday, Aida arranged for me and a handful of other pupils to go to the Palace Theatre in London's West End to audition for one of six roles as orphans in a new musical called *Love From Judy*, based on Jean Webster's popular children's book *Daddy Longlegs*, about an orphan with a mysterious benefactor with whom she ends up falling in love.

I met up with the other Aida Foster girls by the statue of Eros in Piccadilly, and together, chatting excitedly, we walked up Shaftesbury Avenue towards the Palace Theatre at Cambridge Circus. When we got there our hearts sank: outside the theatre and snaking right the way round it was the most enormous queue of girls we'd ever seen, hundreds of them, in an array of different coloured school uniforms, all waiting for an audition. Even if I did manage to wedge my foot in the door, I thought, and was asked to go through even a small part of my repertoire, what hope would I have with so many other girls my age, probably just as talented or more so, going for the same role?

At the audition itself I felt a bit more confident. My jazzed-up version of 'On the Sunny Side of the Street' went down so well that I was allowed to finish it, which made a nice change. Then I was asked to dance, and went through a tap routine, ending with a cartwheel across the stage. I sensed I was in with a chance when I was asked if I could speak with an American accent. 'Yes, I can,' I said quickly, trying to remember how Daddy sounded when he used American slang. I read from the script, then left. I'd rarely felt positive after past auditions, but I did that day, and went back to school really hopeful. I did not hear anything for more than a week, but one morning, while I was in the middle of a dance lesson, a message came over the school tannoy system: 'Barbara Deeks, Barbara Deeks, you are wanted in the main office.'

The tannoy meant one of two things: either you were in deep trouble, or something wonderful had happened. I hurried to the office, filled with an unfamiliar feeling of confidence: I didn't think for a moment that I was in trouble. And sure enough, Aida was all smiles. 'Well, Barbara,' she said. 'I'm so pleased to tell you, you've got the job. You're going to play Sadie Kate.' My size had clinched it for me. Because of the employment regulations, the show could not use children under fifteen, although the orphans were supposed to be ten-year-olds.

'The show is going on a four-week tour, starting with a world première in Coventry,' Aida went on. 'Then it will open in the West End.' The words 'on tour' excited me even more than 'West End': they conjured up images of travelling vaudeville performers, who always seemed like one big happy family. After Coventry we'd be moving on to Bournemouth on the south coast. I loved the idea of living out of suitcases like the Dolly Sisters, and being fussed over by motherly landladies.

And, of course, it would be a relief to get out of London, away from the constant bickering of two disgruntled parents who were becoming more and more miserable living under the same roof.

3

I LEFT FOR COVENTRY ON A SUNDAY IN AUGUST 1952. Apart from when I was evacuated as a small child, I'd never been away from home before, and I'd never felt so excited. Mummy took me to Euston Station to put me on the train. I was wearing a beautiful lemon and grey seersucker outfit she had made for me, a hat and a pair of red shoes with a small heel to make me a little more grown-up. I'd shown the shoes to Daddy, wanting his approval, but, knowing what he thought about heels, I covered those with my hands so that he wouldn't see them.

The first two weeks of the tour were the happiest of my life. The cast quickly became a loving family and Coventry Hippodrome Theatre a haven where I always felt welcome and wanted. I palled up with another 'orphan', Heather Lee, who also had a speaking part, and we shared digs, a twenty-minute bus ride and a long walk to the theatre from the city centre. We had to get out of our lodgings soon after breakfast so we'd go into town and congregate in the Kardomah coffee bar, hoping to spot famous performers working in Coventry – there were four theatres in the city in those days. After an hour or so in there, we'd go to the Hippodrome. It was always open early, and we knew we could count on endless cups of tea and cakes while we chatted to whoever was there. On payday – the one day we had enough money – we'd go to the pictures.

To begin with I thought that appearing on stage would be like the panto, but, of course, there were ten times as many people in the Hippodrome audience and I was totally unprepared for such loud, prolonged applause. On the first night the theatre was packed, and the audience, which included the actress Hermione Gingold and the singer Elisabeth Welch, famous stars of the day, loved the show. The next day the *Coventry Evening Telegraph* declared that it was better than anything the United States had produced. The leading man, Johnny Brandon, and June Whitfield were described as 'two of the brightest features of the evening', and 'beautiful, talented Jean Carson' would, it was predicted, be acclaimed in the West End. It was all terribly exciting.

I quickly developed an all-consuming crush on Johnny Brandon. He was a singer-dancer, and when I saw him on stage for the first time during rehearsals, I literally caught my breath: he was the most gorgeous human being I'd ever seen. It was not a sexual attraction, of course: I was too immature, too unworldly for that; it was more a childish adoration of someone blessed with exquisite good looks and the most dynamic personality and talent. Whenever Johnny was around, I was so nervous I'd start to perspire, and off stage I could never bring myself to look at him, much less speak to him. So captivated was I by his looks and his stage presence that every night – and twice on Wednesdays and Saturdays – I'd go down and stand in the wings to watch him sing his big number before joining him and the rest of the cast on stage for the finale.

After Coventry we went to Bournemouth, arriving in the middle of a heatwave. When the other girls suggested going to the beach, I had to buy myself a swimming costume. The one that caught my eye had criss-cross straps at the back, like the one Betty Grable wore in her famous pose, but not only did it cost £4 – over half a week's wages – but it was maroon, which I wasn't keen on because it was the same colour as my school uniform. In the end, though, I decided to lash out on it because I was developing a bit of a bosom and looked really good in it. Also I felt that Mummy would be proud of me for showing such good taste.

When the tour was over, I left Bournemouth for London, eager to see Mummy and Daddy and to tell them all about it. I jumped off the train at Waterloo, my joy at going home tempered by the usual worries about what mood Mummy would be in. As I walked briskly along the platform with the other girls I could see Mummy at the barrier, with all the other mothers, and she was smiling. Everything seemed to be OK. But as I got closer and she spotted me, her face tightened into a scowl. 'Christ,' I thought. 'What have I done?' I couldn't think what could be the matter. I wanted to tell her what a success the show had been, how excited everyone was about going into the West End, but she got in first.

'What on earth have you done with yourself?'

I didn't have a clue what she was on about.

'Look at the state of you.'

I looked down at my clothes; I was always pristine, and today was no different. 'What?' I said. 'What's wrong?'

'You've put on a lot of weight. You're fat. You're getting just like Fat Nanny.'

'All right,' I said. 'I'll try to lose some weight.' Then, trying to please her, I added: 'Hey, you'll never guess what I bought.' I reached into my bag and pulled out the swimming costume I'd bought in Bournemouth. 'Isn't it smashing?'

Mummy stared at it in disbelief. 'How much did you spend on *that?*' she wanted to know.

'Four pounds,' I said.

'*Four pounds?*' she said. 'You stupid girl. Spending your money – just like your father.'

Heather said: 'Oh, don't say that, Mrs Deeks. We all went to the beach and Barbara didn't have a costume. She was so pleased with it.' But Mummy didn't want to know. She could not bear the thought of me spending so much money on anything. As we headed for the Underground, the warm, wonderful memories of the tour receded and I felt deflated and scared of what lay ahead. I'd hoped that my being away would improve things, give Mummy and Daddy time to resolve their differences, but it hadn't. No sooner was I home than the rows continued, and I started counting the days to 25 September when *Love From Judy* opened at the Saville Theatre a short walk from Leicester Square.

We opened to great reviews and, for the next few weeks, I would hurry away after the show and gush out my excitement to whichever parent met me at Finsbury Park. If Daddy had been working an early shift he'd be there, and, to be honest, I preferred that. He was always in a good mood, keen to see me, and interested in what I had to tell him. I was always thrilled to see him, too, and we'd chat away and laugh so much that we were home before we knew it.

I could not wait to go back to Aida Foster's. I wanted to keep up my dance and acting classes, of course, but if I'm honest, I wanted to show off, too; to savour the adulation of those prettier, more-talented girls who had looked down their rich noses at the short, fat bus conductor's daughter they never expected to get anywhere. I was greeted like some returning heroine: everyone, it seemed, flocked round me, wanting to be my friend. 'What's it like being in the West End?' 'Do you get nervous?' 'Is it exciting getting loud applause every night?' The questions came fast from all angles, and it was terrific being the centre of attention for once. I lapped it up.

Aida and Anita and the teachers were thrilled for me, too, and one of them made my day by asking me to act out an excerpt of *Love From Judy* in front of the class with the help of some of the other pupils. My own stage role was not big enough, so I borrowed some of Jean Carson's scenes and tore at everyone's heart-strings with two of her tear-jerking numbers. I also did June Whitfield's comedy number about blondes, 'Dumb, Dumb, Dumb'. For a little girl of fifteen, being asked my opinion on this and that as if I were some veteran of the theatre was a real buzz, and I left school that afternoon feeling even more important than when I arrived.

I kept up with my classes as often as I could, but it was exhausting doing the show and concentrating at school as well, and I finally left during the West End run of *Love From Judy*, though Aida Foster remained my agent.

One night, as we all came off stage, I found myself next to *him*; just a couple of feet away. 'Hello,' he said. 'Barbara, isn't it?'

Before I had a chance to blush or stutter, I heard myself respond quietly: 'Yes.'

'Are you enjoying the show?'

I gulped. I hadn't expected a second question and couldn't cope with a conversation. 'Yer, yer ... yes, Mr Brandon,' I stammered.

He smiled. 'You obviously like my number. You watch it every night.'

I nodded. 'I think it's wonderful,' I managed to get out.

All the girls were rushing past me, Heather and Pixie and Linda and the others, all giggling. I felt myself going red.

'What do you want to do in the business?' he was asking. 'What ambitions do you have?'

'Just to sing and dance,' I replied. 'I love it.'

'Who's your favourite film star?'

'Betty Grable.'

He smiled again; he was so sweet, so lovely. 'Yeah, she's great.' Then, as he turned towards his dressing room, he said: 'I must take you to tea one day.'

I rushed into our dressing room, tingling with excitement. I could hardly take it in that Johnny Brandon had actually spoken to me. And I had spoken back. I told Heather he had invited me to tea. 'I'm not going on my own,' I said. 'You'll have to come with me.'

The only café we girls used was Valotti's, opposite the theatre in Shaftesbury Avenue. It was pretty basic and cheap. The boys from Italia Conti gathered there and one in particular, Johnny Briggs, stood out because he was always surrounded by admiring girls, me included. When Johnny Brandon took Heather and me to a posh restaurant off Charing Cross Road I was so nervous I wished I was back in Valotti's. The only item on the menu I could find that seemed appropriate for teatime was poached eggs on toast, so that's what I had. But Johnny chatted to us easily, making us feel comfortable and very grown up. He asked me where I came from and when I told him Stoke Newington, he laughed. 'I can't believe it,' he said.

'Why?'

'So do I.'

As they say, it's a small world.

After that, I didn't blush or stutter when Johnny was near; instead we struck up a warm, innocent friendship. I still stood in the wings watching his act every night. During one performance a big, blowsy chorus girl came by. 'I don't know why you waste your time looking at him,' she remarked. 'He's queer.'

'What? Isn't he well?' I asked, concerned.

'Don't be daft,' she said. 'I mean he likes men.'

But I didn't even know much about straight sex, let alone any other variety, so that went completely over my head.

Now that I was in a long-running show, I started giving serious thought to something Aida had mentioned to me when I joined the school. Deeks, she had said, is not a good stage name; there will come a time when you will have to change it. That time, I felt, was now. I was fed up with always being asked at auditions how I spelled my name, and I wanted something simple. Mummy and I put our heads together to try to come up with a stage name that not only was uncomplicated and had a good ring to it, but meant something to us, too. We kicked around loads of ideas, but in the end it came down to two: Ellis, my mother's maiden name, and Windsor, Auntie Dolly's married name. We eventually plumped for Windsor, the name Auntie Dolly shared with the new Queen, as it seemed particularly apt in Coronation year.

Daddy, predictably, did his nut. He would not accept that the change was for professional reasons and accused me of turning my back on a name that had been good enough for his family for generations – and, of course, when he fought for the likes of me in the British Army. He never forgave me for changing it.

At sixteen I was very lucky to look young enough to still be in the show. Many of my fellow 'orphans' had grown too tall to be remotely plausible ten-year-olds. But it seemed I had another problem. One day the wardrobe mistress came into the dressing room barking out my name. She was holding up a band of wide elastic, pinching it between her thumb and forefinger distastefully as if it was something the cat had dragged in. She shook it irritably in the general direction of my chest.

'Barbara Windsor, they're too big now. You do not look ten years old.' With that she thrust the elastic into my hands and marched out. I was so humiliated. She was behaving as if I had deliberately grown breasts to spite her.

I was still upset when I got home and Mummy, for once, was understanding. That weekend she took me to the West End and bought me the most fantastic satin Berlei bra. I still had to flatten my bosom by binding it with the wardrobe mistress's elastic every night to play the part of a character six years younger than me, but it was a small price to pay to stay in the show.

Now that I've got boobs, I thought, I can wear perfume. In the theatre, we used Leichner and Max Factor, but for going out, the make-up of the day was by Elizabeth Arden and Helena Rubenstein, the brands, I was assured, that film stars wore. I went for Elizabeth Arden. Then came the stockings. I could not imagine what it would be like to wear stockings, suspender belt and bra at the same time, and I got myself in a right tizz the first time I did.

I was still immature, but I wasn't a kid any more. In my school uniform – which was all I ever wore during the day and to the theatre – I still looked no more than twelve, but I didn't feel it. I felt very grown up, never more so than on Fridays, when the girls and I slipped into our stockings, low-heeled shoes and 'going out' clothes, collected our £6 7s 6d wages and had a Chinese meal in Soho's booming Chinatown. After those humiliating first days at Aida Foster's, I was 'eating out' at last, though I was still so unworldly that I didn't have a clue how to order. After lunch we would go to the cinema, then back to the Saville for the show. To round off the evening, we sometimes treated ourselves to a 'nightcap' – a milkshake – at a Black and White Milk Bar in Charing Cross Road, but I'd always be on the tube from Leicester Square by 11 p.m. at the latest.

Johnny Brandon was incredibly understanding of my naïveté. Once I saw him chatting at the stage door to a black gentleman who had the most wonderful, uninhibited, wide smile. Later, I said to Johnny: 'Don't niggers have lovely smiles, Mr Brandon?'

He took my hand and looked me straight in the eye. 'You must never say that, Barbara,' he said, quite sternly.

I was embarrassed. 'Have I said something wrong?'

'Well, yes,' Johnny said. 'You must never ever call black people niggers. You must say "coloured".'

I had no idea what he meant. The word 'nigger' was part of the language I'd grown up with. It was just a name, like 'Jew'. I didn't know there was anything wrong with that. I'd been brought up to believe that all people, no matter what their colour or creed, were the same, whatever they were called. Of course, today the word 'coloured' would be considered insulting as well, but in 1950s Britain it was thought polite. The point is that Johnny could easily have put me down and made me feel even more embarrassed, but he didn't.

I was captivated by all kinds of showbusiness and, along with the other girls, made full use of my Equity card, which entitled us to free seats in other theatres. We travelled all over the place, even as far as Streatham in south-west London which, to a north Londoner like me, seemed like the end of the world. Our free seats were always up in the 'gods' – the highest balcony – but we didn't care. We were show people; the theatre was our business, our love, and we soaked up and savoured every magical moment of everything we saw.

The hottest show in 1953 was a musical based on Damon Runyon's classic *Guys and Dolls*, and it captured my imagination so much that I went to see it four times over the next year. During that time the cast changed and I was especially taken by the man who took over as Nathan Detroit. I had seen him many times in pictures playing a wide boy, boxer or gangster, but never singing and dancing on stage. I thought he was wonderful and found his craggy face very appealing. His name was Sid James.

I especially loved the spectacular dance number 'Take Back Your Mink', in which the Hot Box Girls discard, one by one, their mink stoles, hats, diamonds, pearls, high heels and tights. Watching Toni Palmer, Millicent Martin and the American Vivian Blaine pushing their boobs in and out to that raunchy, jazzed-up music set my pulse racing. This was what I wanted to do; this was a world away from playing an orphan scrubbing the floor. Seeing my name up in lights as a solo performer, though, never entered my head; I was still happy to be a bit-part player, one of a team.

By now we had moved from the prefab to a council flat in Bethune Road. I thought the prefabs were lovely, but for some reason they were now generally considered a bit downmarket, and Mummy, of course, couldn't bear that, so with typical determination she had set about getting us a more acceptable home. The rent was higher than for the prefab, but Mummy saw it as a step up.

The cracks between her and my dad could no longer be papered over and that autumn, the atmosphere at home was awful. I'd always thought that Mummy was mostly to blame for the rows, but now that I was older, I could see that often it was six of one and half a dozen of the other. During one barney, I heard Daddy shout at Mummy: 'You won't be much good any more. You'll be past it.' I didn't know what he meant: she was still absolutely stunning approaching forty. But it sounded very unkind and hurtful, and Mummy was very upset.

By Christmas 1953 they had drifted further and further apart and I knew there was a split coming when Daddy admitted to me one day: 'I can't stand your mother.'

'Oh, I know, Daddy,' I said. 'She drives me mad as well sometimes; but she doesn't mean it.'

'I'm going to live somewhere else,' he told me. 'Come and look at a place with me.'

It didn't seem real, my dad living away from us, but I went with him on the 106 bus to Finsbury Park and looked at a room he was thinking of renting. It was awful. 'This isn't good enough for you, Daddy,' I said. 'It hasn't got its own bathroom and toilet.' I never knew whether he took that room or not, because I went straight on to the theatre afterwards and we never spoke about it again. But wherever he went, the next thing I knew he was no longer at home.

When Daddy left, Mummy's proud spirit seemed to go with him. The West End had always been a big deal in her life, a place she adored and always talked about. Now, suddenly, I was the one going there and talking about it, and, instead of being pleased and interested, she was disgruntled and unhappy. She criticised me constantly: my legs were not as shapely as hers; my bust was too big. Once, when I'd had a perm, she scoffed: 'Now what have you done? You look like Harpo Marx!' She constantly complained that I had inherited all my father's worst characteristics: his fine hair, his raucous laugh and the red face when he got angry. It was as if in some bizarre way we were not mother and daughter, but rivals. And it was as if she resented me becoming a young woman and enjoying life in the part of London that had always fascinated her.

Never once, however, did Mummy fail to meet me off the tube at Finsbury Park. She was there in all weathers, once in dense fog even though she was suffering badly from asthma. Usually she was in a good mood, but I was always a little tense because I knew that the slightest thing could set her off. One Friday night, for example, feeling particularly grown up, I decided to pay our bus fares out of my wages. I reached into my coat pocket for my unopened wage packet and, to my horror, discovered it had been nicked. I couldn't see that it was my fault, but Mummy gave me a clout for being careless, and she was still so angry when we got off the bus that she kept pushing me along the street.

I was aware that Mummy must be going through a lot of pain with Daddy going, but selfishly, I showed little concern or compassion. I had been piggy-in-the-middle of their rows for too long, and I was glad to escape to the sanctuary of my showbusiness 'family' where I felt wanted and happy.

And, anyway, I had problems of my own. We were nearing the end of Love From Judy's West End run and would soon be starting a final provincial tour. After that, I would not be seeing my 'family' any more, or Johnny Brandon, and the thought of being without them terrified me.

4

AFTER WE FINISHED AT THE SAVILLE I SPENT A WEEKEND AT HOME
AND THEN TRAVELLED TO BIRMINGHAM FOR THE FIRST WEEK OF THE
CLOSING TOUR OF THE SHOW. Birmingham was notorious in those days
for having the worst digs in the country, and when the other girls said they
were going back to London for the weekend after the Saturday performance,
I jumped at the chance to join them: Mummy was still unhappy, and I thought
it would be a nice surprise for her to have me home. As we still could not
afford a telephone I couldn't ring her to say I was on my way, so the first she
knew about it was when I walked through the door shortly before midnight.
She hurried out of her bedroom, looking flushed and embarrassed, and yelled:
'What are *you* doing here?'

'I've come home,' I said. 'I thought you'd be pleased.'

'No, no,' she said, angrily. 'You shouldn't be home. You've only been
away a week. How did you get here?'

'On the coach,' I told her.

'How much did that cost?'

'Thirty shillings,' I said.

Mummy glared at me. 'Thirty shillings! You're wasting more money.
Just like your father.'

Not knowing what to say to that, I ran into my bedroom and cried myself
to sleep, thinking, 'Why did I bother coming home? I want to go back.'

The next morning, Mummy walked around in a huff, hardly saying a
word, and I went out and roamed the streets, wishing away the time until
Monday, when I could go back to Birmingham and the welcoming warmth
of my 'family'. Lonely and miserable, I went back to the flat to find that
Mummy's mood had lifted. She didn't explain why she had not wanted me

to come home, but she was less aggressive. 'What was the point in travelling all that way, dear?' she said. 'You'll be back for good soon.'

The following month Mummy told me that she and Daddy were getting a divorce, and that I would have to give evidence in court. The show had moved on to Manchester, and I had to travel back by train on a Sunday night to attend the hearing. I had to stand all the way because there was not a seat to be had; the train was packed. I spent the four-hour journey in tears, partly because I'd dropped a drawer on my foot and it was really hurting, but mostly because I would be missing a performance, which seemed a tragedy to me. But my pain was nothing to the anguish I would suffer the next morning.

On the bus to the court in Stoke Newington, Mummy was very kind and gentle and told me I had nothing to be frightened of; all I had to do was tell the truth. As this was something Daddy had drummed into me too, I felt I had nothing to worry about. Mummy said I wouldn't see Daddy until we were in the court. I expected him to greet me as usual and give me a kiss, but when I was called in, I got a terrible shock. I had not seen him for several months and he was like a different person: gone was his happy-go-lucky manner; his face was bright red with anger and, instead of his usual suit he was wearing a hand-knitted, canary yellow crew-necked sweater over a shirt and tie. He didn't even acknowledge me; instead he just stared straight ahead at the judge.

I was asked to step into the witness box. As usual I was wearing my school uniform and I was so tiny I couldn't see over the top. 'She is only a little girl,' the judge said. 'Can someone find a box for Barbara Ann to stand on?' I thought that would make Daddy laugh, but he kept on staring ahead, his mouth shut tight and his eyes full of hate. My father was a handsome man, but now he looked ugly, his face set in the furious expression I'd seen him turn on Mummy in the middle of their blazing rows. Until then, I had not been nervous; I'd thought the judge would say to Mummy and Daddy, 'Now, don't be silly. You love each other. You've got this daughter,' and we'd all walk out and live happily ever after. But now, feeling small and scared in front of my angry father, I was terrified.

'Have you ever heard your mother and father arguing?' the judge was asking me.

'Yes,' I answered.

'Have you ever heard your father swear at your mother?'

'Yes,' I had to say.

'Do you remember the words he used?' the judge went on. Then he added, kindly, 'You don't have to say the words – you can write them down.' The clerk of the court handed me a pen and a piece of paper and I wrote: 'FUC'. Thinking of the little Jewish boy, David Fuchs, who was bullied at school, I paused, not sure whether to finish the word with an 'H' or a 'K'. Finally, I added a 'K', then wrote: 'the neighbours'. I also noted down another word I'd heard Daddy use – BASTARD – and handed the paper to the clerk.

There was talk of Daddy's temper and I was asked if I'd seen anything else. It was like I was on stage – 'Come on, Barbara, tell us all about it, tell the truth about what you saw.' So I told them how Mummy had had this lovely fur coat, and Daddy had chucked it out of the window and it had landed in the mud. All the time I was telling them about Daddy, I was thinking they would ask next about Mummy, and what she had done to him. But there were no questions about her, only about my dad.

'And did you ever see your father hit your mother?'

I had to tell the truth about that, too. 'Yes,' I said.

That seemed to do it. A few seconds later, I was dismissed and left the witness box. Mummy came up to me and said, 'Well done, Babs,' and I went and found a loo, leaving Mummy talking to a solicitor. When I came back, she said: 'Well, Babs, Daddy and I are no longer together. You've been awarded to me.'

'You mean I'm going to live just with you?' I asked.

'Yes. And Daddy is going to pay me five shillings a week to go towards your keep.' Sensing my concern, she added: 'Don't worry, dear, you'll still see Daddy.'

As she said that, I heard the studs of Daddy's shoes on the concrete floor, and there he was, striding towards us, his face damp with perspiration and scarlet with fury. I felt sure he was going to speak to me, to say that he would still see me, that he would take me out once a week, that I would stay with him every so often. But he didn't say a word. He just rushed past like a gust of wind without even glancing at me. Seeing my crestfallen face, Mummy put her arms round me and held me tight. I was shocked, but I was at such a loss to cope with all that was happening to me that I basked in this rare show of affection from her.

Mummy and I hardly said a word to each other on the way home, and for the next few weeks all I could think about was that everything was my fault; that if I had not gone to court and said all those things and written down those words, Mummy and Daddy might have been able to get back together. If Daddy had taken me to one side and explained that the rows were nothing to do with me; that the split would be better for me in the long run; that he had met someone else but would still come and take me to the pictures once a week, then, possibly, I might have understood and come to terms with it. But he didn't. He behaved like a child himself. He walked past this little girl, sixteen going on ten, leaving her to get on with life as best she could. We were peas out of the same proverbial pod, Daddy and me, and until that moment he had always made me feel safe. Now, in the blinking of an eye, he had left me feeling insecure and a little fearful at having to cope alone with a discontented and hypercritical mother for whom little was ever right and nothing ever good enough.

We went into the final week of the tour at the New Theatre, Oxford. My sense of loss over the divorce deepened at the thought of *Love From Judy* closing, but nothing could have prepared me for the emptiness and utter desolation I felt when I left the theatre for the last time with all the friends I'd come to love. It was all over, finished. Never again was I going to walk through a stage door and say 'hi' to all those lovely people who had been my 'family' for two exhilarating, memorable years. Never again would I hurry from my dressing room excitedly to go on stage and do my routine. Never again would I stand adoringly in the wings watching the gorgeous Johnny Brandon weave his special kind of magic. Johnny gave me a beautiful necklace and bracelet as a farewell present, and I spent all my wages on a set of silver-backed hairbrushes for him (something I chose not to tell Mummy). He was very touched. When I got home, I sobbed uncontrollably. How desperately I was going to miss not only the father I idolised, but the loving sanctuary that had comforted me so often in the difficult times.

Alone and sad, I'd find myself wandering along Manor Road towards the Jewish Sector I loved so much, past the baker's, and Stephens', the haberdashers, and my favourite deli with all the different delicacies on display and the big barrels of rollmops outside. I'd hang around where the 643 and 647 buses pulled up by Abney Park Cemetery, hoping to see Daddy. Standing there, I remembered how proud I'd been when I'd watched him clinging to the back of a bus with one hand, cheerfully ushering the passengers aboard with the other. Now that was just a warm memory of happy yesterdays, and I wanted them back. I did see Daddy one day, I swear I did. I waved at him, but he looked through me as though I wasn't there and I walked away, hurting even more inside, not knowing what to do with myself. My daddy had come home to me, whistling, from the war, but now he didn't want me in his life, didn't want to speak to me, didn't love me enough to even wave. What, I wondered, was going to happen to me now that everything I loved and had come to rely on had gone?

One afternoon the following week Mummy told me that there had been a terrible row when she'd come home early from work and caught Daddy trying to remove the radiogram. He said it was his; she said it was hers. Mummy won, and two days later I realised why it was so important to her: she was throwing a little party and needed it for the music. She was in one of her better moods, but I was still feeling down and worried about the future, and suddenly I said the wrong thing. Before we knew it, Mummy and I were in the middle of a blazing row. In a strop, I rushed to the mantelpiece and grabbed one of two orange vases that Mummy adored. She was always talking about how they matched. I threw it on the floor and screamed: 'Now look – you haven't got a matching pair any more. You can't tell everyone about your matching pair now!' Then I stormed out.

I roamed the streets for a couple of hours, terrified that Mummy would give me what for if I went back. But when I finally plucked up the courage to go home and apologise, I found lots of people in the house, all chatting amiably, the music playing – and Mummy all smiles. 'Don't worry about the vase,' she said. 'It's just got a crack down it. We had a row and you were upset.' And then she brought me in and introduced me to her guests. One of them was a friendly, sweet-natured man named Len Atkinson, and it was clear that Mummy liked him. A lot.

For the next couple of weeks, I moped around, feeling abandoned. Even Mummy seemed less interested in me now that she had another man in her life. And then one day a telegram was delivered to the flat, and suddenly the clouds darkening my world lifted and I caught a glimpse of the sunny side of the street again.

The telegram was from Johnny Brandon, asking me to phone him. He didn't say why, but the fact that he had made contact at all was enough to make me jump up and down with excitement. Mummy and I both went to the phone box at the end of Dunsmure Road to make the call, and Mummy spoke to Johnny. I could barely contain myself. The second she put the receiver down I demanded: 'What did he say? What did he want?'

'He's doing a television show for the BBC,' Mummy said. 'He wants you to be in it with him.'

I couldn't believe it. 'Doing what, Mummy?'

'What you said to him when you were in *Judy*,' she said. 'To be the little fan who says she wants to sing and dance on stage.'

I could not have been happier: how terrific to have the chance to work with Johnny again!

The show was called *Variety Parade* and it was transmitted live from the Television Theatre in Shepherds Bush on 3 July. I must have done OK, because Johnny asked for me again the following month for his own forty-minute show, *Dreamer's Highway*, a musical fantasy for teenagers about a nightclub in the stars. *Dreamer's Highway* was broadcast from a TV studio, which was all very different from performing on the stage. Television was not a big medium then, and our classes at Aida Foster's hadn't been geared to it, so I found the lights, the shadows and hitting marks quite confusing, and the cameras intimidating. But I was working again, and with Johnny, and I was over the moon. That summer, all the joy I'd felt in *Love From Judy* returned, and I was in seventh heaven.

After those TV appearances I couldn't wait to work again. Not for a second did I imagine it would be a problem. I thought I was Miss Showbiz and would just walk into another job. Hadn't I been in a hit West End show at fifteen? Hadn't I now been on TV as well, not once, but twice? Wasn't I a cute kid with an enviable, precocious talent that lit up the stage? But after two months of knock-backs I was forced to accept that no one but me thought I was God's gift to the theatre. Aida arranged a few auditions, but I couldn't get that foot in the door: I was quite a brash performer, which was not the flavour of the month. I was back at square one, reluctantly having to admit that landing *Love From Judy* had been more to do with luck than talent, and my TV appearances as much to do with who I knew as how I could perform.

My self-esteem and general confidence was the lowest it had ever been, and to make matters worse, I began to feel embarrassed by my preposterously big breasts. They produced all sorts of saucy comments from groups of men, and I was so self-conscious I had no idea how to respond. Once, when one cheeky bloke on a building site yelled: 'Have you seen your feet lately?', I actually looked down at them. There was a Jewish crowd that used to gather at the E and A salt beef bar at Stamford Hill, among them Neil Osborne, Steven Berkoff and Ronnie Mitchell, who was always nice and polite. 'Hello, Bar,' he'd say, and then, to the others, 'Let the lady pass.'

In the mid-fifties you had to wear what was in fashion, but with such a big bosom nothing seemed to suit or fit me. So every Sunday Mummy would take me to Petticoat Lane to buy material which she made into dresses, skirts and tops. She taught me what looked good on me and what I should avoid: no horizontal stripes, no polka dots and don't mix colours was her advice.

Mummy got fed up with me lounging around feeling sorry for myself, and told me to get off my backside and go on the dole. I had no idea what this was, or how it worked, but I went along to the labour exchange at Hackney to sign on. I stood there in a long queue, not knowing what I was queuing for. Eventually, someone told me how to fill in a claim form and said that my unemployment benefit would be sent on to me in the next few days. Far from being grateful, I was appalled: I hated the idea of being paid for something I hadn't worked for, and I told Mummy so. 'Well, you can't lie around here,' she said. 'You'll have to get a job.'

So I went for an interview at a branch of Littlewood's Pools in Tottenham, but I didn't get the job because I had no academic qualifications. Then, one Friday morning, I saw an advertisement for an assistant at Sherry's shoe shop in Edmonton. I rang for an interview straight away and was given one the same day. I got the job and was asked to start work the following Monday. I should have been pleased – I knew Mummy would be – but on the bus back to Stamford Hill I was more miserable than ever. I didn't want to work in a shoe shop; it wasn't me. Despite all the disappointments, I still wanted to be in showbusiness. It was where I felt I belonged. I poured out my misgivings to Mummy, who, to be fair, was supportive. 'I know, Barbara,' she said sympathetically. 'But you must do your best. Do the job well.'

I certainly did that. One of my first tasks was to remember what shoes the shop carried, and I memorised the stock like a script in one day. Then I learned how to use my sex appeal to encourage men buying shoes for their wives or girlfriends to add matching gloves and handbags, too. I cottoned on to that on my first Saturday, when I caught a bloke eyeing me up as I climbed a ladder to the top shelf. Something in his look told me that I had something he liked, and that I could use it to my advantage. So I started wiggling my bottom a bit more, and directing my sales pitch to the men, not their partners, and it worked a treat. That first Saturday I took a phenomenal £80. I was thrilled, but the manageress wasn't. She was jealous, and when we totted up my sales and she saw how well I'd done, her face was like thunder.

Working in the shoe shop quickly made me realise what a narrow life I'd been leading. For the two years I'd been in *Love From Judy*, all my social life had consisted of was going to the cinema or theatre, or both, and then going home. When one of the shopgirls asked me what I did on Saturday nights, I said: 'Nothing really. I just stay in and listen to the radio or play records.'

'Why don't you come to the Royal with us?'

'What's the Royal?' I asked her.

The girl laughed. 'You don't know the Royal? It's a dance hall. In Tottenham.'

When I told Mummy I was going to my first dance, she dressed me in a black felt full skirt with turquoise hearts and diamonds round the edge to match my tight-fitting, high-necked turquoise sweater, and a turquoise and black petticoat. She even took the trouble to stick little turquoise motifs on a pair of lovely black shoes. And of course I had the immaculate Berlei bra and stockings and suspenders. Mummy pin-curled my hair and helped me comb it out. She liked me looking nice. And as I set off to meet the girls in the Eagle, the pub opposite the Royal, I knew I did.

After a Babycham, I walked across the road and into another world. I'd never seen anything like it. I loved the theatrical air of the dance hall, the lighting and the big orchestra. And I loved the immediate attention I drew from brashly confident young men in long Edwardian jackets with velvet collars and drainpipe trousers and with Tony Curtis curls falling over their foreheads.

It wasn't only my breasts that made me stand out, though: it was the way I was dressed and the way I spoke. I was not the norm, and from the word go I had blokes giving me the eye and chatting me up. The looks I got were different from the furtive glances in the shoe shop. Here they were blatantly sexual, and I hated it. Most of the blokes were cockney, all 'fink' and 'fank' and 'forty-free', and when they made suggestive comments, I responded by going all posh and theatrical. This must have made me more desirable because I was always being asked to dance, and the fact that I was a dancer made me even more popular. When the band struck up the last number, dozens of blokes, it seemed, made a beeline for me. The one I accepted offered to take me home, but he made the mistake of trying to touch me up, so I gave him the push and went home on the bus on my own. I'd spent more than four hours in that dance hall, feeling very wanted. At the time I assumed it was because I was in the theatre, but when I thought about it later, I realised that none of the blokes knew who I was.

I went to the Royal the following Saturday, and the next. It was the beginning of what I felt was a 'normal', non-showbiz, life. I still hankered after stage work, though, and kept in touch with Aida for news of auditions, which I'd go to on my Thursday afternoons off. Until something came along, at least I could put a £5 wage packet in Mummy's hand and have some pocket money back with which to go out and enjoy myself.

Towards the end of 1954 I landed a job singing with the Edmundo Ros band on TV. Ros was very popular, but I found him most unpleasant and I didn't enjoy doing the show at all. I'd been surrounded by lovely people in *Love From Judy*, and for the first time I wondered whether I should forget all about showbiz if it was going to mean having to work with people like him.

But then Johnny Brandon got in touch again.

5

AFTER *VARIETY PARADE*, WHEN JOHNNY BRANDON HAD HAD TO SEND
A TELEGRAM TO GET HOLD OF ME, MUMMY HAD SAID: 'I think it's time
we got a telephone in the flat, Babs.' Since we had, it had been pretty silent as
far as offers of work were concerned, but now it rang, and it was for me, and
it was Johnny.

He wanted me to appear not only on another *Dreamer's Highway* TV
show in January, but also in a stage version of the programme he was
taking on the road in the spring. The TV show, which went out live
on 21 January, was fine. I was thrilled to be on the same bill as Jill
Day, a twenty-three-year-old pop singer making a name for herself in
films. When we did the stage version I was equally thrilled to be on the
same bill at the Grand Theatre in Bolton as a talented young man with
a lovely singing voice who told jokes between his songs. As I stood in
the wings watching him, I noticed that every time he told a joke, a young
woman next to me wrote something down on a notepad. Eventually my
curiosity got the better of me. 'Do you mind me asking what you're doing?'
I asked.

'Not at all,' she replied kindly. 'I'm making notes of how the jokes are
going down, so that we know which gags get a laugh in which town and which
don't. I do this everywhere we play.' I thought, how clever, how professional.
That man was a supporting artiste and closed the first half. He was a huge
hit and even I, a raw seventeen-year-old, could see that he should have been
topping the bill. His name was Ken Dodd.

Dreamer's Highway, on the other hand, didn't work on the stage, and when
we came on after Ken we died on our arses. It was not that *Dreamer's Highway*
was a bad show, but it was too American and too jazzy. Johnny was good,

but quite honestly, people could see much better singing and dancing at the cinema with Fred Astaire and Gene Kelly.

For me, the tour was not a happy experience. The dancers kept themselves very much to themselves and I spent a lot of the time alone. It did have its funny moments, though. During rehearsal, for example, the drummer kept getting something wrong and Johnny went into one. 'I don't have to do this bloody show for a living,' the drummer said. 'I'm a postman as well, I'll have you know.'

I was relieved when the tour ended, but then I was faced with the same problem I'd had after leaving *Love From Judy*: what did I do next? Apart from a pantomime Aida Foster had booked me to do in the winter, there was nothing in the pipeline. I spent the next couple of months going to auditions but there still seemed no room for a tiny blonde song-and-dance girl. If I was given the chance to finish my song, I usually got on the shortlist for a job, but nine times out of ten I was stopped early on and given the usual 'Thank you, we'll let you know.' I was tempted to drop 'On the Sunny Side of the Street' from my repertoire, but knew I wouldn't feel as comfortable with anything else. It was just as well, because one morning in the summer of 1955, that song landed me a spot in a prestigious revue which was to play a vital part in my life.

Many Happy Returns was staged by an eminent producer and writer named Peter Myers at the Watergate Theatre near Charing Cross Station. After I'd sung the song at my audition, he said, with the most unfortunate stammer, 'How ref–ref–ref–reshing you are. S–s–s–s–so dif–dif–different to the other g–g–g–girls.' Then he asked me if I could do the Charleston and, without a second's hesitation, I said I could – 'My dad was a Charleston champion.' He wasn't, actually, but he was bloody good. Next I spoke in some different accents, which Peter thought was my weak spot, but he said that didn't matter and gave me the job. Hallelujah – the brash, ballsy performer was in at last! And it was such a prestigious production, too. The theatre held only a hundred, and on the opening night that select few included, to my amazement, luminaries such as Laurence Olivier. Johnny Brandon came to the opening night and wrote me a lovely letter the next day, telling me I was going to be a big star. I did not understand that: I was still happy to be part of a successful team and on *Many Happy Returns* that team featured the wonderful Edward Woodward, who had a beautiful singing voice; Jimmy Thompson, a renowned revue star, and Thelma Ruby, all very highly regarded in the business. I had no desire to see my name in lights, I just adored the whole process of performing in such exalted company.

Many Happy Returns was a fantastic experience which helped me grow up a bit, and I'll always be grateful to Jimmy Thompson for the part he played in that. He soon noticed how ill at ease I was in the theatre restaurant, always ordering soup, meat, potatoes and peas. 'You aren't used to restaurants, are you?' he said to me one day.

'No. Usually I only ever go to cafés,' I confessed.

The next day he took me to the restaurant on my own, explained the menu and showed me how to order. I was nervous about ordering chicken or fish with bones, but Jimmy helped me, bless him.

I must have made some impact in the revue, because one night an influential showbusiness journalist and former actor named Peter Noble came backstage to meet me. 'You're so cute in this show,' he said. 'I'm producing a film, and I'm going to write you into it.'

I could not believe what I was hearing. To date the sum total of my film experience had been one day's shooting on *The Belles of St Trinian's*, for which Aida Foster had supplied the extras.

'It's only a little part,' he went on. 'But I would like you to come to Shepperton Studios to meet everyone.'

Of course, I took him up on his offer.

I was very excited about going to a film studio for the first time, though it was not quite what I had expected. You imagine you will be running into the likes of Rock Hudson round every corner, but all I saw were lighting men, sound men and chippies going about their business and various people walking around in an assortment of strange costumes.

At Shepperton I was told that the film, *Lost*, was about a police hunt for a kidnapped child, and, yes, there was indeed a small speaking part in it for me. I was thrilled. However, as I was leaving the studio with Noble, my joy turned to fear when suddenly he pushed me against some scenery and started running his hands all over me. As an innocent little virgin I didn't know how to handle this at all. I just kept saying: 'Please, don't do this to me. Please don't do this.' Finally he pulled away, laughing, but I couldn't see what was so funny. I hurried away from the studio, convinced I'd blown my chance of the film part. But a couple of weeks later, I got a call telling me to go to a chemist's in Kensington High Street for a day's shooting. After hanging around for hours I finally uttered the memorable line: 'Can I have a cherry red lipstick?'

My success at the Watergate Theatre also landed me my first cabaret work, at the Côte d'Azur, a Latin-American drinking club in Soho run by a Frenchman we knew as Monsieur Vincent who chose its name in an attempt to create the ambience of a club in the south of France.

I was in a revue with a zany singer-dancer named Una Stubbs and a girl I knew only as 'Fifi', who was married to Digby Wolfe, who wrote and also performed in the revue. Fifi had a mane of red hair, Una had dazzling white teeth and I was blessed with you know what, so Digby wrote a number called 'My Hair, My Teeth, My Bosom', which, as you can imagine, went down a storm.

After the show Una would leave immediately, Fifi would go to the bar and chat with her husband and I would put myself about, talking to the musos and generally enjoying the whole atmosphere. I had no idea that a certain very handsome, Arab-looking young man had what my friend, the singer Georgia Brown, called 'the hots' for me. He came in every night, gazed at me adoringly as I performed, and bought me drinks. The next day he would send me flowers or chocolates and sometimes both. One weekend in October he insisted on throwing a lavish party for the whole cast at his home in Lancaster Gate. Whether or not it was arranged so that he could get closer to me I don't know, but if it was, then the plan worked, because I got plastered and ended up in bed with him. It was a far from memorable experience, but I do have a hazy recollection of travelling home in the early hours aware that I was no longer a virgin and feeling disappointed. 'Is that what it's all about?' I asked myself. The next night I told Georgia. She was not surprised. 'Thank God for that. You were gagging for it,' she said.

'Was I?' I asked. I'd honestly had no idea I was sending out that sort of message.

The following week I came off stage and was mingling with the customers when a smartly dressed man in his mid-twenties came up to me. 'My name is Peter Charlesworth,' he said. 'I'm a song-plugger at the moment, but I'm going to set up as an agent. I'd like to handle you.' I shrugged off his proposal as a pass. 'That's what they all say,' I retorted, and walked off to get changed. But when I came back, he was still there. 'No, seriously, I think you're terrific,' he said. 'I think you've got what it takes.' Before he left, he told me: 'I'm going to bring a friend to see the show. He'll absolutely love you.'

And the following week Peter did come back, bringing with him a face I recognised immediately. It was Benny Hill, who was just starting to become well known on television. Peter had told him: 'There's this little blonde girl who's just fabulous. She sings, she dances, she can do comedy and work the audience. But you've got to see these tits – they're fantastic.' That was the only reason, Peter admitted to me later, that Benny came to the Côte d'Azur that night.

As he left, Peter promised that he would definitely be in touch. There seemed something inherently decent about him that made me feel he could be better for me than Aida Foster. Whatever might come of the relationship, however, would have to wait until the New Year, because I had signed the contract with Aida months before to play Red Riding Hood in pantomime in Liverpool.

I was devastated that I had to leave London. I was earning £10 a week, probably enough to have rented a little flat in the West End had I wanted to. But I had no desire to live there. After the hustle and bustle of Soho, I couldn't wait to get the bus or tube – or sometimes now even a taxi – to the relative calm of Stamford Hill home life and the Jewish area I loved. Best of all, Mummy and Len Atkinson had decided to get married. I was overjoyed. It was clear that Mummy loved and respected Len, and she was so much happier. I thought the world of him, too. And with Len in the flat the atmosphere improved no end.

There was another reason why I didn't want to go away, too. I'd discovered the joys of sex, and I'd become a right little goer, putting it about freely. London, not Liverpool, was where it was all happening and I wished more than anything that I was not contracted to do that panto. But as it turned out, I had a great time in Liverpool. The Shakespeare Theatre, which was due to be pulled down after the panto, was on its last legs. It was running alive with mice and there was water coming through the roof, and as if that wasn't enough to cope with, I was driven mad by a couple of lecherous dwarfs whose heads were level with my chest. But my digs and the Liverpool people were great, and in the end I was having such a good time that I didn't want to come back.

Shortly after I returned to London, in February 1956, Peter Charlesworth phoned me to say that Annie Ross, a great vocalist who sang with Ronnie Scott's famous jazz band, had been taken ill and Ronnie desperately needed a replacement to go on a two-week tour with a new band he was forming, leaving the following Thursday. Was I up for an audition with six other girls? Well, I wasn't a jazz singer, and I knew bugger all about singing with a band, but I had the bottle to tackle anything on stage, so I said: 'Definitely.'

So off I went to Ronnie Scott's first club, which was in a basement in Gerrard Street, off Shaftesbury Avenue, for the audition. The six other girls, who went before me, sang 'The Lady is a Tramp', but I stuck with the tried and tested 'On the Sunny Side of the Street'. Afterwards we stood in a line and Ronnie looked along it, studying us closely. The other girls were all more experienced than me; they all had better, jazzier, voices than mine, too. But Ronnie must have seen something in me he liked. He stopped at me and said: 'You. Little one. Outside the Mapleton Hotel, Leicester Square. Monday morning. Nine o'clock.'

I rang Mummy, all excited, and said I needed an evening dress. The only long one I had was a blue bridesmaid's dress with a high neck and long sleeves. She immediately came to the rescue. It was just like when the commentator on *Come Dancing* used to say: 'And her mother sat up all night sewing.' Except that Mummy spent two whole nights sewing bits of ribbon, sequins and forget-me-nots on to the now scoop-necked, sleeveless bridesmaid's dress to make it suitable for a dance hall.

Ronnie Scott liked it, too – apart from the forget-me-nots. On the first night of the tour he took one look at them and ripped them off. 'The dress is nice,' he said, 'but these flowers are covering up the box office!'

I sang the hits of the day, songs such as 'Band of Gold' and 'Love and Marriage', to a jazzed-up beat. The first night I sat on the bandstand next to the drummer, the great Tony Crombie, and was nearly deafened. On the second night I got into my stride, and Ronnie duetted with me on 'Love and Marriage'. On the third night he came over with a couple of maracas and stuck them in my hand.

'What do I do with these?' I asked.

'Just shake them, Barbara!'

After the show, when Ronnie's musicians found an excuse to knock on my hotel room door at night, I honestly believed that they wanted to talk about my singing or their music. They would plonk themselves down, soften me up with a few complimentary remarks, then suddenly say: 'Are you going to be nice to me?' At first, I would reply: 'Yeah, I'm a nice lady, I really am.' It was only when they said, 'No, I mean *really* nice to me. Are you going to make me a happy man?' that I'd click what it was all about and send them on their way. During that two-week tour I did get it together with the trumpet player and the trombone player, however. I wasn't in love with either of them, and they weren't with me: I was just having a good time with people I liked.

In the first couple of days of the tour I developed a crush on Ronnie Scott himself. 'When the show is over, maybe we'll go out,' he said to me one day. I loved the idea of that: not only was he a very famous bandleader with his own club, but he was very attractive, too. He had the dark, seductive looks of those handsome movie stars of the late forties and early fifties. He was also Jewish, and I had always found Jewish men attractive. On the bandstand, he would look at me and wink and my stomach would turn over. When he phoned after the tour and invited me out, I accepted excitedly.

On the day I made an effort to look really smart. I didn't know where we were going, but as far as I was concerned it was an old-fashioned date, and I didn't want to be caught out by not being suitably dressed for wherever we ended up. We had agreed to meet outside a salt beef bar in Windmill Street, but when I arrived, Ronnie was already inside ordering a salt beef sandwich.

'Half for you and half for me,' he said. I had to laugh: there I was, living near one of the best salt beef bars in London, and I was on a date in a Phil Rabin Nosh Bar! If I thought it was a cheap and cheerful prelude to a romantically exciting evening, I was mistaken. No sooner had we wiped our mouths than Ronnie was leading me into the street and guiding me into a doorway and up some rickety stairs to a dingy little room, bare except for a bed. The next thing I knew, we both had our clothes off and were on the bed. It was very much a wham, bam, thank you, ma'am job, and in no time at all we were back in the street and he was waving me goodbye, leaving me to find my own way to the bus stop.

I was acutely disappointed, but consoled myself that he would not have gone to bed with me if he hadn't liked me. We met twice more like that and I had the same feeling of having been let down each time. Although I didn't relish the confrontation, I knew I had to put an end to it. So as we got dressed after our third 'date', I said girlishly: 'You know, Ronnie, I'm not really enjoying this. It's not a proper date as such, is it?'

He just laughed. I think he was embarrassed. Here was this little shy, immature eighteen-year-old telling him that she expected more from something he saw only as a quick, and very cheap, poke, and he didn't know what to say. He knocked those seedy assignations on the head after that. He probably thought I'd be wanting to go to the pictures next. For me, when I thought back to Ronnie's comments about my dress on the first night of the tour, and some of his gestures with those maracas, I felt that perhaps he had taken me on more for my bosom than for my singing.

The money I earned from the tour soon went and once again I was looking around for work, singing in pubs and clubs for a few quid a night, when I got a call from Bryan Blackburn. I'd never met him, but I knew he was a comedy writer who wrote revues for the Stork Room nightclub off Piccadilly. He said he had been impressed by my performance at the Watergate and wondered what I'd been doing since. He told me: 'I'm putting on a show at a new club in Mayfair and I'd like you to be in it.'

'What sort of club?' I asked.

'Like Churchill's, only better,' he said. 'It'll be the top cabaret nightclub in town.'

I was chosen, along with three other theatrical hopefuls – Barbara Ferris, Fenella Fielding and Jill Gascoigne – for the cabaret at the new club, Winston's. However, the show didn't work, and after two weeks we were given our notice. On the Saturday night of our final performance, I was invited to a party earlier in the evening in Soho. There were many film stars there, including Diana Dors, and I was so awestruck that I started drinking to conquer my nerves. I knocked back so much I passed out, and the next thing I remembered I was waking up in the morning, in my own bed, thankfully, with an awful hangover. Embarrassed at not having turned up at Winston's for the last show, I rang the owner, Bruce Brace, early on the Monday to apologise. 'I'm so, so sorry I let you down, Bruce,' I said, 'but I had a terrible cold and bad chest and just flaked out.'

He burst out laughing. 'What do you mean, let me down? You were there. You took over the show.'

'*What?*'

'You went on stage, rubbished the show, then sang your own stuff.'

I could not believe it. 'What did I sing?'

'"Sunny Side of the Street" and "You Made Me Love You",' he said. 'The audience loved you.'

I didn't say anything. Well, what could I say?

'I'll be in touch,' Bruce told me, and put the phone down, leaving me to wonder what else I'd got up to that Saturday that I didn't remember.

Two weeks later, Bryan Blackburn rang me again. The Winston's customers missed me so much, he said, that he had rewritten the entire show and wanted me to come back and front it. The clubs then tended to feature their own trademark type of performer, and in keeping with the Winston's reputation for cute girls, I was to be joined by Amanda Barrie, who had a similar appeal to mine. It was to be the beginning of a great friendship. For the first time, it was the audience who chose me for a job. Unlike all those casting directors, they did not care that my legs were as short as my vowels. It was the beginning for me of a lifelong affair with the lovely British public.

6

I WAS WORRIED WHEN BRUCE TOLD ME HE WAS CONSIDERING POACHING A FEMALE IMPERSONATOR FROM THE RIVAL CLUB, CHURCHILL'S. The performer, Danny La Rue, was good, but Bruce had got everything spot-on this time. Business was booming and Winston's was always packed, and I thought if it wasn't broke, you shouldn't fix it. I tried to talk him out of it, but he went ahead anyway. He was dead right. In no time Danny helped turn Winston's into *the* club in London. We became great mates, and Danny was very protective towards me. One night when I was on stage with him, a punter kept calling out to me, 'I couldn't half give you one, darling,' and Danny didn't like it. 'Watch it,' he said, 'or I'll be down to see you.'

'Oh, yeah?' the punter jeered. 'You old poofter.'

Danny jumped down from the stage. 'Don't let this wig fool you, mate,' he said, and promptly laid out the punter with a right hook. After that, 'Don't let this wig fool you' became Danny's catchphrase.

Another of Winston's young performers was a very short man, not much taller than me, named Ronnie Corbett. I felt sorry for Ronnie; he always seemed to be on his own. When I mentioned this to one of the hostesses, she laughed. 'Don't worry about Ronnie,' she said. 'He can take his pick of us any night of the week!' He ended up marrying one of the stars of the show, the beautiful Annie Hart.

Early in 1957, Peter Charlesworth came back into my life. He called me to say that he had formed a showbusiness agency with Max Bygraves' agent, Jock Jacobson, and he still wanted to handle my career. He felt he could do more for me than Aida Foster. My instinct was that he was right. So in February I left Aida and went on to Peter's books. It proved to be the best decision of my life.

Peter – or PC, as everybody called him – thought I was wasting my time at Winston's. He saw me as an actress, capable of both comedy and drama, and insisted I went for auditions for stage roles. Towards the end of that year, I passed one for an offbeat revue, *Keep Your Hair On*, with the brilliant Welsh actress Rachel Roberts as the leading lady. The production – a follow-up to *Cranks*, Johnny Cranko's huge fifties hit with Anthony Newley and Annie Ross – was going straight into the West End at the Shaftesbury, and I was thrilled at the thought of performing at a big London theatre again, even though the piece was so off the wall that I didn't understand one word of it.

When I told my wonderful guv'nor, Bruce, that I was leaving Winston's, he came out on stage on my last night, just before Christmas, with a huge cake. 'Well, we've had our little star here for some time, and she's a great favourite with us,' he told the audience. 'But now she's going off to the West End. We want to wish her well.' Everybody cheered and there were kisses all round, with everyone congratulating me, which was lovely.

Bruce was stretching a point in saying I was to star in the West End: I had a fabulous little part that I could score with, and I was excited, but that excitement faded quickly when the cast realised that the whole show was a shambles. After a disastrous and depressing dress rehearsal, we consoled ourselves with the old showbiz adage 'Bad rehearsal, great first night', but we feared the worst. And, as it turned out, we had every reason to worry: everything that could have gone wrong did.

We were given a warning of the fiasco to follow when one of our first 'notes' during the dress rehearsal warned everyone: 'Don't go anywhere near the scenery.' It had been brilliantly devised by the photographer Anthony Armstrong-Jones – who later married Princess Margaret and became Lord Snowdon – using big, blown-up black and white photographs, but everything was so far behind schedule that it was still wet when the curtain went up. We had to concentrate almost as much on not touching the scenery as on our lines. The cues were all wrong, a light fell down and sliced through the scenery – you name it, it happened.

Rachel Roberts was a strong performer and she was playing opposite this rather fey actor. Amazingly, the show got off to a great start, but the mood changed halfway through the second half when the leading man sang a number called 'Crocodile Tears'. We knew we'd lost it when one of the renowned and influential gallery first-nighters, a woman in her fifties, stood up and shouted: 'Crocodile Tears? More like crocodile fucking queers!'

That raised a few embarrassed laughs, but it was the booing that most of us remembered after the curtain came down. That and the lone voice of dear Danny La Rue in the dress circle, shouting at the noisy crowd: 'Shut up, you lot. They are doing their best down there.'

Ten days later, on 23 February 1958, the show came off and I had no alternative but to go to Bruce and ask for my job back. Thankfully, he welcomed me with open arms.

For a young woman not yet twenty-one, Winston's was marvellous because I never knew, from one night to the next, what the audience was going to be like. The club attracted the rich and the not so rich, the famous and the infamous. Some nights heavy underworld figures rubbed shoulders with film stars like Gina Lollobrigida and Victor Mature and millionaire movie moguls like Darryl Zanuck; on others, our own showbiz stars would mix with Fleet Street printers or sales reps in London for a conference.

Now that I had more experience of sex, I was quite carefree. I thought, I like this. And I realised I was wanted, that it was 'in' to look as I did. There were men round me like bees round a honeypot and I took advantage of that and went bananas. And because I was still so naïve, I never bothered with any form of contraception.

I was awestruck when Victor Mature came to the club. He was the Sylvester Stallone of his day, and I'd seen him in *Samson and Delilah* when I was a child. Apparently he said to someone, 'I'd love to meet that little blonde girl – she seems like fun.' Not surprisingly, I was quite silly and giggly when we were introduced, but he didn't seem to mind. He invited a crowd of us out to supper and then back to the luxurious house he was renting in Mayfair. There I was, partying with a Hollywood star and a lot of posh, debby types. It was like another world. I stayed the night at Victor's house, and got a clout from Mummy the next day when he rang to say I'd left my earrings behind.

I was more attracted to a far younger American, Gary Crosby, the eldest son of Bing, the legendary Hollywood star, who was in England on a tour of the US bases. I'd seen lots of Bing's movies and was thrilled when Gary chatted me up after the show then asked if he could take me home. I don't know where he thought I lived, but I'm sure he hadn't bargained for a forty-minute taxi ride out of the elegance of Mayfair and into the drabness of Stoke Newington. The journey seemed to go on for ever and I got really embarrassed watching the meter clocking up. I could sense Gary thinking, 'Jeez, where is this chick taking me?'

At nearly four in the morning, I couldn't possibly invite him in for coffee or anything, so I just kissed him goodnight and he went back to town, promising to see me at the club the following night. When I got in, I was so excited at having met Bing Crosby's son that I woke Mummy up. 'You'll never guess what,' I said. 'Gary Crosby's just brought me home from the club.'

Mummy was less than impressed. 'Fancy waking me up to tell me that,' she said. 'Now, if it had been Bing . . .'

I saw Gary regularly after the show for the next two weeks. I found him very nice and polite, and extremely attractive. One Friday night, I agreed to have dinner at the Dorchester Hotel with him, his godfather and some friends. I arrived at eight o'clock. I'd never been inside a posh hotel and I was very nervous. Gary was so sweet. He was there the minute I walked in and quickly introduced me to his friends and his godfather. One face I recognised from the cinema was the actor Forrest Tucker, who, Gary told me, was in England filming *The Abominable Snowman* with Peter Cushing. There were also some elegant-looking ladies. They could have been brasses for all I knew, but they seemed so self-assured that I felt terribly inferior.

I was given a champagne cocktail – bubbly mixed with a drop of brandy – which I'd never heard of, let alone drunk. Then we sat down to dinner and, of course, the menu was in French, wasn't it. I hadn't a clue what most of it meant. I shyly ordered melon, followed by steak and a salad – items I felt sure must be on the menu somewhere.

Gary did his best to involve me in all the sparkling conversation, but when we had finished eating, he took my hand and said: 'You're feeling very ill at ease, aren't you, Barbara? What's the matter?'

'It's all a bit much for me, Gary,' I told him. 'The champagne cocktails and everything, and the girls – they seem to take it all in their stride. It's all so easy for them.'

'Let me tell you something,' he said softly. 'You are shy. And you are lovely. You've nothing to be worried about. You've got more class than all these women.' I felt he was trying to tell me to relax; that he wanted me there for myself, and he did make me feel better, but I was still relieved when it was time for me to leave to get ready to go on stage. When Gary asked me to go back to the hotel after I'd finished my cabaret, I wasn't sure I wanted to, but he had been so sweet, a real gentleman, that I agreed.

Back at the hotel, he suddenly became very serious. 'I'm flying off to Germany tomorrow to finish my draft service, and I want us to get engaged,' he said. 'But I haven't got a ring or anything.' It was all so quick. I'd known him for just two weeks and now he wanted to get engaged! It was all to get me into bed for the night, of course, and it worked.

The next morning, Gary's press agent asked me to go to the airport with them to be photographed waving Gary off (I was astounded when the picture appeared on the front pages of the papers the following day). By then Gary didn't want to leave. 'I'll write to you, Barbara,' he said. 'And when I come back . . .'

After the plane took off, the press agent looked at me. 'He will write, you know,' he said. 'He's very smitten.'

The press agent was right. Gary did write, several times, and I wrote back. But over the next year or so the long-distance relationship fizzled out and the next I heard he was back in America making a movie, *Holiday For Lovers*. I never forgot Gary Crosby, though, for making a shy young girl's first visit to a posh hotel such an occasion. And I never forgot the Dorchester, either. It was such an elegant, stylish hotel, it seemed so perfect for special moments.

After the show, I would often go on to the Côte d'Azur or another club to unwind and chat with friends. At one club I met a very attractive man whose appeal to me lay in the talent and vitality that shone out of him. His name was Anthony Newley and he was making a name for himself after a wonderful film debut as the Artful Dodger in David Lean's brilliant *Oliver Twist* in 1948. We clicked, and went out on a couple of smashing dates.

A few weeks later, I was drawn to a thin, hungry-looking guy who regularly sang at the Côte d'Azur. His name was Cliff Lawrence and his voice was a cross between Frank Sinatra's and Mel Torme's. When he saw me in the audience, he asked to be introduced, and we fancied each other immediately. My friends warned me off Cliff, telling me that he was unreliable and temperamental with a self-destructive streak, but I found him irresistible and we began a passionate, if violent, affair.

For one reason or another, we were always fighting. Once, when I didn't want to go home, he dragged me along the street by my hair, and it was nothing unusual for me to turn up for work at Winston's with a black eye or a bruised arm. When I introduced Cliff to Mummy, she, too, thought he was not good for me. He never earned any money; he had talent, but wasted it. She tried to stop me seeing him, but the lust was too strong. I couldn't help myself.

Gradually, though, Cliff's erratic behaviour, obsessive gambling and cavalier disregard for his career started to affect me. Before, I'd had a very professional approach to my work, always arriving on time and with the right attitude. But now I began to feel lethargic and often downright lazy. But Cliff wasn't the only reason for that.

One day I was assisting Robert Harben, a well-known magician, in a live TV show at the Hackney Empire, filling in for his regular assistant, who had been taken ill. Of course I knew nothing about doing magic tricks and there had been no time to teach me: I just had to try to take on board what I had to do in a few minutes before the show. Not surprisingly I was hopeless. I had to be 'the lady in the box' – in the box one moment and gone the next – which involved climbing on to partitions which divided the box so that when Robert opened one of the doors at the front I couldn't be seen. I thought I did quite well, but apparently there was always one bit of me – an arm or a foot – flashing across the screen because I hadn't been quite quick enough. Evidently the television audience thought it was the funniest act they'd ever seen. Robert was absolutely furious.

To make matters worse I was feeling ill myself. I kept needing to go the toilet to be sick, and over the next few days I'd throw up every morning. Eventually, Mummy asked if I'd had my period. I hadn't.

'And you're being sick every morning?'

'Yeah.'

'Well, that's it. You're pregnant.'

'Yeah. If that's what it means, I suppose I must be,' I said.

It sounds unbelievable, but it's true. It had never crossed my mind how children came into the world, and for all I knew a woman could get pregnant simply by kissing a man. So when Mummy said I was pregnant, I was terrified. I didn't have a clue what to do.

Mummy admitted that she didn't know what to do, either. She had known someone who performed abortions during the war, but the woman had died. I said I'd speak to the girls at Winston's.

'What happens if you get pregnant?' I asked one of them that night. 'A friend of mine's going out of her mind.'

One girl gave me the number of a woman in Streatham in south London. The next morning I dialled it nervously. The woman seemed very nice and said she would do the abortion for £15. She gave me her address and told me to be there at eight o'clock the next morning. I set off at what seemed like the crack of dawn, feeling lonely and frightened. I had to get one bus after another and the journey took for ever, adding to my anxiety. But when I arrived, the woman was very kind, welcomed me into this beautiful house and did her best to put me at ease. It was almost like going to size up a place for digs while I performed at the local theatre.

The woman did not explain anything to me; she just did the job clinically, with the minimum of fuss or embarrassment, then told me to go home and rest. All I could think on the long journey back to north London was that no woman had ever touched that part of my body before, and what a horrible experience it had been. I had gone there not knowing what to expect, and now I was going home, still in the dark. I was so, so frightened. I knew I'd have to go to the loo, but I had no idea how the baby would leave my body.

Although I had been told to rest, like a fool I went to work at Winston's. Miraculously, I got through the evening with no pain at all, but when I arrived home at about three in the morning it started. Mummy was awake. She got up and held me tightly and advised me on what I should be doing while Len kept out of the way in their bedroom. But over the next three hours the pain got worse and my screams got louder. For once, Mummy was not worried about the neighbours, only about me.

When I was still in agony at 7 a.m., Mummy asked me for the number of the woman in Streatham. At first the woman was obviously petrified to talk, because I heard Mummy say to her: 'No, I'm not going to tell anyone. I'm the mother of the little blonde girl, Barbara Deeks. She's in a great deal of pain and I don't know what to do.'

The next thing I knew I was being told to sit on a bowl of boiling water. It scalded me, but it did the trick. Then Mummy put me to bed and, in a rare moment of closeness and honesty, confided that she'd known all was not well because she had had an abortion herself, shortly after Daddy had gone to war. It was the perfect opportunity for her to tell me, belatedly, the facts of life, but she didn't. After those few minutes of intimacy she became distant once more and neither sex nor its repercussions were ever mentioned again.

In the following months I did quite a bit of TV, including the *Jack Jackson Show*, on which I mimed to hit records of the day, and stood in for Josephine Douglas presenting the hugely popular and high-profile Friday pop record show *Six-Five Special* with the disc jockey Pete Murray. My joy at this lucky break was marred, however, by having to make another emergency trek to Streatham. This time Mummy knew nothing about it.

On my twenty-first birthday, Cliff took me to a party in Knightsbridge with one of his friends, Richard Lyon, the adopted son of Ben Lyon and Bebe Daniels, who were enjoying enormous success with their radio comedy show. Cliff and I were caught up in the heady atmosphere of the night and when he asked me to marry him, I gushed, 'Yes.' The next morning a picture of us with Richard appeared in a daily newspaper, with a small story reporting our engagement. When I rang Mummy to tell her it was true, she did her nut. She didn't think he was suitable for me and that was that; my feelings didn't come into it. She also blamed him for getting me pregnant and had never forgiven him for that. Now, on top of everything else, my getting engaged to him, and behind her back as well, was too much.

I expected a blasting when I got home, and I got one – but not so much from Mummy as from Len. He laid into me, telling me how selfish and thoughtless I was. 'I want you to know how unhappy you've made your mother,' he said. 'You've got no right to do that. She's a wonderful woman. I'll never forgive you, Barbara.'

When he had finished I said: 'Well, that's it. I'm not coming back here again. I'm going to live in the West End.'

I meant it. I stormed out and went to stay with some friends. After a couple of days I calmed down and went home during the day to collect my things, particularly a dress I needed for my first-ever solo singing spot. I got a shock when I put my key into the door of the flat. It didn't fit. Mummy was so angry with me that she had changed the locks. She knew I'd sneak home while she was at work to collect the dress and she wanted a confrontation with me. So I had to go back in the evening. I had it out with her then, promising not to see Cliff again so that I could move back in. It was an empty promise, but I just had to say something to placate her and get off again. I was opening the next night in my solo act and I was sick with nerves. I just had to get myself together.

The job was at the Jack of Clubs nightclub, run by Jack Isow below his famous Soho restaurant, where stars like Cary Grant had their names imprinted on the backs of expensive leather chairs. Not surprisingly, with all the upset and everything, I died on my arse. And it was the first time I felt I could put my hands up and say it was my fault. I was awful, and the experience made me wonder whether perhaps I was only cut out to be a support act rather than a star.

Jack had wanted a thirty-five-minute spot, but I had rushed everything and was finished in twenty. For the next night, Peter Charlesworth suggested that I sang a current Max Bygraves hit, 'Hands', impersonating such stars as Al Jolson, Judy Garland and Sophie Tucker, who were famous for using their hands while performing, and building in a little chit-chat to fill out the show. It went slightly better and lasted slightly longer, but even so, when I came off, Jack said: 'You work the week, and that's it.' Fortunately, I was spared the embarrassment of having to go back. It was a relief when I woke up the next day covered in spots. I had chicken pox. But feeling rough and having to stay in bed was better than flopping on stage.

Cliff and I wanted our own flat, but we both needed to be earning to afford it. One night, after he had performed wonderfully at the Nightingale club in Gerrard Street, I persuaded the owner to give him a regular spot – and to pay him in advance so that he could buy a new suit. The trouble with Cliff was that he liked performing for nothing, but once he got a job he just wouldn't turn up. So I shouldn't have been surprised when I went to the Nightingale on his opening night to find no Cliff and the owner steaming. Boiling mad myself, I said I would find him and fetch him. I trawled all his usual haunts, but I couldn't track him down anywhere. Then, just as I was about to give up, I saw him staggering out of a drinking club in Gerrard Street, only a few doors away from the club. I ran up to him and bellowed: 'How can you do this to me, you bastard?' Before he could mumble any excuse, I spotted the Nightingale's two burly bouncers walking towards us. Cliff started to run off, but one of the blokes grabbed him and pushed him against the wall. I dashed between them, begging the bouncer not to hurt Cliff, but I was a split-second too late. The thump aimed at Cliff caught me in the face instead and I fell to the ground. As the horrified bouncer and his mate bent down to pick me up, Cliff got away.

Early in 1959 I went for an audition for the part of a wacky beatnik – which I wasn't right for – in a play called *The Gimmick*, starring Bernard Braden and Barbara Kelly, a Canadian couple who were making names for themselves in films and television in Britain, Bernard on *Breakfast With Braden* and *Bedtime With Braden*, and Barbara as a panellist on *What's My Line?* There were dozens of girls there, but the shortlist finally came down to two: me and a tall, dark, very beautiful actress named Judy Bruce. We were called back after two auditions because the director and producer disagreed on which of us to cast. At the third audition it was left to Bernard to decide. He chose me.

The play was due to open in the West End after a two-month provincial tour. With things as they were with Cliff, I was relieved to be going away and to be able to put off any decisions about our future together – if we had one. When I handed in my notice at Winston's, Bruce brought out another cake and went through the now familiar 'Our Barbara is off to become a huge West End star' routine. I began rehearsals on a high, but I was quickly brought down to earth when I was told that, as Barbara Kelly was also blonde, I had to dye my hair. I didn't like it, of course, but I had no choice. Dark hair looks terrible on me, so I dyed it red and put a pink rinse through it to make me a strawberry blonde. Then I bought a long hairpiece and dyed it the same colour, and it worked well.

We were a relatively happy team, although I did notice that Barbara Kelly was rather distant and cool towards me.

The play opened in Leeds to good reviews and went on to do good business around the country for the next five weeks. As we arrived in Wolverhampton for the fifth week, I felt a surge of excitement: just two more dates, Newcastle and Oxford, before we hit Golders Green, then the West End of London.

One of the actors, Monty Landis – of *Rowan and Martin's Laugh-In* fame – was a real joker who always tried to make me laugh as we took our final bows. I'd contain myself until the curtain came down, then I'd dash off stage, giggling all the way to my dressing room. The last night at Wolverhampton, a Saturday, was no exception. I was still laughing as I changed out of my costume when there was a knock on the door. It was the show's producer, Charles Ross.

'Hello,' I said cheerily. 'How are you? Great show tonight, wasn't it?'

But he hadn't come to talk about the performance. 'I don't really know how to say this to you, Barbara, but I've got some very bad news. I'm afraid I'm having to give you two weeks' notice.'

I stared at him, not knowing what to say. I'd heard him, but the words did not make any sense, didn't register. All the reviews, and mine particularly, had been great. And we were on our way to the West End, weren't we? All that came out of my mouth, quiet and plaintive, was: 'But why? Why?'

Looking slightly embarrassed, he said: 'I'm terribly sorry, Barbara, it's just something that's got to be done.' And with that, he walked out.

I burst into tears. I was still sobbing when Monty came in, having heard I'd been fired and wanting to know why. I couldn't tell him. I'd never misbehaved, I'd always been on time, my reviews were good, yet I was being kicked out, my dreams of getting back to the West End shattered. Other people heard the news and came to offer sympathy but, significantly, not Bernard Braden or Barbara Kelly.

Monty, bless him, half dressed me as I fought to get myself together and the others helped me to pack up all my things and load them on to the van that was taking everything on to the next town. Suddenly it struck me that I did not want to go to the next town. If I wasn't going on to the West End, I wanted no further part of the show; I wanted to go home and let Nyree Dawn Porter, the assistant stage manager who doubled as my understudy, step into my role. I phoned Peter Charlesworth at home and the second I heard his voice, I started to weep uncontrollably. 'I'm coming home tomorrow and leaving them to it,' I said.

'No,' said PC quickly. 'Now you listen to me—'

Before he could continue, Monty snatched the phone and told him: 'We're going to take Barbara out. We've all been invited to this party.'

'Good,' Peter replied. 'Now put Barbara back on.' To me, he said: 'What you do is go to this party and have a few drinks. It'll make you feel better. Then, in the morning, make sure you're on the train to Newcastle with all the other actors. Show them that you're going to fulfil your contract, your two weeks' notice. Behave like the professional I know you are.'

I did go to the party, I did have a few drinks and I did cry some more, but I was on the train the next day, determined to do what Peter thought best, even though all I wanted to do was run away and hide and lick my wounds.

On the Monday, I did not bother getting to the theatre until around five o'clock; I saw no point doing up my dressing room if I wasn't going to be part of the show any more. When I walked in, I collapsed in tears again. Someone had stuck the cuttings of all our newspaper reviews for the previous six weeks round the mirror, with a note in the middle that read: 'Look at these, darling. It's just not fair. We all love you.' Through my tears, I looked at the biggest review. It was headlined: 'BARBARA NO. 2 OUT-ACTS BARBARA NO. 1'.

On the final Saturday night, the stage doorman rang my dressing room to tell me a gentleman wished to speak to me. I agreed to see him. He was a little, fat Jewish man and he introduced himself as Slim Cattan, a film producer. 'I'm making a film,' he said. 'There's a smashing little part for you. You'll be great.'

Just as I was thinking, oh, yeah, this is either a wind-up by Monty or a repeat of the Peter Noble episode, he added: 'Who's your agent?'

I gave him Peter Charlesworth's address and phone number.

'Lovely,' he said. 'I'll be in touch with him in a month or so.' And then he was gone.

The funny thing is, if I had not been given the sack, and if that little man had not come backstage, I am not sure if the world would ever have heard of Barbara Windsor.

7

'YOU KNOW, BAR, THERE'S A GUY WHO I WENT TO SCHOOL WITH WHO'S DRIVEN UP AND DOWN THIS ROAD THREE TIMES. I think he's trying to pluck up courage to speak to you.'

I was walking along the road with my friend Neil Osborne, who had just taken me to lunch at Montegeno in Stamford Hill. I was still upset about being sacked from *The Gimmick*, and agonising over what to do about Cliff, and he'd been trying to cheer me up. I had no idea how he'd worked out what a stranger in a car was thinking, but I let it pass. Then Neil said: 'His name's Ronnie Knight. We were in the same class.' I looked round and saw a lemon and grey Ford Zephyr cruising slowly past us. A couple of minutes later, a good-looking, smartly dressed and well-groomed young man in his early twenties, with a sweet face and a twinkle in his eye, was walking towards us.

'Hello, Neil,' he said. 'How are you?'

'Fine, Ronnie,' Neil said.

'Aren't you going to introduce me to this pretty lady?'

I thought, pretty? What are you talking about? It was not a word I ever used in relation to myself. And I was not exactly looking glamorous. I was wearing hardly any make-up and as it had just begun to rain, I was pulling on an old plastic see-through mac. I said a polite hello, but my mind was on my troubles, and, after a couple of minutes, he went on his way.

Three days later Neil rang. 'Bar, you remember that guy Ronnie Knight? Well, he came looking for me in the salt beef bar. He wanted your phone number. Hope you don't mind, but I gave it to him. I didn't like to say no.'

I wasn't pleased, but there was nothing to be done about it. 'That's all right, Neil,' I said. 'I know exactly what he's like. He obviously knows I'm in showbiz and thinks we're all at it like knives. He thinks I'm easy.'

Ronnie called the same evening, wanting to take me out. 'I can't,' I told him. 'I'm busy.'

'Oh, all right,' he said. 'Can I phone you again?'

He was so polite that I said, 'OK, if you want. But I'm in the theatre and don't keep normal hours.'

Several days later, he rang again and I said I was still busy. I wasn't, but I had no interest in going out with anyone outside showbusiness. I'd have felt uncomfortable. But after another few days he called a third time.

'You said I could call you again, so I am. Would you like to go out with me one evening?'

I had nothing much going on and thought it was nice that he had persevered, so I gave in. 'Yeah, all right then.'

'Well, there's a turn-up. I wouldn't have phoned again,' he said.

'It's your lucky day.'

'Yeah,' he said. 'I think it is.'

Mummy wanted me to marry money. 'Don't pick anyone like your father,' she'd say. 'Don't worry about good looks.' She had her eye on a wealthy Jewish boy called Johnny Bloom, who lived a few doors away from us. He had made his name as the first man to sell washing machines direct to the public, and drove a Rolls-Royce. I went out with him once to keep her happy, but she couldn't understand why I didn't take things further.

Someone else she would have liked me to marry was another Jewish boy, David Starr, who operated mock auctions in street markets. I had gone out with him after he came to Winston's with Shirley Bassey. He said he wanted to marry me, and gave me a ring, saying he had planned to give it to Shirley but had changed his mind after meeting me. I didn't believe him for a moment: Shirley could have had anyone. David knew exactly how to handle Mummy. He brought her flowers and chocolates and said all the right things – how much he loved me and wanted to take care of me. She had urged me to settle down with him. 'Don't worry about the love, that will come later,' she said.

On the evening of my date with Ronnie, Mummy was excited when I told her I was being picked up in a car. And when she saw him pull up outside the flat in his Zephyr she was impressed. 'What a lovely car,' she said. I knew why she liked it so much. It was the colour – the same lemon and grey as the outfit and little hat she had made for me when I went on tour with *Love From Judy*. It had been my first time out of school uniform and that outfit was her favourite of all the clothes she'd made for me. She was pleased, too, to see Ronnie get out of the car and wipe the windows. She liked that: making everything nice for her Babs.

If Ronnie was nervous about going out on his first date with me, he didn't show it. He saw Mummy and me looking down from the first-floor window and waved nonchalantly. I was nervous, though, and, over drinks at a Tottenham club owned by one of Ronnie's friends, I hardly stopped rabbiting. It was all so strange to me: I was used to dating showbusiness guys in the West End and here I was in north London with a bloke I'd known two minutes, who could have been a window cleaner for all I knew. But I had a lovely evening and was pleasantly surprised by Ronnie's behaviour: he didn't try to grab hold of me once, and when he dropped me at home, he did not even kiss me goodnight. He just said, very politely, 'Thank you for a lovely time. I'll phone you again.'

The following week he took me for a meal in the West End, where I was more relaxed, and over the next few days he phoned me constantly. Evidently Ronnie had had his eye on me well before we had been introduced by Neil. He told me that we had first met me in a pub where my Uncle Ronnie had been singing. He had mentioned to me then that he had often seen me outside the Mapleton Hotel in Leicester Square. 'Yeah,' I'd replied. 'I go to a jazz club there.' After that, he said, he had hung around outside the hotel in the hope of seeing me. Once he had, and he'd come up and said: 'Hi. Remember me?'

Apparently I'd just given him a vague 'Yes, how are you?'

'You didn't want to know,' he told me now.

I was still not what you'd call smitten, but when he invited me out on my twenty-second birthday and said he wanted to take me somewhere special, I jumped at the chance. I thought we'd go to a nightclub in the West End, but he drove out to a restaurant at Heathrow Airport from which we could watch the planes landing and taking off while we ate. I'd never been on a plane and I thought that was terrific. We chatted easily about the places we'd each like to fly off to if we had the money, and then the subject of my birthday came up and Ronnie pulled some notes out of his pocket – £13, to be precise. He thrust them into my hand. 'Here, go and buy yourself something.' It was a strange thing to do – I don't know why he didn't just give me a bunch of flowers or something – and I remember thinking that it was an odd amount, too. Nevertheless, by the end of the evening, I was quite taken with him. He was smart, handsome, clean – and rather shy, which I liked.

One afternoon, later that month, he turned up at the flat unannounced while Mummy and Len were at work. By then we fancied the pants off each other, but I was keeping him at arm's length because he had been treating me like a lady and I didn't want to spoil things. I certainly had no plans to have it off with someone in my mother's house, even if I did live there as well. But when Ronnie made a move towards me, I found myself backing off towards my bedroom. We fell on to my little single bed and went at it frantically. We were so excited by then that it was all over very quickly, but it was enjoyable nonetheless.

However, when we had calmed down, I got a bit defensive. 'This isn't going to be a regular occurrence, you know,' I said. 'I don't want you thinking you can pop by here and have a matinée with me whenever you fancy it.' I was, after all, still theoretically engaged to Cliff Lawrence.

'No, no, that's not what I want,' Ronnie assured me hastily. 'I just think you're lovely. I really think you're lovely.'

We lay there quietly for a bit, and then he said: 'I'd like to come over one day and maybe you could cook me a meal.'

I'd never cooked a meal for myself, let alone anyone else, but I found myself saying: 'Yeah, OK.'

Over the next few weeks Ronnie and I saw more of each other and I slowly began to care a lot for him. He would come to Winston's and run me home afterwards, which was lovely; far better than having to get the bus. He was always charming and attentive, and the sex improved. He didn't talk much about his business – he just said he was a company director involved with toys. I hadn't met anybody else like that; I thought he was quite posh, actually. There were many times in the week when he couldn't see me, but not being a nine-to-five worker myself, I didn't think anything of it. He'd say he was tied up with his business, and I accepted that. He could not see me on Sundays because he played football on Hackney Marshes and that was fine by me too. It suited me not to see Ronnie all the time anyway. I was going out with – and sleeping with – other men when the fancy took me. Ronnie was special, but he was not my one and only.

One lunchtime, I saw another side of him. He had held me to my promise to cook him a meal, even though I'd told him I couldn't cook to save my life – I was an actress, not a housewife, I'd said. I was nervously attempting to grill some lamb chops, concentrating on trying to remember how my mother did it, when the phone rang. It was Cliff Lawrence, and he was steaming. 'I'm in the phone box round the corner and I know you've got somebody there!' he bellowed. 'You're going out with that guy Ronnie Knight. I know him. Tell him I'll shoot him. I'll kill him.'

Ronnie quickly cottoned on to what was happening. He grabbed the phone from me. 'I'm coming down to see you,' he said menacingly. We both ran downstairs, jumped into Ronnie's car and drove off to look for Cliff. Suddenly Ronnie stopped the car.

'I've just realised I don't even know what he looks like,' said Ronnie.

'I'll tell you when I see him,' I promised.

I had no intention of letting Ronnie find him, though – having seen his temper for the first time, I had no doubt that he would give Cliff a good seeing-to if he did. So when I spotted Cliff lurking in the phone box I said nothing. Ronnie drove straight past him and eventually he gave up and we went back to the flat.

Mummy had taken to Ronnie from the start. He was charm itself to her, nicely spoken and respectful, always said the right thing and stood the right way. But it was not long before someone told her the truth about him. In early September, I walked through the door after a friend's wedding in Essex to find that Mummy had gone into one. 'You're going round with a married man who's got a little girl and another baby on the way!' she yelled. She was talking as if this was something I knew, but I didn't. I had no idea, and I was shocked rigid.

I waited for Ronnie to ring, and when he did, I let him have it, using all the colourful words I'd picked up in showbusiness and a few more besides. I blasted him for stringing me along, telling me a pack of lies, treating me like a fool. And then I told him that I never wanted to see him again and he could go to hell.

But he kept phoning and phoning, and, in the end, I gave in and agreed to see him.

When we met up Ronnie told me he had met his wife, June, at school and had married her after she became pregnant. Everything had been fine for a while, but he had outgrown her and now they had nothing in common: he was someone with a few quid who liked the club life; she preferred to stay at home. With June the week was mapped out and organised and he always knew what to expect, whereas with me, everything was unpredictable and exciting.

We talked it all through and I began to believe him. From what I'd seen, he did seem to be more of a man about town than a settled-down dad, and he did seem to be genuinely in love with me. And I agreed to continue the affair because by now I was desperately in love with him.

As I left Ronnie said to me: 'Will you behave yourself this weekend?'

'Why?' I asked.

'Because I want to marry you.'

From then on, my attitude to other men changed dramatically. Now that I realised that Ronnie really did care for me, I elbowed everyone else. No one had a chance; I was a one-man woman.

Mummy was livid. She could not bear the thought of me knocking around with a married man – particularly one who now reminded her of Daddy. She even offered Ronnie £200 – her life savings – to stay away from me. He turned it down, saying he loved me too much to walk out on me.

I'm sure Ronnie felt it was wrong to fall in love with me, that I was not right for him, but he could not help himself. Sometimes he felt out of his depth with the famous people I mixed with; he didn't believe he had anything to contribute. But he did. He had this nice quality, a lovely way, and he was very good for me. He sat me down and told me: 'You're sexy enough, Barbara. You don't have to wear those low-cut, tight dresses. You don't have to put it all in everyone's face, you know.' He was right. I took his advice, and Peter Charlesworth picked up on the change. 'I don't know who you're going out with, Barbara,' he said, 'but whoever he is, he's having a wonderful effect on you.'

Until I met Ronnie I never saw myself as a star, just a steady, reliable performer. But he gave me extra confidence and generally made me believe that I could achieve much more in life. He was lucky for me. And, in a way, I was lucky for him. He did not have a wide vocabulary, so he was always wary of opening his mouth in case he said the wrong thing. I used to encourage him and teach him words he'd never heard before. I taught him to read and write better, too. Ronnie had spent more than three years in hospital as a kid, missing vital schooling, and was virtually illiterate. While playing football on a bombsite, he had fallen into a crater in which six horses killed by a wartime explosion were buried. He cut one of his legs and picked up an infection from one of the carcasses. It was diagnosed as osteomyelitis, a disease that rots bone marrow. He finally left hospital at thirteen after five major operations, and being a rebel who scorned authority, he had never caught up with his education.

There was still a lot Ronnie didn't know about me – how I actually earned my money, for example. One night, we were in L'Hirondelle, a club next to the Stork Room, when one of the band spotted me and called out: 'Come on, Windsor, come on up. Give us a song.'

I went to get up, but Ronnie tugged my sleeve. 'No,' he said. 'You can't.'

'Why not?' I said. 'I do sing, you know!'

Ronnie looked scared out of his wits as I walked up to the stage. He thought I was going to make a fool of myself and of him, too. As I sang 'On the Sunny Side of the Street', and then 'From This Moment On', I watched Ronnie's expression change from shock to amazement. I got a great ovation and when I came back to my seat Ronnie was smiling. 'You were fantastic,' he said. 'I had no idea you did all that.'

'Haven't you seen me at Winston's?' I asked.

'No, I go to the Astor usually.'

There was still a lot I didn't know about Ronnie, either. One day, having phoned to say he was coming round to see me, he didn't turn up. I didn't hear from him until late the next day, when he called to tell me, with some embarrassment, that he had been arrested and charged with receiving £3,000 worth of suit material. He assured me it was all a mistake that would be cleared up, but I was hardly encouraged when he said, 'You know it would be over between us if I went to prison.'

'That's a funny thing to say. Why would you go to prison if you haven't done anything wrong?' I asked him.

'I don't know,' he said vaguely. 'But you never know what's round the corner, do you? Anyway, if it did happen, I wouldn't want you to visit me. It would be over.'

A few days later, I was sitting in Stoke Newington Magistrates' Court with Neil Osborne listening to the case against Ronnie being read out at a committal hearing. Also in court was his heavily pregnant wife, June. Neil pointed her out to me, but I saw only the back of her. I was shown another facet of Ronnie Knight that morning: flash and arrogant. He showed no respect for the law, looking at the magistrate with a bored expression that said: 'You're wasting my time, you stupid old prat.' He was given bail and allowed home, and that night when he came to pick me up I tore him off a strip for his behaviour in court. He just laughed.

The Jewish producer Slim Cattan who had come to see me after I was sacked from *The Gimmick* turned out to be for real. A month after the court hearing,

Peter Charlesworth rang me with the news that Mr Cattan wanted me to audition for a film he was making called *Too Hot to Handle*, starring Jayne Mansfield, a blonde Hollywood actress with a 42-inch bust.

I was working in a new revue at Winston's, but I reckoned I could combine both jobs if I passed the audition. I did get the part – playing a northern lass, who is raped and murdered shortly after arriving in London – and as I travelled by train and bus to MGM's studios in Borehamwood a few weeks later, I pondered this latest twist of fate: if I hadn't lost *The Gimmick*, I wouldn't have been able to do the film. Now, here I was about to share the big screen with a Hollywood star, and who knew where that might lead? It's funny how things work out sometimes.

But fate soon gave me something else to think about. I was about to start work on the film when I discovered I was pregnant again. I was devastated, of course, and ashamed of myself, too – not only for letting it go to four months, but for not bothering about contraception. While I was with Cliff I'd tried the coil, but I'd had problems and had had to give it up. As I was no longer having sex with other blokes, I knew the baby was Ronnie's. But what was he going to have to say about it? And where was I going to go for another abortion?

I told Ronnie at Mummy's flat. He panicked, but I quickly assured him I was going to get rid of the baby, and he said: 'OK, all right, fine.' What else could he say? He was facing a possible prison sentence and already had a child and a pregnant wife.

My problem was not just finding someone who would give me an abortion, but finding someone who could do it quickly so that I would not have to miss a day's filming or an evening performance at Winston's. One of the girls in the cabaret told me about a doctor in Hans Crescent, just behind Harrods, who carried out a new kind of abortion which involved sticking amylnitrates under the patient's nose and scraping her womb, rather like a D&C. The bad news was that the pain was horrendous; the good news was that it was all over in a minute and I'd be able to walk out. I booked myself in with the doctor and the girl was right: the pain was indescribable, excruciating agony. Fortunately, I had a day off from filming, otherwise I'd have been in deep trouble, because there was no way I could have performed in front of a camera.

It took Jayne Mansfield only a few minutes to upset me. She walked on to the set as though she had a nasty smell under her nose, gave me one look and told the director to get make-up to tint my hair light brown. I'd gone along with a colour change for *The Gimmick*, but I was buggered if I was going to do it again. 'You can't do that, I'm afraid,' I said. 'My boss at the club will go spare if I'm not blonde tonight. I'll get sacked.'

It wasn't just me she took exception to. She insisted that all the girls with ample bosoms, including Toni Palmer, one of my pals from cabaret at Winston's, were put at the back during a dance number.

For the rest of the filming, Jayne never once gave me a smile or a hello; in fact she was non-communicative with almost everyone, crew as well as cast. It's a great feeling when the star walks on to the set and says, 'Good morning, how are you, everyone?' It makes the company feel good and encourages a good working atmosphere. However, although she had been a big star, by this time her career was on the wane, and maybe this was part of the problem.

The film, a British gangster story about two Soho strip-club owners who join forces to hunt down a blackmailer, was terrible. And even though I was fortunate to get some lovely reviews, I thought I was terrible in it. With my experience of film being limited to *St Trinian's* and that chemist's scene in Kensington for *Lost*, I knew very little about filming continuity and I'm afraid my Lancashire accent wafted all over the place from Land's End to John O'Groats. But at least the movie gave me some valuable experience, which is why Peter had been keen for me to do it. Mind you, I found it totally exhausting: I was not getting home from Winston's until 3 a.m. and snatched only two or three hours' sleep before I was on my way up the A1 again. The first assistant thoughtfully put a cot on the side of the set so that I could grab a bit of sleep before being called, but to be honest I rarely used it. I was too interested in everything that was going on and keen to learn as much as I could.

It became something of a notorious film, too. PC made sure I got paid, but many of the cast and crew weren't. And halfway through the production, someone kindly informed us they were doing a version for South America at the same time, so would we girls strip off to our panties, please. Some of us did, to earn a few extra quid.

In those great days of British cinema as many as six films could be in production at the same studios at the same time. While we were shooting *Too Hot to Handle*, *Jazzboat*, a comedy about a musician who pretends to be a crook and leads the police to a gang of criminals, was also being made. It starred my East End mate Anthony Newley, Lionel Jeffries, the lovable Bernie Winters and the best-looking guy I'd ever seen since Mr Brandon, James Booth. We would all meet up for lunch in the dining room and I'd have them in fits with funny stories from Winston's and the latest on how Jayne Mansfield's 'bristols' had to dominate every scene of *Too Hot to Handle*, even if it meant putting us behind schedule.

I was completely bowled over by Jimmy Booth. I can remember exactly what I thought when I first laid eyes on him: 'My God, he's gorgeous. Oh dear, I've met Ronnie Knight . . .'

8

RONNIE WAS FOUND GUILTY OF RECEIVING STOLEN GOODS AND JAILED FOR FIFTEEN MONTHS. Although I knew from what had happened at the committal hearing that things were not quite as straightforward as he had painted them, I was shattered. He soon changed his mind about everything being over between us and not wanting me to visit him, though. He wrote me a letter from prison asking me to come and see him. He was in Wandsworth Prison in south London. I had never been near a jail in my life and I was absolutely petrified when I went there. The sound of the warders' jangling keys and the huge door slamming behind me was very intimidating and gave me this cold feeling that once I had gone into that forbidding building I might not be let out again. It was always a relief afterwards to breathe the air outside and find that normal life was still going on.

I carried on visiting Ronnie throughout his sentence, but my confidence in our relationship had taken a knock. First of all I had found out he had a wife, and now this. Although I believed him when he told me it had all been a mistake, I'd been brought up to trust British justice, so I just couldn't understand how he had could have been found guilty. It all left me feeling very mixed up.

Soon after Ronnie was jailed, PC rang to tell me I had an audition at the Wyndham Theatre.

'What's the show?'

'*Fings Ain't Wot They Used T'Be*. It's a musical. It's on at Stratford East. They're recasting it to open in December.'

'At the Wyndham?' I asked.

'No. Theatre Royal, Stratford East.'

'No,' I said. 'Mummy will have a heart attack. All that work she did to get me out of the East End. I'm not going back there.'

'But they say it's a super part, Barbara.' He wouldn't let it go. He went on and on about this fantastic director called Joan Littlewood whose radical and unorthodox approach was shaking up the theatre, and finally, just to shut him up, I found myself agreeing to do the audition, though I still wasn't happy about it.

I stayed overnight with Toni Palmer, who was also auditioning for the show, at her mother's house in Marble Arch, and arrived at the stage door of the Wyndham Theatre in Charing Cross Road, at 9.45 a.m. There was a short, podgy woman in a woolly hat, who reminded me of Fat Nanny, cleaning the steps. 'Hello,' she said. 'What do you want?'

'I've come for the audition at ten,' I said.

'You're early.'

'Yeah, I know. I'm always early.'

'Where do you come from?' she wanted to know.

'I'm from the East End originally, north London now, but I'm working in the West End. I don't want to do this audition or this show. I've only come 'cos my agent made me.'

'Why don't you want to do it?' she asked.

'I don't need it. I'm *West* End. My mother's worked very hard to get us out of the East End so I don't want to go back there now.'

'Aren't you a cute little thing,' the woman said.

'Cheeky!' I retorted.

I went into the theatre and on to the stage. There were a handful of people in the stalls, but I couldn't see who they were because it was dark. Then a voice called out: 'Hello, Bar, I'm here. It's Lionel. Lionel Bart.'

'Oh, hello, darling,' I said. 'How are you?'

I knew Lionel vaguely from Stamford Hill, and had seen him in the Two I's coffee bar in Soho. He was famous now, through writing songs for Tommy Steele and Cliff Richard. I was surprised he was here.

'Fine,' he said. 'You know what the show is about, don't you?'

'No, not really.'

Then a woman's voice. 'Do you know what part you've come for?'

'No.'

'It's the part of Rosie, an Irish prostitute.'

'I can't do an Irish accent.'

'Where are you from?' the woman asked.

'Shoreditch.'

'Have you ever seen a prostitute?'

'Yeah, yeah,' I said. 'I've worked in Soho. I know quite a few of 'em.'

'Come on, then,' the woman said. 'Let's see you do a prostitute from Shoreditch.'

I took a deep breath and strutted as sexily as I could across the stage and back to the centre again. I pouted my lips at an imaginary punter and said: ''Ello, short time, mister? Five bob for a wank, ten bob for a plate and it's a quid for the full card trick.'

I could hear them all laughing in the stalls. Then the woman's voice called out again: 'Can you sing?'

'Yes. Actually, I'm a very good singer. I've sung in clubs and with Ronnie Scott's band.'

'Sing something for us, then.'

I had brought all my music in a briefcase. As I went to open it, I asked: 'Where's the pianist?'

'We haven't got one. If you're that good a singer, you won't need one.'

I belted out 'On the Sunny Side of the Street', ending with a cartwheel. When I finished, there was some gentle clapping, and the woman stood up and came towards the stage. 'Where have you been all my life?' she said, smiling. 'You're wonderful, little bird.' To my astonishment it was the podgy woman in the woolly hat I'd thought was the cleaner.

'Blimey,' I exclaimed. 'I didn't think you were—'

'No, I know you didn't,' Joan Littlewood interrupted. 'And you weren't supposed to. You got the part at the stage door. You're perfect for Rosie.'

I left the theatre pleased to have been offered the role, but still not sure if I wanted to do it. I'd read the script and wondered how on earth it could work as a musical. To me, musicals were all about beautiful songs and lots of dancers and big scenery, like *Annie Get Your Gun* and *South Pacific*. But this one had just twelve actors and crude songs I didn't particularly like. Even the title *Fings Ain't Wot They Used T'Be*, grated on me: I'd been brought up to speak properly and it seemed to sum up everything I didn't like about the show. I was not convinced that the show would make it to the West End, and I certainly wasn't keen on performing every night in Stratford East.

It was Peter who persuaded me, and a few days later I found myself telling my Winston's boss I was off again. 'But do me a favour this time, darling,' I said. 'Can we elbow the big send-off, the cake and all that. Because I'm sure I'm going to be back.'

When I went to the theatre for the first day of rehearsal – with my marked-up script, my music and my toothbrush and toothpaste in my briefcase – I had to walk through a market. Even that did not feel right. I loved the noise and all the people milling around, but it was a long way removed from what I considered theatre.

I had no idea who else was in the cast. There was only one person in the Theatre Royal when I arrived, and it was someone I knew. His name was George Sewell, but everyone called him Chuck. I'd seen him about the West End, but he came from Stamford Hill. I was pouring out my misgivings to him when the other members of the cast began to arrive. Assuming that Chuck was working as a stagehand, I whispered to him: 'I think you ought to leave, Chuck. We'll be starting rehearsing soon.'

He laughed and shook his head. 'I'm in the show, too, Barbara.'

'What? I didn't know you were an actor.'

'Neither did I,' he said.

Apparently, he had been in the Salisbury pub next door to the Wyndham with his brother, who was an actor, and some friends who were talking about this great, but crazy, director, Joan Littlewood, who was at that very moment holding auditions in the theatre, and they persuaded him to go along. Geed up by the group and by a few pints, he had sung the cockney song 'Any Old Iron' for Joan and she had signed him up on the spot. I was so thrilled for him, but I did feel a prat for having thought he shouldn't have been there.

I nearly fell through the floor when I saw who the leading man was. It was none other than Jimmy Booth, the gorgeous actor I'd met at the film studios at Borehamwood when I'd been making *Too Hot to Handle* and he'd been shooting *Jazzboat*.

Once everybody had arrived, we all sat in a circle on the stage ready for the first read-through of the script. I was feeling slightly better now that I was with people I knew, like Miriam Karlin, Victor Maddern, Jimmy Booth and my friend Toni Palmer, who was playing the other prostitute. But when Joan Littlewood spoke her first words to us I wondered what the hell I'd let myself in for.

Throwing her copy of the script in the air, she said: 'Well, this is a load of fucking rubbish, isn't it?'

Shocked, I stared at Frank Norman, who had written the story, then at Lionel Bart, expecting one of them to respond. But they didn't; they just sat there waiting for Joan to carry on. 'Right,' she said. 'We're going to start again.' She went through the story, which I felt was a waste of time because we'd all read the script and knew it backwards. Then she announced: 'We're all going to play other people's parts. Barbara, you play Tosher, the ponce.'

'But I'm Rosie,' I said, confused.

'No, I want you to play Tosher. I want you to find out what his character's about, what his problems are.'

I'd never experienced anything like this. But since no one else was making a fuss, I kept my mouth shut and went along with it. For the next three days, we played what I can only call silly buggers, and I loathed it. This was not what I expected from the theatre. Joan had nicknamed me Bird's Egg, because, she said, I was a funny little bird.

On the third day she came up to me and said, 'You're not enjoying this, Bird's Egg, are you? You're not enjoying yourself.'

'No, I hate it,' I told her.

'So why don't you fuck off, then?' she said, nonchalantly.

'Are you saying you want me to go?'

'I keep hearing you going on about the West End,' she said. 'Why don't you go up there? Go up the West End?'

'OK, I will.' I marched out and went straight to Peter Charlesworth's office, where I got all my anger off my chest. Peter just laughed: he found it amusing that this twenty-two-year-old with just one West End musical behind her had walked out on one of the country's most innovative theatrical directors. He told me to calm down, think of the opportunity I might be chucking away.

Leaving his office in Leicester Square, I found myself in Soho. I decided I may as well do some background research for my part and kept an eye out for the prostitutes who hung around in the doorways. I couldn't find one. Then I began to notice all the signs in windows for 'French lessons' or 'massage' and it dawned on me that this was where they were now. Browsing around there for a while gave me some great ideas for playing Rosie.

The next day I went back to Stratford and said to Toni: 'I've been going round Soho, and you'll never guess what the prostitutes there get up to. They dress up as schoolgirls, charladies and all sorts!'

I thought Joan would give me a hard time, but when I reappeared, she just said: 'Hello, Bird's Egg. Had a nice time up West?'

'Yes,' I said. 'Very nice, thank you. Can I play Rosie now?'

'Yes, of course, Bird's Egg.'

I wasn't the only one to have balked at Joan's methods. While I'd been away Victor Maddern had also stormed off, and had been replaced by Glyn Edwards. But for the next few days, everything went smoothly – until I saw the bridesmaid's costume I was to wear in the final scene. I went spare. It was supposed to be pink, but it had been cleaned so many times that it had faded into something more like grey. It was tatty.

'I'm not wearing that,' I told the wardrobe mistress. 'East End weddings might be flashy or over the top, but one thing they're not is scruffy. And that dress is scruffy.'

Joan overheard. 'You listen to her, she knows,' she said. 'She may be a West End star, but she knows about the East End.' If there was any sarcasm in her tone, I didn't pick up on it. Instead I volunteered to bring in a bridesmaid's dress I'd worn for my cousin Roy's wedding to his wife, Ira.

We were rehearsing on the Sunday before we opened when I was called to see Joan and Lionel.

'Joan asked me to write something for you. Here it is,' said Lionel, handing me several pieces of paper with the words and music to a song on it. He had called it 'Where Do Little Birds Go?'

'Who am I going to sing it with?'

'No one,' Joan said. 'I want you to sing it on your own.'

I was astonished. All Joan's work was about ensemble; nobody ever got a solo.

'How do you want me to do it? Am I going to make an entrance? Dance? What?' I asked.

'No, I want you to sit on a stool and just sing it, sweetly, like a little bird. We'll have all the lights down with just a spotlight on you. And keep still. Sit on your hands.'

I was to do my solo number about twenty minutes into the second half. I didn't know then, but it was a terrific spot to have.

We opened on Tuesday 22 December 1959. I still had little faith in the show. I'd been tempted to phone Bruce and ask him to keep my job open, and I'd even said to Toni: 'We'll be back at Winston's soon, dear, you'll see.' But the moment we all went on stage and sang the opening number, 'Goodnight, Dearie, Goodnight, Darling', my attitude changed dramatically. The show was a joy to do. I didn't know if it would be a hit in the West End, but I loved it. We all did.

I enjoyed my few minutes alone in the spotlight singing Lionel's creation. It was a funny little song, hardly a memorable one, and certainly not what I would have called a showstopper. However, a few weeks later, the night before the show was to open at the Garrick Theatre in Charing Cross Road, one of the cast, Wallace Eaton, who had starred in the great radio show *Take It From Here*, said to me, very earnestly: 'Tomorrow is going to be a big night for you, Barbara.'

'Don't be silly,' I said.

'No, I mean it. The reaction to your number has been wonderful. You sing it so prettily. It's going to be a smash.'

I just laughed it off. If anything was going to get people excited, it was the catchy and downright rude title song, not a sweet gentle one, no matter how movingly I sang it. I was to be proved wrong again.

After I'd finished the number on our first night at the Garrick and the lights came up, the audience were on their feet, almost as one, clapping and cheering wildly, and calling: 'More! More! More!' Other less self-conscious actresses would probably have lapped up the applause and done the whole song again, but I just stood there, embarrassed. I loved the response, of course, but I had no idea how to acknowledge it or what to do next. The ovation went on and on for a full minute or so before I held my arms out helplessly, shrugged my shoulders and shook my head. 'I can't do any more,' I said weakly. 'Lionel hasn't written any more.' Then I gave them the widest smile I could and added brightly: 'Anyway, the next song's even better.' Of course, that endeared me to everyone even more, and there was more wild cheering before the orchestra struck up again and we moved on.

What was it about that song that stopped the show? The timing, I think. During the first half and at the start of the second, the mood had been cockney, very brash and very loud. But when I came on all soft and gentle, and the lights went down and I sang that sweet song, the atmosphere changed and the audience were ready for it.

I can remember hardly anything about that first night. It's all the most amazing blur. Mummy and Len were in the audience and came backstage to the little dressing room I shared with Yootha Joyce, Toni Palmer and the props girl, but I have no idea what they said to me. I imagine Mummy would have cringed when she saw me greeting well-wishers in a nondescript little housecoat. I do remember the great Hollywood legend Bing Crosby coming round and telling me he knew I knew his son Gary. I also have a vivid memory of Peter Charlesworth being so excited that every time he opened his mouth to speak, nothing came out. Dear PC. He had seen this little girl doing her thing in a Soho club and believed in her, and here she was getting a full minute's standing ovation. No wonder he didn't know what to say. I didn't, either.

Fings was a milestone in British theatre. It was set in a West End gambling club and followed the lives of its customers, who included prostitutes, ponces, old lags, a policeman and an old-time gangster. Not only did it break new ground by dealing openly with sex, and in particular with homosexuality – still illegal in those days – but it changed the way actors were expected to talk and look on stage. Suddenly girls didn't have to be chocolate-box pretty with long, curly hair and plums in their mouths, and it was all right for leading men to be rough and ready and to have regional accents. *Fings* did for British theatre what the brilliant film of Alan Sillitoe's novel, *Saturday Night and Sunday Morning*, released in 1960, did for the cinema. And it was thrilling to be a part of it all.

The star of that innovative movie, Albert Finney, was a friend of Jimmy Booth's, and came to see the show one night. Afterwards Jimmy put his head round my dressing-room door. 'Would you like to come down and say hello to Albie? He'd like to meet you.'

The three of us went off to the Stork Room, and the evening developed into the start of a little affair between Jimmy and me. While I'd been dancing with Albie, Jimmy seemed to get a bit of the green eye, and when we returned to our table, he said to me: 'Come and sit over here with me,' and just kind of took over. With the uncertainty I now felt about Ronnie, my commitment to being a one-man woman had faltered, and it was a comfort to have a bit of a fling. And Jimmy was lovely.

Fings was a spectacular success at the box office as well as with the critics, and Joan kept us on our toes. Every day notes in her big, bold handwriting pulling people up on their performances with typical bluntness would appear on the noticeboard for all to see. I never got any, though, and maybe I became a bit blasé.

One night, just before going on, I ran into Joan coming out of the stage door. 'Bird's Egg, remember the little bird,' she said.

'Yeah, OK,' I replied vaguely.

A couple of nights later I was in the middle of singing my big solo number, alone in the spotlight with the lights down, when suddenly Toni Palmer came running across the stage, yelling: 'That home perm – I knew it wouldn't work. It's ruined my hair!' She was followed by Jimmy Booth, who rushed on with another wild ad lib. They both shot me a sheepish look of apology as they came by.

I hadn't a clue what was going on, and just carried on as best I could. When I came off Joan was standing in the wings.

'What was all that about? My number was wrecked!' I said.

'I couldn't get through to you,' Joan told me. 'You'd forgotten the little bird. You've been doing it more like Judy Garland at Carnegie Hall.'

When I thought about it I realised how right she was. My solo spot was not stopping the show any more.

The show hardly needed help with ticket sales, but we got it anyway from a most unlikely source: the Lord Chamberlain, who was responsible for censoring what appeared on the British stage. There was a lot about *Fings* that he considered offensive but which we felt was OK and yet there were bits we thought rude which he found acceptable. For instance, he didn't mind all the camp jokes about homosexuals, but he drew the line at me sitting with my legs apart 'in a pose indicative of copulation'. I'd never heard of copulation, so I asked Joan what it meant. 'Fucking, you silly cow,' she said.

The establishment's verdict on London's shocking new show got us priceless publicity in every paper and the box office tills didn't stop ringing. It didn't do any harm to Max Bygraves' bank balance either: his witty, cleaned-up version of the title song went into the charts a month after we opened and stayed there for thirteen weeks. I'm sure many people who came to see the show expected him to walk on stage any minute and sing it.

One night I offended Miriam Karlin by bending down and showing my bum to the audience to get a cheap laugh while she was singing. I did it deliberately. Joan had told us if we fancied doing something, we should go ahead, and I fancied it. It was unfair, though, and Miriam was less than pleased. She called me to her number one dressing room after the show and said: 'I'm going to point out something to you, Barbara. One day, you will be the leading lady, doing your best, and someone behind you will be trying to get a cheap laugh. It won't be nice. And it wasn't nice for me.' It was a right bollocking, but it was a lesson, too, and one I never forgot.

Never in my most outrageous fantasies could I have imagined how dramatically *Fings* would revolutionise British theatre, much less my own career. If I had not been brought down to earth visiting Ronnie in jail, it might all have gone to my head. As it was, I'd arrive at the Garrick every evening and gaze up at the big picture of me and Toni on the poster outside advertising the show and think how lucky I was. My name wasn't there, but so what? To do what I loved more than anything in the world, and be paid for it – a non-negotiable £28 a week for the whole run, however long it lasted – was more than enough.

How had it happened? I knew the answer. And I knew who I had to thank. At my audition, I'd asked Lionel Bart why I'd been approached. He said a mate had gone on about this comical little bird who had him and his film star pals rolling about with stories about Jayne Mansfield's tits. She sounded ideal for Rosie, so he and Joan had decided to take a look.

The mate turned out to be dear, sweet Bernie Winters. I'm so glad I didn't let him down.

9

I FELT IN THE WAY AT THE FLAT IN BETHUNE ROAD. It was probably unintentional, but Mummy made me feel she didn't want me there. When I suggested renting a flat of my own, she persuaded me to go for one like hers in Camden Town. To her it was perfect, but I hated it, and when she and Len went away on holiday, I found a bigger one, in Harringay, that suited me better. Mummy made a big fuss about wanting to see it so I invited her round the following Sunday. The flat had an unsightly back entrance which I was afraid Mummy wouldn't like, and I was not wrong. She sat in the flat, po-faced, for several hours, then phoned me when she got home. 'Don't think I'll ever visit you again, because I won't,' she said.

'Mummy, it's lovely.'

'What?' she said. 'That back entrance? And I believe there's a green-grocer's stall at the bottom of the stairs during the week.'

How she knew that I had no idea, nor did I care. I was just relieved to be away from her while I waited for Ronnie to come home.

While I was appearing in *Fings*, Bryan Blackburn offered me a spot in a new revue he was writing for the Stork Room. I lasted only ten days – not because of my performance, but because of what I did to the owner, Al Burnett, in the course of a blazing row.

I'd been there a week or so when the manager came into the cramped little room beside the tiny stage where the revue cast changed and told me there was a customer outside who wanted to meet me. 'Do I know him?' I asked.

'No, you don't,' he told me. 'But the man is a good punter who spends a lot of money.'

'Will you tell him, thank you very much, but, no,' I said.

'The man likes you, Barbara. All he wants is for you to have a drink with him.'

At Winston's girls had never been pressurised to drink with customers; it had always been left up to us. So I decided I wasn't having any of it. The next thing I knew, Al Burnett came marching in and glared at me. 'You,' he said aggressively. 'What's all this, you won't go out there and have a drink?'

'Well, I don't know the person,' I said.

'It doesn't matter,' Al fumed. 'He's one of our customers. Now, get out there and have a drink with him. He'll give you a oner.'

'No. I don't want to. I'm a performer, not a hostess.'

'Get out there, or you'll get the sack,' he insisted.

I picked up the bucket of ice we used to cool ourselves between numbers and chucked it at him. Then I stormed out of the room and out of the club, leaving him drenched.

Sod it, I thought, I couldn't care less. I'd gone there thinking the Stork Room would have a family atmosphere like Winston's, but it didn't, and I was glad to be out of it.

One night I had just come off stage after another belting performance of *Fings* when Chuck Sewell poked his head round the dressing-room door. 'Have you a moment, Bar? I'd like you to meet some good friends of mine.'

'Of course, darling. Bring 'em in.'

Three extremely smartly dressed young men in dark suits, crisp white shirts and sober ties came shyly through the door. Two looked identical: dark-haired, strongly built and in their mid to late twenties; the third was older, taller, slimmer and had lighter hair.

'Let me introduce the Kray twins, Ronnie and Reggie, and their brother, Charlie,' said Chuck.

He spoke as if I should have known their names, but I didn't. They meant nothing to me. I just smiled at them and moved forward, expecting the customary showbiz kiss on the cheek, but they just wanted to shake hands. The twins were very polite, respectful and softly spoken as we exchanged the usual pleasantries. To be honest, they seemed a bit overawed at being in a performer's dressing room.

Charlie, the older brother, was strikingly handsome – a bit like Steve McQueen – and had a lovely relaxed, confident air about him. After ten or fifteen minutes' chat, they said their goodbyes and moved towards the door. Charlie went out with Ronnie and Reggie, but then came back and, in a soft voice, asked me if I would have dinner with him one night. He was charming, and I heard myself saying: 'OK. Why don't you give me a ring here?' Toni Palmer and Yootha Joyce, who were also in the dressing room, laughed knowingly.

Charlie did not waste any time. Within a few days he had phoned and we went out for a meal. He was everything I found attractive in a man: he had Ronnie's gentle approach and Daddy's giggly, happy-go-lucky nature, and I fell for him immediately. I was perfect for him, too: I was something of a celebrity, performing in a West End show, but I was also an ordinary, down-to-earth London girl with no airs and graces who enjoyed a rabbit. We started going out regularly after the show, always to the same place – the Astor, London's most expensive club. But you'd hardly have described these nights out as romantic dates because, for some reason, Charlie always had a mate in tow – Limehouse Willy or Big Scotch Pat.

For the first couple of months, I had no idea that Charlie was married, but the closer we became, the more the deceit played on his mind and he owned up. Oh, God, I thought. Another married man. When he said he was thinking of leaving his wife and two children for me, I began to feel awkward and told him we had to stop seeing each other. Charlie was a gentle soul who treated me well, but I always saw my future with Ronnie; my whole life was geared to him coming home. He had told me that he was returning to me, not to his wife, and as the date of his release drew nearer, I just prayed he was a man of his word.

After I finished with Charlie, his brother Reggie invited me out to dinner in the West End. Naturally, some of his friends came, too. Later we moved on to a small hotel and, after an hour or so, everyone made their excuses and bowed out, leaving Reggie and me alone. We chatted for a few minutes, and then I stood up to leave. 'I must be going now, Reg.'

'I'd rather you stayed,' he said. His voice was quiet but persuasive.

I knew exactly what lay ahead of us if I did. Reg made it quite obvious that he found me attractive and, to be honest, the attraction was mutual. He didn't put me under any pressure to stay; I chose to. In my heart of hearts, I did wonder whether perhaps my disappointment at the way things had worked out with Reg's brother Charlie influenced me. Whatever the case, I had no regrets.

When Ronnie was released from Wandsworth at 6 a.m. one morning in October 1960, he found two of us waiting at the prison gates. I'd arrived to collect him in a minicab and his brother Johnny had driven down to pick him up as well. It occurred to me that perhaps Johnny had come to take him back to his wife after all. But Ronnie went over and had a word with him, and then came and got into the minicab and we drove off together to north London.

Though I'm not a great cook, I felt Ronnie needed a good English breakfast after all that time in prison, so I made him a huge helping of eggs, sausages, mushrooms, bacon and tomatoes. He ate it all, but a few minutes later, he threw it up. It wasn't my cooking, he was quick to point out, just that he wasn't used to good food, or so much of it. We spent the rest of the day in bed and I didn't get up until it was time for me to go to work. All the way to the Garrick, I felt so happy. All my worries about Ronnie and me had vanished. I had this great show, and now I had the man I truly loved back again. Life was good.

Those early days living with Ronnie were lovely. I'd never had a man who had been so good for me, had my interests at heart; never shared a home with someone who cared for me. I didn't know anything about being a housewife, but I threw myself into it. I learned to cook and iron, and after watching Ronnie wallow in the bath every morning, I'd put rollers in his hair and blow-dry it for him. Ronnie was meticulous about his barnet: he would spend an hour in front of the mirror making sure not one hair was out of place. While he was fussing with it, I'd lay out his clothes. He never wore the same outfit two days running and, no matter whether it was smart or casual, everything – suit, shirt, tie and shoes – had to match, and I made sure they always did.

My fussing over Ronnie drove Mummy mad. She didn't stick to her vow never to come to the flat again, but she didn't visit us very often, and when she did, she'd say: 'I can't believe you. You've made your bed and now you've got to lie in it. He sits on that couch and you run around him, all soppy, asking if everything's all right, does he need anything.'

'But that's the way I am, Mummy. That's what I like to do.'

I loved Ronnie, and I honestly felt he loved me. We couldn't keep our hands off each other and the sex was wonderful. But he couldn't handle my past. He hated my free and easy attitude to sex, and that I'd done anything with other men before I met him. I wanted an open and honest relationship, so I told him the truth, particularly about my wild time with Ronnie Scott's band.

'How many did you go out with?' he asked.

'I can't remember,' I said. 'A couple, maybe three.'

'Did you have sex with them?'

'Yes,' I said.

'With all of them?'

'Not all at the same time,' I said. 'On different nights.'

Ronnie looked at me, horrified, then stormed out of the house and drove off in his car. He did not come back for two days.

At first I was flattered by Ronnie's jealousy. But once we had committed to each other I felt he should not keep going on about the men in my past.

One night in March 1961 Dennis Main Wilson, the BBC producer who had given me my *Six-Five Special* TV spot three years earlier, came to see *Fings*. His prime reason was to see Miriam Karlin, who had signed to do a new sitcom he was producing about streetwise girls working in a dressmaking factory. But two other girls caught his eye that night – me and my mate Toni Palmer, and he asked us if we wanted to be in the show, too. To be honest, we didn't really. We were starring in a hit West End musical and neither of us felt we needed television work. But the money was too good to pass up – £50 an episode, almost double our wages – so we signed up for *The Dress Factory*, which later became a popular Sunday-night comedy series called *The Rag Trade*. Along with us came another girl, who was performing as the second lead in a West End revue. Her name was Judy Carne and, like us, she didn't really like playing a bit part on TV even though the money was so good. We all felt we were, in some way, prostituting ourselves.

When Dennis had first told us the show was about a dress factory, I said: 'My mother's a dressmaker.' He asked if he could take the designers of the show to Mummy's factory for a look round. Mummy's boss was all for it, so I took them to the factory in Langham Place, by Broadcasting House in Upper Regent Street, for some lessons in dressmaking. Mummy of course knew that I was no seamstress, and when I was put on the buttonhole machine she remarked: 'She'll never learn to work that in a million years.' But I knew she was quietly thrilled that a bigwig from the BBC was modelling his show on her place of work, and I'm sure she was proud of me, especially as I arrived wearing lots of make-up and looking like a star.

Miriam, Toni and I were all still appearing in *Fings*, doing a couple of matinées a week as well as the evening shows, and in addition we were rehearsing all week for *The Rag Trade*. At 10 a.m. on Sundays, Ronnie would drive me to the BBC for the studio rehearsals before we performed the thirty-minute comedy in front of a live audience at 7.30 p.m. The show was transmitted on a Friday evening and was an instant hit.

My joy at the success of *The Rag Trade* was shattered one August evening after Ronnie drove me home from the theatre. We had just got in when there was a loud bang on the front door. I opened it, thinking it was a friend who had been looking after our dog. Instead I was confronted by half a dozen tall, heavily built blokes, who brushed past me with the curt explanation that they were the police. You could have fooled me: they looked so menacing I thought they were gangsters. They pulled out drawers, opened cupboards, even poked around in a new and expensive decorative fireplace. They said they were investigating an armed robbery, but I thought Ronnie was being victimised, and started screaming: 'How dare you? I'm going to see my MP! I'm going to do something about this!'

'Your missus,' one of the coppers said to Ronnie. 'Don't she shout?'

Little good it did. Within minutes they were taking him away. 'Phone Jimmy!' he yelled as he was marched out of the door.

I didn't have home phone numbers for Ronnie's brothers, so I had to sit up all night waiting until his elder brother, Billy, arrived at work in the morning. He gave me a number for Jimmy. Jimmy got in touch with a lawyer, Ellis Lincoln, who recommended a barrister named Nemone Lethbridge to represent Ronnie. When I met her I had my doubts. I told Lincoln: 'She's too young, too pretty and doesn't look experienced.'

'But she's red hot,' he said.

He was right. Ronnie was charged, with others, of stealing £8,000 from a power station in Lots Road, Chelsea, and when the case was heard at the Old Bailey five months later, her brilliance earned him an acquittal. What it earned me, however, was less positive. Because of my stage and TV success, the case attracted a lot of publicity and even though Ronnie was found not guilty, I'm sure that in many people's eyes I came over as some sort of gangster's moll.

The power of television changed my life in other ways, too. Now passengers on the bus recognised me and were always keen to talk to me; some even asked for my autograph. It was the same on the tube. I liked the fame, but I didn't much care for that bit of my ordinary life being taken away, and I had to start taking taxis everywhere. Ronnie found it hard to cope with me being recognised, too. If I said hello to someone, it would be: 'How come you know him?' Usually I didn't, but I suppose my face was familiar and people imagined they knew me. It caused so many arguments. I thought that kind of jealousy was ridiculous, and Ronnie was now becoming so paranoid he began to bug me. We were in a Turkish restaurant in Harringay once when this guy, with a girl, smiled and said 'Hello, there.' Immediately Ronnie wanted to know who he was and where I'd met him. When I said I hadn't a clue who he was, Ronnie went into one, accusing me of lying. 'You *do* know him, but now you're denying it.'

▲ My parents on their wedding day in 1935. On the left are my cousins Rose and Dolly Ewin, and Auntie Ivy, with my cousin Kenny in the front. On the right are Uncle Alf and Auntie Mae, and cousin Roy.

◀ Mummy made her own dress, as well as those of the bridesmaids and the pageboys' outfits.

▼ My grandparents, Charlie and Eliza Ellis.

▲ Me, aged eighteen months. Mummy hated my fine hair so insisted on tying it back with ribbons and bows.

▲ Dolly and Charlie Windsor. I adopted my aunt's married name because I wanted something simple with a good – royal – ring to it.

▼ With mummy and daddy in 1939. Daddy was called up when war broke out and I missed him terribly when he went off to fight with the Eighth Army in Egypt.

◀ ◀ *I joined Madame Behenna's Juvenile Jollities when I returned to London from Blackpool, where I had been evacuated during the war. Here I am, aged nine, already the veteran of numerous charity shows at Stoke Newington town hall!*

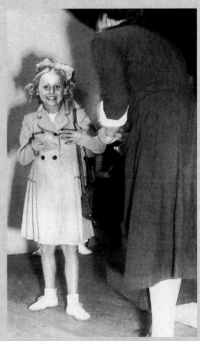

▲ *'What, me?' The look of surprise and delight as I'm awarded first prize in a talent competition at the age of ten.*

▲ I nurtured my early stage career at Aida Foster's school in Golders Green, where at first I felt very much out of place. This photo was taken around 1950 – I'm in the front row on the left.

▲ When I joined Love From Judy *I became besotted with leading man Johnny Brandon. Here we are together on television when I was about seventeen.*

◄ On tour in Bournemouth with Love From Judy.

▲ *With Jeannie Carson (on the far right) and the chorus of* Love From Judy.

▼ *Striking a pose with Amanda Barrie in this wonderful poster for the New Year's Eve gala at Winston's in 1957.*

▲ *Mummy and Len on holiday in Capri in the seventies. Len Atkinson was the lovely man who became my stepfather after my parents divorced.*

▼ *A picture taken on my first date with Ronnie Knight.*

▲ *With Ronnie in Seaton, Devon, in 1960, shortly after we first met.*

▲ *The Knight brothers – Jimmy, Ronnie, David and Johnny – on David's wedding day. His bride was also called Barbara.*

◀ *With Ronnie outside the Old Bailey after he was acquitted of the Lots Road armed robbery.*

▲ *Ronnie, me and Reggie Kray at the première of* Sparrows Can't Sing *in 1963.*

▼ *Pay-back time: a charity function at the Krays' club, the Kentucky, in Mile End Road. Frances and Reggie Kray sit either side of me and Ronnie.*

One night he started questioning me again at home, when I was making some sandwiches, and I got so angry I hurled the bread knife at him. The villain in Ronnie saw it coming and he blocked it with a cushion. 'You're bloody crazy, you are!' he yelled. 'I'll have to watch myself with you.' He kept on and on and on about men until, in the end, I thought, what the hell, if I'm going to be accused of having it off with another man, I might as well go ahead and do it. Be hung for a sheep as a lamb and all that.

Another day I came home to find Ronnie going through my drawer in the bedroom.

'Where is it?' he asked.

'Where's what?'

'You know, the thing you wear when you have sex.'

'It's in my handbag,' I said.

He glared at me accusingly. 'Why are you carrying it around, for God's sake?'

I felt my face redden as Ronnie brushed past me and drove off once again. When he came back the next morning, he asked me point-blank if I'd slept with someone else. I had, but I denied it. Ronnie kind of accepted that, but I don't know if he really believed me.

Despite the success of *The Rag Trade*, I saw myself as a theatre comedy actress and felt demeaned to be playing a soppy bimbo in white stilettos. All I seemed to do throughout the first six-part series was chew gum, giggle inanely and warn other girls: 'Sshh, here comes Mr Fenner.' I much preferred stopping the show in front of 700 people at the Garrick to uttering that banal line in front of millions on TV. Toni was happy enough, but Judy felt the same as me – she saw her future in America. So when Dennis Main Wilson asked us to sign for another series, Judy and I went to see him together to tell him no.

Dennis was a marvellous producer with a string of successes to his credit, including *Steptoe and Son*, *Till Death Us Do Part* and *Hancock's Half Hour*, and I admired and respected him. But he got it wrong that day. When we told him we wanted to be comediennes, he pooh-poohed us. 'That's something you'll never be,' he said. 'You're far too young. And far too pretty.' He did have a point, because the funny females then were amply proportioned ladies like Peggy Mount, Irene Handl and Hattie Jacques, but things were about to change.

So, as *Fings* closed, the second series of *The Rag Trade* went ahead without me. When a third series was being planned, it was decided that a new character should be written in: a girlfriend for the popular Reg Varney. When Reg was asked if he had any ideas as to who might play her, he immediately suggested 'little blonde Barbara from the first series'. So I returned in a starring role, which was much more rewarding.

From the moment *Fings* hit the stage, everyone talked about it being turned into a movie. It was so over the top that it lent itself to the big screen, and, of course, it had the hottest director in town who could do no wrong. So you can imagine our surprise when Joan Littlewood turned her back on *Fings* and decided instead to make a film of *Sparrows Can't Sing*, a play that had flopped when she directed it on stage.

The producers did not want me for the film. In their eyes I was now typecast as the scatty blonde in *The Rag Trade* and they could not envisage me as a strong-minded woman in what was to be a hard-hitting, controversial movie making serious social and political comment as well as comedy. I couldn't see myself in it either, but for a different reason. Joan wanted me to play Jimmy Booth's wife and I felt it would not work. With him being so tall and me so tiny, I felt we would look ludicrous on screen. But Joan loved the idea of the little lady giving the big guy what for, and told the producers, 'Either Bird's Egg does it or I don't make the film.' They grudgingly gave in, and we started filming on location in Stepney in the summer of 1962. Joan backed me up again when she heard a cameraman telling me I was doing too much with my face in a close-up. 'This is a movie, not the theatre,' he said. Joan gave him one of her steely looks and said: 'Fuck off. Don't tell my little actress what to do.'

I found *Sparrows* quite an important piece, very much of its time. A husband (Jimmy Booth) goes off to sea and, after bonking his way round the world, returns home to find that not only has his house been flattened to make way for a high-rise block of flats, but his wife has gone too. It was Joan's first film, and she made a great job of it.

It was down to Ronnie that I wore a high-necked, frilly blouse in *Sparrows* rather than some revealing sweater or a number with a plunging neckline. I wanted to please him so much that I persuaded Joan to let me dress demurely. It worked because it made my character sweet without detracting from any of her sexiness. As Ronnie maintained, you don't have to put it in people's faces.

Joan needed a nightclub for the final scene of *Sparrows*, so I called Charlie Kray and asked him if his brothers would allow the film to be shot in the Kentucky, their new drinking club they had opened in the Mile End Road.

With characteristic (though often unintentional) wit, Ronnie Kray told Joan that he did not normally allow shooting in the club, but that on this occasion it would be a pleasure. The club was no more than a long narrow bar, but Joan thought it was perfect and, in return for the favour, agreed to allow the three brothers to watch the club scenes being filmed. Even then, the twins and Charlie had stars in their eyes, and when Ron heard that *Sparrows* was to have a royal première at the ABC Cinema directly across the road, he suggested that the Kentucky should throw a party afterwards for the stars of the film and their guests, which were due to include Princess Margaret and her husband, Lord Snowdon. Joan thought this was a great idea, and of course the mere mention of royalty coming to the East End hyped the première, so on the night of Wednesday 27 February 1963, the Mile End Road was lined with many hundreds of people cheering and waving flags.

In the event, Princess Margaret caught a diplomatic cold and missed the movie, but Lord Snowdon came, and joined us at a post-film reception at Stepney Town Hall. He and I had a good laugh about the disastrous *Keep Your Hair On* for which he'd designed the scenery. Lots of celebrities – among them Roger Moore, Stanley Baker and Ronnie Fraser – went on to the Kentucky, where we had fish and chips, jellied eels and other cockney fare, and drank, courtesy of the brothers Kray, until the early hours.

Sparrows was being distributed in America, and in May I had to go there to promote it on TV and radio and in the press in New York, Boston and Washington. Ronnie hit the roof, not so much because I'd be away for a week, but because Peter Charlesworth was going with me. There was no question that PC had to go: he was my agent and manager and I needed him with me, particularly as I was still so unworldly and gauche. I had never even been abroad before, let alone to the States. But Ronnie could not understand it.

I should have been excited about going to America, but I was terrified. What on earth was I going to say and do? I should have been thrilled at flying for the first time, especially as it was first class, but I was nervous. And overawed. When I learned that the champagne was free, I showed myself up, guzzling it down as though it might run out before I'd had enough. And then, just in case there was anyone who hadn't noticed there was an idiot on board, I summoned a stewardess and asked her to open a window because I was hot. Imagine, then, this naïve little bird sauntering into a luxurious suite at Manhattan's legendary Plaza Hotel overlooking Central Park and discovering a telephone in the toilet!

The movie promotion went smoothly as far as radio interviews were concerned, but we ran into a problem with the hugely popular *Johnny Carson Show* in New York which was intended to be the climax of the trip. I'd been warned that the American Federation of Television and Radio Artists might make trouble and, sure enough, three hours before I was scheduled to appear, the union put the block on me, saying that Barbara Windsor failed to meet their requirement 'that she be an alien artist of distinguished merit and ability'. PC spent two days trying to get in touch with officials to sort it out. I even offered to join the union, but they did not want to know.

PC and I went to Birdland for the jazz and were fêted at the slick musical *How to Succeed in Business Without Really Trying*, the hottest show in town at the time. We also had dinner with Peter's best mate, Anthony Newley, who was appearing on Broadway in *Stop the World, I Want to Get Off*, to celebrate his success and his recent marriage to the lovely – and pregnant – Joan Collins. 'Two little people from Hackney, here on Broadway,' Tony said to me as we clinked glasses. 'Who'd have thought it, eh?'

I had not been back in England long before I realised that all was not well with Ronnie, though it had less to do with his jealousy of Peter than with my swift rise in popularity. Suddenly I was no longer the little lady running around doing a bit of this and a bit of that. I was getting busier by the day, and everybody, it seemed, wanted me. Ronnie did not understand that at all. Maybe I should have sat him down and said, 'Don't worry about how much work I've got. You know I'll always be here for you.' But there again, I didn't know myself just how busy I was going to be.

One day the film producer Oscar Lewenstein rang PC to ask if I would do a screen test for Ionesco's *Rhinoceros*, a film that was to star the comedian Tony Hancock, a hero of mine. I'd never done a screen test before and, although I agreed, I lost my bottle on the day and phoned to cancel. But Oscar wouldn't let it go: he persuaded me to go to a studio in Shepherd's Bush at the end of the day, after four other actresses had done their tests, just to have a chat with Tony. He quietly filmed me and Tony chatting and then, without making a big deal of it, asked me to read a bit from the script with Tony.

When we finished, Tony's famous hangdog expression vanished and he smiled. 'That was nice,' he said. 'I've only seen you do *The Rag Trade* as that dumb bird. Let's go and have a drink.' Over that drink we talked about actors being locked into their image and Tony confided that he loathed his character in the hit TV show *Hancock's Half Hour*, the role that had made him famous. He liked to try a variety of mixers with his vodka and I saw them all that afternoon as he drank himself into oblivion. Even so, I had no idea that he was an alcoholic.

I was thrilled when Oscar called PC the following week to say that I'd got the part. It was not to be, however: before long the movie was shelved because Tony went into a clinic to dry out. But there was plenty of other work for me in London that summer – cabaret, recording and countless personal appearances. Then Peter Charlesworth rang with the offer of a movie called *Crooks in Cloisters* to be filmed on the Cornish coast. The producers had been after Diana Dors, but she did not want to do it, so they had settled on me. I didn't care a bit about being second choice. The film – about a gang of forgers who go on the run, posing as monks – was to star Ronald Fraser, Bernard Cribbins and Wilfrid Brambell – and promised to be a giggle. I jumped at the chance. *Crooks* lived up to my expectations. For two carefree weeks, cast and crew never stopped playing pranks on each other and laughing over the silliest thing. We were just like schoolkids. One day, while filming on the beach, I chatted up some young hunk and agreed to go out on his boat with him at four the next morning. Well aware of my cavalier attitude to sex, the actors and crew knew where the assignation would lead, and when I got the hunk back to my hotel room, we were met with the most overpowering smell of fish. Someone had also thoughtfully deposited a load of sand on the bedsheet. Happily, neither got in the way of the matter in hand, and I recorded a memorable catch of the day.

Later that year Ronnie Fraser phoned me. He was filming *The Beauty Jungle* with Jeanette Scott and Ian Hendry at Pinewood, and wanted me to join him for lunch. I accepted immediately: we'd had a real laugh on *Crooks* and liked each other a lot.

Ronnie had left a message with Tom, the commissionaire at the main gate, asking me to meet him in the bar. To get there I had to walk through a long dining room full of people. Suddenly I became very nervous and self-conscious. I was reasonably well known, but hardly a household name, and although I'd made films, I'd never set foot in such grand studios. I clip-clopped through on my stilettos, praying that I wouldn't trip and hoping that one of the many famous faces might recognise me and call out a friendly 'Hello, Bar,' but no one did.

But Ronnie's thoughtful invitation was to change my life in the most spectacular way. For among the scores of people in that long and impressive dining room were two gentlemen who were on the look-out for a busty blonde actress to replace Liz Fraser in the next in a series of long-running comedy films they were making. Those gentlemen, a producer named Peter Rogers and a director, Gerald Thomas, thought the pert little blonde who had tottered self-consciously past their table fitted the bill perfectly.

When they approached PC about a month later to ask if I was interested, he was wildly enthusiastic. 'I know that you find filming difficult, Barbara,' he said, 'but these Carry On producers really are the best. It'll be valuable experience for you and it'll teach you the tricks of the trade.' And that was how I came to sign up for *Carry On Spying*.

I was having such a fabulous year that I was chosen to appear on *Night of 100 Stars*, which was compered by four young men who were having a pretty good year themselves – the Beatles. For the finale of the show, at the London Palladium, each female star had to be escorted down a long flight of stairs on to the stage by one of the Fab Four. To my delight, I was chosen as one of John Lennon's ladies. Unfortunately I could not attend the rehearsal because I was away filming *Crooks in Cloisters*. But that was good news for everyone working on the show, because they were treated to a magical moment of Lennon humour that had everyone in fits. When it was John's turn to rehearse walking an imaginary me down the staircase, he bent his knees so that he was barely four feet tall, lifted up his chest and wiggled across the stage, imitating my giggle; then, in an uncanny impersonation of my voice, he said: 'I'm Barbara Windsor.' He had me off to a T, apparently, and everyone who saw it said it was a pity it was not captured for posterity on film.

I was also invited, with more than 200 other celebrities, to a Variety Club charity gala in Battersea Park's pleasure gardens, which had been designed for the Festival of Britain in 1951. We spent a lovely warm afternoon signing autographs and posing for photographs, and when I was asked to take a ride on the boating lake with a craggy-faced actor I'd seen on the cinema screen and on stage, I happily obliged. We pulled away from the side and motored towards the middle of the lake, waving to crowds of onlookers and cameramen. The actor shifted closer to me and gave a throaty chuckle, then put an arm round me and squeezed. 'I do think you're lovely,' he kept saying. I thought he was being sweet and acting up for the photographers, so I just giggled.

That was my first meeting with Sid James.

10

Life changed dramatically when June suddenly demanded a divorce from Ronnie and he and I bought a maisonette in Hendon, north-west London. All the time he was married and we lived in rented accommodation, Ronnie was happy with the status quo. But when I had to pass him off as Mr Windsor to get a mortgage and my name began to appear on all the household bills, Ronnie started to get the hump. One day early in 1964, he said: 'I can't be doing with all this Mr Windsor stuff no more. Let's get married.'

I did not want to get married. I was more than happy the way I was, working in showbiz and having a sweet man to look after when I got home. But Ronnie was adamant. 'Either we get married, Bar, or I'm off,' he said. I thought: 'If I'm not with him, what will happen to me?' I'd never had a man like him in my life. Maybe if I'd had a year living by myself, I'd have realised I could cope on my own. But I could not bear the thought of Ronnie leaving; he had been so strong and good for me, and I could not picture a future without him. So I agreed.

It should have been simple, but it wasn't. After we had arranged to get married at Wood Green Register Office, we were told that, as we now lived in Hendon, we did not come under Wood Green's jurisdiction. Then we booked a wedding in Tottenham, our previous borough, for Monday 2 March. However, having signed to do *Carry On Spying* I was told – on the Friday – that I would be on standby for filming until midday that Monday, and to stay at home and wait for a phone call. I didn't know what to do. The wedding seemed doomed, but Ronnie would have gone spare if we'd postponed it again. I decided to go ahead and leave the phone off the hook all Monday morning. But first I had another problem to solve: Mummy. I had not told her I was getting married and, knowing how much she disliked Ronnie, the thought of doing so filled me with dread. I could not go through with it without telling her, though, so at nine o'clock on the Sunday night, I went into the hall and picked up the phone. 'Oh, dear,' said Ronnie. 'The shit's going to hit the fan now.'

But it didn't. Mummy was very nice about it. I think she had to acknowledge that Ronnie had not let me down, and we'd been together such a long time by then that she was probably resigned to our relationship. However, she did not ask to come to the wedding. She just said: 'It's a bit short notice. Too late to get a hat now, isn't it?'

It was just as well she didn't come. I'd lost so much weight dieting for the film that the cream suit I'd bought a few weeks before hung on me like a sack. I actually had to hold it together at the back with a safety pin. And it rained from start to finish. Driving all the way to Tottenham through rush-hour traffic to be at the register office by nine was a nightmare. By the time we reached the top of Muswell Hill, it all got on top of me and I burst into tears.

Ronnie stopped the car and asked me what was wrong.

'I don't know ... I don't know,' I wailed.

'You don't want to get married, do you?'

'I do, I do,' I sobbed. 'But it's all wrong. My suit doesn't fit. It's pouring with rain. And we're going to bloody Tottenham.' I was also feeling a bit guilty about not telling Mummy until so late. In a way, I wished she had blasted me. When we arrived, the witness Ronnie had arranged was someone I didn't know. And the so-called reception was a couple of very swift drinks in the nearest boozer, when they opened, because I had to rush home and put the phone back on the hook. Sod's law, I wasn't phoned until 2 p.m., when I was told I wasn't wanted until the next day.

Obviously the honeymoon had to be put on hold. Instead I went to Pinewood the next day to make my Carry On debut. I was very nervous and Bernard Cribbins, like the good friend he is, did his best to calm me down. 'Don't worry, Babs, they're a good lot,' he said. 'Watch Kenny Williams, though. He doesn't like new people and he'll try to get you at it.' Unfortunately, that was probably the worst thing Bernie could have said, because I was a huge fan of Kenny's work, and very keyed up at the prospect of acting with him. I'd ached with laughter at him in *Hancock's Half Hour* on the radio, and had seen him many times on the stage. He had the most wonderful talent.

My first scene on *Spying* was with Kenny and I fluffed my lines. Everybody went quiet, waiting for the inevitable.

Kenny, who was playing a bearded secret agent, didn't let them down. 'Oooh, da-ah-ling, do please get it right,' he said snootily from beneath the black false whiskers. Out of sheer embarrassment I went on the attack. Having heard he had fallen out with the actress Fenella Fielding, I pulled myself up to my full four feet ten and a half inches and replied, in my poshest voice, 'Don't you yell at me with Fenella Fielding's minge hair stuck round your chops. I won't bloody stand for it.'

For a moment I thought he was going to say: 'How dare you! Get her off the set!' and I'd be out of a job. But he just stared at me, then flared those famous nostrils, and clapped his hands. 'Haaaahh,' he said, grinning broadly. 'Isn't she wonderful?'

After that, we got on fantastically. He just took to me, which I treated as a compliment, because I'd been told that you didn't choose Kenny as a friend, he chose you. Although he came from London's Caledonian Road, the son of a barber, he was a terrible snob. One day on our way back to the set, he put his arm round me and said: 'I really love you, Bar. You're the only person round here who cleans their teeth after lunch.'

Kenny, I discovered, could be outrageous, particularly if members of the public visited the set. One day, despite Gerald's warning to behave himself, Kenny walked over to a group of punters who had won a competition to look round the studios. He turned his back and dropped his trousers, inquiring: 'Anyone want to see my lovely bum?'

Amusing though Kenny was, for me, the funniest on-screen actor in that Carry On team was Charles Hawtrey, who had learned his craft playing an ageing schoolboy in films with the unforgettable Will Hay. In *Carry On Spying*, Charlie and I played the spies, and at the end of the film we were captured and held over a vat of boiling oil to force us to reveal our identities. We were strapped on to a sort of conveyor belt, but it was still a scary scene to do. Afterwards, just as we were being unstrapped, Charlie collapsed. He was as white as a sheet and his eyes were glazed over. Thinking he had fainted, I called for someone to get some brandy, but Gerald Thomas said: 'You're joking, aren't you, Barbara? It's the brandy that's done it!'

Apparently he was an alcoholic, and once on every film he made, he would go on set the worse for wear. Feeling sorry for him that day, I went over with a bucket, in case he felt like throwing up. I shouldn't have bothered.

'Why don't you piss off?' he slurred. 'You're always trying to be so nice to everyone.'

I quickly learned that Charlie did not court friendship; in fact he was most unsociable. While waiting for the technicians to set up the cameras and lighting, he would sit on his own far away from the rest of us, very aloof, smoking Weights, the cheapest cigarettes you could buy, with an expression of disdain on his face. It was as though he was thinking: 'I've been with the greats of British comedy. Why am I part of this rubbish?' He liked me, though, and I got on really well with him.

We always knew when Charlie had come straight to the studio after a bender. He'd saunter in, looking grand, with his chauffeur behind him lugging a crate of R. White's lemonade. We'd all groan: 'Oh dear, we're in for trouble today – Charlie's on the R. White's.' He was so dehydrated he'd drink bottle after bottle of the stuff.

One day towards the end of shooting, Kenny and I were sitting in our chairs with our names on the back having a chinwag. He asked me what I was doing after the film. 'Going on my honeymoon, of course,' I said.

'How long were you with Ronnie before you got married?' Kenny asked.

'Three years.'

'Honeymoon? It's an 'oliday. And I shall come with you.' I thought he was joking, but he was deadly serious.

'Kenneth Horne and Stanley Baxter say there is a marvellous hotel in Funchal, Madeira,' he went on. 'It's all lovely and on a Wednesday night you get a free buffet. You fly, then you get this boat that goes across at midnight. All very romantic. All these lovely dark-haired young Portuguese men waiting for you.'

'Well, I won't need them now, dear, will I?' I said.

But there was no arguing with Kenny, and I found myself going along with the idea. Happily, Ronnie did, too, although neither of us expected Kenny to invite his mother, Louisa, and his sister Pat as well.

Like our wedding, the honeymoon was a disaster. We were delayed in Lisbon for two hours, then a second plane flew us to Porto Santo in Madeira, where we picked up a ferry for the capital. It was a filthy ferry, full of people with chickens and pigs and God knows what other animals. To put the tin lid on it, a violent storm broke as we set off at one in the morning. Ronnie was not good with boats, and spent the entire journey hanging over the side throwing up, his face literally touching the waves, wailing: 'Let me go, let me die,' as I held on to his legs.

In the middle of all this, I could hear Kenny complaining that he had not been given what he'd paid for. 'Where's my food? It's all included in the ticket. I should have three courses on this ferry. The food, where is it?' And then his mother's little voice: 'My Kenny wants his three courses. You let him have it.'

There was worse to come. When we finally got to the hotel Ronnie and I discovered that the bridal suite was a tiny room with no bathroom or toilet. Flopping, exhausted, on to the hard bed, Ronnie groaned: 'Fucking 'ell. Prison's beautiful compared with this.' Then he started throwing up again.

It proceeded to rain on and off for the next ten days, but we'd given up trying to have a good time by the third anyway. Looking out at yet another downpour one morning, Kenny produced some huge, torpedo-like capsules. 'I've come well equipped, Windsor. I've got the very latest in sleeping pills. Made in France, they were. They'll see me through this misery.'

'Bloody hell, Kenny,' I said. 'They're a bit big. How on earth do you get them down your throat?'

'You don't swallow them, you silly cow,' he said. 'You shove 'em up your arse.' With that, he flounced off to his room, announcing that he hated the place, and stayed there for most of the rest of the holiday. The few times he did venture out to sit with us by the pool when the sun did come out, he kept his suit on. In fact I never saw him in shorts the whole time we were there. And he refused point-blank to sign autographs for anyone. His distinctive voice was instantly recognisable, and of course people would come up and ask him to sign something for them or for their mum or their daughter. Kenny would just look down his nose at them, and say, very brusquely: 'Piss off. I'm on holiday.'

I think it takes a certain amount of courage to approach a well-known person and ask for an autograph, so I'm always polite to people who do. But Kenny didn't give a monkey's if he hurt anybody's feelings. I was appalled. 'Kenny, you can't do that,' I told him one day. 'They're our fans.'

But he just huffed: 'I've come here to relax, not sign autographs.' He looked at Ronnie. 'Come on, Ron. Let's go.' Then his mother launched into me. 'Don't you have a go at my Kenny. If he doesn't want to sign autographs, he doesn't have to.' Then off she went, too, and I was left sitting there with Kenny's sister, Pat. 'Now you know what I've lived with all my life,' she sighed.

If the weather had been good, we could probably have got through the holiday OK, but the constant rain heightened the tension between Kenny and me and we ended up not speaking. As it turned out he spent more time with Ronnie than I did. He liked Ronnie enormously – he thought he was a dish – and early on pulled me up about the way I spoke to him.

'You mustn't keep picking him up on things, Barbara,' he said.

'What?'

'Well, twice you've said, "No, no, Ronnie, it's not 'off of' him, it's 'from' him." You shouldn't say that. Ronnie's OK as he is.'

'He doesn't write very well, so I've been helping him,' I explained.

'Well, you shouldn't. It doesn't matter. Ronnie copes very well. He's got a lovely manner.'

The weather finally let up and we were able to escape to Lisbon, where the sun was shining. We checked into an expensive hotel and did our best to salvage something from what had been a most miserable experience.

When we got back Peter Charlesworth rang to say that Joan Littlewood was taking her stage show *Oh What a Lovely War* to America and wanted me to take over from Avis Bunnage, who had been doing the musical at Stratford East. Knowing how much I'd enjoyed the States the previous year, Peter felt I'd jump at the chance to go back, but he was wrong. I wanted to appear on Broadway – of course I did, who wouldn't? – but I wasn't prepared to go there just for the sake of it, in the same way I wouldn't do a West End play if it wasn't right for me. And I didn't think *Oh What a Lovely War* was right for me. I loved the show: it made a trenchant comment on the 1914–18 war by contrasting the on-stage action with haunting images of the war, and it was powerful, provocative and worthy. But it was very much a company production, a director's piece, and I felt I had moved on from being part of a company.

Besides, the Swinging Sixties had hit Britain and it was all happening on this side of the water. I liked being a big fish in a small pond, and a bit of me was afraid that, even if I did well in the States, few people in Britain would know about it. I wanted Mummy to be proud of me. I knew she'd love people to go up to her and say: 'Your Babs is doing well,' and, as I was young and on my way up, I had no reason to doubt that something else that suited me better would turn up another time.

But the next thing I knew, Joan was on the phone determined to talk me round. 'What's all this about you not wanting to do the show?' she snapped.

'I just don't think it's my cup of tea, Joan,' I said, sweetly. 'Anyway, you don't need me. You've got Avis.'

Joan was never one to mince her words. 'I'll tell you something, Barbara. You've become a very boring actress. You're always playing it safe with the same little parts. *Fings* was your best, but you've been playing that part ever since. I think you're afraid of the challenge. You just want the spotlight on you.'

Joan was wrong about the spotlight, but right about me playing the same type of part. I hadn't played a brass since *Fings*, but I couldn't deny that my characters had all been similar 'blonde floozies'. And maybe she was also right about me fearing a challenge. Whatever the case, I allowed her to change my mind. Even though I had been offered a part in a movie, *John Goldfarb Please Come Home*, with Shirley MacLaine and Peter Ustinov, I heard myself telling Joan, OK, I'll do the show. Then I would have to clear it with Ronnie. Although we had been living together for three years, we had only just got married, after all. How was he going to take his young bride saying: 'I'm off to America for four months'? As it happened he took it remarkably calmly. 'If that's what you want to do, babe, then do it,' he said.

Before I left for the airport that September, I felt I needed to clear the air about something that was bothering me. 'If you feel you need to get your rocks off while I'm away, darling, I won't mind, you know,' I told Ronnie.

He glared at me as though I was a stranger. 'What the hell's that supposed to mean?'

I thought I was being mature and up-front. I never for a moment thought I wouldn't have affairs in New York. I didn't believe in all that 'absence makes the heart grow fonder' rubbish; 'out of sight, out of mind' was more my line of thinking. And I felt that if I was going to be unfaithful, it was only right to give Ronnie permission to do the same. I knew I would not think about him or suffer any guilt about having it off with other men, because to me sex and love were two different things. But Ronnie didn't see it that way, and we had a bit of a row about it.

Before opening on Broadway, we played two weeks in Philadelphia to smooth out the rough edges. We just could not get it together. And that sent Joan Littlewood off the dial.

On the second night she took the almost unheard-of step of coming backstage during the interval to have a go at us. The person in the firing line was Victor Spinetti, who was sharing a dressing room with me. I felt she was totally out of order. I could have understood it if she had given him a note saying, 'Keep it down a bit,' or 'You can afford to go up a bit,' or whatever, but instead she came rushing in and tore into Victor as though he were some know-nothing amateur. 'What the hell do you think you're doing?' she fumed. 'You're going way over the top. You're not giving a true performance.'

OK, Joan was the director, but it was still a terrible thing to do to an actor when he had the rest of the show to do. I knew what her problem was: it was a director's piece and she didn't want the actors overshadowing her. Victor had been scoring as the sergeant-major and she was pissed off. I couldn't just sit there and let it go, so I chimed in: 'You shouldn't come round here and have a go at my friend like that. Fuck off back to the front stalls and sit with the spotlight on you, because you're obviously missing it far more than we are.'

I don't know if Joan picked up on the irony of that remark, but she half-grinned as she strode out. Maybe she just admired me for sticking up for my friend. But Victor was wrecked. That he pulled himself together quickly and got through the second half showed what a strong character and highly professional performer he was.

It took less than a week in New York to convince me I'd made a mistake going to the States. I was not on an all-expenses-paid promotional trip, staying in a posh hotel, as I had been the previous year. Instead we actors were put into a cheap hotel on the poorer west side of town, where the rooms didn't have toilets, let alone telephones in them. And whereas before I'd found Manhattan exciting and invigorating, now it was all too fast, too noisy and too rude. I was so tiny and everything was just so big. Every time I went out to eat, for example, I never seemed to get what I thought I'd ordered, and it was always too much for me. And I didn't know that it was acceptable to pick up chicken or spare ribs with your hands, so I ended up not eating much and losing a lot of weight. To make matters worse, all my misgivings about the show resurfaced. I knew I wasn't going to score in it. I knew I wasn't going to be happy. I knew I should have stayed at home.

My unhappiness must have been obvious, because after rehearsals one day, Shepard Coleman, the musical director, came up to me and asked me what was wrong. I poured my heart out to him, particularly on the subject of where I was living.

'Well, you don't have to live in a place like that, Barbara,' he said. 'I'm staying in an apart-hotel uptown. It's like having your own apartment, but you've got the facilities of an hotel.' A week later, along with Victor and two other actresses, Valerie Walsh and Fanny Carby, who also wanted to move, I checked out of the grubby little off-Broadway hotel and moved into a swish apart-hotel block uptown on West 73rd Street. After that things started to go a bit better.

We opened at New York's Broadhurst Theatre in front of a specially invited VIP audience. The production was never going to be a smash hit, more a prestigious show, but we all got a standing ovation when we walked into the legendary Sardi's restaurant opposite afterwards and the manager called out: 'Ladies and gentlemen: welcome, please, the cast of *Oh What A Lovely War!*'

No sooner had we sat down than all sorts of people who had seen the show came over to tell us how superb we had been. I felt like the cat who had got the cream, and the more I was told how wonderful I was, the more I lapped it up. Having noticed my surname, one woman even asked me if I was related to the royal family! As we left to go to a first-night party at the top of the eighty-storey Pan Am Building over on Park Avenue, PC – who had come over for the opening – gave me a nudge. 'There's someone else who'd like to meet you, Barbara.' He motioned to a man behind me, so close I was actually backing into him. 'Oh, no, darling,' I said dismissively. 'Let's get on to the party.'

'I think you'll want to meet this gentleman,' Peter insisted, swivelling me round.

I found myself looking into the bluest eyes I'd ever seen in my life. 'Barbara, this is Paul Newman,' Peter said. 'Mr Newman, meet Barbara Windsor.' It was all I could do not to wet myself with excitement. Paul Newman was one of my favourite film stars at that time and I couldn't believe that we were a couple of feet apart in the most famous restaurant in New York and he was wanting to speak to me. Any bit of starriness I felt at having just performed on Broadway went out of the window and I started behaving like a fan.

'Oh, hello, Mr Newman, I think you're great,' I gushed. 'I saw you in *Somebody Up There Likes Me* and *Hud*. You were fantastic.' Grabbing a napkin from one of the tables and a pen from Peter, I asked: 'Would you mind signing an autograph for my mother? Please. She'd love that. Her name's Rose.' While he was writing I seized another napkin and as he handed me his autograph said: 'You wouldn't mind doing another, would you? It's for my Aunt Ivy. She's a great fan, too. She won't believe it when I tell her I've actually met you . . .'

A lovely woman by his side smiled warmly at me and said: 'We loved your performance tonight and we thought you were wonderful in the baby carriage movie.' I had no idea who she was or what she meant: I was too caught up with meeting Paul Newman. 'It's so wonderful to have met you, Mr Newman,' I stammered.

'Have a great time here,' he said as Peter ushered me outside.

'Good God, what a state you got in,' he told me. 'You've got to get your act together, Barbara. You're going to meet lots of people like that.'

My head was in too much of a spin from the excitement of it all for me to reply.

'You know who that lady was, don't you?'

'No, I couldn't concentrate.'

'That was his wife, Joanne Woodward.'

'What did she mean by the baby carriage movie?' I asked.

'*Sparrows Can't Sing*. You with the pram.'

I should have been flattered that such a great actress remembered my role rather than the title of the film. I was really embarrassed that I had not recognised her or acknowledged her compliments.

Peter was right about the people I was going to meet. During a matinée performance the following Wednesday, I was in the middle of the opening number when I looked into the wings and saw the most stunning-looking young man standing there. The face was familiar, but I couldn't place him. As I walked off stage with Victor after the final curtain, he grabbed me, laughing. 'Hi, Barbara,' he said, then held out his hand to Victor. 'Hi, Victor.' He introduced himself as Warren Beatty and said he had popped in to see the show and to have a chat with some English people. He had spent time working in England and had fallen in love with the country and the people, he told us.

We nattered in our dressing room for a while, then, as he was leaving, he said: 'We must have tea at Sardi's.'

'That would be lovely,' I replied. 'Can I bring Victor?'

'Of course you can,' Warren said. 'And I'll bring Leslie.' We made a date for the following Wednesday.

When Warren had gone, Victor shook his head at me. 'You're so stupid, Bar,' he said. 'It's obvious he's got the hots for you.'

'Nah,' I said. 'Not little me.'

The following Wednesday we met at Sardi's for tea as arranged and Warren introduced us to his girlfriend, the French actress Leslie Caron, who, nine years before, had starred in *Daddy Longlegs*, a screen version of the story from which *Love From Judy* had been adapted. Warren had a wonderful smile and was easy to talk to, but he was so dazzlingly good-looking that I was too nervous to contribute much in the way of teatime banter. It reminded me of being taken out to tea by Johnny Brandon. Again I recognised little on the menu and ended up ordering poached eggs on toast. Leslie told us that she was going to England shortly. As we left, I said I hoped she would have a good time.

'Thank you, Miss Windsor, I will,' she said, adding tartly: 'But remember, I have my spies!'

Not that this seemed to bother Warren much. Somehow he got my phone number at West 73rd and called me three times to ask me out. I never went because I would have been a bag of nerves. After starring in *Splendor in the Grass* with Natalie Wood, he was one of the hottest Hollywood properties around, and he was also just too drop-dead gorgeous.

The dressing room I shared with Victor was so near the street that we could hear people's voices outside as we got ready to go on stage. Hit shows including *Funny Girl* with Barbra Streisand, *Hello, Dolly* with Carol Channing and *Golden Boy* with Sammy Davis Jr were playing on the same street, and we could hear theatregoers who had not been able to get tickets for those shows discussing whether or not to come and see ours. It was billed as a 'musical fantasy', and those New Yorkers who thought they were in for a light-hearted production were obviously disappointed. Many of them walked out, and although that wasn't a nice experience for us, I could understand why. The piece was one for the ardent theatregoer, not for your average person looking for a fun night out, and the subject matter did not always strike a chord with a nation that had never fought a war on its own soil.

A month into the show, Shepard Coleman and I began an affair. My old man was miles away and, as Shepard's beautiful wife, Gretchen, a striking, six-foot Broadway star, was on tour, we had ample opportunity, especially as we were both living on West 73rd Street. Shepard, in his early forties, was a big name on Broadway. He was a shortish, elegant gentleman with a little beard, and handsome, but it was not so much his looks I fell for; it was that he took an interest in me and was so good to talk to. This was something I did not have with Ronnie: a good sex life is all very well, but you've got to be able to talk to each other when you are not bonking, haven't you?

Although I'd got married only a month or so before, Shepard and I became very close and I began to look on him more as a boyfriend than as a musical director. Thanks to him and his wide circle of friends, I was invited to loads of sophisticated parties at wonderful houses by New York's rich and famous. I went to one given by the director Mel Brooks and his wife, the actress Anne Bancroft, and another at the invitation of the film star Lee Remick. She actually rang me herself at my apart-hotel. I was caught a little off balance and addressed her as Miss Remick. 'Oh, call me Lee,' she said. 'We're having a get-together and we want to make sure you English people feel welcome here and are having a good time.'

The more I saw of Shepard, the more I realised that marrying Ronnie had been a mistake. I knew now that I could live without him. My dislike for New York and its noisy, overbearing character vanished and I started to enjoy myself as a carefree, bachelor girl. New Yorkers were not used to seeing such tiny, busty girls and Shepard would ask me to walk down the street ahead of him so that he could watch people's reactions. I'd wiggle along, then turn round to see him doubled up with laughter. I think he saw me as something of a trophy, someone he could show off, because one evening, he took me to an extremely posh party at an art gallery, where I was clearly out of place. Shepard was a cellist and the party was full of equally gifted people. I was overawed by such talent and had trouble even opening my mouth, let alone saying anything remotely interesting. But Shepard just said: 'Don't worry about saying anything, darling – you're contributing a hell of a lot!'

I kept telling Shepard I was a city type, but, one weekend, he insisted on taking me to his farm in Warwick, New Jersey, an hour and a half's drive out of Manhattan. The beauty of it all took my breath away; I'd never known places like that existed. Having no experience of country life even at home, it never occurred to me to buy flat shoes or wellies, so I teetered around in high heels all the time, which Shepard found hilarious. Weekends in Warwick while Gretchen was away became a regular thing and they were bliss. I loved that part of the country so much I jumped at the chance to spend Christmas there with two mates from the show, Chuck Sewell and Murray Melvin.

I met Shepard's wife once when she was in New York for the day. She knocked on my dressing-room door and introduced herself. 'So you're Barbara. Shepard has told me all about you.' We had a brief chat and, after asking me to take a hairpiece to her hairdresser's, she went on her way, leaving me wondering whether she knew I was her husband's bit on the side.

As well as Shepard, I was seeing a beautiful, twenty-one-year-old guitarist called Vince. I was having a fabulous time, but my visa would expire two weeks after *Oh What a Lovely War* closed and as we neared the end of the run I had to face the prospect of returning to England to a husband I had not missed for a second. Yet, much as I now loved the States, there was never any question of me not going back. Shepard felt that I belonged on his side of the Atlantic, but I wanted to be a success in my own country.

I did not speak to Shepard for twelve days after the show closed, preferring to travel to Boston and Philadelphia then back to New York to watch Vince perform. I rang him to tell him that I'd run out of time and would not be able to get to Warwick as I had hoped. Two days before my visa ran out, Gretchen Coleman phoned me. 'Shepard is devastated, Barbara.'

'What do you mean? Why?'

'You're going tomorrow, and you haven't even called him to say goodbye.'

'I was going to,' I said.

'You must see him,' she told me. 'You've got to get out here.'

I told her that was impossible – my flight was the next day. But a few minutes after I put the phone down, it rang again. This time it was Mary Ellen, a close friend of the Colemans I knew from Warwick, telling me I *had* to say goodbye to Shepard and that she and her husband were coming to New York to pick me up. When we arrived at Mary Ellen's house I was astonished to find Gretchen there. 'I hope you weren't going to leave without saying goodbye to Shepard,' she said to me.

Later that day, I saw Shepard and we had a few words. He seemed to think I'd been cruel. I suppose I had, but we both knew the affair had to end more or less as soon as the show finished, and that I was also seeing Vince. In fact one night Shepard had walked me to watch Vince perform. 'I can't believe I'm taking you to a date,' he'd said. 'I really shouldn't let you go.'

Those last two days in New York were very hectic and I had Immigration on my back making sure I was not planning to outstay my welcome. By now all I wanted to do was get on a plane. On my last day I went on a wild shopping spree round all the famous stores, such as Macey's and Bloomingdale's, buying presents for Ronnie and Mummy and Len. I also wanted something for myself; something special that would symbolise the sweet smell of success I'd experienced working on Broadway for the first time. I treated myself to a bottle of Guerlain's Shalimar, promising myself I would use it as my trademark for the rest of my life. And, as I saw myself returning to a life of relatively quiet domesticity, I also bought some cookery books and kitchen gadgets I knew I'd never see in England.

I wanted to look nice for Ronnie, so in Saks on 5th Avenue I splashed out on a classy but demure dress: it was a plum colour, with vertical stripes, long sleeves with frills and a high neck. Watching the shop assistant pack it, I hoped Ronnie would like it.

But my homecoming was nothing like I had imagined. To start with Mummy had a go at me for 'wasting money' buying so many presents. As for Ronnie, well, he was just Ronnie. I'd wanted him to say, 'Oh God, I've missed you so much,' but he didn't express any such thoughts to me. It was as though I'd never been away.

As Ronnie had not been to New York, I thought he'd be fascinated to hear about it, but he wasn't. I started to miss those lovely conversations with Shepard: he had such an intellect, was such stimulating company, and Ronnie now seemed dull by comparison. If I used a word he didn't understand, he'd say: 'Stop using long words – you know I don't understand what they mean.' It was all such an anticlimax that I felt very flat.

Then, on the first Saturday after I got home, Ronnie said he was taking me out to a party. I cheered up a bit, thinking that he had deliberately tried not to appear overexcited by my return because he had laid on a surprise do for me and didn't want to give the game away. When I got all made up and put on my new dress for the party, Ronnie barely looked at me. I'd really made an effort, even combing my hair off my face, to show my forehead, just as he liked it, but he didn't say a word.

As we got into the car, it all became too much for me and I started to cry.

'What's wrong with you?' Ronnie said.

Through my tears, I said: 'I've been away *four* months and have bought this dress, and you haven't even told me how I look.'

'Don't be daft, you look great. I'd have told you if you didn't, wouldn't I?' He laughed, making me feel even more stupid than I did already.

As we headed towards Dalston in north London, I thought I'd tumbled where we were going. There was a pub there we often used, and I felt sure Ronnie would be taking us there, and that when we walked in, a crowd of our friends would be waiting to shout: 'Welcome home, Babs!' But we drove past the pub and ended up instead at the home of one of Ronnie's pals, Clifford Saxe. Apparently it was his birthday. All night they played the Tom Jones hit 'It's Not Unusual'. That was quite apt, wasn't it? It certainly wasn't unusual for me to be doing what suited Ronnie Knight.

But Ronnie was not much of a man for surprises. He never turned up unexpectedly to meet me where I was working because of his suspicions about other men. 'I would never know what I was going to walk into,' he'd say. He did not understand that showbiz was not a nine-to-five business, that rehearsals could go on until late and that performers would want a drink to relax afterwards.

People would comment on the way Ronnie looked at me and say: 'That man loves you a lot.' I could never see it. He did not have wandering eyes, but if I did catch him admiring another woman, she would invariably be tall, with long legs and dark hair. I did say to him once: 'When you said you loved me and wanted to marry me, were you looking over my shoulder at someone else?' It seemed to me that I was everything he didn't fancy. In fact I didn't think he even liked me much. I felt I aggravated him.

11

After I came back from New York, I was visiting family in Stoke Newington when a woman I'd never met came up to me. 'You're Barbara Deeks,' she said. 'My name's Julie. And I'm married to your father.'

I was astounded. Not only by this bolt from the blue, but also because Julie was everything Mummy wasn't: tall, slim and Jewish.

When I'd recovered my composure, I asked: 'How is Daddy?'

'He's had a very bad heart attack. He's in hospital.'

'Can I go and see him?'

'I'm sure your dad would be very glad to hear from you,' she said. 'Why don't you write?'

I took her advice, and my father wrote back saying he'd like to see me. I wanted to see him too, but I felt duty-bound to ask Mummy how she felt about it. She was very understanding. 'It's your choice, Babs,' she said.

Daddy and Julie lived in a flat in Stoke Newington and invited Ronnie and me there for dinner. It gave me a wonderful warm feeling to see Daddy again after all the silent years, and it seemed he felt the same. We were both keen to put the past behind us and begin afresh; to try to pick up the pieces and enjoy a loving father–daughter relationship.

Ronnie found the whole evening 'eerie'. He said that my dad was a male version of me, and that watching us together, anyone would have thought we'd seen each other every day of our lives, we had so much in common.

Ronnie and I then invited Daddy and Julie to Hendon and enjoyed a similar, friendly evening. Daddy complimented me on my good taste in everything, and kept telling me how pretty and intelligent I was. All the time he was gushing over me, Ronnie noticed that Julie was giving me dirty looks, as if she were thinking: 'This little lady is taking away a bit of my husband's love.'

I wanted to build a relationship with Daddy. At some point, when I felt comfortable and confident enough, I wanted to ask him why he had ignored me at the court and when I'd seen him afterwards at the bus stop. But we never got that far. Julie was a very possessive woman: if she wasn't working, she would travel on Daddy's bus, up and down the whole route, just to be near him. It was an unhealthy love, in my opinion, and whenever we saw them after those first two evenings, I always got bad vibes from her. She clearly didn't like me one bit.

After New York, I was eager to get back on stage in another big musical, so when my old mate Lionel Bart told me he was going to do for Robin Hood what he had done for Oliver Twist, I was excited. The plot had nothing to do with the original Sherwood Forest escapade, but it didn't matter: Lionel had the musical Midas touch and I felt that anything he wrote was bound to be successful. PC was not so sure. He tried to talk me out of it but I told him I wanted to do it, come what may. I was still on a high because I had been nominated for a Tony Award for Best Featured Actress in a Musical for my appearance on Broadway. I didn't win, but even being in the running was a fantastic boost for me – definitely a sunny-side-of-the-street moment.

The show was called *Twang!*, and neither Lionel nor I saw how it could fail to hit the target, particularly with the talent he was assembling round him on stage and behind the scenes. He had Joan Littlewood directing; Paddy Stone, one of the world's top choreographers; the great royal designer Oliver Messel and writer Harvey Orkin, who had scripted the Marx Brothers. With Jimmy Booth as Robin Hood, and Ronnie Corbett and Bernard Bresslaw among his Merry Men, the show had all the hallmarks of a West End hit. Lionel was so convinced it would be a roaring success that he was backing the show with thousands of pounds of his own money.

I had a lead role playing Delphina, a cockney nymphomaniac who is saved from marrying Roger the Ugly, and I signed my contract full of confidence and enthusiasm. It did not take long for me to lose both. There were so many things wrong: too many egos in one basket, for a start. Everyone putting the show together thought they knew best, and the arguments raged from day one. What shocked me were Joan Littlewood's shortcomings. As I'd witnessed at first hand, she was terrific with a few actors. In that situation she could make something out of nothing, but given more than sixty performers, she had no idea what to do with them. During a rehearsal, one of ten statuesque showgirls who had to run through a make-believe forest dressed as reindeers asked her: 'What do I do here?'

'Just do your own thing, dear,' said Joan.

I was appalled. She could have been excused for saying that to me because by then I was an experienced actor and would improvise. But the poor showgirl just got herself in a right state.

There was a lot wrong with my own part, but I swallowed it – except for a one-liner in the second half. I was in a cage, having been captured, and I had to say: 'I don't know what's going on here.'

'Do you mind if I don't say that?' I asked Joan.

I got the usual abuse: 'Oh, you've lost it, have you? Frightened of your audience, are you? Yes, I *do* mind. I want you to say it.'

'To be honest, Joan,' I said, 'I don't know what the fuck *is* going on here! None of us do.'

It was true. The whole thing was a shambles. We didn't know the next line, the next song, who was supposed to be doing what. It was all over the place. What made it worse was that all the bigwigs blamed each other. Oliver Messel had bought some wonderful, but weighty, costume material in Paris, and when Paddy Stone pointed out that it was too heavy for us to dance in, Oliver snapped: 'You'll have to change your choreography.'

'No,' retorted Paddy angrily, 'you'll have to change your costumes!'

But what made it a real nightmare was that Lionel was out of his head on drugs all the time and giving Joan rewrites that made little sense. It all got too much for Joan. In the middle of a blazing public row, she screamed at Lionel: 'It's that fucking LSD, isn't it?'

I said to Jimmy, 'That's not fair. We're all in it for the money, aren't we?'

'She doesn't mean that, stupid,' he said.

'What *does* she mean, then?' The only LSD I knew about came in my wage packet. It was the abbreviation for pounds, shillings and pence.

Jimmy said he'd tell me later, but I was so intrigued that I buttonholed Joan after the row had died down, and asked her: 'Is it all about money?'

'No, you silly cow!' she said. 'Don't you know? He's into acid.'

I was none the wiser.

'The rubbish that makes people hallucinate and believe they can fly out of windows. It's called LSD.'

Most of the cast were so terrifed about what kind of fiasco we had signed up for that we turned to each other for comfort, and affairs were rife. Everyone felt they needed all the love they could get to lift their spirits.

Predictably, the opening night, at Manchester's Palace Theatre in October 1965, was a disaster. Dancers came skipping on in too-heavy, outsize costumes and kept bumping into each other. The Merry Men went into the audience, even the box seats, 'looking for Robin' and got dirty looks from punters who did not find it funny. And when I gritted my teeth and spoke my unenviable line, 'I don't know what's going on here,' someone shouted a reply that summed up the whole miserable occasion: 'Neither do we, Babs. It's not as good as *The Rag Trade.*'

Alone on stage in front of 3,000 silent, stony-faced paying customers, I didn't have the presence of mind to say anything other than: 'Don't worry, we'll work on it. That's what first nights are for.' Which upset Ronnie Corbett terribly. He couldn't forgive me for coming out of character on stage, and refused to speak to me when I came off.

'What could I do?' I asked him. 'I couldn't ignore it.'

The whole show was so terrible that Jimmy Booth told me he couldn't face going on stage for the finale; he was too fed up, too humiliated, to confront an audience which was by now baying for our blood. 'Bollocks you are, Jim,' I said. 'We've done our best. It's not our fault the show's a mess.' So we all went out for the big finish and performed to the backs of hundreds of people flocking to the exits. By the time we got to the end of the last number, the theatre was empty.

Not surprisingly, the critics slaughtered the show. The next morning Joan called us all in for a meeting. The theatre has a wonderful atmosphere when the lights are up and the sweet smell of success is in the air, but when you've had a huge flop, it's a horribly cold place. That day, as disgruntled punters queued at the box office demanding their money back, we sat sombrely in the stalls with one of the producers, Bernard Delfont, to hear what Joan had to say. She sat on a stool on the stage, looking down at us very despondently, and said how disappointed she was for everyone that the show had not worked. She held her hands up, blaming herself for the flop, and said she had agreed to quit and to let a 'theatre doctor' try to get the production back on its feet. That person, we learned later, was an American named Burt Shevelove, who had made his name with *A Funny Thing Happened on the Way to the Forum.* His verdict was that there was a lot of wonderful stuff and some fine performances, but the production was totally wrong. Burt was to have the final decision: if he felt the show could be saved, we would rework it and finish the scheduled four weeks in Manchester; if he felt it couldn't, then it would close immediately.

We were saved from the instant axe, but Burt warned us it was going to be a mess: he would rewrite ten minutes of the show every day with Harvey Orkin, but after performing the rewrite we would have to revert to Joan Littlewood's version. It was so crazy that at one point one of the cast 'died' in the show and reappeared later. If it was difficult for Burt and Harvey, it was a nightmare for us. To keep abreast of the rewrites, we resorted to jotting down our lines on the scenery, but this had its problems. Poor Jimmy Booth. He wrote a long, totally new speech on the back of a tree, but when he came to say it the tree had been moved off stage and Jimmy was literally lost for words. The reviews wrecked the box office. Hardly anyone booked, and when any of my friends or acquaintances suggested coming, I'd say: 'Don't bother. We're still trying to get it right.'

Slowly, though, we did get it right. Everyone's hard work started to bring results, although I did try to resist one of Burt's suggested improvements. He thought my Delphina was too 'ballsy' for Elrick Hooper's Alan A'Dale and wanted to replace him with Bernard Bresslaw. My heart sank: whenever I have even a faintly serious love scene in a show, someone always wants to put a gag in it, make a joke of me. Memories of my initial reaction to playing opposite Jimmy Booth in *Sparrows Can't Sing* came flooding back. This time it would be worse: Bernie was six foot six.

'No, no, *no*, Burt,' I wailed. 'We'll look bloody stupid.'

'Hold on a minute, honey,' Burt said. 'I'm going to show you something.' He arranged for Bernie to walk on stage in his Little John outfit, complete with tights and told a short girl, not dissimilar to me, to stand next to him.

'Now, there,' Burt announced triumphantly. 'That's what I call a couple. That's the kind of man you should be working with. No chance of you cutting *his* balls off.'

I saw what he meant. He changed the script to involve Delphina with Little John, and it worked brilliantly.

To us, the show got better and better, to a point where we almost felt good about it. Now, when our friends asked about it, we'd say, 'Yeah, it's fine now, come and see it.' It was nowhere near good enough to go into the West End, however, which is what Lionel wanted. We all begged him to let us take it on tour to tighten the parts that still weren't right, but he had invested a lot of money in it and he was dead set on London.

I had my own reason for not wanting to go into the West End. I was pregnant again. And, this time, I wanted to have the baby. I told the management that I wanted to leave. I didn't explain why, and they persuaded me to stay. 'If you leave us now, Barbara, the show will have no chance,' they said. I had no option: I had a contract to honour. So, very, very reluctantly, I had another abortion – unnecessarily, as it turned out, because *Twang!* failed to hit the bullseye when it opened at the Shaftesbury Theatre.

Christmas week was a dreadful time to open, particularly when the panto at the Palladium that year – *Robin Hood*, would you believe – not only starred the highly popular chart-topping Australian singer Frank Ifield but had also received great reviews. We took our final bows to a crescendo of boos: many people, it was clear, had come along simply for the sport. As ever, Danny La Rue was a lone supporting voice amid the barracking. In the pub afterwards, Joan Littlewood was sympathetic, too. 'It's still not right, Bird's Egg,' she said, consolingly.

Not surprisingly, *Twang!* closed after four weeks, leaving poor Lionel close to bankruptcy. He had invested most of his savings in the show and he said he was down to his last grand piano and stool.

That Christmas I had a dreadful confrontation with my father that brought back frightening childhood memories and killed off all hope of a long-lasting relationship between us.

I had gone with Ronnie to the card shop where Julie worked to give her some presents for herself and Daddy: a matching shirt, tie and sweater from Cecil Gee for him and a blouse for Julie. Daddy was there, looking at a card, and I went up to him, smiling, and said: 'Hello, Daddy.'

He glared at me, his face terrifyingly angry. 'What do you want?' he shouted.

'I've come with your Christmas presents,' I told him, and handed them to him.

He chucked them back at me, right in my face.

'Hold up, John,' said Ronnie. 'What are you doing?'

'Get out!' Daddy yelled at me. 'I don't want to see you again. You haven't been to see me for weeks now.' And as his face went red, then purple, with anger, and he started foaming at the mouth, those terrible old memories flashed into my mind. I was horror-struck, and humiliated, too: my face was well known to the public now and the shop was packed.

'If you wasn't an old man, John, I'd smack you one,' Ronnie said. Then we went out, leaving the presents on the floor.

At the door, I turned to see Julie laughing, a look of enjoyment and triumph on her face.

To this day, I don't know what provoked Daddy's reaction. The only reason I hadn't been to see him was because I had been working away, and he knew that. He'd been to see me in *Twang!* and I'd kept in touch by phone, which wasn't always easy – something that Mummy always understood. She appreciated how things were with work and never put any pressure on me. Julie's expression, however, seemed to indicate that his attack on me was all she could possibly have wanted for Christmas.

With the nightmare of *Twang!* over, I broke out in everything. I had conjunctivitis, spots all over my face, a streaming cold. I even had cystitis. I was still feeling emotional after the agonising decision to have an abortion I did not want. My eyes like slits and my head throbbing, I dragged myself up to Peter Charlesworth's office in Whitcomb Street the following Wednesday morning. He was shocked at the state of me. 'You look awful, Barbara,' he said. 'But the main thing is, we've got to get you back in the West End. In another show. Quickly.'

'What?' I said, horrified. It was the last thing I expected or wanted to hear. 'You must be joking. I don't ever want to see a theatre again. I don't even want to go and see a show, let alone be in one.'

Peter shook his head, then smiled soothingly. 'There's a saying in the theatre that if you're going to have a flop, have a big one. And, boy, have you had a big one. People will remember you for that. Now you've got to make them forget it.'

But I wasn't having any of it. *Twang!* had done me in, and I didn't want to go through anything remotely like it again. 'No, Peter,' I said, firmly. 'I want you to get me a movie.'

'I thought you didn't like filming,' Peter said.

'I don't,' I agreed. 'But it's better than what I've just been through.'

PC was wonderful. He didn't push me that morning, he just let me pour my heart out, then told me to go home and rest and let him speak to some people and see what came up. He didn't find me a movie; he found me another bloody musical, in which I'd play a jittery lift operator called Mavis who suffered from claustrophobia and a fear of heights.

'I can't believe you think I could do that,' I told him. 'It's not me. It's not me at all.'

'I know it's not, Barbara,' he said. 'But it'll be a challenge.'

Having no answer to that, I found other reasons why I shouldn't do the show, which was to star my mate, Danny La Rue. 'Danny's great in cabaret,' I argued, 'but do you think his style will work in the theatre?'

'That's not your problem. It's a really good little show. I think you should do it.'

He told me that it had been written by Bryan Blackburn, who'd produced and written my shows at Winston's.

'Who else is in it?' I asked.

'Gary Miller.'

'But he's a recording star, not a stage performer.'

'He's just done *She Loves Me*, remember?'

'Oh yes, of course he has.'

I still didn't want to do it. Then PC said: 'And the great Ned Sherrin is directing.'

I gave in.

When we opened with *Come Spy With Me* at Oxford's New Theatre, it didn't quite work, but as we had with *Twang!*, we worked on it every day. At the time Danny had his own club, where he appeared in cabaret at midnight, so he'd finish our show at 10.30, drive to London, do his cabaret, drive back to Oxford, grab three hours' sleep and be at the theatre again for rehearsals at ten.

By the time we moved on to our next venue, the Theatre Royal in Brighton, our hard work seemed to have paid off. The audience there was more responsive, and we went into the last week of the tour in Golders Green knowing we had a smashing little production that would meet the high standards set by the wonderful Brian Rix farces at the Whitehall Theatre, where we were to open the following week.

It was a joy to be back at the Golders Green Hippodrome Theatre where my stage career had begun. This time my name was up there with Danny's and it was lovely knowing that all my misgivings had proved unfounded. Nothing, it seemed, could go wrong. But it did. And in the most worrying, upsetting and ultimately tragic way.

Towards the end of the play, meek, mild-mannered Mavis takes a wonder drug and is transformed into a Wonderwoman figure in red leather and thigh-length boots who falls in love with a British spy, played by Gary Miller. It was a great scene for me: after spending most of the show as a timid lift operator, I came out and started throwing Gary around in an energetic song-and-dance sequence. On the final night at Golders Green, we were into the last number, with only minutes to go before the final curtain, when Gary fell on me like a dead weight. I thought he was going to collapse. I coped, as one does, but the moment we came off I said anxiously, 'Are you all right, Gary?'

'No,' he said. 'I feel ill. Very ill.'

I helped him to his dressing room and said, 'Right, Gary, let's get you home.'

But he wouldn't have it. He reminded me that his wife, Joy, was coming and that they were due to have dinner with Ronnie and me.

'Forget it, Gary. You're unwell. Ronnie won't mind.'

'No, I'll be all right,' he insisted. 'I haven't been eating properly on tour. I expect I was just faint with hunger.'

Ronnie and Joy arrived and we went to Derek Stoller's fish restaurant opposite the theatre. When it got to midnight, I said we should be going, but Gary did not want the evening to end, and we stayed there until around 1.30. An hour or so after Ronnie and I arrived home, the phone went. It was Joy. Gary had been rushed to hospital: he had had a massive heart attack.

He survived the night and the doctors said he had a good chance of recovering, but he was clearly not going to be well enough to do a charity performance on Sunday and open at the Whitehall the following Tuesday. The producers did not feel that Gary's understudy, Craig Hunter, was powerful enough for such a big part, so they called in Biff Maguire, a Canadian singer-dancer who was married to my fellow *Love From Judy* orphan Jeannie Carson. But after three days' rehearsal, Biff held his hands up and said: 'I can't tackle this,' and the producers had to go with Craig.

Opening nights are always exciting but *Come Spy With Me* was extra special for me, a real buzz. I think it was because I was so happy being back on the London stage in a smashing little show that stood a real chance of a long, successful run. The dressing rooms were at the top of the theatre, but microphones relayed the sound from the auditorium, and I actually heard the audience gasp as somebody walked into the auditorium to take his seat. It was Noël Coward, who had arrived with Rudolf Nureyev. They both came backstage afterwards, and Rudolf made my night when he told me how much he'd enjoyed me singing 'I'll Never Forget Whatsisname'. I feared what Noël, so celebrated for his acerbic wit, would make of the show, having written and starred in so many himself, and I prepared myself for a cutting remark. But he, like Rudi, said he loved it, which endorsed what we all felt about it.

Two months later, as the country was celebrating the England football team's World Cup triumph at Wembley, Gary returned to the show.

It was exciting to be in the West End again. I was for ever being invited to the openings of clubs and shops and to all sorts of star-studded parties, usually hosted by Danny or by my other great mate, Lionel Bart, where the champagne never ran dry. At one party, at Danny's home in Hampstead, Dusty Springfield got hammered and left a diamond ring in the bathroom after washing her hands. A little while later, she noticed the ring was missing and went into a drunken rage, screeching: 'My ring! My ring! Somebody's taken my ring!' Amid all the predictable jokes – 'Who'd want *your* ring, dear?' and so on – Danny got very upset and rushed upstairs. He came down with the most enormous diamond ring from his own collection and shoved it on to Dusty's finger, saying: 'There you are, darling. Have that. *Nobody* steals in my house.'

Of course, Dusty's own ring eventually turned up.

Ronnie was not in any way theatrical, but he did like being in the company of the stars at that party, and he was spellbound, along with the rest of us, when the great Noël Coward christened Danny's new white piano with the most memorable impromptu performance. Peter O'Toole was there, too, with his wife, Siân Phillips, and he got on so well with Ronnie that he invited us both back to his house nearby for coffee on our way home. I was mesmerised by Peter's incredible charisma and charm, as much as by his blazing blue eyes.

I was always proud of Ronnie: he always dressed immaculately, spoke quietly and conducted himself well, although one actress, Judith Bruce, confessed to me once that she expected him to carry a knife.

'What do you mean, a knife?' I asked.

'Well, he's got a club in the West End, hasn't he?' she said. 'I've heard he's a bit of a gangster.' How stupid can you get?

Ronnie did indeed run a West End club. It was a new business venture he had gone into with Mickey Regan, a wealthy pal who owned a string of betting shops. I'd been pushing the two of them to work together and when Malcolm Allison, the flamboyant football manager, decided to sell a club he owned in Charing Cross Road, Mickey bought it, renamed it the Artistes and Repertoire Club and installed Ronnie as the manager.

Quiet and unassuming as he was, Ronnie was not slow to speak up if somebody was out of order. He couldn't abide swearing, particularly in female company, and at one Lionel Bart party, Dave Davies, guitarist with the Kinks pop group, was well over the top. Ronnie put up with it for a while but eventually felt compelled to do something. He went over to Dave and said, quietly, politely, but very, very meaningfully 'Please don't talk like that in front of the ladies, there's a good chap.' Thankfully, Davies took the hint.

When we weren't partying on Saturday nights, Ronnie would leave the club early so that he could cook a meal for me when I got home. I'd have a taxi waiting for me at the stage door at 10.30 p.m. and was nearly always home by 11. It was late to eat a steak with chips and salad, but cooking for me was something that Ronnie enjoyed, and I was always starving. They were happy days indeed.

During the rest of the run of *Come Spy With Me*, Gary Miller showed no sign of the trauma he had experienced until, on the second Saturday of May 1967, he arrived at the theatre looking pasty and decidedly unwell. He would not tell me what was wrong, but later I twigged. That day, the papers had been full of the news that Sid James and Don Arroll – the comic who replaced Norman Vaughan on *Sunday Night at the London Palladium* – had had heart attacks. Don did not recover. It was a year to the day that Gary had had his own coronary, and all the coverage had brought home to him how close to death he had been.

I left the show shortly before the end of its fifteen-month run. A few months later, I read that Gary was appearing at the Pigalle in cabaret and making a film. I said to Ronnie: 'Gary will have to watch it, you know. He might be doing too much.' On Sunday 15 June the following year, Ronnie and I were sitting in bed reading the papers. 'I don't think you should read this,' he said to me. 'You're going to be really upset.'

Gary had had another heart attack the previous night after breaking an arm on stage. He never recovered and died aged just forty-two.

In 1968 I was a guest artist on the wonderful *Dad's Army*, playing a music-hall artist who was a crack shot. A lot of the cast were old-age pensioners and they treated me with an old-fashioned courtesy that really took me back. From the moment I arrived at rehearsals they were vying with one another to fetch me tea and biscuits and to make sure I was comfortable. It was a programme that was a real joy to work on.

Peter Charlesworth's next move was to persuade me that playing Lucy Lockett in *The Beggars' Opera* in Worthing for relatively poor money would be good for my career. But no sooner had I signed for it than Gerald Thomas called, saying he wanted me for another Carry On, *Carry On Doctor*. It had been four years since *Spying*, and it was too good an opportunity to turn down, so I agreed and spent ten days travelling to and from Worthing by train and then getting up at 5 a.m. or so to be at Pinewood for a whole day's filming. It was punishing, but I was only thirty-one and bursting with energy.

Ronnie took a night off to be at the opening of *The Beggars' Opera*. Peter sat beside him, and told me the next day that he had never had an experience like it in the theatre. In one scene I had to spend more than five minutes raunchily snogging my leading man, Freddie Jaeger. Peter said Ronnie spent the whole time biting his nails, rubbing his arms and generally fidgeting. 'He does love you, Barbara,' said Peter. 'He got himself into a terrible state.' Ronnie, not the most tactile of people, hated public shows of affection, so I wasn't surprised that he was so uncomfortable watching that sexy scene.

In spite of Sid James' heart attack, Gerald Thomas desperately wanted him in *Carry On Doctor*. Sid agreed on one condition: that he appeared only in bed. For someone who had nearly died a few months before, he looked astonishingly well – deeply tanned and lean after a holiday in the sun. The scene in which I, playing a nurse, cause his temperature to rise and the medical equipment to explode as I wiggle sexily up to his bed was the first we had together.

One of the films being made at Pinewood while we were shooting *Carry On Doctor* was *Chitty Chitty Bang Bang*, written by Roald Dahl and starring Dick Van Dyke and Sally Ann Howes, which had been in production for nearly a year. I was intrigued when I was asked to go and meet the movie's director and producer. To my astonishment and delight, they asked me if I would like to do a cameo in their film. I was completely bowled over at the prospect of working with Dick Van Dyke, who was one of the most popular television performers in the UK at the time.

'We'll send you the script,' they said, adding apologetically, 'there won't be many lines for you.'

'I don't need to see the script,' I replied quickly. 'I don't care if I don't have any lines.'

'We'll negotiate your fee with Peter Charlesworth.'

'I don't want any money,' I said. 'I'll pay *you* just to work with Dick Van Dyke.'

I was to play the girlfriend of Arthur Mullard – another case of big, slow-witted man with tiny girl – in a fairground scene in which Dick Van

Dyke, as the inventor Caractacus Potts, is demonstrating his miracle-working hair-restorer. In the process he manages to burn off Arthur Mullard's hair, which results in a furious chase through the fair.

I was only supposed to be doing one day's shooting, but when Dick said how much I cheered everyone up, the fairground chase was lengthened to extend my role a little, and I ended up working on the film for three or four days. *Chitty Chitty Bang Bang* was a great success, and not only was I overjoyed to have the chance to work with Dick, but the film was a valuable addition to my CV.

The following year, 1969, I did two more Carry Ons: *Camping* and *Carry On Again Doctor*. For obvious reasons *Carry On Camping* was set in the summer, but we shot the film during a bitterly cold February and March with the mud sprayed green to make it look like grass. *Camping* was, of course, the film that featured the famous scene in which the bra of my bikini had to come off while I was doing a physical workout in a field with other female campers. It was decided that it should be pulled off with a fishing line and hook and the first assistant director started getting everyone in place for the shot.

'Hold on a minute,' I said. 'I don't want anyone watching. I want the field cleared.'

'We've got to have camera and sound men, Barbara,' Gerald said. 'And what about me?'

'You're all right,' I said. 'Who's going to hook the bra off?'

Gerald said it would be Bert, a lovely old props man on the point of retirement.

'That's fine,' I said. So, with only Kenny Williams and Hattie Jacques in front of me and the other girls behind me, the camera rolled. Bare boobs were not shown in family films and Gerald told me to remember to cover mine with my hands when the bra flew off.

On the first take, as Bert pulled the fishing line, the bra failed to detach itself from me and I was pulled with it, headlong into the mud. 'Get her up, mop her down and let's go again,' said Gerald.

On the second take, the bra came off successfully, but when Hattie came over and grabbed my right arm to lead me off, she pulled my arm and exposed my right breast.

'Oh God, we've got to go again,' said Gerald.

'Oh Gerald!' I yelled. 'Look at my feet. They're sinking in the mud!'

'I'm not employing you for your feet, Barbara,' he told me.

The third take was spot-on. However, surprisingly, the censor passed the bare-boob one. 'I don't think Miss Windsor's right nipple is going to corrupt the nation,' he ruled.

Another scene in *Camping* involved me having a St Trinian's-type fight with a tall, buxom lady I faintly recognised. Just before we started, she came up to me, all nervous. 'You will tell me if you smell anything not very nice, won't you?' she said quietly.

'What do you mean, darling?' I asked.

'Well, we'll be fighting. There'll be body odour. I've sprayed myself everywhere, but . . .'

'For goodness' sake, don't worry, sweetheart,' I reassured her.

We did the scene in one take and, afterwards, she said: 'We've met before, you know.'

'I thought I recognised you.'

'I did a striptease at the Panama Club. I remember you because you starred at Winston's and everybody knew you.'

I took to her immediately. Her name was Anna Karen and we became good friends.

That year I was delighted to read that my idol, Betty Grable, was coming to London to perform at the Palace Theatre in a show called *Belle Star*. As soon as she arrived, I sent her a telegram telling her how much I'd admired her since seeing *The Dolly Sisters*, how much I was looking forward to coming to the show and how I hoped she would enjoy her time in England. I say telegram, but it was more of a fan letter, really, and it cost me a small fortune.

A couple of days before I was due to see Betty's matinée performance, I was sitting in Danny La Rue's nightclub in Hanover Square with Ronnie, when my friend Val Walsh walked in. My jaw nearly hit the floor, for with her were none other than Betty Grable herself, along with another Hollywood star, Rory Calhoun.

If that wasn't enough of a surprise, Val brought them straight to our table and gave me the most amazing build-up by way of introduction. She told Betty that we'd worked on Broadway together and said, 'Barbara's one of Britain's leading ladies in comedy.'

'Barbara Windsor?' Betty said. 'I know that name. You sent me a wonderful letter. Thank you so much for that.'

Of course, I went all starry-eyed and behaved just like a fan. When I told Betty that PC and I were going to the Wednesday matinée, she invited us backstage for tea and cakes in her dressing room. Me having tea with Betty Grable? It was almost impossible to believe.

I was devastated for her when I saw the show. It had done fantastically well in Las Vegas, but it was not right for London and had some dreadful reviews. That afternoon the theatre was virtually empty. But Betty, being the trouper she is, strutted her stuff as though she was playing to a packed first-night audience, which endeared her to me even more. Backstage afterwards Betty and I got on so well it was as if we'd known each other for years. Ginger Rogers was in *Mame* at Drury Lane and there was a story about her doing the rounds that made Betty and I giggle like a couple of schoolkids. She was just like an older sister.

Betty wasn't that bothered when the show closed after a few weeks because she was missing the horses she kept back home terribly. She was a delightful lady and more than lived up to my expectations, and she must have been a nice person to work with because, when the show closed, her colleagues on *Belle Star* placed an advert in *The Stage* thanking her for all she had done.

I was in Danny's again, one Friday in June, with Ronnie when a woman not much taller than me came in. I knew who she was, and that she was appearing at the Talk of the Town, but I hadn't gone to see her perform; I had seen her at her best and did not want to spoil the image. As she passed our table, very unsteady on her feet, I was appalled at how thin and frail she was. I wanted to get hold of her and hug her, but I felt that if I did, she would disintegrate; that even if I blew on her she would fall over. She had been one of Hollywood's brightest stars, and I felt she should have been given a pension, not forced to carry on performing when she was messed up with drink and drugs.

She said she'd found happiness in London after marrying for the fifth time only three months before, but Judy Garland never saw the bluebirds over the rainbow she sang about so poignantly. Just two days later, she was found dead in her flat, aged just forty-seven.

After *Carry On Camping* I did a short tour, opening in Coventry, of *The Wind in the Sassafras Tree* with Simon Oates and the wonderful Frankie Howerd. The play was a huge success in Britain and the American producer David Merrick wanted to take it to the States. PC advised me against going with it: he felt that Frankie wouldn't transfer well to the other side of the Atlantic. Once again, his instinct was dead right: the play went to the USA but closed within a week.

I was delighted to be able to work with Frankie again not long afterwards as a guest star on his TV comedy series *Up Pompeii*. On that show I had to seduce him by doing the Dance of the Seven Veils. In view of Frankie's sexual preferences we both found the idea so ludicrous that from the minute I peeled off the first veil we went into hysterics. I'm ashamed to say the scene went to twelve takes and got us both a reprimand from the floor manager. What made it worse was that every time we got the giggles the audience started laughing too.

Next I was signed to do *Wild, Wild Women*, a TV series about a millinery factory, like *The Rag Trade* but set at the turn of the century. I suggested to Anna Karen, who I'd met on *Camping*, that she auditioned for it, and she was successful. We were working in the same studio where I'd filmed *The Rag Trade*, and it had the same type of set. I told her to sit where I had on that show. The seat had proved lucky for me; maybe it would be lucky for Anna, too. One day the two scriptwriters, Ronald Chesney and Ronald Wolfe, mentioned to me that they were writing a new series for Reg Varney, called *On the Buses*, and were looking for 'a big lump who likes her food' to play Varney's scruffy, plain-Jane sister Olive. 'You've got someone here, haven't you?' I said, quickly. 'Anna.'

Having little to do on the show, she was always sitting around munching something and drinking Coke, while she read Mills and Boon novels. With no make-up on and her hair scraped back, she looked ideal for Olive, so the two writers arranged for her to audition for the directors of the new series. But when she turned up at the studios, she arrived looking very glamorous. When the writers saw her, they made her go to the loo and screw back her hair, scrub her face and take her bridgework out. Anna got the part and was wonderful in the role.

I'm OK at learning my lines, but not very good at taking in the little bits in between. So when the script of *Carry On Again Doctor* said I had to wear three hearts over my breasts and private parts, I assumed they would be part of a costume. When I went for a fitting, however, the tiny hearts were just plonked straight on me. I was horrified. I wasn't sure I wanted to expose my whole body to millions of strangers.

Ronnie, not surprisingly, wasn't keen, either. 'Are you going to turn it down?' he asked, making it sound more like a request than a question.

'I can't, darling,' I said. 'I'm committed.'

I then went on a strict diet and had slimming injections as well. It worked: within a month I'd lost a stone and my boobs had shrunk to about half their previous size. Gerald, of course, was not pleased, especially because of a joke he particularly liked. The doctor in the film, Jim Dale, was to ask what I did for a living, and I would tell him I was a model and on a calendar for Bristol Bouncing Baby Cream. 'Well, the Bristol gag's going to fall flat,' Gerald said, looking at my chest. 'You haven't got anything there!'

I loved working on those Carry Ons. I'm sure that, given the scatty nature of the films, many people think everything was thrown together haphazardly. Nothing could be further from the truth. Comedy is a serious business and everyone involved in the Carry On success story was at the top of their profession. That's why all the scenes were usually shot in no more than two takes and the films completed in just six weeks, if that. You could also be forgiven for imagining that making those films was just one long giggle. In fact they were bloody hard work. We had a joke between scenes, of course, but once the cameras were rolling, no one was allowed to mess around. It's the only way to work.

In the autumn of 1969, Charlie Hawtrey and I were walking into a Manchester cinema for a midnight première of *Carry On Again Doctor* when we heard the crowd outside screaming and squealing. I looked round to see what all the fuss was about, and there were handkerchiefs and knickers flying through the air and commissionaires battling to keep hundreds of girls – mostly blonde, it seemed – outside the velvet rope of the VIP area. 'Georgie! Georgie!' they were chanting. Coming along behind us was the sensational George Best, the first footballer to be idolised like a pop star.

I got chatting to him at the reception afterwards and all the time these gorgeous girls were crowding round him, trying to touch him. 'Oh George, don't let me keep you,' I said. 'You can't be here talking to me with all these stunning birds around. It's ridiculous.'

'Oh, no, Barbara,' he said. 'How often do I get to talk to a lady like you? It's lovely. Why don't we go off and have a quiet drink somewhere?'

As we edged our way towards the exit, I noticed that the comedian Jimmy Tarbuck had a look of surprise on his face. The next day, I was performing with Jimmy in *The Good Old Days* music-hall show for BBC TV in Leeds and the first thing he said to me was: 'Where did you get to last night?'

I smiled and said nothing. But it *was* a great night!

Towards the end of 1969, I felt that the time had come to part company with Peter Charlesworth. He had been a brilliant agent, and had been very good for me; he had always made decisions with my best interests at heart, and more often than not they had proved to be the right ones. There were two reasons why it seemed to me I should move on. First, Ronnie was jealous that I spent more time talking to PC than to him and was pressurising me into it. Secondly, and probably more importantly, PC had been representing me for a long time and I had the feeling that he had lost just that slight edge of interest in my career.

With hindsight, I think I should just have let it ride for a bit and things would have righted themselves; certainly, with no disrespect to the people who have helped me since – Richard Stone, my next agent, recommended to me by Benny Hill, represented me extremely well until his retirement – it was a decision I came to bitterly regret.

But as it was, not relishing the prospect, I went to Peter's office to break the news. It was a highly emotional meeting and there were tears on both sides: we had come through a lot together. Peter, bless his heart, was smashing about it. He left the door open for me to go back if things didn't work out, and the last thing he said was: 'You have this wonderful varied talent, Barbara. Don't let them pigeonhole you as that Carry On bird. And never take her on stage.'

Ronnie was pleased that Peter was no longer a fixture in my life. What he did not foresee was that losing the man who had been such a rock throughout my career would make me insecure and more likely to seek attention and understanding elsewhere.

12

SHORTLY AFTER CHRISTMAS 1969, THE DIRECTOR AND PERFORMER NED SHERRIN CONTACTED ME TO SAY HE HAD CO-WRITTEN A MUSICAL ABOUT MARIE LLOYD AND WANTED ME TO BE IN IT. I went to Ned's house in Fulham to meet the producers and Ned's co-writer, Caryl Brahms, and to sing a few songs round a piano. One of them, 'Sing a Rude Song', was a rousing number that seemed to sum up Marie's bawdy life. I thought of dear Grandad Ellis, who had sat me on his knee and told me to model myself on Marie, as I sang that song, and a poignant ballad, 'This Must Be Happiness'. It was a cosy, friendly, if nerve-wracking little session, and when we were sitting around afterwards, I asked Ned: 'Which sister?'

'What do you mean?' he said.

'Which of Marie's sisters do you think I could play?'

'No, Barbara,' he said. 'This is for Marie herself. We want you to play her.'

All of them, it seemed, had made up their minds before I came, but had wanted to hear my singing voice again. I was, as they say, gobsmacked. And terribly thrilled. I love the period and the pretty Victorian costumes; I would have liked to have lived in those times. I knew I'd be happy and comfortable performing in a show set in that era.

I knew a fair bit about Marie already, but I set about adding to that by researching as much as I could about her. There was limited film footage, but I read everything I could get my hands on, and as *Sing a Rude Song* went into rehearsal prior to opening at Greenwich in February 1970 in front of Princess Alexandra, I felt I could not have been better prepared.

Someone who was not prepared, however, was the actor playing Marie's husband, Jockie. When I'd been told that producer Robert Stigwood was bringing in a pop star, I thought it would be Davy Jones of the Monkees, because he fitted the bill perfectly: he was small, he could sing and he was a good actor, having held down a job in *Coronation Street* before embarking on a musical career. But the role went to Maurice Gibb, one of the Bee Gees pop group, which Stigwood had managed until their recent break-up. Maurice was very nice, very sweet, but he did not know the theatrical side of showbusiness and clearly did not want to be in the show. He was a pop singer, not an actor. He lacked theatre experience and had no stage presence when he made an entrance. He just did not have it in him to come on stage and ask of the audience, 'Wow, look at me!'

Ned suggested I took Maurice in hand, so one day early on in the run, I invited him for a meal. I always went out of my way to get on with my leading men, you know, make them happy, and I thought it might help Maurice if he went to bed with his leading lady. At first, Maurice had no idea what was on my mind, but it dawned on him over dinner, and suddenly he said: 'Where are we going afterwards?'

'Do you want to go on to a club?' I asked.

'No, no,' he said. 'Where are you going to take me back to? Isn't that what this is all about?'

Seeing that I was embarrassed, Maurice said: 'Come on, Barbara. You want to do it. And I want to do it.'

He was so forthcoming that he threw me totally. I had not been banking on anything happening the first time. But Maurice was up for making a night of it. So I called my hairdresser, Sandra, who kindly lent me her flat, and we went back there and indulged ourselves. We went out again the following week, and I like to think our little dalliance eased his worries about the show and helped his performance when we finally opened, to amazing reviews, on 17 February.

Marie Lloyd was a role I felt I was destined to play, and I threw myself into it with all the energy I could muster. *Rude Song* was a great success, and everyone was keen for it to transfer to the West End, but unfortunately there just wasn't a West End theatre to be had until the Garrick was available again in May. Still, I was delighted to be back there for the first time since *Fings Ain't Wot They Used T'Be*, when I'd shared a dressing room with three other girls. Now I was in the number one dressing room. With such recognition, however, came self-doubt, and I suffered the most chronic attack of nerves. I couldn't eat. I couldn't sleep. I came out in a nervous rash. And all the confidence and exuberance I'd had during the Greenwich run suddenly vanished. Before, I'd always been first support in the West End, never the lead; I'd always had someone else to lean on. But now I was the star, the one carrying the show, and its success or failure rested on my shoulders. If it was a hit, lovely – I'd get the credit. But if it flopped, I'd get the blame. The familiar insecurity, the feeling that I was not worthy of it, took over and I got in a right state.

I gave an interview to the *Daily Mail*'s Lynda Lee Potter baring my soul about all this, and a couple of days later received the most amazing letter from the actress Honor Blackman telling me that I *was* worthy, and that the reason my name was above the show was that I had earned it. The letter was six pages of glowing praise and it gave me a real boost when I desperately needed one.

But then, on Thursday 7 May, a couple of weeks before opening night, something happened that completely overshadowed everything I was going through. I'd been making a record album for the show and had gone home early. Ronnie and his brother Johnny had gone out for a drink with their youngest brother, David, who had come into town. Ronnie rang me a little later to tell me not to bother about dinner for him: he would have a bite to eat with David and Johnny and be home around midnight. Ronnie thought the world of David but he didn't see him that often, and I thought it was good that they were having a few drinks together. So I went to bed early, hoping that the day's recording had exhausted me enough to get a good night's sleep. Around midnight, I was woken by the phone. It was Ronnie, and he was sobbing. Hysterically. I had never heard Ronnie cry like that before.

'Ronnie, Ronnie,' I said. 'What on earth's the matter, darling?'

'It's David, Bar,' he sobbed. 'He's been stabbed. He's dead.'

I couldn't believe what I was hearing. I asked Ronnie exactly what had happened, but he couldn't speak. He just said: 'Please, please, Bar, can you speak to Johnny?'

But Johnny was no calmer, and I couldn't get any sense out of him, apart from the fact that there had been a fight in a club in Soho and David had been knifed. From what I could gather, Ronnie and Johnny were at a hospital and David had died. I asked if they wanted me to come to the hospital, but Ronnie said no, he would be home later. He arrived in the early hours, in the most awful state, and he broke down and wept uncontrollably. He told me that David had been stabbed twice, once through the heart, with a carving knife. He was just twenty.

The murder was big news the next day and there were pictures of me, as the victim's sister-in-law, all over the papers. Ned rang me immediately, concerned for me and anxious to know if I was going to be OK to carry on with the show.

'Of course I am,' I assured him. Amid all the trauma at home, I put my sadness for Ronnie and his family to one side, conquered my fears and self-doubt and performed in a glorious opening night just over two weeks later.

Rude Song was a personal milestone for me in that it saw the prediction Miriam Karlin had made about me ten years earlier come true. Shortly after we opened, I was doing my bit out front when the audience started laughing unexpectedly at something behind me. I turned round and saw that one of the actresses had let her dress slip down and was juggling two of the biggest bosoms I'd ever seen to get a cheap laugh. After the show I asked her to come to my dressing room and repeated everything Miriam had told me, and in the very same dressing room, when I'd been the cheeky young actress.

It was not the only echo of the past. One evening one of the producers came to my dressing room during the interval. 'What *are* you doing?' he demanded to know. 'Keep it down. You're frightening the audience. You're trying too hard, dear.' It put me off my stroke completely and gave me first-hand experience of what poor Victor Spinetti had suffered at the mouth of Joan Littlewood in *Oh What a Lovely War* in America.

Around this time, I met a diminutive but good-looking young record plugger just down from Paisley in Scotland, who told me he'd seen *Come Spy With Me* several times and was very complimentary about me. John Reid was only eighteen, but he had a drive and ambition I found very attractive. He was ballsy and had a sparkle, a twinkle in his eye. He wanted it all, and you could see he had the chutzpah to go out and get it. We soon fell madly in love; more importantly, we liked each other and remained great friends.

Sadly, the delay in getting *Rude Song* to the West End eventually proved fatal. In the intervening three months the tide had changed in British theatre, as it does from time to time, and we'd been left stranded. To make matters worse, that May was hardly the ideal month to be opening. We were competing against a general election, the England football team's World Cup campaign in Mexico and – the kiss of death for any show – a newspaper strike, and we had to close after just two months. I was particularly upset because I'd put everything I had into it and I honestly felt it was the best work I'd ever done.

That autumn, Ronnie and his brother Johnny appeared at the Old Bailey accused of an affray at the Latin Quarter nightclub in Wardour Street. The jury could not agree and Judge Sir Carl Aarvold ordered a retrial, at which both were acquitted. Another man, Alfredo Zomparelli, known as Italian Tony, was jailed for four years for manslaughter after the jury found that he had stabbed David Knight in self-defence.

In 1971, I was back at Pinewood shooting another Carry On, *Carry On Henry*, in which I played Delphina, Lady Bristol, to Sid James' King Henry VIII. Our first scene together involved dancing the gavotte, and we did it in one take after a brief rehearsal. When the cameras stopped rolling, we laughed like drains, pleased with ourselves, and as we prepared for the close-ups, Sid said: 'That was great, Barbara. You can really dance, can't you?'

When I told him I'd been in showbusiness since the age of thirteen and earned my living from musicals, he was surprised. He was even more amazed when I said I'd seen him in *Guys and Dolls* and knew he had done *Kiss Me Kate*.

In another scene King Henry wants to fondle Delphina's breasts. She tells him to close his eyes and hold his hands out, plonks two huge marrows in them and runs off. The morning after we shot that scene, Sid came on to the set and handed me what looked like a prune.

'Hello, Barbara,' he said. 'I've bought you a present.'

'What is it?' I asked.

'Have you never seen one of these before?'

'No, I haven't.'

'It's called a passion fruit,' Sid explained.

'Oooh, is it?' I said.

'Aren't you going to eat it?'

'I've never seen a passion fruit before. How do you eat it?' I said. 'Do I just bite into it, or what?'

Sid peeled the skin with a small knife, then split the fruit open. I still didn't know how to deal with it.

'Let me show you,' said Sid. He stuck his tongue into the fruit and started licking it, slowly and suggestively.

'Ah, yes,' I said, slightly embarrassed. 'I know what you mean, dear.' I'd heard nothing about Sid's reputation as a ladies' man, and had seen no sign of girls going to his dressing room. But that morning, there was no doubt he was coming on a bit strong.

'It's very, very nice,' he said. 'Aren't you going to have some?'

'No thank you, darling.' Oh dear, I thought. I'll have to keep well away from him. He was a nice, sweet man, but I was not physically attracted to him.

After that, Sid always seemed to be around when I was doing a scene, even if he wasn't in it. And he became more and more protective of me. Once I had a scene where I had to step into a bath naked. The set was cleared, except for Gerald Thomas and the essential technicians, but Terry Scott was still hanging about, determined to get an eyeful. Suddenly I heard Sid shout: 'Come away! Hey, Terry, I'm not going to tell you again, come *away*!' He made sure Terry was off the set, then said: 'Bloody people. They've only got to hear that you're going to show your bum, and they're like bees round a honeypot.'

I thought that was rather sweet.

No one actually said so, but everyone knew that Sid was the number one man. They were all a bit in awe of him. He didn't have a dominating personality, and he wasn't a bully, but there was something about him. When he walked on set you could sense the respect. He had made so many films, people would listen to him.

A few days later I was invited to join Sid and our producer, Peter Rogers, at the Mirabelle, a highly fashionable Mayfair restaurant, for lunch. I was sat next to Sid and got terribly embarrassed when I realised that some fluff from my angora outfit had got in his eye. I apologised and he just gave me a lovely smile and told me not to worry. Halfway through our starters, Sid lowered his voice and said to me: 'Do you know something, Barbara, they're not as big as they look on screen.'

'What aren't?'

'Your bosoms.'

'No, they're not,' I agreed.

'How do you explain it?'

'Well, it's called acting, darling,' I told him. 'It's all to do with how I hold myself. And I've got tiny feet and a little waist, so it looks like I'm top-heavy and about to teeter over all the time.'

That day, and during the rest of the filming of *Henry*, I was aware of a change in Sid. The jokes went out of the window and I began to notice that he was looking at me more or less all the time. It was the start of a love that would become an all-consuming, suffocating obsession.

Also being made at Pinewood while we were shooting *Henry* was Ken

Russell's *The Devils*. Hearing they were doing some sexy stuff, I cheekily went over to the neighbouring set for a peep, and there was Vanessa Redgrave stretched out, naked, on a slab, and a hooded monk masturbating under his habit. At the end of the scene Vanessa jumped up and rushed off, saying she couldn't stop, she had to fetch her daughter Joely from school. Quite bizarre.

There was I for ever worrying myself silly that someone might catch sight of part of my bottom or a boob, while here it was all going on like some Roman orgy. I came back all shock, horror and told Kenny Williams what I'd seen. 'Oooh,' he said, giving the nostrils a good airing, 'it's a disgrace.'

A couple of days later, I was called to the phone. 'This is Ken Russell's office,' a nicely spoken male voice said. 'Mr Russell is casting for his next film, *The Boy Friend*, and would like to speak to you about a part.'

'Is that right?' I replied, not believing it for a moment.

'When will it be convenient for you to see Mr Russell?' the gentleman asked.

'Oh, I can see him at six o'clock tonight after I finish filming.'

I put the phone down and immediately looked around for Kenny. When I couldn't see him anywhere, I was sure that he had made the call to wind me up.

At lunch in Pinewood's restaurant the next day, however, Ken Russell came over to my table, looking cross. 'What happened to you last night?' he wanted to know. I felt myself going scarlet: it had never occurred to me that the great director might really have wanted me. But he did: he thought I was right for the part of a saucy French maid Hortense in Sandy Wilson's *The Boy Friend*. He asked if I'd learn a song for an audition. I thought I'd left auditions far behind, but in the circumstances I didn't have much choice.

'I'd be delighted to, Ken,' I said.

A couple of weeks later, when I had a day off from *Henry*, I went to Pineapple Studios and was relieved to find some other acting pals, Bryan Pringle, Murray Melvin and Brian Murphy, also there to audition. I sang 'It's So Much Nicer in Nice', finishing with a little dance routine and a couple of cartwheels across the stage. Ken was amused. 'If you promise to do those in front of the camera, you're in,' he said.

The Boy Friend was due to be shot at my old stamping ground, the Theatre Royal, Stratford East, but the arrangement fell through and Ken was forced to take over a disused theatre on the south coast instead. At this news Ronnie went into one, accusing me of having known all along that the film wouldn't be made at Stratford. He complained that I was buggering off again and didn't care about him and all the rest of it. I was very unhappy. I felt that he should have been proud that I'd landed a part in a film by such a prestigious director, but all he wanted was me to be at home to wait on him. To humour him, I promised to come home at weekends. But in the end things didn't work out that way.

Before we started filming at the run-down Theatre Royal in Portsmouth in April 1971, Ken Russell took each of the leading cast out to dinner separately to get to know us individually. When he asked me about the Carry Ons, I told him about how, due to the hectic schedule, no scene ever went to more than two takes. On my first day's shooting, Ken arrived looking like the silent-movie director Erich von Stroheim, wearing riding boots and carrying a riding crop. 'Ladies and gentlemen,' he addressed the crew, 'I'd like you to meet Miss One-Take Windsor.'

'That's only when I have a director who knows what he's doing,' I quipped cheekily, to much laughter.

From day one, the film was a nightmare. Ken would be constantly rewriting the script and would sack people on the spot. He had been keen to do something quintessentially English after *The Devils*, but quickly got bored with the tame story of *The Boy Friend*, a period pastiche set in the twenties about a tatty theatrical company with backstage problems putting on an empty-headed musical. So he was always looking for ways to spice it up and make it more interesting.

On my big number, 'It's So Much Nicer in Nice,' it took 'One-Take Windsor' thirty-two takes to satisfy Ken. In what turned out to be the last, my beaded head-dress broke during one of my cartwheels. As the beads scattered all over the stage, Ken yelled: 'That's the take!'

'What?' I said. 'My head-dress has broken.'

'That's what I wanted,' Ken said.

'If that's what you wanted, why didn't you tell me? I could have done it on the first take.'

'I didn't *know* I wanted it until you did it.'

He would also insist on us watching his old films in the evenings when we were knackered from filming all day. We wanted to scream, 'We're tired! We're going to bed!', but Ken Russell was not a man you said no to. There was too much drinking and not enough sleeping and, not surprisingly, things got fraught. In fact Brian Murphy had a sort of breakdown: he was so stressed out that he took off on his own and was missing for two days.

Ken is a terrific director, but his quest for perfection and high demands made the movie traumatic for virtually everyone. Certainly all I kept thinking was: 'I'll never work for this fucking man again.'

During the first week of filming, I'd just finished a number, tap-dancing and jumping on hatboxes and was on a break, sitting in the dress circle, when I became aware of someone a couple of seats to my right looking at me. A few seconds later, a young man in his early twenties leaned across and said: 'Forgive me for talking to you.' He looked like Paul Newman. He had long hair, pulled back to make it seem short, and was dressed in period costume.

'That's all right, darling,' I said.

'I didn't know you did all that,' he said. 'I only know you from the Carry Ons.'

He told me that his name was Thomas Powell and that he had got a job as an extra after seeing an ad in a local newspaper. I liked him on sight and I enjoyed talking to him. He was very sweet.

A few days later I was running up some stairs and saw him again. Almost without thinking, I called out to him: 'Some of us are going out to dinner tonight. Would you like to come?'

'I'd love to,' he said. 'That would be great.'

Suddenly I felt the need to backtrack. Thomas was so much younger than me, I didn't want him to feel awkward. 'There will be a couple of other ladies there,' I explained.

'No, no,' he said. 'I would love to sit and have dinner with you. Where would I get to meet and talk to a lady like you?'

I assumed that Thomas was out of work, but he told me he was a musician, and played the guitar and harmonica in a little group, and of course I found that attractive. He was intelligent and easy to talk to, and we went back to my hotel after dinner and went to bed. My marriage was so unhappy that a serious affair was on the cards, and when I heard Thomas play at a local pub the following week, I was completely bowled over. There was something vulnerable about him that suggested he might be a damaged person, and he was. At eighteen he had gone to Paris and got hooked on heroin. He went into a clinic to recover and fell in love with and married the girl who nursed him. But the marriage had not worked out, and now he was unhappy and wondering whether he should try to repair it. I found myself thinking that maybe he had fallen for me on the rebound.

One day we were due to go out for the evening and Thomas didn't show. He didn't turn up for work for two days after that, and when he finally did, I feared the worst: he looked so awful I was sure he was back on drugs. When we finally talked, he admitted that his feelings for me had confused him and he'd decided he had to trace his wife to find out how he felt about her. She was out of his system, he said. Now we both threw ourselves even deeper into the affair.

Six weeks into the film, Ronnie called to say he was going on holiday to Hawaii with two friends from the club. The second week he was away, he rang wanting to know why I had not been at home at the weekend when he had phoned there. For selfishness and arrogance, I thought, that takes the biscuit. I'm not going back. I'm finished with him.

I could not forget Ronnie that easily, of course. I had increased the dosage of my sleeping pills to help me cope with both the worry that our marriage was in real trouble and the punishing work schedule. One night, I awoke with terrible tummy pains, something I'd lived with for years, and took two pills, one to ease the pain and the other to get me back to sleep. The next thing I knew, Thomas was splashing water on my face, trying to bring me round. He had woken up at 3 a.m. to find me sprawled on the bathroom floor, unconscious. I vaguely remember being carried into an ambulance, but then everything is a blank until I came to in hospital, alive and well, but feeling a complete prat.

Ken Russell was one of my first visitors. 'What the hell happened, Barbara?' he was anxious to know. 'What's wrong?'

'It's my husband,' I told him. 'We're breaking up.'

I was kept in hospital for two days and by the time I left Ronnie was home from Hawaii. He called the hotel, wanting to know why I hadn't been home. I went bananas. We had a terrible row and I screamed at him: 'That's it. We're finished. The marriage is over. I've found someone else. I'm not coming back.'

It was the first time I'd ever said anything like that, and it hit Ronnie hard. The next minute, his sister, Patsy, was on the phone, telling me that he was in a terrible state. I knew she must be telling the truth because it was very unlike Ronnie to discuss our business with anyone, even family. Patsy obviously advised him to make a fuss of me, because the next day he sent me the most massive bouquet and asked if he could take me out in London on my next day off. I agreed, and a few days later, we had lunch at the Chop House in Panton Street near Piccadilly. Ronnie proudly gave me a watch, the first present he had bought me in ages – usually he gave me money. And then, the following week, he called asking if he could drive down to Portsmouth to see me. I said yes, even though I knew we would be working on location in a forest. It turned out to be the worst day for a visit because Ken had rewritten the script for the umpteenth time and when Ronnie arrived, at 8 p.m., he found me perched up a tree, playing a Greek muse in a dark wig, still filming.

We had been shooting all day in the sweltering June heat, and when I finally climbed down, covered in insect bites and sweaty and exhausted, Ronnie was not a happy bunny. He had made the effort, though; he was doing his best to recapture my heart by doing all the things I'd wanted him to do. But it was all too little, too late. I'd now fallen deeply in love with a gorgeous young man I wanted to talk to as much as sleep with, and I could not imagine saying goodbye to him.

But in the end, I did say goodbye when filming finished and went home to Ronnie, not so much because I'd changed my mind and forgiven him, but because he had tried so hard and I didn't have the heart to hurt him. There was also a bit of me that was scared of walking out and committing myself to someone as vulnerable and unstable as Thomas, who, by his own admission, could slip up and revert to his old habits at any time. However, we said we would keep in touch. I knew I'd miss him too much not to. He said he would try to get his act together and come to London.

Thomas kept his promise. He found himself a small flat in Westbourne Grove, a fashionable part of west London, and we picked up where we had left off in Portsmouth. With Ronnie occupied every afternoon and evening at the club, we were able to see a lot of each other, and I revelled in his company. The physical attraction remained strong, but with Ronnie as uninterested as ever in anything I had to say, it was the fact that Thomas and I could chat for hours, about anything and everything, that made me really adore being with him. Our affair was marred only by my concern that he was drinking too much and smoking too much dope, and by his constant nagging about me leaving Ronnie and setting up home with him.

The drinking had first become a worry when Thomas had arrived in London. To begin with he drank beer, but now he was knocking back any spirit he could get hold of and would get very drunk. It was then that he would badger me about leaving Ronnie, and I'd have to cool it and not see him for a day or two. I was feeling under pressure: I wanted to live with Thomas, and felt that if I gave him the stability of a permanent home it could sort him out. But at the same time, I was worried about jumping out of the frying pan into the fire. Ronnie had made me feel that home was safe, and the thought of moving in with Thomas and something going wrong, and then being left on my own, terrified me.

I was given some breathing space to think it through when I had to go to Liverpool to play an Ugly Sister in *Cinderella*. Thomas came with me and we got on so well that I started to think that perhaps setting up home with him could work. I had little time to do anything about it, however, after I got a call in Liverpool to say that the director Tony Richardson wanted me to appear with his wife, Vanessa Redgrave, in *The Threepenny Opera*, Brecht's version of *The Beggars' Opera*, which I'd played in Worthing. And it was due to open in the West End in February 1972, less than three weeks after I finished panto. I was to play the same role, Lucy Lockett, and it was a part to die for. I would come on in the second half, eight months' pregnant, and yelling at the top of my voice because my man, Macheath, was being unfaithful. I'd start shouting in the dressing room, so the audience would know I was on my way, and I'd arrive on stage screeching at the top of my voice – to loud, hysterical applause, I hoped.

From the first day of rehearsal, the show was joyous, and working with Vanessa, Annie Ross, Hermione Baddeley and Joe Melia was a dream. I loved playing four-foot-ten Lucy to six-foot Vanessa's Polly Peachum. We had to sing a duet and, as you might imagine, I did not have to work hard for laughs. We'd often get the giggles ourselves as well.

'Stop it, I'll get the sack,' I'd say.

'What about me?' Vanessa would reply.

'You're OK – you sleep with the director!'

Vanessa is frightfully posh and comes from a distinguished theatrical family, but she has a wonderful common touch. She adored the lovable East Ender Arthur Mullard, who was also in the show, and when we went out to dinner, she would usually get him singing cockney songs. More often than not, she'd call on me, too, and I'd belt out 'My Old Man'. They were fun times. Vanessa is a politically motivated lady, but she always left her opinions at the stage door, and I admired and respected her for that.

I became good friends with Annie Ross, too, and sometimes would go on with her to her club, Gerry's in Shaftesbury Avenue. She very kindly took on Thomas as a barman and he repaid her by locking himself in one night after everyone had left and drinking himself into a stupor – not only from every optic in the bar, but from bottles in the cellar as well. Annie was understanding, but I was embarrassed. And Thomas was fired.

Thomas let me down again in August at a party at Robert Stigwood's country estate in Hertfordshire after the opening of his West End production of *Jesus Christ Superstar*. Everything was fine until he got drunk on the free booze and started a row with John Reid, by now Elton John's manager, who Thomas knew I'd been to bed with. I had to nip off into the bushes for a pee, and Thomas, noticing where I'd gone, came after me, shouting: 'Who have you got behind there with you?'

John leaped to my defence. 'Don't you speak to her like that.'

'What's it got to do with you? You're not with her any more,' snarled Thomas, and lashed out at John, who retaliated.

The pair of them ended up with grass stains and blood all over their lovely white suits.

That month I was asked to star in a two-month tour of *The Owl and the Pussycat*, a demanding, two-handed comedy, with one of my favourite leading men, Simon Oates. I had just ten days to learn the part and was scared witless, not only by the amount of dialogue, but by Simon's desire to deliver it in an American accent. I'd wake up in the middle of the night in a panic, work on the script for two hours, go back to bed, then start on it again as soon as I woke up.

The script was not my only worry. A few years before, during our short tour with *The Wind in the Sassafras Tree*, Simon and I had had a little fling, and I was concerned that our attraction for each other might make an already difficult piece even harder. Yes, I know I was involved with Thomas, but I also know what I'm like when my leading man is as dishy as Simon and we've been to bed together before. We talked it through at rehearsals and made a pact to keep sex off our agenda. To be on the safe side, we also agreed to stay in different hotels.

In the event, Thomas joined me after the start of the tour at Sheffield's Crucible Theatre and stayed with me for the whole run. Chastened by the Annie Ross and John Reid episodes, he wasn't drinking and we became really close. We were living together as a couple and he was a wonderful help, always doing the things that Ronnie didn't. By now I'd lost it with Ronnie and was more in love with Thomas than ever. When we returned to London I decided to leave Ronnie once and for all and to move in with Thomas. All I had to do was sign the flat in Hendon over to Ronnie and start looking for a new place.

I found the most wonderful flat, in Dolphin Square, a prestigious block in Pimlico, but, even as we looked over it, I knew in my heart that if I found an excuse not to go ahead, I wouldn't. As fate would have it, I was given one: tenants, I was told, were not allowed dogs. That was it as far as I was concerned. If I could not have my poodle, Freddie, I did not want the flat. That convinced Thomas that, as much as I wanted to be with him, I was not ready to make that final leap. Our relationship continued, but I stayed with Ronnie and Thomas never mentioned us living together again. Instead he started drinking even more, and the more he drank, the more I realised it would never work with him. He was a beautiful person, but he was so damaged that he could not cope with life without something to blur the edges.

13

WE RARELY FILMED ON LOCATION ON THE CARRY ONS, BUT FOR
CARRY ON GIRLS IN 1973, WE HAD TWO DAYS' FILMING IN BRIGHTON.
Normally, we all made our own way to the location, so I was surprised to be
told that this time I would be picked up by car. Then I learned that I would
be travelling with Sid James. A chauffeur would pick me up in Hendon, then
drive to Sid's home near Pinewood. That's a bit strange, I thought. Surely
Sid warranted a car of his own. And why drive north from Hendon when
we were going south?

I soon learned that this special treatment was Sid's idea, not the producer's,
but it had more to do with business than pleasure. The Carry On team had
been asked to perform in a revue at the Victoria Palace Theatre. Most of the
cast had agreed, but I'd refused. I remembered dear Peter Charlesworth's
parting advice not to take that Carry On bird on stage. He hadn't wanted
me to be the butt for jokes, and neither did I. But the Carry Ons' number
one star was about to make use of this trip to Brighton to try to change
my mind.

The chauffeur pulled up outside a luxurious house and Sid came out with
his wife, Val. As Sid got into the back of the car with me, Val handed me
a barley sugar sweet, as if she thought I was a little girl who might suffer
from travel sickness, which made me laugh. 'That's nice,' I said.

After we drove off neither of us spoke for a while. We just smiled politely
at each other. Sid noticed my spectacles. 'My goodness, I didn't know you
wore glasses,' he said suddenly.

'I'm long-sighted,' I told him. 'When I go on long journeys, I like to read
without straining my eyes too much.'

'They suit you.' Then he added: 'I like your rings.'

'They're not expensive,' I said quickly. 'Just costume jewellery.'

'Don't you have any nice jewellery?' He sounded surprised.

'I've got some. Not much.'

I'd dressed smartly that day in a trouser suit and high-necked sweater. Looking me up and down, Sid said: 'I don't see you much outside the studios, do I? This is the way you look, isn't it? This is you.'

'Yeah, I suppose so,' I agreed, for want of something more profound to say.

We chatted about this and that for about an hour. And then, just as we were heading out of London towards the A23, Sid said: 'I know what I was going to say to you, Barbara. This show, *Carry On London.* I've only just heard you won't do it.'

'That's true. It's not right for me.'

'Why's that, then?'

'Well, I'm doing OK as I am,' I said. 'I'm doing films, theatre, a bit of telly. I don't want to do the Carry On girl on stage. The theatre's too special to me to play that character there.'

'I'm very disappointed,' Sid said, sounding it. 'We've decided to do it à la Crazy Gang. And they were the most successful revues the Victoria Palace ever had.'

I knew he was right. Mummy and Daddy had taken me to see them, and yes, they were certainly funny. But I also remembered a bosomy girl running on as the stooge. 'Yes, I know, Sid. But I'd still be the Carry On blonde. And I don't want to take her on stage.'

'It's very sad, Barbara.' He shook his head. 'We do need an attractive, young, funny woman, and you fit the bill.'

'I'm so sorry, Sid, but I honestly don't want to know. Why don't you ask Joan Sims? She's great on stage.'

'You're part of the team.'

'Joan is more part of the team than I am. She's been in more of the films than me.'

'We need you,' Sid insisted. 'If you don't do it, it won't be the same.'

I was feeling a little pressurised. 'From what I've heard, the show has no format. We'll all be coming on as glorified campers, introducing various acts. It's not what I want to do.'

'I'm sure if we talk to the producers, they'll allow you to do whatever you want in the show,' he assured me.

We carried on talking about it for the rest of the journey. He was a very persuasive person, Sid James, and by the time we pulled into the Metropole Hotel on Brighton's seafront later that May afternoon, he had made me feel so bad about my refusal that I was now nodding and saying, 'Yeah, OK then, I'll ring my agent and tell him I'll do it.'

As we got out of the car and walked into the hotel, Sid was smiling.

My room was a few floors below Sid's and as I got out of the lift, he suggested we should have a glass of champagne together.

'That would be very nice,' I said, and sauntered off happily to my room. Yes, it would be *very* nice, I thought, as I unpacked: it would be a lovely way to round off an enjoyable journey. I was feeling good about being in *Carry On London*, on my terms. Besides, a glass or two of bubbly would be the perfect way to relax before the pressures of filming began the next day.

Half an hour later, Sid phoned me and I went to his room. I thought a couple of other Carry On people might be there, but he was alone. He had changed into a new set of matching clothes and I could see a bottle of champagne in an ice bucket on a table near the balcony. Sid poured two glasses and we were sitting at the table, chatting about nothing in particular, when the phone rang.

Sid picked it up. 'Hello,' he said. 'Oh, hello, Val.'

Looking sort of panicky, he put his finger to his lips and shook his head, signalling to me not to make a sound. I was surprised. Why didn't he want his wife to know I was there? We had nothing to hide. Sid was on the phone for ages, and all the time I was sitting there like a lemon, wanting to get back to my own room and ring Thomas to find out when he was going to come down and see me. Finally, Sid came off the phone. 'That was Val,' he said. 'She wouldn't like it if she knew you were here.'

'Why not? I'm your leading lady. You invited me for a drink. Why would she be concerned about that?'

'Well, that's the way Val is,' he said. 'It's best for her not to know.'

'OK,' I said. 'Anyway, thanks for the champagne. I've got to go now. I've things to do.'

Sid's face dropped. 'We haven't finished it. I'll put a spoon in the bottle.'

'What does that do?'

'Keeps it fresh. I hope, Barbara, you'll come back later and finish it off.'

I smiled sweetly. 'Yeah. OK, darling, 'bye.' I walked out of the door, thinking, oh no I won't.

The next day Sid was very nice to me. In one of my scenes I had to start a motorbike and ride off a few yards. I'd never ridden one in my life before and was worried about Gerald finding this out. I didn't want him to be angry with me for not having owned up earlier. 'Can you tell me how to start it, Sid?' I asked.

'My God, I've just realised, you don't drive, do you?'

'How do you know?' I asked.

'I just know,' he said enigmatically. Then he went off and arranged for filming to be delayed while someone got hold of a mattress, so that if I came off I'd have a soft landing. After we did the scene, he asked me to join him for dinner at the hotel. I couldn't because Thomas was coming down. There was only one restaurant in the hotel, and Thomas and I were at a table not far from Sid and Gerald's.

The next morning, while we were filming at Dora Bryan's hotel in Brighton, Sid came over and asked if I'd had a nice evening and who the young man with me had been.

I told him that Thomas was my boyfriend.

'But you're married.'

'Yeah, I know. But that's the way it is.'

Thomas returned to London, and that night I went out with Tony Wells, the film's publicist – he and his wife Barbara were very close friends of mine – and some other mates. 'You know Sid's got it really strong for you,' Tony said.

'At the end of the day, he only wants to go to bed with me,' I said. 'I think he knows he's got no chance. So there you go.'

I meant that. Sid was not embarrassing me or being a pest. We did our work, and that was that.

Everyone else went home after the second day's filming, but Sid and I stayed on to open a cinema complex. There were three cinemas in one and we had to run from one to the other to open them all within the space of a minute or so. We popped into the first, said, 'Hello, everybody,' then raced to the next and did the same. As we came out to do the third, Sid suddenly swept me off my feet, plonked me over his shoulder and ran towards the last cinema, laughing. Don't ask me why he did it, because I don't know. I just put it down to him being a showman and wanting to give everyone a giggle. I certainly didn't read anything into it.

If he was expecting me to stay another night in Brighton, which the cinema owners suggested, he was disappointed. I didn't want to wake up there when we weren't working the next day. So I just waved him goodbye and went home.

Back at Pinewood to put the final touches to *Carry On Girls*, Thomas came on to the set for the day. In one scene, Sid had to kiss me passionately on the mouth and on his way back to his dressing room, Thomas saw him wipe his mouth. 'You must be mad, wiping her lipstick off your mouth,' he remarked. Sid gave him one of his throaty chuckles: 'Yeah, yeah.'

After lunch Thomas went on to see some friends who were working in another studio. They obviously made a fuss of him, because when I finished filming at 6.30, I found him in the bar, paralytic. He had just got a job at the Mandrake Club, off Wardour Street, but I knew he didn't have to be there until 11 p.m. 'Do me a favour, Thomas,' I urged him. 'Promise me you'll go home and sleep it off.'

'No, I won't,' he slurred. He got so stroppy when he was in a state that I could never make him do anything he didn't want to do. So I just said: 'Let's go now. My driver will drop you off after me.'

I was in bed reading over my lines for the next day when I got a phone call from a policeman at the Middlesex Hospital, apologising for ringing so late. He said he was with a Thomas Powell, who insisted I was told he had been injured in a fight at a club. Apparently, he had staggered into the Mandrake, drunk, and upset a bloke by constantly badgering a number of girls, and one in particular, to dance. Thomas, who could be flash when he had drink inside him, ignored several warnings and finally the bloke picked up a knife and slashed him across the face. He had had to have forty-two stitches.

The following day I disguised myself with a hat and glasses and went to see him in hospital. He looked terrible, poor dear. He had been so good-looking, my Paul Newman, but now he was scarred for life. As if that wasn't bad enough, his facial nerves were damaged, which would make it difficult for him to play the harmonica.

I was worried about what would happen to Thomas when he was discharged. I couldn't look after him because I was working, so I asked Anna Karen if she and her husband, Terry, would do me a favour and let him stay at her house. She and Terry thought the world of Ronnie, but they liked Thomas and knew how unstable he was. Anna and Terry, bless them, looked after Thomas for four days.

The next time I saw Sid was in an upstairs room at the Palladium when we all met up for the first day's rehearsal of *Carry On London*. He breezed in straight from London Airport after a trip to New Zealand, and greeted everybody warmly with his familiar chuckle. I sensed there was something missing – he had no enthusiasm, and didn't seem to care – but I put it down to jet lag.

I'd arrived bubbly as ever. First days are usually quite fun and I was looking forward to going through the script, written by Eric Merriman, who wrote for the BBC radio series *Round the Horne*. He was one of my favourite writers and I was sure his script would be good. When I read it, though, I shuddered: it was appalling. Clearly Eric's ideas had been cut without giving us a chance to try them out. Bernie Bresslaw's face was a picture of gloom. 'We're nothing but glorified compères,' he groaned. I chimed in: 'You don't need me – you can get any chorus girl to do what's here.' What, I wondered, had happened to Sid's promise that I could do what I did best?

The problem was that the show was being produced partly by people representing Sid. The Crazy Gang approach that had seduced me had gone out of the window and instead there would be lots of continental variety acts. It seemed we were just a warm-up act for them.

'My God,' I thought. 'Why did I let Sid talk me into this?'

If we thought it was a case of them and us, lunchtime proved it. Normally, on first days, everybody lunches together, but Sid and Jack Douglas, their agent Mike Sullivan and the producers, went off on their own, leaving the rest of us to do our own thing. Bernie, Kenny Connor, Peter Butterworth and I went to a little Jewish restaurant by the Palladium and sat there so miserable we could hardly speak.

It had sounded a good idea to bring another Crazy Gang back to the Victoria Palace, and it should have worked, but now we feared it had all the hallmarks of an embarrassing disaster. For me, there was an early indication of what little standing I had when I learned that I had to provide my own dresses for the big opening number and finale. One of the loveliest moments on a new show is being given sketches of your costumes; this time, it was as if I'd been forgotten – even though the production was billed as 'the costliest in England' with a costume budget of more than £50,000.

We travelled to Birmingham for a three-week run filled with pessimism, and the audience reaction was everything we thought it would be. We took our bows to polite, lukewarm applause. No actor ever likes that, of course, but since I was well aware that I could have phoned in my performance, personally, I felt it was all we deserved.

It was no surprise, then, that meetings were frantically set up the next morning. Something had to be done, and fast. It all brought back memories of *Twang!*, but at least with that shambles, we had gone into it believing it would work. We all knew that *Carry On London* had been wrong from the word go, but no one listened to us. We were called to rehearsals to discover that the whole of the first act was being changed. Something was still missing, though. 'Why don't we have a music-hall section?' suggested Jack Douglas.

The director looked at me. 'You sing, don't you, Barbara?'

'Well, I've been known to earn a crust through singing, thank you very much,' I said sarcastically.

Everyone, it seemed, was now looking at me. 'Will you do something, then?' they asked.

I could not believe that, with a top West End show in the making, they were being as vague as this. 'OK,' I said. 'Fine.'

From that moment on I went into overdrive. I'd been associated with one major flop and I didn't want another one. I was completely fed up with Sid and kept my distance from him, afraid that I might turn on him and tell him: 'If it wasn't for you, I wouldn't be in this sodding place.' Instead I threw myself into helping the rest of the cast turn the show around.

I went to Richard Holmes, our dishy musical director, and suggested a musical routine ending with a big version of 'You Made Me Love You'. We had a twenty-piece orchestra but no time to rehearse for that night, so I volunteered to go on with just a trio. I had a sketch in which I played Cleopatra to Sid's Caesar, and I had the idea of opening it with a huge number I'd seen Barbara Harris perform on Broadway in *The Apple Tree*. No one knew the song – 'I've Got What You Want, I've Got What You Need' – so I arranged for my copy of the album to be collected from Hendon and delivered to Birmingham. Then, getting carried away, I insisted that four male dancers carried me on and rolled me out on stage à la Eartha Kitt.

What was basically wrong with the format was that none of the sketches had been set up. In a camping piece, for example, we all came on cold, with a lazy and obvious line: 'How far is it to the camp site?' We changed that so that people dressed as Girl Guides and Boy Scouts came on first to set the scene. All it took was a little thought. Jack Douglas, who had more or less come over to our side, drove to London to collect all his old props. It was very frenetic, but we got through that second night and, over the next few days, improved everything to a point where we all thought we had quite a good show. Not as good as we would have liked, admittedly, but one that, with a few further touches, would be OK to take into the West End.

With the show saved we all lightened up. Sid's enthusiasm returned and he got involved again. He was appreciative of my input and tenacity, nicknaming me Tiger. On stage, he had to pick me up. I was wearing only a handkerchief skirt and little bra, and I'd feel his hands going where they shouldn't have. I didn't mind. I thought: 'That's no big deal. I'll let him get away with that. It'll keep him happy.' Maybe I should have stopped it there. Maybe I should have said: 'Look, don't do that.' But I didn't. Off stage, he started paying me more and more attention, watching intently from the wings as I went through my routines, and telling me he kept thinking about me during the day. And then, one night as I was waiting to go on stage, he whispered: 'I dreamed of you last night.'

'Did you?'

'No,' he said. 'You wouldn't let me.'

He delivered the line like a Carry On gag, but he was only half joking. I thought: 'I can handle this. I've been down this avenue before, and I've only got another week to go before I'm back in London.'

One night towards the end of the run, we all went out for a Chinese meal. I must have eaten something with squid in it by mistake (I'm allergic to it), because within ten minutes of getting back to my hotel room I had to rush to the loo. I was in the middle of throwing up when the phone rang. It was Sid.

'Can I come down and see you and make my dream come true, Barbara?'

'Thank you so much, darling,' I said. 'But can we take a rain check, please? Number one, I'm being sick. And two, Thomas is coming tonight.'

'All right, darling. Good night, God bless.'

The next morning, Sid was waiting at the bottom of the hotel stairs, looking a little embarrassed. 'I just want to apologise for last night,' he said.

'No, darling,' I told him. 'Don't worry yourself. It was a compliment.'

'That's nice,' he said.

And we walked off, laughing and talking about the show. He was very sweet, very nice. I wanted to say. 'You've got to get me out of your system, because nothing's going to happen.'

When *Carry On London* opened at the Victoria Palace the following month, the first two days were a nightmare for me. Nothing to do with the critics this time – they were disappointed and picked up on the faults we knew were still there, but we didn't get panned. No, my problem was Thomas.

It all started when he turned up at the theatre the day before we opened, saying he wanted to come to the first night.

'I'm sorry, Thomas, you can't. Ronnie will be there. Anyway, I never know how you're going to be. You'll get so drunk.'

'I give you my word I won't,' he said.

I couldn't risk it. 'No, Thomas, you can't come.'

But somehow he got a ticket. I saw him there at the end of Act One when I sang from a narrow walkway stretching out from the stage into the audience. He was in the front row, in his white suit, and Ronnie was just two rows behind.

Afterwards I was in my dressing room, having drinks with Ronnie and some friends, when there was a loud banging on the door and someone shouting my name. My pal Anna Karen whispered to me: 'Thomas is outside. He's in a terrible state. Says he should be here because he's been on tour with you.'

Oh, God, I thought.

Fortunately Anna's daughter persuaded him to go away, arguing that he would show me up, and he was passed off as a troublesome drunk. But an hour later he turned up at the Embassy Club in Bond Street and tried to gatecrash the celebrity after-show party. I heard some loud banging and Thomas's voice at the door, screeching and shouting my name, but again, he was treated as a drunk and spirited away, leaving Ronnie none the wiser.

The following day Thomas phoned me at my hairdresser's flat. He was very apologetic, and promised never to get that drunk again, but the previous night had convinced me that we had come to the end of the road. 'I mustn't see you any more, Thomas,' I told him. 'I'm obviously not good for you.' He pleaded with me to give him another chance, but I said I wanted to sort things with Ronnie and find out if we still had a marriage.

But Thomas didn't get the message. Somehow he got past the stage door and burst into my dressing room, steaming drunk, as I was getting ready to leave.

'What are you doing here?' I said. 'I told you not to come here any more.'

'I'm sorry, I'll never do it again,' he begged. 'Please forgive me. I know

I'm drunk, but I had to get drunk to come and see you because you've said it's over. But, believe me—'

'No, Thomas,' I broke in. 'It's over. Once and for all. This is wrong.'

That seemed to sober him up and he went quiet. 'OK,' he said eventually. 'I can see you mean it. Can I just wash my hands before I go, please?'

'Yes, of course you can.'

I started gathering my things together as he filled the sink. When I turned round, he was holding his head under the water. Jesus, he was trying to drown himself! I seized his long hair and tried to pull his head up but he kept forcing it back under the water. I put a foot against the wall behind the sink for leverage, but he was too strong. Suddenly I noticed blood all over the edge of the sink and on the floor. Somehow he had got hold of my scissors and slashed his wrists. I finally summoned the strength to wrench his head out of the water and he stared up at me, a terrible look in his eyes that seemed to say, 'I'll do it another fucking time when you're not around.' I grabbed some towels and cotton wool and tried to wrap them round his wrists, but he kept pulling them away, screaming, letting the blood run. I tried to reason with him, to let me help him, but he was too drunk, beyond reason. I eventually managed to bandage him up and get him out of the door. Bernie Bresslaw was coming out of his own dressing room. 'Are you all right?' he said to Thomas.

'It's nothing, Bernie,' I said hurriedly. 'We'll be fine.'

Bernie looked worried. 'Are you sure?'

'Yes, thanks, Bernie. Goodnight.'

Fortunately, Thomas had come with a film extra pal who was waiting for him outside, and he took Thomas to hospital. Over the next few days, I made discreet inquiries about him and was relieved to learn that he had been discharged from hospital and was OK. Physically, at least. I hoped that Thomas could get his mind sorted out and knock the booze on the head, but I was afraid that he was too far gone for that. I heard he was hanging round the Stage Door pub opposite the theatre, hoping to see me. I kept out of the way. Our affair had run its course. He would always have a place in my heart, and I'd never turn my back on him if he was in trouble, but he had to get on with his life and I had to get on with mine.

Meanwhile, life at home with Ronnie had not so much gone from bad to worse as plunged into a well of indifference where we didn't know who each was any more. I had no idea what he got up to at the club and he knew nothing of my life outside Hendon Hall Court. Even as separate lives go, it was pretty distant: we were worlds apart. What either of us wanted to do about it was another matter. I could see no signs of restlessness in Ronnie. He'd never wanted a lot out of life, and all the time I was coming home on Saturday nights and cooking him a Sunday roast and laying out his clothes and generally running around after him, he was probably content. He didn't like me – I was pretty sure of that – but while there was no one else on the scene to make his life better, he seemed happy to toddle along, doing what suited him and not caring about what I might want. For me, finishing with Thomas had changed everything. No way was I going to walk out and live on my own – things were not so bad that I would wave goodbye to a lovely home unless I knew it was going to make me a lot happier. We probably needed to sit down together and say: 'Hey, this ain't working for either of us – what are we going to do about it?' But we were both so single-minded in the pursuit of our own happiness that neither of us thought it was worth rocking the unsteady marital boat still further.

With Thomas off the scene, for the first time in a long while my life was all about work, with no pressures on my private life from anyone. I threw myself into *Carry On London*, now loving every moment of it. One night Sid invited me, Jack and Bernie to his dressing room for a drink after Act One. None of us was back on stage until the camping sketch twelve minutes or so into the second half, so it gave us a nice long break to have a natter, and it became a routine, something we all looked forward to. Sid regaled us with salacious stories about Diana Dors in the fifties, and her husband's two-way mirrors; about how he had gone to Egypt and seen orgies, with donkeys and goodness knows what else. But he was the perfect gent to me, never making suggestive comments as he had in Birmingham, never pressing me to see him after the show, and I was able to enjoy his amusing company without the constant feeling that he was trying to think of ways to get me into bed.

But then, in late October 1973, Sid got a chance to make his move when Pete Murray's morning radio show, *Open House*, asked us to appear on a live broadcast from Victoria Palace. As this was scheduled for 9.30 a.m., the cast were given the opportunity to stay overnight in London. When Sid heard I wasn't taking this up, he asked why.

'There's no point, Sid,' I said. 'I'm only half an hour away, and Ronnie doesn't really like me staying out. He's not seeing a lot of me as it is.'

Sid dropped the subject, but a little later, my pal Tony Wells, the publicity man, had a quiet word with me and asked me to reconsider.

'What for?' I asked.

◀ Ronnie and I on honeymoon in Lisbon, with Kenny Williams, his mum Louisa and sister Pat – and Lance Percival, who we bumped into quite by chance!

◀ ▲ At home in Stanmore: Ronnie and I loved our dogs, Freddie the poodle and Blue the collie.

◀ Larking about with Ronnie in Las Palmas in 1977 on a TV Times *cruise.*

▼ We were a huge hit on the TV show Mr & Mrs. *Ironically, Ronnie and I got all the questions right!*

▲ *I received hundreds of letters and cards of support when Ronnie was sent to jail.*

◀ *Thomas Powell in 1991, his face showing the signs of a troubled life.*

▲ ▶ *In Australia: sightseeing at the Sydney Opera House during my visit in 1981, and with Robert Dunn. My great mate Danny La Rue was booked to appear on the same TV chat show.*

◀ *With Robert in the Bahamas in 1998.*

◀ *With my second husband, Stephen, outside our pub-restaurant, the Plough, in Winchmore Hill, near Amersham, Buckinghamshire, in 1985.*

◀ *In Jersey, where I was appearing in* The Mating Game: *me, Stephen and Lulu backstage.*

Dancing the night away: with Starsky and Hutch *star David Soul at the Sun TV Awards in the 1970s and Vinnie Jones and Ross Kemp in the 1990s.*

ROBIN KENNEDY

PIC PHOTOS

▲ *With Charlie Kray at the Peggy Ashcroft Theatre in Croydon, in 1993, where I was appearing in* Entertaining Mr Sloane.

▲ *At the première of the movie,* The Krays, *with Martin Kemp, who also later joined* EastEnders.

◀ *A chance to get close to George Best – again. We bumped into each other at Butlins, Bognor Regis, where we were both booked to judge a glamorous granny competition.*

◀ *Outside London's Ivy restaurant in 1996: Joan Collins, make-up in place, gives me a lesson in how to meet the media after a night out!*

BIG PICTURE

▶ *In true Hollywood style Oliver Reed and I put our hand prints in a pavement in London's Leicester Square in 1992.*

MSI

'Well, it would be nice,' he said. 'We could go out and have supper, have a laugh. We haven't done that since Birmingham. Jack's staying.'

'It's different for Jack,' I pointed out. 'He lives way out.'

Tony said no more about it. But two days later, he came to see me again in a terrible state. 'Look, Bar, do me a favour. Please stay in town with us.'

'Tony, *why?*'

He put his head in his hands. 'It's Sid. He's really getting at me. It's him who wants you to stay. He wants to take you to dinner. You'd be doing me a great favour, Bar.'

'What do you mean "getting" at you?' I didn't understand. What was any of this to do with Tony?

'It's all the time, Bar. He keeps nagging me about it, and to be honest, it's becoming a real problem. He seems to think I can make you change your mind.'

The whole business was clearly getting totally out of hand, but there was no mistaking the trouble it was causing Tony. Sid's persistence was putting him in a difficult position and I was the only one who could get him out of it. And it was just dinner, drinks and a few laughs, after all, not a lot to ask of a mate.

I sighed. 'Oh, all right, then. I'll have dinner.'

But when I walked into Sid's dressing room in the interval that evening and saw his face, I knew there was more to it than that. Greeting me with a lovely, warm smile, he said: 'I'm so glad you're going to stay, Bar. We're going to have a wonderful night.' His expression was one of total relief that at last he was going to have me.

I realised that the only way he was going to get this infatuation or whatever it was out of his system was to give him what he wanted.

The moment the penny dropped, my heart sank and I thought: 'Oh, God, I'm going to be such a huge disappointment, a terrible let-down.' I had this intense, overpowering anxiety that he saw me as a red-hot sex bomb, and that I would not match up to his fantasies; that he would be expecting a mind-numbing experience I wasn't equipped to deliver. As the day drew nearer, I started getting into a state, worrying about what to wear. My hair was very short and I could put a piece on and wear it all up in a hat, with all the pins in. But the second I thought of that, I remembered the scene in *Charlie Bubbles* when Liza Minnelli's hairpins get caught up and her hairpiece comes off while she's in bed with Albert Finney.

Yet strangely, by the time the night of the dinner arrived, I'd calmed down and was quite relaxed: it was a bit of whatever will be, will be, I suppose. Maybe Sid simply wanted to look at me across the table after all. Maybe it was as if I'd given him permission in some way to admire and fancy me.

Sid had suggested that we all assembled in his dressing room for champagne after the show, and when I walked in I was thrilled to see John Inman there with his friend, Barry Howard. They regularly played Cinderella's ugly sisters in panto. I'd known John for ages and we were very fond of each other. Sid watched us hugging and kissing and said: 'Isn't she beautiful? Look at her. Isn't she gorgeous?' You'd have thought he was talking about Audrey Hepburn.

'Oh, yes, we all love Barbara,' said John in that camp way of his. 'She's lovely, she's absolutely wonderful. We all love working with Bar.'

But that wasn't what Sid had meant. He hadn't been talking in the general flattering showbiz way; he'd said it as if he really believed it. And the sweet look he gave me seemed to confirm he did. I was not so much flattered as touched. I found it very moving.

When John and Barry left, Jack, Tony, Sid and I went on to a lovely restaurant. It was very quiet, with a man playing the piano. As we walked in, I saw Sid nod to the pianist, who stopped the tune he was playing and went into the haunting ballad 'The First Time Ever I Saw Your Face'. Jack was too busy admiring the place to notice, but as we were shown to our table, Tony whispered to me: 'Oh God, you're in for it, Bar.'

We had the most superb meal, with beautiful wine chosen by Sid, who was something of a connoisseur. I'd gone into the restaurant a bag of nerves. Knowing how carried away I can get after one too many, I took it easy, drinking just enough wine to relax me, and I thoroughly enjoyed myself. It wasn't the right occasion to get out of it but a few glasses made me feel good and I responded when Sid flirted with me.

At the hotel I was booked into the room next door to Sid's. We went up in the lift together and stopped at mine. Sid said: 'It's been a lovely night. Goodnight, Bar. God bless.'

'Night, night, Sid,' I said, and slipped my key in the lock. So I'd got it all wrong. All that anxiety had been for nothing. Sid just liked me a lot. It was as simple as that. Good, I thought. I'm off the hook.

And then Sid said: 'I'll ring you.'

Fuck it. I wasn't.

14

I UNPACKED, SORTED OUT MY BITS AND PIECES AND SAT DOWN ON
THE BED, WONDERING WHAT TO DO NEXT. I put the telly on: nothing
worth watching, and I couldn't concentrate anyhow. I switched it off and
turned the radio on. Some debate I wasn't interested in. I put the telly back
on again and stared at it, my mind whirling with all sorts of emotions. For
about forty-five minutes I kept getting up, walking round the room and
sitting down again. Then I thought: 'This is crazy, I'm going to bed.' I had
just taken my shoes off when the phone rang.

'Sorry I've been a long time, Bar,' said Sid. 'I had to phone Val and then
I had to wait for her to ring back. I'm coming round now.'

Good grief, I thought: she was on his case all the time. I assumed she'd
called back because she'd caught him out before lying about where he was.
It occurred to me that it would have been easier if I'd gone to his room, but
I guessed that Sid would not have liked me to have been there if Val did
phone again.

Suddenly, I was nervous. The effects of the booze had worn off
by this time and I was stone-cold sober. I dialled Room Service and
ordered two large Scotches. Don't ask me why – I don't drink Scotch.
And I don't know why I didn't order a bottle, either. I was distracted,
I suppose. Sid came in, and a few minutes later, the waiter knocked at
the door.

Sid stepped out of sight. Rattled, I blurted out to the waiter: 'Oh, two.
You've brought two Scotches. Well, er, they're both for me.' I was in such a
mess that with that, I plonked the tray on a table, signed the bill and threw
one of the drinks down my neck. As the waiter turned to go, I said: 'Hold
on, darling. I've got to give you a tip.' I couldn't find any change, so I handed

him a fiver. No wonder he smiled: in those days it was more than the drinks had cost.

I closed the door after him and turned round to see Sid standing there with a broad grin on his face. 'I thought one of those drinks was for me.'

'Well, I'm in a state, aren't I?' I said.

'Didn't you think of looking in the fridge?'

'What?'

'The mini bar.'

'Didn't give it a thought,' I said.

We both knew what we were there for, and I just wanted to get it over with, so I took the initiative. I was still so nervous that getting my clothes off, and his, and getting into bed was awkward.

In the end, in a strange kind of choreographed movement, I whipped off my hat, slipped out of my dress and pounced on him on the bed. Naked before me, the first thing he said was: 'Oh, Barbara, I wish you were seeing me as I used to be.'

That made me feel I should make a huge fuss of him so he'd feel attractive and wanted. Once we were in bed, it wasn't difficult. I'd thought, because of his lecherous, leering Carry On image, he might grab me and be forceful and rough, but instead he was sweet and gentle and very loving. I thought I was the jittery one, but he was even more nervous and vulnerable.

When it was all over and we were lying there in each other's arms, he laughed. It was all down to me, he said; I'd sorted it all out. I was embarrassed then; I couldn't really believe I'd been so active, taken the bull by the horn, so to speak. To cover my blushes, I giggled. 'Yep. That's me. That's Barbara Windsor. That's my little lot.' And we laughed loudly together and lay there for a long, long time. Finally, I said: 'Sid, you're going to lie here and get yourself in a state. Nervous that you're going to snore. Worried Val may call back. Please, please, don't worry about it, darling. Go back to your room and have a good night's sleep. It's all right, I don't mind, I promise. And I'll see you in the morning.'

The next morning the theatre was packed with die-hard Carry On fans who all screamed with laughter when Pete Murray introduced me and I bounced on to the stage wearing a see-through crocheted dress. I had an all-in-one body-stocking on underneath, but that didn't stop one woman chucking a pair of drawers at me. I immediately put them on over the dress and pranced around the stage to more howls of amusement. I looked to the wings and there was Sid, who had just arrived. He was laughing, but I suddenly felt embarrassed. Oh my God, I thought, I made love with you last night. What are things going to be like between us on the stage? But everything was fine. We exchanged a bit of banter, then he did his spot with Pete and we all went our separate ways.

That night, I was nervous going to Sid's dressing room during the interval. I didn't want anyone to mention the previous night, or what might possibly have happened. Later, I found a moment alone with Sid and made him promise not to tell a soul about it. He agreed. 'It'll be our little secret,' he said. For the next two weeks we carried on as usual and I was relieved that Sid did not refer to what had happened even to me, let alone anyone else. He didn't say a word, not so much as 'It was lovely seeing you', or 'That was a great night.' I thought, well, he wanted to make love to me, and now he has, it's cured his infatuation.

But then one night when we were in his dressing room on our own, he leaned across and said something that made me tense up with fear. 'You know I'm in love with you, don't you, Barbara? You know I love you. I want to see you again, make love with you again. Please. When can I see you? Please.'

'I thought you just wanted to give me one,' I said.

'I know that's what you thought,' he said. 'But it's more than that.' And then he started to unload himself, telling me that I'd blanked him when he showed out to me on *Henry*; how I didn't seem to notice him; how sometimes he had sat at tables admiring me from afar because he'd get upset sitting next to me and getting no reaction.

Oh dear, I thought. I've got a problem now.

He went on and on, and it was quite disturbing. I wasn't flattered, I was confused. All I could think was: 'What the hell am I going to do? I'm working with this man. We're sharing the same stage.'

I glanced at his dressing-room clock. 'Sid, stop,' I said. 'We've got to go on stage.'

'Just let me take you to dinner one night, Barbara,' he pleaded. 'Please find a night. Please, sweetheart.'

'All right,' I heard myself saying as we walked out of the door and headed towards the stage, him in Boy Scout uniform, me in Girl Guide gear, for the camping sketch.

*   *   *

It was difficult for Sid to take me to dinner because of having to come up with an excuse to Val, but he managed it and we had a lovely, romantic meal at an Italian restaurant near the theatre. Unlike Ronnie, Sid was very demonstrative about his feelings for me, and over the next few weeks he made me feel marvellous. He oozed love for me. I'd never known anything like it. Yes, I'd felt great love from Thomas, but Sid made me feel like Monroe and Streisand and Bassey all rolled into one. He kept telling me how much he wanted to make love to me again, but he was terrified to take me to an hotel in case we were recognised. He wanted to have sex in his dressing room, but I told him I was not the kind of girl who did that. In the end, I called my hairdresser, Sandra, who had given me the keys to her flat for my tryst with Maurice Gibb.

'Do you mind if I use your gaff for the afternoon, love?' I asked.

Sandra laughed. 'Oh, Barbara, not again.'

Sid and I did go to the flat a few times, but I began to feel embarrassed about it with Sandra, so I went back on my word and agreed to meet him at the theatre early in the afternoons. I'd leave shortly after Ronnie went to the club at midday and spend some time with Sid before the rest of the cast started arriving at 5.30. I found this very sordid, but it was either that or not see him, and, to be honest, I wanted to see him. He had terrific sex appeal and knew what making a woman feel wanted and wonderful was all about. By Christmas 1973, I knew I was falling in love with him.

Early in 1974, the Conservative government was forced to put the country on a three-day week to cope with the gravest economic crisis since the war. In the great tradition of its legendary proprietor, Lord Beaverbrook, the *Daily Express* mounted a 'Get Britain Back to Work' campaign featuring a photograph of me sitting beside the River Thames dressed as Britannia. Being a Tory myself and a fervent nationalist, I loved the idea, but whatever good it did for the country, it had a catastrophic effect on me personally. After sitting around for over an hour weighed down with a breastplate, steel helmet, trident and heavy Union Jack, I could hardly move after the photographs had been taken. When I did, I tripped and hurt my back. I managed to get through the two performances of *Carry On London* that night, but afterwards my back seized up completely and I couldn't walk. Bernie Bresslaw was giving me a lift home, as he sometimes did, and although I was able to get into his car, I had one hell of a struggle to get out. Somehow I negotiated the lift at Hendon Hall and hauled myself through the front door of the maisonette, but climbing the stairs was out of the question. I just had to sit at the bottom of the staircase and wait until Ronnie came home.

My doctor told me that the only cure was rest, so my understudy, Anita Kaye, took over in *Carry On London*. The irony of the campaign made me smile: there was I, unable to do my job, while my Britannia was urging the country to get back to work!

Surprisingly, Ronnie turned up trumps. The thoughtless, uncaring husband I'd come to know was suddenly replaced by one who showed the utmost concern. When it became clear that sitting around doing nothing was having no effect, he lifted me down the stairs and drove me to an osteopath. When that didn't do the trick, he took me to a physiotherapist, but he could not straighten me out either. Then my dear friend Katie Boyle recommended a faith healer she knew in Essex. Ronnie drove me there and carried me into this woman's house. As I stood there hunched over like a cripple, he burst into tears. 'Do something for her, please,' he begged her. 'I want my Barbara back the way she was. Make her well again, *please*.' Somehow the laying on of hands did seem to do some good and I managed to straighten up a bit and walk a few steps. Ronnie was so thrilled that he grabbed hold of the woman and embraced her. He kept saying, 'Thank you, thank you,' over and over again. 'How much do I owe you?' he asked.

'There's no official charge,' she said. 'Give whatever you feel.'

Ronnie thought nothing of handing her £50. It was over the top in those days, of course, but that was Ronnie all over. He did have a generous nature where cash was concerned. As it turned out, though, it was a waste of money because, when we got home, I found once again that I couldn't walk. I think I was so embarrassed that the faith healer was trying so hard and not getting anywhere that I'd forced myself to take those steps. I don't like to be a nuisance.

A specialist finally got to the root of my problem: it was not so much a physical condition as stress-related. The strain of performing two shows every night, plus filming a Carry On special for TV, and coping with an emotionally exhausting affair at the same time had finally taken its toll.

I was out of the show for three weeks and when I went back, I had the most wonderful surprise: there were hundreds of flowers spread out across the whole stage. Sid and Peter Rogers had bought the entire stock of a flower stall outside the theatre and had wheeled it in by the barrowload.

That February we were starting *Carry On Dick*, which meant getting up at 5 a.m. and working all day at the studios, then going on to the theatre in

Victoria for *Carry On London*. It provided Sid with a legitimate excuse to tell Val that he needed a flat where he could crash immediately after the show so that he could get some rest. Of course it involved an earlier start for Pinewood in the morning, but she must have felt it was more important for him to get to bed at a reasonable time at night. He rented a little place in Dolphin Square, where I'd nearly taken a flat myself with Thomas. It was the perfect love-nest and I'd often stay the night there with Sid after dinner.

Our affair might have been the worst-kept secret in the theatrical world, but on the movie side of the business no one knew about it. Until we started *Dick*, that is. Although Sid knew how anxious I was that people shouldn't find out about us, no sooner had shooting started at Pinewood than he started pushing notes under my dressing room door. He would write 'I Love You' hundreds of times on any piece of paper he could lay his hands on: Kleenex tissues, studio stationery, even toilet paper! I wouldn't have minded if he had put the messages inside envelopes, but he didn't, so it was hardly a surprise when the wardrobe lady went in one day to lay out my costume and discovered one of them. When I arrived she handed it to me, saying apologetically: 'I found this on the floor. I'm sorry, I shouldn't have read it.'

Sid's behaviour on the set was a giveaway, too. Before we became lovers, he'd usually played poker with the technicians during breaks in filming and certainly never joined the rest of the cast. Now, he made a beeline for me when our scenes were over, and always joined us for lunch. It was only a matter of time before someone put two and two together, and in the end it was Kenny Williams. He looked at me one day and said: 'You're having it off with Sid, aren't you?'

'Don't be stupid,' I laughed.

'Don't lie to me, Bar,' he said. 'I was making these Carry Ons before you came on the scene, dear, and Sid James never came to lunch. I find him a much nicer person now. I can tolerate him. And I can see it's all down to you.'

I wouldn't admit it but Kenny knew. Having a wicked streak, he decided to stir it. Well aware of how jealous Sid could be, Kenny said to him one day: 'You know Barbara's had it off with Elton John's manager, don't you? And you know she loves fellatio, don't you?'

'Don't be silly, Kenny,' I said. 'What are you talking about? I don't even know what it means.'

'Yes you do. It's a blow job.'

Sid's face was like thunder. Kenny's remarks put it in his mind that I was easy with my favours, and he didn't like it at all. Neither did I. But that was Kenny. He could be fun and hilariously witty, but he could be very spiteful and malicious, too. And totally fearless. Whether Kenny's jibes were to blame I don't know, but Sid started acting oddly, out of character, on *Dick*. One scene, in which I had to seduce him, went to an unheard-of four takes before I realised what was going on and called a halt to it. In the first one, I jumped all over Sid and thought we both did a convincing job. But Sid looked at Gerald and said: 'I don't think that was very good, do you?'

'It looked all right, but if you want to go again, we will,' said Gerald.

This time Sid fluffed his lines so we had to do a third take. I couldn't understand it: Sid was always red-hot with his lines. When he complained again that something was wrong, I twigged: he was enjoying it. I wasn't having any of that, and after the fourth take, I said to Gerald: 'I don't want to do it again. Is that all right, sir?' It was, and we did not reshoot the scene again.

Sid was not pleased. 'It didn't light up the screen, did it?' he said. 'It's like you don't want to come near me. Do you find me unattractive? Have I got a disease? Am I some kind of monster?'

I didn't know what to say to him. It was awful, him bringing his feelings for me on to the set. I thought: I've got to back off. I've got to get out of this.

With my six-month contract due to expire in April, I decided the best thing would be for me to quit *Carry On London*. But when I told Sid a few nights later, he was devastated. 'If you leave, I'll go as well, and then the show will fold,' he said.

'Oh, Sid, don't get yourself in a state. I'll stay. But, honestly, you've just got to cool it. It's bad for you. I don't want you making yourself ill again.'

That April I had a two-week holiday from the show and when Ronnie suggested that we went to stay at his sister's villa in southern Spain, I jumped at the chance: lying in the sun and recharging my batteries was just what I needed. Sid was not keen on me going away and immediately wanted to know when I'd be back. Then he went to Harrods and bought me a load of highly expensive suncreams and moisturisers.

'You've got such fair skin, Barbara,' he said. 'You've got to be careful.'

I couldn't believe it. 'Sid,' I said, 'I have been abroad before, you know.'

But he still insisted on giving me instructions on what I must and must not do in the sun.

The villa, in the village of Benalmadena, high in the hills above Fuengirola, was perfect for us and we had a lovely, relaxing time. Ronnie was so taken with it that he suggested we had our own villa built in Spain. I thought it was a great idea, so he got on to it straight away, and by the time we were back in London the wheels were in motion.

I returned so heavily tanned that under my dark Cleopatra wig I looked like an Italian. After the show, Sid wasted no time. 'The only way to keep a tan is to put moisturiser all over you,' he said. 'You've got to take a shower, then lie down and rub it all in. But you can't do it properly yourself. I've got loads of it back at the flat. I'll do it for you.'

So that's what he did.

Given Sid's jealousy of the men who had featured in my life, when John Reid asked to take me to dinner, I thought it best to run it by him first. 'It's OK, Sid,' I told him. 'John licks the other side of the stamp now, but we were friendly once.'

'Yeah, all right, then,' Sid said.

When John turned up in his white Roller, I took him in to meet Sid before we went on to dinner. They exchanged a few pleasantries and Sid told John to look after me and make sure I got home safely. Walking to the car, within Sid's earshot, John got a whiff of my perfume and sighed: 'Oooh, that gorgeous Windsor Shalimar. I love it. Whenever I smell it, I always think of you.' It was something Sid had heard Thomas say, and he didn't like it.

The next day, there were twelve different perfume samples in my dressing room.

'I'm not keen on the smell of Shalimar,' said Sid. 'I think you should have something else, so I've given you some to choose from.' To keep him happy, I chose L'Air du Temps, but I only wore it for a week. I'd used Shalimar since I'd first bought it in New York in 1964, and I was very hurt that he wanted to change something I felt was a part of me.

It even got to the stage where Sid started to show his jealousy in public. One night, he went into one when Ronnie was only a few feet away. We were at some charity ball at the London Hilton and I was bopping away with Ronnie on the dance floor. Somebody sitting at a table behind ours called out: 'Lovely, Barbara. Go on, jiggle them about.' Sid swung round angrily and glared at the man. 'Don't you dare say anything like that again, or you'll have me to answer to.'

Ronnie couldn't believe it. When he got back to the table, he made a point of telling Sid: 'Don't fight over my wife, Sid.'

One of the casualties of Sid's jealousy was our musical director, Richard Holmes. When Richard came to see me, astonished that his contract was not being renewed, I suspected that Sid had something to do with it. And the moment I saw his replacement, I knew that he had. I confronted him about it.

'It was obvious you were attracted to him,' he said. 'You were always looking at him.'

'Don't be bloody stupid,' I said. 'Of course I looked at him – he's my musical director.'

I've had a lot of men fall in love with me, but Sid was crazily, madly, in love with me. He seemed to want me to be jealous too and could not understand it that I wasn't. On the day before Sid and Val were going on holiday to the south of France we were having a cup of tea at our favourite little Italian café in Victoria. He was telling me about the hotel where they'd be staying when he suddenly remembered something he'd forgotten to do. He put his hand to his mouth and gasped: 'Oh God, I haven't arranged for any champagne to be put on ice in the suite. I must ring the hotel.' Then he looked at me. 'I'm sorry, Bar. You're not jealous of that, are you?' He assumed that, as his mistress, I'd be thinking I should be the one drinking champagne, rather than a cup of tea.

'No,' I said. 'I think that's wonderful.'

I can be as green-eyed as the next person, but I just couldn't be jealous about him laying on champagne for his own wife on holiday.

How much Val knew or wanted to know about all this I was never quite sure, though I had a suspicion she was well aware of it. Sid told me once that they had had a blazing row about me. But Val was a strong woman, and perhaps she just took the view that his obsession would burn itself out eventually and that there was no point in doing anything drastic in the meantime. Who knows?

After the show had been running six months, Sid's adoration for me became obsessive. He would stand in the wings, night after night, watching me perform. Eventually I had to tell him he was putting me off and he agreed not to do it any more. A few days later I came off stage and bumped into him as he reached the foot of the stairs leading to the top of the theatre. He was badly out of breath. 'What's wrong?' I asked him. 'What are you doing?'

'Nothing,' he said. 'I'm OK.'

Later the stage manager told me that Sid had been out of breath because he'd been running up and down the stairs to watch me from the gallery because I'd told him not to stand in the wings. I went to his dressing room. 'Look, Sid, you're going to have another heart attack,' I said. 'Stand at the side of the stage, if you want.'

The weight of Sid's obsession was confusing and overpowering me. I hated everyone knowing how he felt about me and I began to be afraid to talk to anyone because of his jealousy. It all came to a head during the finale one night, when something happened on stage that prompted such a wild reaction from him that I blew my top.

As we all came to the end of the catwalk, Bernie Bresslaw turned and helped me off. On the way to our dressing rooms, he was very apologetic. 'You know, Bar, we've been doing this show twice nightly for six months and that's the first time I've ever helped you there. I feel dreadful I haven't done it before. You must think I've no manners.'

I'd never even given it a thought. 'That's all right, darling,' I said. 'Don't worry about it.'

Bernie was giving me a lift home that night and he didn't seem his usual cheerful self.

'Anything wrong, Bernie?' I asked.

'As a matter of fact there is,' he said. 'Before we left, Sid called me into his room. Tore me off a strip.'

'What?' I said, shocked. Bernie was one of the easiest-going actors in the business; I couldn't imagine him upsetting anyone or doing anything out of order. 'In what way?'

'He told me never to lay one finger on you.'

'When have you done?' I asked.

'Tonight. When I helped you off the catwalk. He told me never to touch you again.'

I was so angry I felt like going back to the theatre and asking Sid what he thought gave him the right to say that to anyone, particularly someone as lovely and well-meaning as Bernie. But I decided I'd sleep on it and see how I felt in the morning. I woke up still angry. And I stayed so angry that I didn't speak to Sid for two days. It was hard for me because I hate falling out with anybody, but I simply could not bring myself to say anything to him. I just went in, did the two shows, then went home, as usual, in Bernie's car. Finally, I told Sid I was knocking the interval drink on the head. 'You promised me you would keep quiet about you and me. But when you start letting it affect your work by having a go at someone like Bernie, you're making it public. It wasn't a nice thing to do. And I don't like you for it.'

Sid wanted me to stay and discuss it, but I just said goodnight and went home. The next night, I came down the theatre stairs to find Sid at the bottom, waiting for me. 'Please let me talk to you, Barbara.'

He looked so sad, I didn't have it in me to do what I felt like doing, which was to brush past him. 'All right,' I said.

We went into his dressing room. The moment he'd closed the door he broke down in tears. 'I'm so, so sorry, Barbara,' he sobbed. 'I love you so much, I can't bear anyone touching you. Even getting near you.'

Bloody hell, I thought. This was ridiculous.

'So what's next?' I asked him. 'Are you going to stop the boy dancers coming near me? Or anyone else on stage? It's crazy, Sid.'

Carry On London was due to close in the autumn, and with it would go the cover for our affair. He knew he would have to give up the Dolphin Square flat as well. Late in the summer, he suggested an idea he said he'd been toying with for several weeks. 'I want you to leave Ronnie,' he told me. 'I'll put you up in a flat. I'll go to a hundred quid a week.'

I have this thing about pleasing men, and because I knew this was something Sid wanted, I agreed to look for a flat or house to rent, even though I hadn't made any decisions about what to do. I found an ideal mews house in Kensington. Sid had to see the place, so I told the estate agent I was viewing it for one of my leading men, who lived in the country and urgently needed a place in town. I loved the house. And when he saw it, so did Sid. To my surprise, I found myself getting caught up in the idea of moving. And when Sid said it was time I got my act together and sorted out my life, I said: 'OK. I'll tell Ronnie next weekend.' I did find it strange, Sid asking me to leave, but not being prepared to get out of what was obviously an unsatisfactory relationship himself, but I never once asked him to leave Val.

But fate stepped in again, making me wonder whether I was destined never to leave Ronnie. First, that very weekend Ronnie's father collapsed and died and it was impossible for me to do anything other than comfort him. Then, one awful Wednesday night two weeks later, there was a shooting in Soho that would put him in the dock, accused of murder, and turn my life upside down.

15

THAT WEDNESDAY OF 4 SEPTEMBER, I WAS LEAVING THE THEATRE TO GO TO DINNER WITH SID WHEN THE STAGE-DOOR PHONE RANG. It was for me: a reporter from the *Sun*, wanting to know how I felt about Zomparelli being killed. I caught only the 'elli' bit and, thinking he was talking about the film director Franco Zeffirelli, said: 'I never worked with him.'

'Not Zeffirelli, Zomparelli. The man who killed your husband's brother.'

I sort of squealed in shock and Sid took the phone. He spoke to the reporter for a few seconds, then took me into his dressing room and explained that Alfredo Zomparelli had been shot dead in the Golden Goose Arcade in Soho earlier that evening, a few months after being released from prison.

I was shaking. 'God, this is awful,' I kept saying.

'Now don't worry, it's got nothing to do with you,' Sid told me.

'I've got to get home, darling,' I said. 'Ronnie's going to want me there.'

I knew that, as the person with the strongest possible motive for killing Zomparelli, Ronnie was bound to be a prime suspect. Sure enough, he was pulled in for questioning. He admitted he had wanted Zomparelli dead, but denied he had pulled the trigger or that he knew who had. And he had a cast-iron alibi: at the time of the killing, in Old Compton Street, he had been in his club in full view of dozens of customers. After three hours' grilling he was allowed home. He swore to me he knew nothing about the murder, and I believed him.

As the end of *Carry On London* approached, Sid's health deteriorated. He was in agonising pain with his back and he turned an awful yellow colour. Concerned about his heart, I told him we should take it easy. 'I'm worried for you,' I said. 'Our love life is wonderful, but it can't be doing your heart any good. And you won't even have a check-up.'

At ten o'clock the next morning, a man rang me at home, saying he was Sid James' doctor. 'Mr James has had a very honest chat with me,' he said. 'He is suffering from exhaustion, but his heart is fine, and unless he is going to throw you around the room or swing from the chandeliers, he'll be perfectly all right.'

Then Sid was on the line. 'Are you satisfied now?'

What could I say? For all I knew, Sid had called in an actor pal to impersonate a doctor, but I wanted to believe him, so I said. 'Yes, sweetheart, I am.'

I wasn't convinced, though. His back got worse and he started to limp, and we had to go through every routine in the show to see where we could make things easier for him. Remembering what the doctor had said about throwing me around, I suggested cutting a sketch where he had to run off stage with me over his shoulder.

'No, no,' he said hastily. 'You're as light as a feather. We're not cutting that.' Dear Sid. He didn't want to lose anything that meant physical contact with me.

With just a week to go before the show closed, Sid started drinking more, and when we were talking he would take my hand, tears in his eyes. 'What am I going to do when the show ends?' he'd say. What was making it worse for him was that he knew work would keep us apart for most of the following year. Sid was going on a long tour to Australia straight after Christmas, and I would be leaving to tour New Zealand in February with my own show, *Carry On Barbara*, taking it on to South Africa after a short British run.

He had been advised to take a long holiday in the sun and, in a desperate bid to prolong our affair, he begged me to go with him. I told him not to be so stupid. 'How can we go on holiday together? You've got a wife, and I've got a husband.'

He broke down. 'What am I going to do without you in my life? How am I going to cope? Look, when the show finishes, why don't I tell Val and you tell Ronnie and we'll live six months in the south of France or Spain and six months here. I think I've got ten years left, Barbara. That way I can give *you* ten good years.'

I didn't know what to say; I was too confused. I didn't know where I was any more.

In the event, Sid got himself so worked up that he ducked the final

Saturday night of the show. The audience was told he had suddenly been taken ill, but we all knew that it was because he would find it too painful; that he couldn't face the thought of Monday and not seeing me.

Two days later, a dozen red roses arrived. They were from Spain and were signed: 'Love, Romeo.'

On his return, we were both asked to judge a beauty contest at the Savoy and I will hold my hands up and admit that it was the only time I felt jealous. Sid voted for one particular beautiful girl and I asked him why.

'Because I liked her,' he said.

I got into a right old strop. 'Oh, you fancy her, do you?' I challenged him. 'You like 'em tall, with dark hair.' But a few seconds later, realising how stupid I was being, I burst out laughing. 'You're actually pleased I'm jealous, aren't you?' I said.

Sid laughed. 'Yes, I am.'

I had to go on to the Hilton, where Anna Karen and her husband Terry were celebrating the birthday of a friend of ours. Sid offered to drop me off. As he escorted me in, Terry was coming out of the Gents'. I introduced them, and then Terry and I headed into the party. Sid called him back. I thought he was checking that Terry was who I'd said he was, but later Terry told me that all Sid wanted to say was: 'Look after her, mate. I love her so much. She's my life.'

Now that *Carry On London* had ended, I felt that, for the sake of everyone's sanity, the affair had got to stop. It was making us both unhappy, and it was clear that Sid's jealousy and obsessive behaviour were not controllable. And whether or not his marriage was happy, it was certainly a strong one which it would be difficult, if not impossible, for him to leave.

But the only way I could see it ending was by making sure we didn't work together. So when Sid and I were offered *Carry On Laughing*, a series of half-hour Carry Ons for TV, I turned it down. Gerald Thomas told Sid, who rang me immediately. 'You can't do that,' he said. 'You can't.'

'Yes I can. And I am.'

'But you're part of the Carry On team now.'

'It's not like that,' I reasoned. 'This is just a comedy series. You can get Liz or Joanie or any of the other funny ladies. It doesn't have to be me. Anyway, I don't like television.'

The next thing, Gerald Thomas was on the phone, asking me if I would change my mind. I said I was sorry for letting him down and explained my reasons. He was very understanding. 'I do realise you're the only one who can end the affair – Sid won't,' he said.

I had not bargained for how determined Sid would be. He persuaded me to meet him at a friend's flat in West Hampstead and came straight to the point. 'You're not being fair to the show, Barbara. The whole series has been written with us in mind. I understand that TV is not your big money-earner. You get more in the theatre. So I'm going to talk to them about money. What are you getting now?'

'Three hundred.'

'I'll get you more than that,' he said.

'It's not just money, Sid,' I told him. 'I want us to stop seeing each other. I can't handle it any more.'

'We'll just be good friends, Barbara.'

'Will you promise me that?'

'I *promise* you,' he said.

Sid did keep his word about the money. He arranged for my fee to be trebled to £900 for each of the five shows I'd be in, which meant I'd be getting a fortune for what would be no more than six weeks' filming. I was thrilled, particularly as we'd never done a half-hour TV Carry On, and the scripts were great. But the minute I walked into the ATV studios at Elstree on the first Monday morning and Sid saw me, I knew I had made a mega mistake. 'A round of applause for our beautiful Miss Windsor,' he said loudly. 'Doesn't she look wonderful?'

I smiled, of course, but inside I was cringing. By the end of the day, he was demanding to see me. 'You made me a promise, Sid,' I said, furiously. 'You promised that if I did the show, we'd just be friends. Right?'

Sid didn't say anything. He probably didn't know what to say. He just looked at me adoringly, and I knew it was hopeless. I was back to square one. He was constantly phoning me, following me, checking up on me. I couldn't even have a chat with the cameramen without him going into a sulk.

Once we ran into Danny La Rue in a restaurant. 'Hi, Sid. Hi, Bar. Going to join me?' he asked.

'No, no,' said Sid hastily. 'We want to be on our own.'

A couple of days later, I bumped into Danny again. 'I can't believe what I'm hearing about you and Sid,' he said. 'Is it true?'

I admitted that it was and, as Danny is one of my oldest and dearest friends, I offloaded my anxieties on to him. I confessed that I had got myself into an impossible situation and didn't seem to be able to get out of it. I got no sympathy there. 'Don't be a prat,' he said. 'You're a married woman. Ronnie comes first. If it's over, tell Sid. And don't see him any more.'

I could not wait for my five episodes of *Carry On Laughing* to finish. I was on tenterhooks all the time, wondering and worrying about what Sid was going to say and do next.

That November, I was asked to go to an awards ceremony at the London Theatre in Drury Lane, to present Michael York with a Best Newcomer award for his role in *The Three Musketeers*. It was a great honour for me. I told Gerald three days in advance and he agreed to shoot a scene early so that I could get away. Sid was quickly on the case. 'Why do you have to leave early that day? Where are you going?' he wanted to know. I told him why – it was no secret.

Three days later, I arrived at the London Theatre to find Sid and Gerald at the ceremony with their wives. I gave them my usual friendly greeting as though there was nothing wrong, but you could have cut the atmosphere with a knife. I felt terrible: there was my leading man, who I was involved with, and there was Gerald, my director, who knew all about it.

Sid, Val, Gerald and his wife Barbara were going on to dinner afterwards. When I got home that night, Sid phoned. 'You looked so lovely tonight,' he said. 'That dress was beautiful. I love you.'

'Where are you ringing from?' I asked him.

'A restaurant.'

'Where are the others?'

'Eating. I talked the manager into letting me use his office. I told them I was going for a pee.'

I just hated that. It was so controlling.

As Christmas drew near, Sid was growing stronger while I was getting weaker. I seemed to be under his spell. He always wanted to know where I was going, and if I wasn't going to be with him or Ronnie, he insisted I stayed in. And, you know, I did. He even rang once and asked me to speak to Val and plead with her to let him go. I even did that. The conversation with Val is all a bit of a blur now, but I do remember that it made me even more determined to cut Sid out of my life. I felt he was chickening out of saying himself what it was his responsibility to explain to his wife.

Yet as soon as I talked to him again, my resolve would crumble. As I listened to him saying that we would definitely be together again by the same time the next year, after our respective tours of Australia, New Zealand and

South Africa, I believed he meant it, and a bit of me thought he might actually make it happen.

On Christmas Eve, while Ronnie was at the club, a friend of mine, Beryl Fordham, who knew about my affair with Sid, popped round with some presents. She took one look at me and exclaimed: 'Goodness, Barbara, what's wrong? You look terrible.' I pretended I was just worn out, but she saw through that. 'Why are you sitting in here on your own on Christmas Eve?' I shrugged. 'It's Sid James, isn't it? He's not good for you, Barbara.' Just then the phone rang and it was Sid, no doubt checking that I was in. Beryl couldn't stand listening to me sounding like some downtrodden wife. She snatched the phone from me and gave him a right earful about how wrong it was that I should be stuck at home because of him.

'Bar's making cock-and-bull excuses, but I know it's because you've told her not to go out,' she said.

Sid desperately wanted to see me before he left for Australia, and I agreed to meet him at the Dorchester Hotel on the day before he left. I did not particularly want to go: all that needed to be said had been said, but it was going to be a year before I'd see him again and I saw no reason to part on a sour note after all we'd been through. I arrived at eleven o'clock, wearing a leopardskin coat and matching trilby hat, and bringing with me a heart full of mixed emotions.

He was sitting just inside the front entrance, where there was a piano. A walking stick lay against his chair. He looked absolutely dreadful. He ordered a pot of tea and scones and cakes and we giggled a bit over some silly things, and then he started on the old story. 'I want so much to be with you. If I can't be, I don't want to live. I assure you I'll be dead in a year.'

'Charming!' I said, trying to make light of it. 'You invite me to the Dorchester for tea and cakes, I've put me best hat on, and now you're telling me that. Thanks very much.'

It relieved the tension for a moment, but then he said: 'I feel trapped.'

I knew he meant he could not cut himself free from Val.

'Sid, my marriage has gone from bad to worse because of you,' I told him. 'I wouldn't blame Ronnie if he found someone else.'

When we left the hotel Sid was crying. He asked me where I was off to and I said I was going shopping in the West End. He offered me a lift and his chauffeur drove to Selfridges. When I got out, Sid said to him: 'Look at her. Isn't she lovely? Cross my heart, I love her. Know something? She won't have me.'

When Sid was in Australia he phoned me every night. 'You're going to have to stop at Sydney on your way to New Zealand,' he said. 'I'll be at the airport to see you.'

'Don't be daft, Sid. You're a famous face, and your wife's in the country. How can you possibly go to a big airport?'

'I'll be there,' he promised.

Two nights before I was due to fly to New Zealand, he called to say he had got my itinerary so that he could keep tabs on me.

Oh, shit, I thought.

Late on the night before my departure, Sid's director, Bill Roberton, rang with a message from Sid. 'He wants you to know that he won't be able to meet you in Sydney.'

'Tell me something I didn't know,' I said.

That pissed me off. Why say he was going to meet me in the first place? And why, if he was so concerned, get someone else to phone me when he could have done so himself? It was a side of Sid's personality I had come to dislike. And on the opening night of my show, in Invercargill, he did something else he damned well knew I hated: yet again, he sent me a love note without having the thoughtfulness, let alone the discretion, to put it in an envelope. Phil Norman, my producer, brought it to my dressing room a couple of hours before curtain-up, along with a crate of champagne. Sid had given him the note and the money for the bubbly before he had left for Australia. Written on a plain piece of paper, folded in half, were the words: 'To the most wonderful lady in the world. Wishing you all the success you deserve. I love you. I'm waiting for the day we can be together.'

Phil was clearly embarrassed. 'I don't want you to think I opened the note, Barbara,' he said. 'That's how I got it.'

'I know, sweetheart. Don't worry. It's just Sid's way.'

I was making light of it so that Phil would feel less awkward, but inside I was seething. What did Sid think he was playing at? A wardrobe mistress knowing about us was one thing; an eminent, influential, well-connected theatrical producer was another. And all that old shit about waiting for the day we could be together! He knew that was not going to happen. And surely he knew by now that I didn't *want* it to happen. Yes, there had been that time, back in the summer, when I'd been caught up in it all and prepared, eager, even, to leave Ronnie and go for it. And who knows, if Ronnie's dad hadn't died that weekend, and if Ronnie hadn't been pulled in by the police, I may well have gone through with it. But even then there had been no plan beyond

Sid installing me in a flat like a kept woman. Who's to say that he would have been true to his feelings and left Val? He was always talking about it, and almost certainly wanted to, but he was too weak, too cowardly, to actually do anything about it, preferring to have his cake and eat it.

It was this, more than anything, that had made me lose respect for Sid. But there was something else I didn't like, and that was the selfishness his obsession with me nurtured; the feeling that if he couldn't be with me, then no one else should, not even my girlfriends. Only Ronnie or him. But Sid didn't care: all that mattered was that I was safely tucked away in my box, unable to talk to anyone he didn't want me to speak to. With someone like me, who loves to have a good time and a real gossip, this was cruel; it seemed like he was changing me as a person, making me lose a bit of my identity. I didn't like him for that, and I was unhappy with myself, too, for allowing him to gain a hold over me and going along with his demands.

There had been a lot of love, along with the lust, in our affair. But all that pressure, all that relentless checking up and all the rest of it, had drained me. Quite how stressed I was, how much I was bottling up, didn't hit me until one of the dancers in the show made a play for me one night two weeks or so into the tour. His name was Earl Adair. He was blond and very good-looking, and we were back at the hotel, both quite drunk after we'd all been out to dinner. One minute we were laughing over something silly, the next he had his arms round me and was pulling me towards him and trying to kiss me.

What did I do? I burst into tears. I sobbed my heart out, unleashing all my hurt and anger and disappointment in a torrent of pent-up emotion. All the time, Earl, bless him, the sweet man, cuddled me tight, saying over and over again: 'Oh, Barbara, oh, Barbara,' for what seemed like hours. What I said, how I'd felt, was a blur the next morning. Earl told me it had been all about Sid and Ronnie, and what I felt about each of them, and what I should do for the best. But whatever it was that brought on those tears did me good. It got a lot out of my system and made me lighten up.

Until then I'd just been doing the job on autopilot, which was very unlike me. We were playing one-nighters all over the place and I'd sit on my own at the back of the coach, reading or sleeping, until it was time to put my face on and be Barbara Windsor and go out and say 'Hello, everybody, here I am,' and do the promotional interviews. Then I'd do the show and crash out at the hotel.

After crying on Earl's shoulder, however, I felt better about myself. I heard no more from Sid, and to tell the truth, it was a relief. I started going out with the boys after our evening performance and, during the day, taking in the spectacular sights New Zealand had to offer, and before long my worries seemed a million miles away, and I had put Sid right to the back of my mind.

Towards the end of the tour we travelled to Wanganui, a tiny, remote town in a beautiful mountain region in the south-west of North Island, 200 miles from Auckland. When we arrived we spent a few thrilling hours pitting our wits against some nerve-jangling rapids, and I went off to the theatre feeling invigorated. In my dressing room I was thinking ahead to our next venue, Wellington, and wondering whether anything would come of some talk there had been of taking *Carry On Barbara* to Australia.

My phone rang. 'Sydney is on the line,' said the operator. I felt a rush of excitement. Something must be happening with Australia, I thought. A crazy image of *Carry On Barbara* playing at the Sydney Opera House flashed through my mind.

'Hello?' I said eagerly.

'Hello, darling.' It was Sidney, not Sydney.

I fought to hide my disappointment and shock. 'Oh, er, hello, Sid. This is a surprise. How did you find me here, in the middle of nowhere?'

'I've known where you were since you arrived.'

'Oh, yeah. Right.'

'I told you I'd be at the airport. I'm sorry I didn't get in touch.'

'That's OK,' I said wearily. It all seemed a terribly long time ago. I didn't even want to think about it any more.

'I hear you're a big success. Phil's told me all about it.'

'Yeah, it's going well,' I said. 'Thanks for the champagne, by the way. That was very sweet.'

'Nothing's too much for my beautiful and talented lady.' He was building up to his favourite subject: us getting back together. He then went on and on about how he couldn't wait to get to London to start seeing me again and all the rest of it. I was waiting for a chance to jump in and say my piece when he suddenly shut up. After a short pause, he said: 'Just a minute . . . Val's coming.' And plonked the phone down.

He had not moved on. After all that happened, he was still treating me as someone who ceased to exist when it suited him. That did it for me; made up my mind, focused me. I knew for certain I didn't want to live with him. I also knew I'd never let him control my life again. Ever.

The next day we set off for the south-west tip of North Island and the beautiful city of Wellington, where we had a day off before we opened. The others were keen to take a trip into the mountains to see the hot springs in Rotorua, but I had an important letter to write, and all of a sudden I felt it couldn't wait. So when we checked into our hotel I unpacked and sat down at a little table in my room with a pile of hotel notepaper in front of me. I've never been one for writing: if something needs to be said, I prefer to say it. But this was a matter that had to be put down in writing because no amount of talking had made the point, and it was now clear to me that it never would. And it was going to be a long letter, because I had a lot to say.

I picked up a pen and, in my ludicrously large handwriting, began: 'Dear Sid'. And then I poured out my heart. There were not enough words to tell him how unhappy we were making each other, I wrote, and our love, no matter how great, wasn't meant to be. If he loved me, *really* loved me, as much as he said he did, then he would do what was right for me, not for him, and let me go.

Once I'd started I let it all out. I found I couldn't stop writing. When I'd finished, I read the letter through and decided it covered everything I wanted to say in the way I wanted to say it.

I posted the letter to the Melbourne theatre that was Sid's final venue. Immediately, I panicked. What if Val opened it? Almost as instantly I put the thought out of my mind: it was too late now. And what if she did? She would know me for what I was and for what I meant to Sid: a nice lady, not just an uncaring bit on the side. And, maybe, no matter how angry she was, she would understand that I genuinely loved him.

I'd tried hard to make the letter final, to put a full stop to everything, once and for all, and I prayed I would not get a response. I didn't – not even a phone call through a third party – and when I arrived home in April there was no letter waiting for me. At last, it seemed, he had heard me. Thank God.

Back in London the atmosphere between me and Ronnie was strangely quiet, almost polite. He seemed pleased I was home, although typically, he showed little interest in where I'd been, what I'd done, who I'd seen. He didn't even quiz me on any dalliances I may have had. We were like ships that passed in the night. When I reminded him I was taking the show to South Africa in the autumn after an eight-week British tour, he raised barely an eyebrow.

The British producer, Cameron Mackintosh, changed the title from *Carry*

On Barbara to *A Merry Whiff of Windsor* for the tour. The words 'Carry On' were now synonymous with the films in the minds of the British public, and if we kept them, people would be expecting a farce when, in fact, it was a well-choreographed musical revue. *A Merry Whiff of Windsor* went down well at home, and we set off confidently in the autumn of 1975 for South Africa. On that tour I had a fling with the drummer in the show, a South African called Cecil, who first showed an interest in me when we were playing the coastal town of East London. On the way to Port Elizabeth, where Sid had been born, Cecil brought down my defences with a romantic ploy even I, with all my experience of men, had never come up against. 'Can I stop the coach?' he said suddenly. 'I want you Brits to see how wonderful Africa is.' We all trooped off and stood there looking up at the stars. They were so big they seemed to be almost on top of us. The feel of the warm night air, the sound of the Indian Ocean lapping the shore and the beautiful South African night sky put me in a romantic mood. It made me realise just how much I'd put my feelings on hold while I put up the shutters on Sid.

The last performance of the tour was on Saturday 11 October at the Civic Theatre in Johannesburg. During the interval a call from the *News of the World* in London was put through to my dressing room. They had belatedly picked up on a rumour that Sid and I were having an affair. The reporter had already rung Sid, who had merely laughed and said, 'We're just good mates.' He didn't get much more joy out of me. 'Are you joking?' I asked him. 'I haven't seen Sid for nearly a year – we've both been on tour.'

The paper had absolutely nothing to go on, so I wasn't concerned, but when I arrived at Heathrow on the Monday morning I had to think on my feet, because waiting there was Ronnie, with my press agent, Margot Lovell, and they both looked as though someone had died.

Ronnie stared at me. 'Yesterday the *News of the World* said that you and Sid James are having an affair,' he said icily. 'Are you?'

'Don't be daft,' I dismissed him. 'It's a stupid story.'

It was, too – just a picture of us with a lame report that there were rumours of an affair between Sid and me which we both denied – and Ronnie seemed satisfied.

I'd been back in London a couple of weeks when I had a call from the producer Duncan Weldon. Duncan was an old friend who'd been very good to me in my career, and who had produced several pantos and shows I'd been in. He was in a bit of a panic: he had lost the actress due to play Aladdin at Richmond Theatre. Would I step in? I was happy to. I would be appearing with my old pals Una Stubbs and Jon Pertwee, as well as Jack Douglas, and it was bound to be fun.

Jack lived near Teddington TV studios, where Sid was making his hit series *Bless This House*. One day, during rehearsals, he came up to me, looking slightly ill at ease. 'You'll never guess who I've just seen.'

'Who?' I asked.

'Sid James.'

'Oh, really?'

'I said I was just off to panto and you'd come to our rescue,' he said. I didn't reply.

'Sid asked me to tell you to phone him,' Jack added.

'Oh, did he?' I said, and turned away.

But Jack must have seen the look on my face because he was clearly embarrassed. 'I'm just passing on the message, Bar, OK?'

'Thanks anyway, Jack.'

I didn't ring, and a couple of days later, I received a telegram from Sid with a Teddington phone number on it. 'Please phone me. I love you,' it read.

Over Christmas I was on stage, rubbing Aladdin's lamp, when Keith Michell, an eminent Australian stage and screen actor turned theatrical director, came to see the show. He must have seen something in me that no one else had, because he came backstage afterwards and asked me if I would like to play Maria in his production of *Twelfth Night* at the Chichester Festival the following May.

I thought he was mad. 'I can't do Shakespeare,' I giggled. But he seemed to think I could, and with some persuasive charm he talked me round. To be honest, I'd always had a secret yen to have a go at the Bard, but, as usual, the next day, I thought: 'Oh, God, what have I let myself in for?'

After *Aladdin* finished, I was thrilled to land a lucrative commercial for the Milk Marketing Board's advertising campaign 'Watch out, there's a Humphrey about.' On the way to the shoot at Shepperton I could tell the driver was bursting to tell me something. 'It's going to be nice for you today, Babs,' he said.

'Why's that, then?'

'Well, you're going to meet one of your best friends, aren't you?'

My first thought was that Kenny Williams must be working there too. 'Who?' I asked.

'Sid James,' he said. 'He and Arthur Mullard are doing a milk commercial, too.'

'*Sid James?*'

It was bloody awful timing. What was I going to do if we bumped into each other? As the driver chatted on, I conjured up pictures in my head of how it would be, imagining Sid driving into the studios and, seeing me, winding down the window, giving the old, familiar chuckle and saying: 'Hello, Bar. How are you?' And then we'd part as friends. That was what I really wanted. But the driver had mentioned that Sid was not due in until after lunch, so maybe we might not meet at all. Oh, well, what will be, will be, I consoled myself.

The commercial was a bit of a farce. I was in a bath filled with milk, like a scene from *Carry On Cleo*, and was asked to say my lines in different ways: soft and breathy like Monroe; in a sexy French accent à la Bardot; deep-voiced like Fenella Fielding. None of them worked, so we took a break for lunch while the advertising executives thought it over. In the restaurant a waitress came over and made an enormous fuss of me. 'We're so pleased to see you here, Barbara,' she said, all smiles. 'We're all such great fans of yours. We think you're lovely. You don't work here often enough.'

'That's very sweet of you, darling,' I said, and we had a little chat as the ad guys looked on. They seemed amazed, and impressed, too. As soon as the waitress went away, the top man said triumphantly: 'That's how she's got to do it. Like Barbara. The public identify with her.' So after lunch I reshot the commercial as myself – and it was all over in just a couple of takes.

Relieved that I hadn't bumped into Sid after all, I went back to my dressing room to change and wait for my car. One of the studio runners then asked me to do something very odd. 'Would you stay in your room until your car's here, Barbara?' she said. 'Please don't come out of the room.'

'OK, fine,' I agreed, wondering what on earth was going on. As I sat there, I heard a woman's voice, terse and insistent, in another dressing room. 'No, Sid, no. *No.* We're staying here.'

Then what was unmistakably Sid's voice. 'Look. If I want to see her ...'

I was listening to an argument between Sid and Val. From what I could gather, Val was insisting that they stayed in their dressing room until I had gone. I got so upset, I could stand it no longer. I stood up, grabbed my things and marched along the corridor to Reception, announcing in my loudest theatrical voice: 'Barbara Windsor Has Now Left The Building.'

I got into the car to find the same driver who had brought me there that morning. He was smiling. 'So, was it nice, seeing your old mate?'

'Yeah, lovely,' I said. 'Fantastic.'

I slumped back in the seat, very melancholy, regretting writing that letter; regretting not knocking on that dressing-room door and acting like a mature grown-up and saying: 'Hello, Sid. Hello, Val. How are you? All right? Nice to see you. God bless.'

I felt very, very sad and sorry for myself all the way to Hendon.

It was 26 April 1976, a Monday, to be precise. I'd been to Chichester by train for the first day of rehearsals for *Twelfth Night* and to do a heavy round of publicity work. I was in a taxi, leaving Victoria for Hendon. The time on the station clock was 8.50 p.m.

Driving past the Victoria Palace Theatre, the cabbie said: 'The last time I picked you up, you were with Sid James. I brought you here from Dolphin Square. That was a lovely show, wasn't it? How is he, old Sid?'

'Oh, Sid? He's fine, lovely. He's very happy, he's touring in a play.' That cabbie, like millions of people, wanted to believe that the Carry On team lived in each other's pockets off the screen. I wasn't about to shatter that illusion.

Seeing the theatre, happy memories flashed through my mind like little film clips: the walks on Saturday afternoons, having tea and all the rest of it. We weren't talking because of the letter, and Val hadn't let me see him, I know, but those memories of Sid were safely locked away in my mind and nobody could take them away. Reminiscing with that taxi driver was lovely, and made it a nice journey home.

Indoors the phone was ringing. On my way to answer it, I switched on the TV to catch the news.

'Hello?'

'Hello, Barbara, it's the *Daily Express*.'

'Hello, love.' Inwardly, I groaned: not more publicity. 'I've done loads of interviews already.'

'You've heard the news, Barbara?'

'What, darling?' I said. 'Heard what?'

'About Sid James.'

There was a cold feeling in the pit of my stomach. 'Why? What's happened?'

I looked across at the TV and found myself staring at Sid's face. 'Oh, I'm sorry, I thought you'd know,' the reporter was saying. 'He died tonight. He had a heart attack on stage in Sunderland.'

I went cold all over. I couldn't speak. Then I started shaking. Somehow I got myself together just enough to say something nice for the paper. Then I rang Ronnie's club. For some reason, Freddie Foreman, a friend of Ronnie's, answered.

'I need Ronnie to come home, Fred,' I said. 'Sid James has died.'

'Oh, no. I'm so sorry, Bar. He was lovely, Sid.'

Ronnie came on the line. He said he was sad, too.

'Will you come home, Ronnie?'

'No, Bar. You'll be all right.'

'OK,' I said, hanging up. Why I thought Ronnie would spoil his Monday night with the chaps to comfort me over Sid James, I don't know. I didn't really care anyway. I was better off on my own, anyway, free to wallow in self-pity. I sat in my front room and sobbed my heart out until my eyes stung and my throat ached. All the time, a nagging thought kept turning over and over in my mind, forcing its way through my grief: We didn't talk. We should have talked. Why, oh, why, didn't we talk about it all and stay friends? After all that had happened, after all the joy we'd given each other, we should have stayed friends, at least.

I was still crying when Ronnie rolled in at 3 a.m.

He took one look at me and said: 'My God, you *are* in a state. I hope you cry like this when I go.'

I slept downstairs that night.

The papers were all full of it, of course. The horrid facts were that Sid had collapsed with a heart attack on a sofa on stage at Sunderland's Empire Theatre at 7.45 p.m., roughly fifteen minutes into the touring play, *The Mating Season*. A doctor in the audience fought to revive him on stage and in the ambulance taking him to hospital, but Sid never recovered.

He had died three weeks before his sixty-third birthday. And sixteen months after he had told me he would last only one year without me.

I wasn't invited to the funeral and understood why. Instead I lit a candle for Sid and said a quiet prayer for him in my own way, alone in my home. I thought about the caring side of his nature and how happy he had made me, not the maddening obsession that had stifled, and finally strangled, our love.

16

THE CHALLENGE OF SHAKESPEARE HELPED ME COPE WITH SID'S DEATH. I was terrified, of course; in all my work, I'd only ever spoken modern dialogue. Keith Michell was confident I could manage on my own, but it was the lovely Bill Fraser, who won TV fame with Alfie Bass in the hilarious sixties sitcom *Bootsie and Snudge*, I had to thank for the praise I received for my role as Maria. Bill was playing Sir Toby Belch, and during rehearsal one day, he told me: 'You're struggling with the text because you're trying to speak it the way you think Shakespeare wanted it spoken. You'll find it easier if you read the lines as though you're in a Carry On movie.' Bill was right, bless him. And I was OK after that.

During those three stimulating months at Chichester, I was approached to make *Carry On Emmanuelle*, a spoof on the soft-porn movie *Emmanuelle*, which had rocketed a sexy Dutch lady, Sylvia Kristel, to instant fame two years before. The idea was to take the original storyline – the bored wife of a French ambassador seducing almost every man she meets – and make it funny. But the script wasn't funny; it was pathetic. And crude. More importantly, the producers were deviating from a tried and tested formula that had worked for thirty Carry Ons before. Sid would not have touched it with the proverbial bargepole and neither would I. My agent, Richard Stone, agreed with me, and wasted no time telling the producers, in Sam Goldwyn's immortal words, that they could include me out. The next moment I was reading in the papers that I'd described the film as 'soft porn' and had walked out, even though I hadn't been near the studio.

My instincts were proved right. The film was made, but it flopped big-time. It was the worst Carry On to date, prompting one critic to snipe:

'It's rather like watching endearing elderly relatives disgracing themselves at a party.' It was one party I elbowed, thank God.

That year Ronnie and I were invited to appear on a TV show, *Mr and Mrs*, in which a celebrity and his or her spouse demonstrated how much – or little in many cases – they knew about each other by answering six fairly intimate questions. Being so shy, Ronnie laughed at the idea at first, but after his mum and I both had a go at him, he gave in. I particularly wanted him to do the programme because it was an ideal opportunity for him to show the public that he was not the gangster the newspapers labelled him. Surprisingly, we got all the questions right and were so popular that we were invited back for a festive special, coming on as Mr and Mrs Christmas Knight. The presenter, Derek Batey, remarked, in blissful innocence, how well tuned-in we were to each other.

I did want to make it work with Ronnie: although he never demonstrated it, I'm sure he appreciated what I did when I was at home. So to try to bring us closer together, that autumn, 1976, I suggested we should buy our first house. Mummy had been going on for ages about how I surely could afford a house after so many successful years. It wasn't enough for me to be a star: she wanted me to live like one. Ronnie was up for a move, so I started looking around. I took Mummy to view the first likely sounding property, which proved to be a mistake. It had tiny, leaded, church-like windows, which I adored, but Mummy said it was creepy. So, of course, I didn't take it any further. But I didn't ask her to come to any more viewings.

Ronnie and I finally settled on a house in Aylmer Drive in a wonderful part of Stanmore: a spacious, four-bedroomed property in a cul-de-sac on the edge of a forest, with an apple orchard. Although it was only six miles from Hendon, Mummy was worried that we weren't close enough to where she and Len were living in Rayleigh, in Essex. To make her feel better, I persuaded her and Len to sell up and move nearer to us, and helped buy them a flat nearby.

Sadly, upping sticks brought us all nothing but bad luck. It started on the first weekend in December as I prepared to go to Bradford for panto – *Aladdin* again – at the Alhambra Theatre. All week Freddie, our beloved, sweet-natured poodle, had been throwing up. The vet gave him some pills, but he was so ill on the Saturday that Ronnie took him back and the vet kept him in. I wanted to take him to Bradford with me on the Monday, so I rang the vet on Sunday to arrange to pick him up. To my horror, I was told that he had developed cat flu. There had been nothing they could do, and he had died. I was so, so upset. Why, I wanted to know, had no one rung us and given Freddie the chance to spend his last hours being fussed over by the people who loved him most?

I travelled to Bradford knowing it would be tough bouncing out on stage when my heart was breaking. But it was not only my heart that would end up broken. During the panto I tripped on stage and broke a wrist as well. The audience fell about, thinking it was all part of being the funny Carry On girl, but I was in agony. Somehow I got through the show, then went straight to hospital. I was in plaster for three weeks.

Len was spending a lot of time at Aylmer Drive, doing odd jobs and driving Ronnie about because he'd lost his licence through drink-driving. Len was a dear, sweet man and it was a joy to have him in the house. Shortly after I finished the panto, I came home to find him doubled up in pain over the kitchen table.

'Oh, Len,' I said. 'What's wrong, sweetheart?'

'I don't know, Bar,' he said, grimacing. 'I've got these terrible pains.'

'How long have you had them?'

'Some while now. I haven't told your mother. I don't know what's wrong. I think I may have an ulcer.'

'Have you been to the doctor, darling?' I asked him.

'Oh, yeah. I've seen him. He gave me some pills.'

I shook my head. 'We've got to get you to a specialist, Len.'

The specialist admitted Len to hospital for an exploratory operation. On the day before, Ronnie and I and Len's two lovely sons, Michael and Donald, and daughter, Lorraine, went to see him in Edgware General Hospital to cheer him up. I asked him if he was nervous and he said: 'Not in the least. I can't wait to wake up tomorrow for them to tell me what's wrong with me and sort it out.'

And then he smiled that sweet smile and said, 'Look. I've got all my family here. Isn't it lovely?'

Poor Len never really did wake up after that operation. When they opened him up they found that he was riddled with cancer. They sewed him up again, saying that there was nothing they could do; it was only a matter of time.

That Sunday should have been the time Len passed on, with all of us round the bed and that contented smile on his face. He should have left us happy and optimistic and feeling loved. And that's the way we would have wanted to remember him. But life seldom gives you what you want, does it? It took three months for the cancer to claim Len, three cruel agonising months during which he was in such pain that it seemed there wasn't enough morphine in existence to relieve it. None of us saw Len any more. The drugs took away the personality we all adored and in its place left an irascible creature we didn't know.

Mummy barely left Len's bedside. She did everything she could for him and never complained, not even at those times when he surfaced from his drug-induced state not knowing who she was, or even who he was himself, and shouted the most appalling things at her.

It was so unfair that he was taken from Mummy so soon after he retired, just when they were planning to do so much together – the tea dances and all the rest of it. But at least they had a good twenty years together and, in Mummy, he had someone he cherished and adored, and who loved and respected him. And for me, Len was just the best, the father I wished I'd had.

After Len died, we extended the house to include a granny flat for Mummy and she sold the flat in Bushey. Apart from panto and a TV version of *Come Spy With Me*, with Danny La Rue, I had not had much work and Ronnie seemed to enjoy me being around more. He'd always get out of bed in the morning singing, have a bath, then go and sit in his favourite antique armchair, beside the baby grand piano in the lounge, and read the papers. Often he would cast his eyes around the room and say proudly: 'This is all mine.' He liked being a house-owner.

In the summer of 1979 I was offered a part in a children's TV series. Despite having a chest that might appeal to sailors, I never dreamed I'd ever play a ship's figurehead, but that's exactly what I became in the captivating *Worzel Gummidge*. The figurehead was on the *Saucy Nancy* – actually a replica of the *Golden Hinde* – and it miraculously left the ship from time to time to compete with Aunt Sally, played by my old friend Una Stubbs, for the affections of Worzel the scarecrow, brilliantly portrayed by Jon Pertwee.

When I told Ronnie I had to spend a week filming in Brixham on *Worzel*, he didn't react. But when I started sorting out his clothes and asking him what he wanted to wear that week, he realised I was not going to be home every night to pamper him. 'What are you talking about?' he said. 'You're only going to Brixton.'

'No, darling, it's *Brixham*, in Devon. I'll be away all week.'

He started accusing me of lying about the location. 'I suppose you're meeting somebody there,' he snapped.

'I told you I was filming by the sea,' I said. 'Have you ever seen any sea in Brixton?'

We had a blazing row and when my car arrived, Ronnie was so steamed up that he refused to see me off. Nonetheless I promised to call him as soon as I reached Brixham. Unfortunately, that proved to be easier said than done. We were checked into a lovely, but small and old-fashioned hotel, which didn't have phones in the rooms. When I went downstairs to see if there was a public telephone, I bumped into Una, who said: 'Don't bother, Bar – it's out of order.'

It was ages before I could find a phone that was working and call the old man. 'Been making all your arrangements, have you?' he said sarcastically when I did.

Fuck you, I thought.

The next morning I was having my hair and make-up done when Jon Pertwee came in with a tall, dark-haired, bearded guy, a dead ringer for Al Pacino in the film *Serpico*. Beside me was a plate of sandwiches I'd ordered, and as I chatted to Jon, I saw 'Pacino' stretch out a hand to take one.

'Do you mind?' I said. 'They're my sandwiches.'

'I'm so sorry,' he said. 'I thought they were for everybody.'

Cheeky bastard, I thought. I'm old-school, me, well mannered, and I felt he should have asked, whatever he assumed.

I didn't take much notice of him: he was Medallion Man, covered in gold chains, and I can't stand them. That evening, however, I changed my mind about him. After filming all day, I went back to the hotel to put on my Barbara Windsor look for a press reception. As I came down and headed for my car, I saw 'Pacino' eating with Jon in the restaurant. He noticed me and smiled. 'Mmm,' I thought, suddenly seeing him in a different light. 'He's rather nice after all.' The next night I had dinner with Jon and 'Pacino', whose real name was Robert Dunn, and he owned a nightclub in Southampton. We got on well in spite of our shaky start, and began an affair which was to last, on and off, for many years.

The filming was fun, too, except for the final day, when we shot a scene in which Saucy Nancy had to return to the ship before anyone noticed she was missing. When the stunt girl discovered she had to be strapped to a little trolley and hurtle down a hill at 30mph towards Brixham Harbour, her bottle went and I had to do it. I ended up with a badly gashed leg, high up into my groin, and when I got back to the hotel I found I was bleeding from internal injuries.

If I'd found playing Saucy Nancy gruelling, it was nothing compared with my next role, Calamity Jane. As a sixteen-year-old I'd adored Doris Day in the movie and I was thrilled to be playing the pistol-packing tomboy in a three-month UK tour. It was the most physical performance of my life, but great fun, too: I learned how to twirl guns round my fingers and wield a whip, and I had to master leaping on to a real stagecoach. When Mummy came to see the show in Brighton, she could not believe how hard I had to work. Not knowing what else to say, she told me, 'Oh, Babs, I wish I'd never taken you away from the convent.'

The local media gave us some great publicity for the show. I did an interview with one Radio Trent disc jockey who was surprised to learn that I'd known his mother, a beautiful, blonde actress called Sheree Winton (tragically, she had killed herself only four years before). And he was even more surprised that I remembered her introducing him to me when he was a plump little boy. That DJ was considered the best in the Midlands and I felt it would not be long before he broke into the big time down south. He said he wanted to get into TV and, even then, I could see he had the personality to do it. That young man was Dale Winton.

During the tour I got an odd phone call from Ronnie early one morning. He rarely rang early, so I sensed something was wrong.

'It's your mother,' he said. 'She's not her usual self. She's been acting a bit strange. Imagining things.'

'Like what?' I asked.

He would not tell me over the phone. He just asked me not to mention it to Mummy. When I got home late the following Saturday, Ronnie fussed round me, which made me suspicious that something was up. Mummy, on the other hand, seemed perfectly normal. The next morning I asked Ronnie: 'What's Mummy been imagining?'

'Well, she reckons she saw me in bed with a girl.'

'What!'

Ronnie shrugged.

'Where?' I asked.

'Here.'

'*In this house?*'

'Yeah. I told you not to—'

'Have you had a girl in bed here, Ronnie?' I interrupted, trembling with anger.

'Of course not,' he said. 'I told you, she's imagining things. She's on those silly pills.'

I didn't want to hear any more. I needed to speak to my mother. I told her what Ronnie had said and she looked embarrassed.

'Come on, Mummy,' I said. 'I need to know what's going on in my own house.'

'I can't say anything, Babs,' she said. 'He said he'd chuck me out if I did.'

'He's already told me you said you saw a girl. So you might as well tell me everything.'

Mummy said she had heard noises upstairs at three in the morning and had gone up to find Ronnie, very drunk, in bed with a young blonde woman. Seeing Mummy, the woman jumped out of bed, laughing, 'Oh, we've been caught out.' Far from being worried or embarrassed, she seemed triumphant. She dressed hurriedly, then ran out and drove off in a car which had been parked further up the road. Mummy said Ronnie had told her not to mention it to me 'or you'll never live here again'. The next day he had cried and said: 'Rosie, I'm sorry. I was drunk. I didn't know what I was doing. I only love Barbara.'

My mother had promised Ronnie not to tell me, so I would probably never have found out if Ronnie hadn't been stupid enough to ring me with that daft excuse. It was too outrageous not to be true, and if I did have a lingering doubt, the little girl who walked my collie, Blue, dispelled it.

'I met your sister,' she said one weekend.

'Oh, really?'

'Yes. Your husband answered the door and I saw a lady inside. She had a skirt split right up the side. She was blonde like you. That's why I thought it was your sister.'

'That was Ronnie's sister,' I assured her.

But it couldn't have been. Ronnie's sister was dark, and would never have worn a skirt like that.

I had another blow that autumn. I found I was pregnant. I had had sex with Ronnie only once in the previous couple of months – an impromptu romp one Sunday morning – whereas Robert Dunn had come to see me several times during the *Calamity Jane* tour. In my mind I knew the baby was Robert's, but in my heart I wanted it to be Ronnie's. I thought I still needed Ronnie and he needed me, and wondered whether maybe this would help solve all our problems and bring us closer together.

Robert said that if that was the way I truly felt, I should go home and have a good, honest heart-to-heart with Ronnie and see how he felt.

Robert drove me down after the show the following Wednesday, but all I got from Ronnie when I walked in was: 'What are you doing here?'

'I've come home because I want to talk to you,' I said.

'What about?'

'About us,' I told him.

It was clear from Ronnie's offhandedness that my surprise visit was not welcome and that a cosy tête-à-tête about our possible parental future was not on the agenda. I did try to talk to him when we went to bed, but he didn't want to know. I got a minicab back to Nottingham the next day deeply saddened that, at forty-two, I was going to have to have my fifth abortion.

That Christmas I was working in panto – *Dick Whittington* – with Dickie Henderson, at Richmond. My only break was Christmas Day, a miserable affair: Ronnie's mind was elsewhere. It was obvious to me that he was involved with someone else. I thought we might spend New Year's Eve together, but he didn't want to. Our marriage, it was clear, was finished. I decided I had to get out and, in the first few days of January 1980, I put our Stanmore house on the market and found a small studio flat to rent close to Harrods.

I planned to move in on 16 January. But then there was yet another development in our lives which kept me and Ronnie together, and this time, it brought us so close, it made me believe that, despite everything that had happened, he really did love me after all.

At 5 a.m. on the very Wednesday I intended to leave, I was woken by the doorbell. Blue started barking. Groggy with sleep and not registering that it was still dark, I went downstairs thinking it must be the postman. Immediately I opened the door I was almost blinded by a row of dazzling lights. As I put up my hand to shield my eyes six policemen and policewomen with guns and dogs charged past me and pounded up the stairs. I heard one of them say, 'Get dressed, Ronnie.' Following them up I begged them in a low voice, 'Please, please don't make a noise. My mother is asleep – I don't want her to hear all this.'

But Mummy did hear, and came in asking, 'What's going on? What's he done?' She was crying.

'Don't worry, Mummy, it's all a mistake,' I told her.

A nice policewoman sat her down and made her a cup of tea.

While Ronnie struggled into his clothes, the police swarmed all over our home, emptying out drawers and rifling through wardrobes. At one stage one of them said excitedly, 'I've got something here,' but if he was hoping to find drugs he was disappointed: it was just some powder that had leaked out of one of those sachets you hang up to keep your clothes fresh.

I was still trying to make some sense of what was going on, and wondering whether it was all a dream, when they trooped out, taking Ronnie away with them. Once again, the last thing he said was: 'Phone Jimmy.' I found myself shaking with shock, still with no idea what it was all about, sitting with Mummy and waiting for the world to wake up so that I could do something.

Putting the move on hold, I called Jimmy, who told me to ring Anthony Blok, a solicitor who had represented Ronnie on his drink-driving charge. Mr Blok discovered that Ronnie was being held at Savile Row Police Station off Regent Street, but no one was saying why. He explained that it could be one of three things: murder, arson or drugs. I didn't consider the first two for a second. 'It's drugs – it has to be,' I said, knowing there was a drug rehab place above his club. Mr Blok asked me to ring him at 11 p.m. after the curtain came down on *Dick Whittington*.

Somehow I got through the show and called him as soon as I came off stage. Apparently Ronnie had been accused, along with another man, of murdering Alfredo Zomparelli, and of arson as well. I didn't hear any more because I passed out. The next morning, I was booked to appear again on Pete Murray's *Open House* at the BBC. I didn't feel I could face it. So I rang Dickie Henderson and asked him if he would appear in my place. He told me it would be best for me to do the show, and to be seen in public. 'Go out and hold your head up high, Barbara – that's what our business is all about,' he said.

Splashed across my morning paper was a picture of my husband hand-cuffed to a copper, but I knew that Dickie was right and I had to put a brave face on it. So, hiding my red, swollen eyes behind a huge pair of dark glasses, I set off for Broadcasting House. I arrived to find the place crawling with photographers. Pete, as charming as ever, did not embarrass me with any difficult questions, but what worried me for the rest of the day was how my panto audience would react to hearing that the husband of the star of the show was accused of murder and arson.

That night, trembling with anxiety, I ran out on the stage fearing boos or, worse, an embarrassed silence. But I appeared to a crescendo of cheers and a standing ovation. It seemed to go on for ever. Eventually I held up my hands and said: 'Thank you, ladies and gentlemen. But my name's Dick Whittington, and I've come to London to seek my fortune.'

Bail was set at £250,000. Mr Blok urged me to give him the names of anyone who might be willing to put up sureties if the opportunity arose at the next court hearing. At the top of my list was Tony Chatwell, who was married to Ronnie's sister Patsy. Ronnie and I were close to them both, and had even looked after their children while they sorted out some marital difficulties. They were pretty wealthy and, being family, I was sure they wouldn't let Ronnie down. The next day I was mortified to learn that Tony had refused to put up a penny for his brother-in-law's bail. But I had no time to be angry: I had to chase round to find people who *were* willing to put up some money. It was no easy task. I was doing two shows a day, so spending most of my time at the theatre, which meant the usual headaches finding a working phone – and I needed to speak to Mr Blok every couple of hours or so as well. I got nowhere: everybody, with the exception of my pals Anna Karen and Peter Charlesworth, found some excuse not to help. By this time I'd been living on my nerves for six days and was depressed, dejected and disenchanted with people I'd known all my working life and considered my closest friends.

I tried to contact Tony Chatwell to find out why he had let us down and persuade him to have a rethink, but the family's au pair always answered the phone. Neither Tony nor Patsy ever returned any of my calls. Boiling mad, in the end I said to the au pair: 'Tell Mr Chatwell that if he doesn't ring me tomorrow, I'm going to stand outside his factory with a banner saying that he is Ronnie Knight's brother-in-law and that he won't stand bail for him.'

At nine the next morning Tony was at my front door, sweating like a pig and looking worried. I invited him in, but offered him nothing, not even a glass of water.

'I'm sorry, Barbara, I can't be associated with Ronnie,' he said. 'It would be bad for business. But I'll try to find someone to help out with the bail.'

I never heard from him again. Or from Patsy.

Things were looking bleak until, out of the blue, I got a call from Harry Hewson, a successful businessman and an old friend based in Birmingham who, in the past, had paid me to promote some of his ventures. Harry said I could count on him for £100,000. Then his wife, Phyllis, and her son-in-law,

David, offered the same amount. I told them they were wonderful people and that no words could express my gratitude.

I met Robert Dunn the next day feeling a little brighter. 'All I need now is fifty grand,' I said.

'You haven't asked me yet,' Robert said. 'You're welcome to the deeds of my cottage. I can't see Ronnie doing a bunk.' I was touched and so, so grateful to him.

The police objected to bail twice but, on 2 February, it was third time lucky when their legal representatives were held up in traffic and failed to get to the court in time for the hearing. They came into the building as we left, having heard the judge say that he was always sceptical of cases that rested on the evidence of only one person, which was the situation with this one. So Ronnie walked out of Brixton, thinner than when he'd gone in, but jaunty nonetheless. Asked what he was going to do next, he replied, typically: 'Go home and have a bath.'

First, though, we went to the Savoy Hotel. I'd promised to attend a reception there to mark 100 years of *The Stage* newspaper, and wanted to throw a little party of my own to celebrate Ronnie's release and thank the kind people who had made it possible. We had another party later at the theatre. It was the last night of the panto and I persuaded Ronnie to bring Mummy along to meet Dickie Henderson, Arthur Askey, and the other members of the cast who had comforted me and helped me through the show.

Having Ronnie home was great. The nasty memories of the blonde in our bed faded and I felt closer to him than I had in years: the terrible events of the previous two weeks seemed to have thrown us back into each other's arms, and I believed he needed me more than ever. Feeling that he needed a firm, familiar base, I abandoned my plans to move and took our Stanmore house off the market.

The previous year, during the *Calamity Jane* tour, Robert, who was interested in showbusiness, had suggested that he should manage me. I'd never had a manager – just an agent – and I didn't really feel I needed one, particularly one I was involved with. But I agreed to think about it. In the spring of 1980 I decided to accept his offer. He'd been so kind to me, driving me around and offering moral support, and although I still wasn't convinced that a manager was essential, there was no doubt that I was too distracted by all that was going on with Ronnie to give work my full attention. It wasn't an arrangement that lasted, though.

Sadly, within four months the closeness with Ronnie had worn off and we seemed to be drifting apart again. In an attempt to stop the rot I suggested he came with me to Southampton, where I had another week's filming on *Worzel Gummidge*. A break in the fresh country air, I said, would do him good. But Ronnie didn't want to know. So I went alone and, not surprisingly, ended up in bed with Robert instead. He had a live-in girlfriend named Lynne, but from what I'd been told, she knew about our affair and was not intending to do anything about it.

At the end of the week, with filming over, Lynne went out with some of her friends, taking one of Robert's cars, while he took me to dinner in a nippy green sports car he had bought from Jon Pertwee. Also joining us was a friend of mine, Graham Roberts, who had driven down to take me back to London. As there was no work the next day I happily got plastered. I had drunk far too much to realise that Robert was in no condition to drive. Normally I hate speed, but I was so out of it that I wasn't aware how fast he was going. One second we were on a narrow country lane, the next we were in a ditch. How Robert got the car out I don't know. I was catapulted forward and hurt the lower part of my body, but I was so anaesthetised by alcohol that I had no idea of the extent of my injuries until I got to Robert's home and saw blood running down the inside of my legs. Graham, who had driven there separately, quickly ran a bath. I got in, blood pouring from me, and conscious of Robert standing there worried that the blood would drip on to his white bathroom carpet. Then the phone went. I heard Robert answer it, then say to Graham: 'Christ, Lynne's been hurt in a crash. God knows what she's done to my car.' Within minutes he was gone, leaving Graham to get me into his car and back to London. I slept all the way and had sobered up by the time we reached Stanmore at around 3 a.m. Ronnie was in bed, wide awake.

'What time do you call this?' he demanded.

'I'm sorry, sweetheart,' I said. 'I've had a bit of an accident. I'll explain in the morning. I've just got to get to bed.'

I awoke in agony: my lower back was swollen and the bed was saturated with blood. Ronnie, who perhaps didn't realise how badly I'd been hurt, had gone out, but fortunately Graham, who had stayed overnight, rang my doctor. The next thing I knew I was being taken to Northwick Park Hospital in Harrow with serious internal injuries. I came round to find Ronnie at my bedside. 'What has been going on, Barbara?' I just said I'd been in a car crash, but that I couldn't remember anything about it. Thankfully he didn't ask me any more. Perhaps he didn't want to hear the answers.

Five days later I haemorrhaged and was whipped into the operating theatre for emergency surgery. For a while it was touch and go whether I'd make it, but I did and then, of course, immediately started worrying about Ronnie and the murder charge. With the committal hearing set for 14 July, I wanted to be up and about and doing things for him. I should have been resting, but instead I was in and out of bed making phone calls, feeling that I had to be there for him. In the end I discharged myself from hospital in spite of the warnings of the medical staff about the long-term effects I might suffer as a result.

The committal hearing lasted three days. The case against Ronnie and the other man, Nicholas Gerard, rested on the evidence of a George Bradshaw, a gangland killer who had turned Queen's Evidence and claimed that Ronnie had paid him and Gerard to shoot Zomparelli. On the final day, Ronnie and I went to lunch with Harry and Phyllis Hewson. When it was time for Ronnie to be back in court, he said he wanted to go in alone. He left the restaurant having discreetly settled the bill. When the hearing resumed bail was withdrawn and Ronnie was remanded in custody pending an Old Bailey trial. I was devastated. Before he was taken to Brixton Prison, I saw him in a cell below the court and broke down. 'We should have come back with you, Ronnie,' I sobbed. He shook his head. 'I knew what was going to happen. And I wanted to remember you giggling and happy.'

While we awaited the trial, fixed for Monday 10 November, I made sure that my working schedule enabled me to visit Ronnie every day. He was allowed food from outside, so I would take him meals I'd either prepared at home or bought from a local café, and a quarter-bottle of red wine to go with them. Being a famous face, I attracted a lot of attention from other visitors, some of whom seized this unexpected opportunity to audition for me! I did my best to be warm and friendly, but it wasn't always easy. I was pleased that the prison staff seemed to like me, though. 'She's a lovely lady, your missus,' they'd say to Ronnie. 'No airs and graces. She talks to everyone.'

The enormous publicity brought out of the woodwork a few nutters who found my phone number and rang me with supposedly vital information that could help Ronnie. They sent me on quite a few wild goose chases. Once I was told to go to Camden Town at 1 a.m. I wandered around there for half an hour, no doubt while the cranky caller was secretly watching and getting a thrill out of seeing a famous person making an idiot of herself.

By the time of the trial Ronnie's nerves were shot to pieces and his self-confidence was all but gone. 'Isn't it terrible?' he groaned one day. 'In a few days I could be doing twenty years.' Ronnie had sworn to me he had nothing to do with Zomparelli's murder, and I had such faith in British justice that I was convinced the jury would believe him. The weakness of the prosecution's case had always been the absence of any witness to corroborate Bradshaw's claim. Everything he said in court could be torn to pieces by Ronnie's barrister.

I urged Ronnie to be more positive. 'You'll be back home with me, and that's the end of it,' I said.

On the Friday before the trial, I called to see Anthony Blok to ask if there were any last-minute things he wanted me to do. I'd been to visit Ronnie and he was now quietly confident, too. But Anthony's face was pinched with worry. 'We're in deep trouble, Barbara,' he said. 'The police have found someone who backs up everything Bradshaw says. They didn't disclose it until today to stop us checking him out.'

My heart sank. I began to panic.

'The man's name is Knight, ironically,' Anthony said. 'Gerald Knight. Do you know him?'

'Yeah, we knew him when we lived in Hendon. We called him Gerry. He brought us new-laid eggs. He and Ronnie talked about buying a joint property. He gave us a cheque for £5,000 which bounced, and we never saw him again.'

Anthony looked through some papers. 'He denies ever meeting Ronnie.'

'Bloody liar,' I retorted.

'Do you still have the cheque?' Blok asked.

I was sure I did. Being a meticulous person, I knew I would not have thrown it away.

'That cheque can show that Knight *did* meet Ronnie,' Anthony reassured me. 'It will prove he's a liar, and therefore a witness not to be trusted. You must find that cheque, Barbara.'

I raced home. I knew just where the cheque was: in a desk drawer in the office, inside a white envelope along with all the other bounced cheques and IOUs from Ronnie's club. I pulled out the envelope and emptied everything on to the floor. To my horror, the one cheque I needed wasn't there: every other bleeding worthless cheque was, but not the one that mattered. I'd never been in the loft, but I had to now. It was the only other place it could be. I went through everything I could lay my hands on – even photographs of me as a kid I hadn't seen for years – but there was no Gerald Knight cheque.

Beside myself, I went back to the office and started searching through the contents of the envelope again, chucking bits of paper all over the place. Hearing me huffing and puffing, on the edge of hysteria, Mummy came in. 'Calm down, Babs,' she said. 'Don't get yourself in a state.'

'*Sod off and leave me alone!*' I bellowed.

I don't know who was more shocked I'd sworn at her: me or her.

In the middle of all this, Ronnie's brother Jimmy phoned and warned me to prepare myself. 'Ron could get twenty-five years. At least.'

Well, that finished me right off. With my head pounding like it was going to explode, I went through the papers from the envelope yet again, then charged round the house searching every item of clothing – even stuff I'd worn the day before. Finding nothing, I flopped on the floor, exhausted, and would probably have started all over again if Mummy hadn't gently insisted that I left it until the morning when my head would be clearer.

The next morning I got up, went straight to the desk and yanked the drawer right out. And there, stuck at the back of it, was another, smaller, envelope containing the precious cheque. Mummy came running when she heard my screams, not realising they were screams of relief.

I was not allowed to sit in court until I had given my evidence relating to the cheque. Nobody knew I was going to be called as a witness, and Mr Blok did not want to lose the advantage of surprise this gave us. However, my absence from the public gallery was likely to arouse the suspicions of the police. The problem was solved by my commitments: the first day of the trial was also the day of Hattie Jacques' funeral, which I attended with Kenny Williams.

I was still dressed in black when I visited Ronnie in his cell below the Old Bailey at the end of the day's hearing.

'I've been to Hattie's funeral,' I said.

'Really?' Ronnie replied only half listening. 'How was she?'

'Dead.'

For the second and third days I was out of London filming *Worzel Gummidge*. On the Thursday, the day I had to give evidence, a man I'd never seen before came up to me as I arrived at the court and said: 'Do you know your old man's got another woman?' Whether he was a detective trying to turn me against Ronnie or just rattle me I don't know, but whoever he was, he didn't get any joy. I just looked at him and said: 'I hope he's got several.'

My unexpected appearance in the witness box caused a certain amount of confusion, especially since the defence referred to me as Mrs Knight and the prosecution as Miss Windsor. 'Which is she?' asked the rather stroppy judge testily.

'I'm Mrs Knight,' I told him. Ronnie remarked afterwards that he felt this subtle show of support did him some good with the jury.

Giving evidence was far worse than any first night. I heeded the advice of a private detective who had been helping us, and just told the truth, answering yes or no to every question, without commenting further.

Then Gerald Knight went into the witness box to deny ever having met Ronnie. His face was a picture when the defence counsel, Ivor Richards, proudly, and a little smugly, held up the incriminating cheque and dismissed everything Knight had said about Ronnie as worthless.

Once I'd given evidence I made sure I arrived at the court early to be at the head of the queue and get a seat in the front row of the gallery. After a few days the effects of my recent accident began to take their toll and I was relieved when Graham Roberts offered to queue for me. The trial lasted for ten days and, like most major court cases, went this way and that, leaving Ronnie confident one day and in the depths of despair the next. In the end, Gerald Knight's bounced cheque proved crucial. With the prosecution's important witness hugely discredited, Bradshaw's testimony was far less damning and the jury found both Ronnie and Nicholas Gerard not guilty. Ronnie was free.

That night we clung together; we had weathered the storm and not even the dark cloud of this other woman was going to spoil my outlook for the future. Ronnie and I were due some time on the sunny side of the street.

17

I THOUGHT RONNIE WAS TRYING TO KILL ME. We had been out to dinner in Denham and he was driving like a maniac along the country lanes, cornering too fast and narrowly missing oncoming cars. Memories of the crash with Robert flooded back as Ronnie hurtled on, ignoring my pleas to slow down. I was scared out of my wits, and at a loss to understand why a man who had been given his life back only days before seemed hell-bent on destroying it now.

He had been in a strange mood all evening, as though his mind was elsewhere, and now, having drunk too much, he was in a vile temper. When we finally got home he leaped out of the car, ran indoors and went upstairs. I found him in the bedroom, sobbing.

'For God's sake, Ronnie,' I said, putting my arms round him, 'what's the matter?'

'I'm so unhappy, Windsor. Our marriage was nearly gone. I nearly lost you.'

'I know, darling. But you're home now. We'll wipe out everything that's happened.'

'You can make it right. You're my whole life. It's you I want.'

'And it's you *I* want,' I told him, meaning it. 'God's given us another chance. We're meant to be together.'

I was due to leave for Newcastle the next day to start rehearsals for *Jack and the Beanstalk*. 'Tell you what, darling,' I suggested, 'why don't you come up to Newcastle for Christmas? It'll be different. We'll have a great time.'

'What a good idea,' he said. I could hardly believe it. In previous years, I'd always had to travel home for Christmas Day, cook the turkey, then dash back to wherever for the Boxing Day performance. This year, though, Ronnie made the journey north and we had a lovely time. It seemed he had sorted out what was troubling him. But early in the New Year he came home one evening badly beaten up, refuelling my suspicions that he was leading some kind of double life.

Ronnie was always on time for dinner, but that day he was late. When I finally heard him drive into the garage and he didn't appear, I went to see what was keeping him and found him half-conscious in the car, blood all over the place. I got him into the bath, washed him and was helping him into bed when the phone rang. On the other end was a woman, crying for Ronnie. I handed the phone to Ronnie. He had been drinking and could hardly speak. 'No, I'm all right,' was all he said. Then he put the phone down.

Who the hell was this woman? Was she the mysterious blonde who'd been in my bed? Was she just a bit on the side, or something more than that? I needed answers, but now wasn't the time to ask the questions. Obviously Ronnie had upset someone big-time. Was it the woman's husband? I wondered.

A few days later, a BBC TV team arrived at the house to film me and Ronnie for a programme called *Fame*. Ronnie's face was still so swollen that I asked the reporter, John Pitman, if we could postpone it for a week. Ronnie didn't think it would do his reputation much good if he appeared on national television looking as if someone had given him a good hiding. We told Pitman that Ronnie had walked into a glass door, but I don't think he believed us for a moment.

Again, I had to put my fears about Ronnie on hold when Kenny Williams rang to say he was directing Joe Orton's classic black comedy *Entertaining Mr Sloane*, and wanted me to play the frustrated, middle-aged, sex-mad landlady, Kath. Although the thought of being compared with Beryl Reid, who was stunning in the 1969 film version, was daunting, I was very keen. It was a chance not only to work with Kenny as a director, but to play the part in a way Orton himself had envisaged. Joe had been a great friend of Kenny's, and over a drink years before he had told me that it was important people believed Sloane wanted to fuck Kath, and he'd said I'd be perfect for the role when I was in my forties.

I had got to grips with this demanding part and was looking forward to the opening night at Hammersmith's Lyric Theatre when the jinx of Aylmer Drive struck again. I'd put the house back on the market, and Mummy had decided to go and live near her sisters Mae and Ivy in Herne Bay on the Kent coast. I was only relieved she wasn't there.

Returning after a preview performance, I found the house ransacked. We had been burgled. Whoever had done it must have known where to look because the last bit of money I had, and all my jewellery, was missing from a bedroom drawer with a well-concealed false bottom. A diamond heart pendant Sid had given me was gone. So was a bracelet made by Frank Sinatra's jeweller, and an antique necklace from Danny La Rue, as well as lots of wonderful jewellery Ronnie had bought me over the years. I rang the police immediately, of course, but Ronnie came home from the club before they arrived, and when they did he refused to let them in. 'It's only possessions, and we'll get them back,' he kept saying. I couldn't understand his attitude. Neither could I understand why a thief would leave beer cans all over the place, a knife on the piano and a pair of my knickers and worry beads on the bed, or rake over his footprints on the shagpile carpet. It was a very strange robbery indeed, and a mystery I never solved. And none of the stolen jewellery ever turned up.

The bad luck did not end there. Shortly afterwards, I collapsed during a performance of *Sloane* and had to be given oxygen in the wings. I was run down, in need of a holiday, and when *Sloane* finished at the end of April, we flew to Spain, intending to do nothing but soak up some sunshine at the villa. But the moment I stepped off the plane at Malaga Airport, I seized up; I couldn't move my arms or legs or anything. Ronnie helped me through the arrivals lounge and into a car, and we got to the villa, but there, the opposite happened: I couldn't sit still. I felt sick, but I couldn't vomit. A Spanish doctor gave me some vitamin pills, but they didn't help, and that night as I was getting ready for bed, my body sort of disintegrated and just gave up. I stood up and every excretion you can imagine streamed out of me, from my nose, my bladder, my bowels. Poor Ronnie. He stared at me, horrified. 'Bar, what's happening to you?' I only wished I knew.

We didn't have any faith in Spanish hospitals, but we had no choice: I was too ill to fly to England. Eventually, a German doctor who spoke English listened to my account of the events of the previous five months and diagnosed a nervous breakdown. After the trauma of Ronnie's arrest and the anxiety of the trial, my body had simply said enough's enough; it couldn't cope any more. I remembered the medics warning me to rest after my car crash. Was this what they had meant by 'long-term effects'?

I desperately needed to return to England to get myself better. I was due to perform as Marie Lloyd in a gala show in front of Prince Charles in Blackpool, and was contracted to do a summer season of *The Mating Game* there with Jack Smethurst. When I was well enough to travel, Ronnie agreed to bring me home, but then flew straight back to Spain. He had business to see to, he said. He had mentioned nothing to me about any business, and I did wonder what could be that pressing, but I didn't think much more about it until that June, when I gave a press conference in Blackpool to promote *The Mating Game*. Although I had made it clear I would only be talking about the play, not about Ronnie, a *Sun* reporter confronted me afterwards with a sickening question: 'Do you know that your husband is having an affair with a barmaid called Susan Haylock?'

I tried to laugh it off with a joke, but I'm sure I wasn't convincing. The next day, the *Sun*'s front page carried a big picture of Ronnie with a quote from him: 'I do employ a girl called Susan Haylock, she's a barmaid. But Barbara is the only one in my life. I love her.'

Ronnie was on the phone straight away, denying that he was having an affair, and the way I was feeling, I just let it go. I thought he'd come back from Spain, but he didn't. I'd get the odd phone call – he rang on 6 August, for example, to wish me a happy birthday.

'What's so fucking happy about it?' I snapped.

'What's the matter?'

'You should be here with me, convincing me it's not true about Susan Haylock,' I said.

Ronnie promised to fly home and to come to Blackpool to see the show and take me out. I wanted him there, but I was in a real mess. I'd lost more than a stone in weight, I had bags under my eyes and I'd been getting panic attacks; only the day before Ronnie arrived, I'd been too terrified to go on stage. When he saw me he couldn't hide his shock. 'Good God, Barbara, what is *wrong* with you?' he said.

I told him I didn't know, but I did: I had all the symptoms of another nervous breakdown.

Ronnie stayed for a couple of days but then said he had to get back to Spain. I was too weak, too worried about myself and the show, to argue. To make matters worse, my understudy was taken ill as well and it looked as if the show would have to come off unless I went back that night. My doctor gave me two options: I could quit and go home, or he could give me something to get me through the show. 'Only you know how important it is,' he said.

I hate letting people down, so I did the show that night and got through the following three weeks with the doctor's help. But it was the first time my private life had interfered with my work, and I didn't like it.

When *The Mating Game* finished, I decided to go to Spain to sort everything out with Ronnie. I needed to know if we had a future together or not. We had accepted an offer for the Stanmore house, and I'd been offered two first-class air tickets to go to Australia to appear on a prestigious TV chat show in November. It would, I thought, be an ideal opportunity for us to mend the cracks in our marriage.

At Heathrow I decided it would be sensible to invest in some extra medical insurance for my visit to Spain. The woman behind the counter said to me, rather cheekily, 'Who'd have thought *you* would have trouble in your marriage?' I bit my lip. She went on: 'I'll never forget that evening. I was in a club in Ruislip and your husband was there with this blonde. Three blokes didn't like him cheating on you after all you'd done for him in that murder trial. Laid into him, they did.'

So that was what it had all been about that night Ronnie had come home all bashed up. This news made my trip to Spain even more important: if Ronnie was involved with another woman – whether it was Susan Haylock or anyone else – he needed to make his mind up who he wanted to be with, me or her.

He insisted, of course, that I was the only one in his life. But I found it hard to believe he hadn't been with someone else, what with all the time he'd been spending in Spain. I'd also found a bikini that didn't belong to me at the villa. We were back to being two polite, distant people who happened to live together and share the odd conversation. If I doubted that, I got the message when I asked Ronnie about the Australia trip. 'No, Bar, I don't fancy that,' he said. 'Why don't you take Robert Dunn?'

Robert and I had made it up since the car accident, so I took up Ronnie's suggestion. But within the first three days of arriving in Sydney, all the tension of the past eleven months, all the worry about my marriage and health, caught up with me and I started taking it out on Robert. He was no shrinking violet himself when pushed, and we were having one barney after another before I even set foot in the TV studio. We had a big row while Robert was driving over Sydney's famous Harbour Bridge. I was really laying into him, screeching into his face and telling him what a bastard he'd been. I have a good right hook and I swung it: he thumped me back and I gave him another one. Before long we were having a right old ding-dong. The car was swerving all over the place, and in the scuffle, Robert accidentally caught me with a ring, splitting my face open. Of course, that made me bellow and lash out all the more. How we didn't career off the road into the sea or get arrested for dangerous driving, I don't know.

When we got back to the Seaboard Towers Hotel, Robert stormed up to our room and started throwing his clothes into a suitcase. 'I'm off,' he said. 'No, you're not,' I retorted, and started taking his things out. 'I've had it, I'm off,' he insisted, and started packing again. And so it went on: I kept unpacking as he packed. If it hadn't been so awful, it would have been funny, a bit like the last scene in *Fings Ain't Wot They Used T'Be*.

We had a big function to go to that night, but by the time we'd finished yelling at each other we were too exhausted and had to cry off with an excuse. We ended up saying sorry to each other and making up in the best way possible – in bed.

I was looking forward to the TV show, hosted by Mike Walsh, but a little worried about explaining the cut on my face and the bruises on my arms, from where Robert had grabbed me. I was given the perfect answer, however, when I came out of the hotel into a downpour and slipped on the marble steps. I got a terrific ovation from the studio audience. I had had no idea how popular I was down under, or how much interest there was in my private life. Danny La Rue was also on the show and we had a lot of fun doing a couple of Marie Lloyd numbers, accompanied by the popular Aussie pianist Wayne King. So in the end, in spite of the dodgy start, the week was a great success and Robert and I were back on an even keel when we left for Los Angeles on the first leg of our trip home.

In fact, in LA he made me feel he really did care for me. We were walking along the legendary Rodeo Drive in Beverly Hills, fascinated by the ludicrously over-priced goods in the shop windows, when a passerby stopped, stared at me and said in a loud voice to her companion: 'My, doesn't she look like Dolly Parton?'

Robert rounded on them. 'Dolly Parton? I'll have you know this is Barbara Windsor, one of Britain's most famous stars.' And he went into one, implying that I was far lovelier and more talented than Dolly. I thought that was sweet and it made me feel terrific. I had been feeling so down, what with one thing and another, and Robert boosted me at just the right time.

I'd always wanted to stay at the Beverly Wilshire – the initials BW, see – and we checked in there under our own names in separate suites. We planned to stay a day or two in LA and then fly to Las Vegas to spend some time with Liberace, who I'd met in London. The night before we were due to leave for Vegas, I phoned Ronnie. He was unpleasantly offhand.

'What's the matter?' I asked.

'Your mother's been taken to hospital,' he said. 'If you care so much, you'd better get home, hadn't you?'

'What's wrong with her?'

'I don't know. She's very ill, that's all,' said Ronnie. And then he just put the phone down.

I looked at Robert, my eyes full.

'Every time you come off the phone with that man, you're in tears,' he said wearily. 'He shouldn't do this to you.' I explained what Ronnie had told me. 'I think we should go home,' he said.

We took the earliest flight to England we could get the next day. I'd rung Ronnie with the details, not expecting for a minute that he'd be there to meet us, but there he was. He immediately took my arm, and Robert was left standing there. The next day a picture of Ronnie and me leaving the airport appeared in a newspaper with the caption: 'Barbara Windsor and her husband, Ronnie Knight, return from Australia.'

I knew Mummy would want to be visited by Barbara Windsor, film star, not Barbara Deeks, so I dolled myself up in a really nice suede outfit to see her in hospital, just as if it was a personal appearance. I also knew that I would not be able to handle her finding fault with me. Since Len had gone, she had slipped into her old ways and little I did pleased her. When I'd taken her for a little break at the villa, I was thrilled to be able to spoil her, but as soon as we got home, she told me curtly that she would never visit Spain with me again because she was ashamed of me for having worn the same bikini all week. When she stayed overnight with us in Stanmore I upset her by standing on the doorstep chatting to the milkman in my dressing gown. At every opportunity, it seemed, she would find something to criticise, and if I reacted, she would immediately tell Ronnie she didn't know how he put up with me.

Driving to the Kent and Sussex Hospital in Canterbury, I put all the bad things out of my mind. I was determined just to do what was right for Mummy. When I arrived, the ward sister made a point of telling me that Mummy had been saying: 'My daughter's coming today. Everything will be fine once Babs is here, you'll see.' That's a good sign, I thought.

The first thing Mummy did was to turn to the other patients and say: 'Look at my daughter. Everyone who sees her on telly thinks she isn't pretty, but she is in real life.' Then she asked me to speak to a woman in another bed and I did all the usual 'Hello, darling. How are you? Everything all right?' It was a bit daft saying that to someone who was in hospital, but there you go.

When we were on our own, Mummy said, a little proudly, 'You look a proper film star.'

I smiled, so glad I'd made the effort to please her. 'Now, come on, Mummy, what's wrong with you?'

'I don't know.'

'Are you in pain?' I asked.

'No,' she said. 'I just don't feel well. And my legs ache and my ankles have all swelled up.'

The doctors hadn't yet done any intensive tests; they were going to do them later in the week. Since there was nothing to discuss on the question of her condition, we just chit-chatted about this and that and when I left, I promised to visit her with Ronnie at the weekend. On the Friday evening, around 6 p.m. my Uncle Ronnie rang to say that he and my cousin Roy were on their way home from visiting Mummy and wanted to pop in to see me. They arrived looking sad. 'We've got some bad news about your mum,' Roy said. 'Some really bad news.'

'What?'

'They say she may have only ten days, Bar,' Roy told me.

I stared at them, not believing what he had said. Aching legs and swollen ankles and now ten days left? It didn't seem possible.

'What is it?'

'Cancer, Bar,' said Roy.

'Cancer? Where?'

'All over.'

Instantly I thought of the pain that had crucified Len so heartbreakingly that you were begging God to take him away.

'I don't want her to suffer,' I said. 'That's all I want. Not like Len.'

Ronnie and Roy offered to stay with me, but I told them not to worry, I'd be OK.

'Can you get hold of Ronnie?' Roy asked.

'Yeah, I'll ring him at the club.'

They said they would wait while I phoned him.

'I've got some terrible news, Ronnie,' I told him. 'Mummy is dreadfully ill. She may have only ten days.'

Silence.

'I need you, Ronnie. Can you come home? Please?'

'What do you want me there for?'

I wasn't sure what to say to that. What *was* there to say?

'Well,' I said, 'I could do with you here. I just need you.'

'Oh, you'll be all right, I'll be home later.'

Now I had to put on an act. I didn't want Uncle Ronnie and Roy to know his reaction.

'Yeah, OK,' I said. 'Fine, all right then. Good.'

When I hung up, Uncle Ronnie asked if he was coming.

'Yep. He's going to get straight in the car and come home.'

'Good,' they said. When they left, promising to be in touch over the weekend, I rang Anna and my cousin Kenny and unloaded myself: I needed people to talk to.

When Ronnie rolled in at four or five in the morning, I pretended to be asleep: I didn't want to know what he'd been doing that was more important than being with me.

What I didn't need was extra worry, but I got it: the sale of our house in Stanmore was about to complete and we would have to move into temporary accommodation until we found a house we wanted to buy. So, in between hospital visits the following week, I chased around looking at properties. Ronnie didn't fancy any of them until we viewed one in Edgware. I thought it was awful, cold and damp, but Ronnie persuaded me it would do.

I had not given any thought to the possibility of Mummy spending her last days with me until she told me she knew how serious her condition was. The next time I went to the hospital, I asked her: 'Would you like to come and stay with me? I'll turn the study into a nice bedroom for you.' It was the first time, I think, she didn't question anything I suggested. She just said: 'Yes, Babs. Oh, I'd love that.'

Ronnie drove me to Canterbury to pick her up, and on the way home, I looked at her sleeping in the back with the sun on her, and her face was soft and peaceful, with the hint of a smile. 'I wish she could go now,' I said to Ronnie.

Mummy stayed with me a week. It was a lovely week, actually; I felt I got very close to her. We didn't mention her illness, just chatted about life in general and what had happened to both of us, and, for the first time, it seemed, she talked to me without a trace of the usual criticism in her voice. Don't forget, eat three meals a day, and cream your face every night, she'd say, and there was none of that toughness I'd come to expect. 'You won't cry, Babs, will you?' she said one day, squeezing my hand.

'Cry?' I said. 'Cry over you? I should cocoa. You're going to get better and drive me mental again, just like always.'

But we both knew it wasn't going to happen.

Her condition worsened and I knew she was slipping away. It was a Friday night and Ronnie was out. Mummy was sleeping peacefully, but at the thought of her dying, I panicked. I'd never seen anyone dead, and this was my mother. I phoned Ronnie at the club. 'Please come home, Ronnie,' I pleaded. 'You must come home. Something could happen tonight.'

'You'll be all right,' he said.

'Ronnie, I need you here,' I begged him tearfully.

'I'll be home as soon as possible.'

Lying in bed, I was worried that Ronnie might wake Mummy by opening the garage door, so I got out of bed and went down and opened it myself. I went back to bed, but then I worried about burglars, so I went down and closed it again. I kept going in and out of Mummy's room to make sure she was still breathing, fretting all the time that she might wake up and realise that we were alone in the house. I didn't want her to think badly of Ronnie for staying out.

Ronnie finally got in at 6.30 a.m. He fell in the door, reeking of alcohol.

'You're a lousy shit,' I told him. 'Mummy could have died tonight.'

'Well, she didn't, did she?' he said. And he staggered off to bed.

Two days later Mummy got so bad she had to go back into hospital. The previous night, she asked me to wash her hair for her – something she'd never asked me to do before. As I rolled and set her hair afterwards I thought of all the times she had done this for me when I was a young girl and reflected on the poignancy of this reversal of the mother and daughter roles. The next day I went with her in the ambulance while Ronnie followed behind. 'He used to be such a good boy,' she said. 'What's happened to him?'

Anxious to defend him, as usual, I replied: 'It's six of one, half a dozen of the other, Mummy. You know what I'm like.'

'No, Babs,' she said. 'I don't think it's your doing.'

As I was about to leave the hospital, she said: 'Oh, by the way, there's a box.'

'What do you mean, a box?'

'It's just some things. You've got to make sure the house insurance is kept up and the rates paid.'

I didn't understand what she was talking about.

Five days later I was with Mummy at the hospital when she fell into a coma. She never came round. There was a huge bunch of red roses by the bed, but only one was alive. I took it and placed it in her hair. I wish I'd told her I loved her, I thought. And heard her say she loved me.

I found the box she was talking about and, of course, it was a kind of will. She had left me all the little things she had saved over the years: all her jewellery, even the first record I'd made in a record shop for nineteen shillings, which I'd loved and she'd hated. There was a letter, too. It was addressed to 'my darling Babs, who has been the most wonderful daughter and who I am so very proud of.' And then I realised that she did think a lot of me after all, and that, in her own way, she had loved me, even though she never showed it.

18

Although Mummy's death, in November 1981, affected me deeply, I had no time to allow myself to grieve properly. I was appearing in *Aladdin* in Nottingham and the show had to go on, even on the day of her funeral – that night I went out on the stage as usual. In fact it wasn't until 1983, when I was interviewed by Bel Mooney for a TV programme called *Mothers By Daughters*, and allowed the cameras to film the tears pouring down my cheeks as I talked about Mummy, that I truly began to face my feelings of bereavement.

That production of *Aladdin*, with the ventriloquist Keith Harris and his duck puppet Orville, and Billy Dainty, made the *Guinness Book of Records* that year as the longest-running out-of-town panto. While I was in Nottingham I became so suspicious of Ronnie that I have to admit I hired a private detective. I needed to find out, once and for all, what he was up to. At the end of 1981 I was about to go on stage when the detective phoned the theatre. 'Your husband has been to a woman's flat in Edgware four times in one week,' he said. 'The woman's name is Susan Haylock.'

So it *was* Susan Haylock. And now I knew why he had been so keen to rent the house in Edgware. I felt sick and dizzy and not at all like performing in panto, but, remembering the advice Dickie Henderson had given me after Ronnie was arrested, I took a deep breath, composed myself and ran on, smiling. 'Hello, everybody. My name's Aladdin.'

The following weekend, I asked Ronnie directly if he was having an affair. 'Don't be daft,' he said. 'After all you've done for me? You're my life!' At a loss as to what to do, I decided to throw myself into work and let the relationship burn itself out. But then, one Bank Holiday Monday morning a few months later, Ronnie made a mistake that enabled me to catch him out. I was at home, watching Marlon Brando in the 1957 film *Sayonara*, when Ronnie walked into the lounge, all suited and booted, and announced that he was off to a club. It struck me that 10.30 in the morning was an odd time to be going to a club, and even odder that any club would be open on a Bank Holiday. After he left, I threw on the first clothes that came to hand and called a taxi to take me to the Edgware address the detective agency had given me. To my relief, I couldn't see Ronnie's red Honda outside the block of flats where Susan Haylock lived. But when the taxi reversed down the side of the building to take me home, I spotted it in the courtyard. Asking the cab driver to wait while I viewed a flat that was for sale, I rushed round to the entrance.

One of the residents came along and let me into the lobby. I was about to knock at the first flat I came to and ask where Susan Haylock lived when, conveniently, a door further along the corridor opened and the lady herself, accompanied by my old man, an elderly woman and a child, emerged. Ronnie's face was a picture when he saw me, but he thought on his feet. 'This is Tommy Haylock's missus, Barbara,' he said. 'I'm doing her a favour.'

I bet you are, I thought. 'Yeah? Don't bloody lie to me,' I said, and then I lunged at Ronnie, belted him one, and started screeching at him, telling him what I was going to do to him.

When we got outside, Susan Haylock ran off towards a black Mini parked in the courtyard beside Ronnie's Honda. I ran after her, grabbed her hair and wrestled her to the ground. I wanted to give her a smack, not only for having an affair with my old man, but also for not having done anything to help him the night he was beaten up in Ruislip.

Ronnie pulled us apart and I told him to get in the car. He paid off my taxi driver, who now had a story to tell his mates, and Susan Haylock drove off with the other woman and the child.

I demanded that Ronnie drove to his brother Jimmy's house, where I yelled at Jimmy: 'Look at your arsehole of a brother. I've just caught him red-handed with another woman. I hate him.'

'She's just a friend,' Ronnie protested, but Jimmy wasn't having any of it. He looked at Ronnie with contempt and said: 'After all Bar's been through for you? You're a silly bugger, Ronnie. You really are.'

When we got home I glared at Ronnie with all the hatred I could muster. 'That's it. I want you out.'

'It's not what you think, Windsor,' he began. 'She's only—'

But I didn't want to hear. I charged upstairs and pulled all his suits, shirts, ties and socks out of the wardrobe and drawers. Then, remembering what Daddy had done during his rows with Mummy, I opened a window and chucked them all out.

'Now, fuck off,' I said.

Every night for a week, Ronnie phoned me denying he was involved with Susan Haylock and begged to be allowed to come home. Then the phone calls stopped, so abruptly that I began to fear he might have upset someone and been bumped off. I made inquiries, but no one seemed to know anything. Beside myself with worry, I started taking Valium and for days I became a kind of zombie, neglecting to wash or comb my hair, hardly eating, just sitting in an armchair for hours on end, not wanting to speak to anyone. And then Ronnie phoned – from Spain. 'I hear you've been wanting to speak to me.'

'Why haven't you been in touch?'

'You didn't want me to, did you?' he said. 'Anyway, I've run out of clothes and I'm coming home to get the rest.'

When he turned up, he came over to me and put his arms round me and tried to kiss me. I threw the phone at him.

'What's wrong, Windsor?' he wailed. 'What's got into you?'

I was just too ill, too weak, to fight with him and when he asked again if he could move back in, I found myself giving in. I was feeling so miserable and unwanted that anything was better than being on my own, I suppose. I started getting terrible stomach pains and feared I had cancer. Ronnie took me to hospital for tests and he was so supportive and caring that it was hard to hate him. Over the next month or so he seemed a different person, and when he suggested that we bought a penthouse flat at Hendon Hall Court, where we had begun our married life and had been at our happiest, I began to think that the affair must have burned itself out as I'd hoped it would. So we did buy a flat, and when he said to me, his eyes full, 'This is what I want – just me and my Bar,' I was convinced that it was.

I embarked on a six-month tour of *The Mating Game* with Norman Vaughan and Peggy Mount while Ronnie went off to Spain to make improvements to the villa. He had been spending more and more time there for a couple of years, and was now keen to turn it into more of a home than a holiday retreat. That made me wonder whether perhaps all was not as rosy between us as it appeared. But we spoke regularly on the phone and when I collapsed with 'nervous panic' at the Yvonne Arnaud

Theatre in Guildford in November 1982, Ronnie flew to England and took me back to Spain to recuperate.

Early in 1983, however, after I finished playing Aladdin again, this time with Keith Harris in Oxford, I had a sense that I was being watched. If I went to the chemist or to my favourite boutique, I'd see this blonde woman I recognised looking at me. Once she drove past Hendon Hall Court in her Mini as I was driven in. I thought perhaps I was imagining it all until she appeared at my health club. Then I was able to check the visitors' book and confirm that the mystery blonde was indeed Susan Haylock. I realised that Ronnie's affair with her was far from over, and that the cosy home in Spain he was putting so much into was not for us, but for them.

Yet amazingly, Ronnie and I staggered on, and I went to the villa again to relax before opening in *The Mating Game* – again. By this stage I was so nervous and lacking in confidence that I could handle only scripts I knew backwards. But I was not comfortable at the villa and returned home early, knowing that it was probably the last time I'd go there.

Ronnie did visit me one weekend in Scarborough, the first venue for *The Mating Game*, and strangely, we had a nice time together, playing crazy golf, chatting and generally getting on well. I think it was because by now we both knew that it was all over, and so the pressure was off. He still wouldn't admit to the affair, and there was no definite moment when we split for good, but the relationship had just run its course and finally ground to a halt.

It might not sound like it, but we did have some fun together, Ronnie and I, and we laughed a lot. I remember the first time we took the dogs to Hampstead Heath for a picnic, for example. It poured down just as we had got the wine and all the food laid out on the tablecloth. We should have wrapped everything up again and taken shelter, but we were determined to see it through and just sat there as though it were a beautiful summer's day. Peter Cook, who lived nearby, spotted us as he hurried home across the heath. He gave us an odd look. 'Barbara, what on earth are you doing?' he asked me. But Ronnie and I just laughed.

It was in Scarborough that I would fall in love with a man who would change my life completely. His name was Stephen Hollings and he reminded me of Ronnie's youngest brother, David, who had been so tragically murdered. He was tall, slim, very handsome and immaculately dressed and groomed. He was also young – more than twenty years younger than me.

I was feeling sad and old and unattractive and unwanted, forced to accept that my husband of nineteen years had found another blonde more desirable than me. Although I was not aware of it, that summer in Scarborough I was ripe for the attention and adoration of a vibrant young man who was going places. And Stephen Hollings, the highly respected manager of the Corner, a thriving leisure centre in Scarborough, and a qualified chef, fitted the bill down to the tip of his highly polished shoes. He asked to meet me at one of the parties to promote *The Mating Game*, in which I was appearing with Kathy Staff and, once again, the lovely Jack Smethurst, and I liked him on sight. When I met Stephen again, at another do, at the Grand Hotel, a few days later, I realised that, despite the huge age gap, I fancied him, too. With typical Windsor exuberance, I took him back to the flat I was sharing with Carol Ann Darrock, another actress in the show, where we enjoyed a thrilling encounter that helped to change my whole outlook on life.

The next morning, I dashed to the Corner like an excited schoolgirl. 'I don't know what I'm doing here,' I gushed to an embarrassed Stephen. 'I just had to see you again.' It was the start of a brief, passionate affair that came to an abrupt end when I discovered that he had a steady girlfriend and was due to marry her in August. When I confronted him, however, I was astonished by his reaction. 'I don't feel I should be getting married, feeling as I do about you,' he said. At that point, few people, let alone Stephen's parents, knew of our relationship. But he was going to tell them, he said. And he was going to come clean to his girlfriend, a local waitress named Lorraine Nicklin, and tell her the wedding was off.

Unfortunately, someone tipped off the *Sun* newspaper about our affair before he had a chance to tell anyone. After a photograph of Stephen and I appeared on the front page, all hell broke loose: reporters and photographers from the *Sun* – and from rival tabloids eager to catch up with the story – descended on Scarborough, ravenous for any tittle-tattle about this local kid's love affair with a well-known star. Poor Stephen didn't know what had hit him. 'I had no idea you were that famous,' he said. The journalists besieged the Corner. They found out where Stephen's parents lived and wanted to know what they thought. And they got hold of Lorraine's address and pestered her for the story of her heartbreak at being jilted for an older woman. Scarborough, and those poor innocent parties, had probably never seen anything like it and I felt responsible. I decided I had to be mature and think of others, not myself, so I told Stephen that although I was very fond of him, I was going home to London to give him time to sort himself out.

If he still felt the same way about me in, say, a month or two, then he knew where to reach me. If he didn't, no problem: we would consider it a short, if memorable, fling that was not destined to go any further.

Brave words, but in my heart, I felt I genuinely loved Stephen, and as I left him that September, my tears said it all: I hoped and prayed I would hear from him again.

Well, I didn't. Not for three months, anyway. Then, to my delight, he rang me during my first week as Aladdin at Chichester, where I was working with Christopher Timothy and Aubrey Woods, saying he wanted to see me. I arranged a ticket for the panto and told him to come backstage afterwards and we'd go out to dinner. I was wonderfully on edge, really looking forward to seeing his lovely smile again. But he didn't turn up. He didn't phone or write to say why, and although I sent him a Christmas card, I didn't get one back. It knocked me for six. Once again I felt unloved, unwanted and totally at a loss to understand what was happening to me. I could not wait for the year to end and promised myself that 1984 would be a better one. Mark Furness, who had produced *The Mating Game* in Scarborough, had booked me for a three-month tour of a lovely old play, *Rattle of a Simple Man*, and that would sort me out. Performing something I enjoy usually does.

With Ronnie now out of my life, I sold the penthouse flat in Hendon and bought a four-bedroomed townhouse in Swiss Cottage. I'd asked him for a divorce but he didn't seem to want that. 'We don't have to, you know,' he said. I was pleased when Ronnie rang one Saturday in January, asking if he could pop over, because I loved the house with a passion and wanted him to see it. He arrived with a king-size hangover from celebrating his birthday the night before, but he was very sweet and kind to me. He thought the house was lovely and I got the impression he was feeling a twinge of regret; that he would have liked to have been back with me and living there. Although I was suffering from a heavy cold I had a personal appearance lined up for the next day. 'Don't work too hard,' he said before he left. 'Please don't do that PA tomorrow. You don't look well.'

I was surprised when he rang again the next morning. 'Bar, don't do that PA,' he said again. 'You look tired.'

But I did go off to Brighton to do it, and when I got back that night, the person looking after my dog said that Ronnie had called and had said he would ring again later. When he did he told me he was back in Spain. 'The Old Bill are after me,' he said. 'They've picked up Johnny and Jimmy for the Security Express job, and they want me an' all.'

I knew about the Security Express robbery. It had taken place in Shoreditch, near where I was born. Over Easter the previous year, a gang of six men wielding shotguns had terrified the life out of one of the company's employees by pouring petrol over him and threatening to set him alight unless he opened the strong rooms. They had got away with more than £6 million in cash. I didn't believe for a second that Ronnie – or his brothers, come to that – could possibly have been involved in such a ruthless operation.

Ronnie had got out of the country by the skin of his teeth.

Rattle of a Simple Man is a bit of a sixties classic, a play about a shy football fan who spends the eve of the Cup Final with a prostitute for a bet. The tart was a role I'd always wanted to play. I'd seen Sheila Hancock do it on stage and Diane Cilento in the movie, and for me, it would be a piece of cake. Or so I thought until I started to learn the script. It's not that it was difficult: I just couldn't take it in. Every time I looked at a line it would go all funny and make no sense. It was as if, having always read a lot and been a quick learner, I had developed dyslexia overnight. I sat up in the early hours trying to get to grips with it, but the more I read it, the worse the problem became, and with rehearsals due to start in February, I got in a right two and eight. I was literally sick with anxiety, fearing not only that I couldn't do the play, but that I wouldn't have the confidence to perform on stage ever again. I needed a total break, a change of environment. When the BBC disc jockey David Hamilton enthused about Cedar Falls, a health club in Somerset, I decided to give it a go.

The place was ideal, lovely and relaxing, and within no time I was looking and feeling great. But the script still seemed like Double Dutch: hardly a line was sinking in. I began to panic. I had to make a decision: should I press on in the hope that whatever was going on in my head would clear? Or should I come clean to Mark Furness? In the end I told Mark, who, bless his heart, was kind and understanding: he let me off the hook and authorised a press release announcing that, due to a viral infection, Barbara Windsor had had to pull out of the play and Dilys Watling was taking over. Well, I could hardly admit, after thirty-three years in the business, that I couldn't learn a script, could I?

'I owe you one, Mark,' I said gratefully.

'You owe me one,' he confirmed, meaning it.

It was clear that the emotional turmoil I was going through was threatening not only my private life but my career as well. I was gutted that Ronnie had gone and wounded by Stephen's indifference. I'd always thought Ronnie would be unable to survive without me, and that was evidently not the case. He still wasn't admitting that he had fallen for Susan Haylock, but it was obvious he had. And the fact that she was probably dishing out endless helpings of sex and sangria in a villa I had helped to pay for didn't do much for my self-esteem, either.

With Stephen, it was different, of course. He didn't need me in the way I'd always believed Ronnie did, but I'd seen enough during our brief affair to suggest that, if we did get together, he would care for me in a way Ronnie never had. I'd believed the attraction between us was so strong that he would want to be with me when he had sorted himself out, and his phone call had raised my hopes sky-high. The cruel silence that had dashed them had hurt me deeply. Stephen, I felt in my heart, was someone who could provide that warm, safe, cosy feeling of being truly wanted that I craved. Whether I'd fallen for him on the rebound from Ronnie's humiliating knock-back, I didn't know; only time would tell.

What was certain was that, in early 1984, I was a shadow of the Barbara Windsor the public knew. I weighed only six stone. Friends encouraged me to go out with them, but I rarely did. Christopher Biggins introduced me to a couple of guys, convinced that sex was what I was missing, but I didn't click with either of them. I didn't seem to know who I was any more. In a moment of extreme desolation, I wrote a long letter to my father. I hadn't seen him for nearly twenty years, but I was sure he would respond to my cry for help and offer the comfort and kindness I wanted.

'Barbara?' said a strident voice when I answered the phone a few days later. 'It's Julie here. Your father's wife. What do you want?'

'I'd like to speak to Daddy, please,' I said.

After a few seconds, my dad was on the line. 'What do you want?' His harsh tone shocked me as much as Julie's had.

'I just wanted to talk to you. I thought we might—'

I didn't get to finish the sentence. He had already launched into an attack, shouting and screaming like he had in those rows with Mummy. I listened for a while, then tried to break in and say my own piece, but it was no good. He wasn't listening.

Tears streaming down my face, I put the receiver down gently. He hadn't been there for me as a child or a young woman. Why had I thought he would be there for me now?

Each night, as I went to bed, I would see this pathetic little face reflected back in my mirror. I felt so unloved, so unattractive, at such a pitch of exhaustion that one night I prayed: 'Please God, if you really care about me, don't let me wake up.' Fortunately, He was busy that night.

I was finally jolted out of my self-pity as a result of a call from a dear friend, Davy Kaye, a diminutive comedian and actor I'd worked with on *Crooks in Cloisters*. I respected him not only as a performer, but for the charity work he did for the Water Rats, the showbiz charity organisation, and for the Variety Club. He wanted me to help the Water Rats raise money for an old folks' home, but for once I was saying no. 'I'm sorry, darling, but I couldn't face anything at the moment,' I said.

'Blimey, you *are* feeling sorry for yourself,' Davy said. 'What's the matter?'

I spared him the miserable details, just said that things weren't too good; that I hadn't been out in ages and didn't want to. And then I started crying, which, of course, prompted Davy to be kind and sympathetic and to say all the things I wanted to hear. Naturally, that made me feel a lot better and I ended up agreeing to help him. But in the end it was Davy who helped me rather than the other way round; Davy, that is, and the underprivileged and disabled people I met through him. 'How dare you sit at home feeling sorry for yourself when others are far worse off,' I said to myself. 'Count your blessings.' I took stock of my life, of who I was, and what I'd achieved. I reminded myself that I'd always been a grafter, not a whinger; always got out there and done it when the chips were down. I put everything into perspective and soon I was feeling much more positive. All I needed, I felt, was a kick start: something or someone to come along and give me the confidence to get off my backside and back to work. I got it, and in the form of the most unexpected, though welcome person.

In March Stephen Hollings called me, right out of the blue. He immediately apologised for his behaviour before Christmas. The media attention had freaked him out, he said, and he'd spent most evenings during the intervening six months getting smashed to blot it all out. He had even been away to Ibiza to try to forget me, which proved no more successful: no sooner had he arrived than he had been approached by a man in a restaurant with the words: 'May I shake the hand that has touched Barbara Windsor's bosoms?'

He had returned feeling certain that he wanted to see me. We arranged

▲ *The poster for* Fings. *My name isn't mentioned but my picture was everywhere!*

▼ *The opening night of* Come Spy With Me: *backstage at the Whitehall Theatre with Rudolph Nureyev, Noël Coward, Danny La Rue and Peter Charlesworth.*

◀ A series of posters advertising my first big film, Sparrows Can't Sing.

▶ With director Joan Littlewood, who insisted that I play the wife Jimmy Booth comes home to in Sparrows.

◀ Renewing my acquaintance with Lord Snowdon at the première of Sparrows.

▲ The Rag Trade *was based on the
dress-making factory where my mother
worked. The line-up: Miriam Karlin,
Esma Cannon, Rita Smythe,
Toni Palmer, Peter Jones, Reg Varney,
me, Ann Beach, Judy Carne and
Sheila Hancock.*

▶ *'Me Tarzan, you Jane': Cliff Richard
as you've probably never seen him
before!*

MSI

◀ *In the USA: Shepard Coleman, musical director of the Broadway production of* Oh What a Lovely War.

▼ *In South Africa: with the dancers and musicians on tour with my show,* A Merry Whiff of Windsor, *in 1975.*

◀ *Backstage with Lionel Bart during the production of* Twang! *in 1965.*

▶ *Publicity for* Sing a Rude Song: *being helped from my carriage by my co-star, Bee Gee Maurice Gibb, outside the Garrick Theatre.*

I was a huge hit with the Calamity Jane fan club: Norman Vaughan poses with me outside the New Theatre, Cardiff.

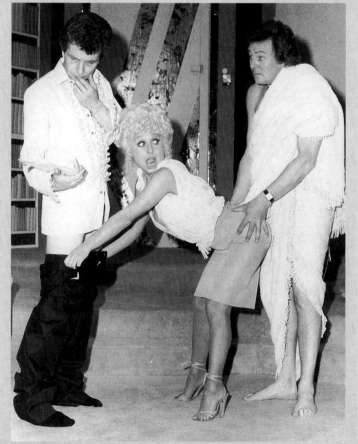

◀ Performing in The Mating Game at Blackpool in 1981 with Peter Denyer (left) and Trevor Bannister. Believe it or not, I was having a nervous breakdown at the time.

▲ *Playing Maria in Keith Michell's production of* Twelfth Night *at the Chichester Festival in 1976, with Andrew Sachs (left) and Bill Fraser.*

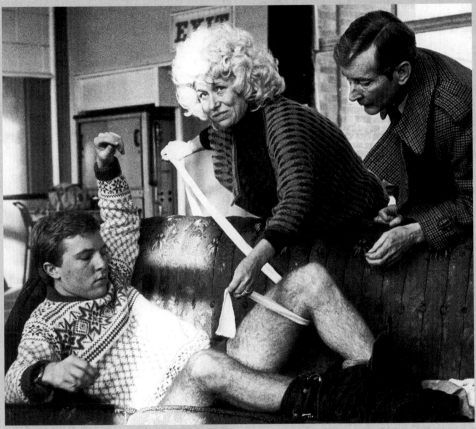

RAY ABBOTT

▲ *Rehearsals for* Entertaining Mr Sloane, *with Kenny Williams and Glyn Grimstead, who played the title role.*

MSI

◄ *With Joe Melia and Vanessa Redgrave in the* Threepenny Opera.

to have dinner the following Saturday, and for Stephen to say he was my hairdresser if anyone was rude enough to ask questions.

I was waiting for him at the barrier at King's Cross Station, but he walked straight past me. I knew he'd seen me, so I ran after him, yelling: 'What are you playing at?'

'Sssh,' he said, looking around furtively. 'The press might be here.'

I had to smile: Stephen was originally from the small Yorkshire town of Malton, and understandably naïve about how things worked in the big city.

We went to Peter's, a quiet, cosy French restaurant in Swiss Cottage, and picked up where we had left off in Scarborough. Stephen was very honest: his parents and friends had wanted him to marry Lorraine. They saw no sense in him getting involved with a showbiz star almost twice his age who was probably going to dump him when the novelty wore off. I was unlikely to bear him children, whereas there was every prospect that Lorraine would be a loyal wife and mother.

Looking at Stephen over that table, I felt that he was the man I wanted to spend my life with. It was going to be up to me to convince his parents that, despite the obvious difficulties, I would be good for him. If I had any subconscious worries or fears that my infatuation was more to do with Ronnie's rejection than Stephen's appeal, they were not evident that night – especially when, as we got up to leave, Stephen handed me a red rose from one of the tables and then swept me off my feet, declaring: 'I love you.'

'You idiot,' I yelled, as intoxicated by romance as by alcohol.

'I don't care,' said Stephen, looking round and smiling at everyone. 'I want the whole world to know I love you.'

With Stephen back in my life, my confidence and self-esteem soared, and it was with great joy that I accepted Mark Furness's offer of a four-month summer season of *The Mating Game* in Jersey with my mate Trevor Bannister. Stephen would be able to come with me, and such a long time on a romantic island with someone I loved sounded idyllic: an ideal trial, I felt, for the marriage both Stephen and I were sure would follow.

With that in mind, I phoned Ronnie at the villa. 'I'm coming over with the divorce papers I want you to sign.'

I arranged to stay with friends who lived a couple of miles away from our villa, and Ronnie turned up there, hot and sweaty, in an old tracksuit and in need of a shave. It was completely unlike him to look so scruffy. I could only assume that Susan didn't know I was in the country and that he had nipped out on the pretext of going to the shops or something.

I took out the divorce papers and put them on the table. 'You don't really want me to sign these, do you?' said Ronnie.

'Of course not,' I joked. 'I just used them as an excuse to get a bit of sun.'

'Seriously, Bar, you don't want a divorce, do you?'

'Yes, Ronnie, I do.'

'But why?'

I couldn't believe we were sitting there having such a ridiculous conversation, when I'd come all the way from England to bring him the papers to sign. 'Because I've found someone else. And you've found someone else. And we're living miles apart, out of each other's lives.'

'I haven't met anyone. I haven't,' he kept saying.

I had no idea why he was still denying that he was having a relationship with Susan, but I knew why he didn't want a divorce: he was afraid that if he was extradited and charged over the Security Express business, I might testify against him. While I was still his wife, I wouldn't be allowed to do so. He wasn't going to bring it up, so I did: 'If you're worried about me giving evidence against you, forget it. I'd never do that. Anyway, I don't know anything about what's gone on.' It was true. I had no idea what Ronnie got up to when I wasn't around, any more than he had about what I was doing when I was away. I must have hit the nail on the head, because he then happily signed the papers.

That done, he stood up. 'Well, I must be off. I've got a long journey.'

'Oh, where are you off to?' I asked. 'I thought you'd come from the villa.'

'No, I've rented the villa out. I'm staying with some friends in Estepona.'

It was the first I'd heard of him letting the villa. The next day, I asked my friend Gina to drive me round there. I didn't want to disturb anyone; I just wanted to have a look at the changes Ronnie had made. We got a shock. The place was empty: gates padlocked, windows shuttered. We looked at each other in disbelief, not knowing what to make of it. Ronnie had lied when he'd insisted Susan wasn't living there. He had lied about letting the villa out. And he had probably lied to Susan as well. Who knows, he might well have told her that I wouldn't give him a divorce, and then had to get her out of the way in case she and I bumped into each other and I told her the truth. Why Ronnie didn't just admit what he must have suspected I knew already is beyond me. Well, it isn't actually. I know the reason and so does he: he's weak. He may be handy with his fists and well able to have a row, as they say in the East End, but when it comes to telling the truth and owning up when his deceit has hurt those he has professed to love, he is a coward. He was a coward with his first wife. He was a coward with me. And he would probably turn out to be a coward with Susan Haylock as well.

Anyway, having got what I'd come for, I cut short my holiday and flew home, consumed with an overwhelming sense of relief that Ronnie Knight was out of my life at last. When I arrived in London, I phoned Stephen with the good news. He had already given in his notice at the Corner, and within a week he had sold his bungalow and his car and was on my doorstep in Belsize Avenue with all his bits and pieces.

A new, far happier, era was dawning.

19

APART FROM THEIR LOVELY SMILES, RONNIE AND STEPHEN WERE LIKE CHALK AND CHEESE. Ronnie often forgot birthdays and anniversaries, but Stephen always made a note of important dates and got a buzz out of springing elaborate surprises. I got an early indication of this lovely side of his nature when my forty-seventh birthday came round in Jersey. We decided to have a few drinks and go out to dinner after the show.

'Do you think it would be nice to ask the company?' I mused.

'Yes,' said Stephen. 'Why not?'

As he knew Jersey well, he offered to find a place for us to go. But then he vanished, and I had no idea where to tell the rest of the cast and crew to meet us. After the performance, more or less everyone had gone by the time Stephen came backstage to tell me he couldn't find anywhere suitable for a large party. 'Do you mind if we just go out on our own, Barbara?' he asked.

I was a bit put out because I'd promised the kids a night out, and we were barely talking as we drove off. When we got to the restaurant he'd chosen, it was in darkness. But as we walked in, I realised that the whole company was there, amid a mass of lighted candles. When they saw us, they started singing 'Happy Birthday'. I was so touched: Stephen had obviously done lots of wheeling and dealing behind the scenes, because he had taken over the entire restaurant, arranged for flowers and chosen the birthday cake himself, as well as ensuring that all the people I wanted to come were there.

If that summer season was a trial marriage, it could not have turned out better. Stephen and I were very compatible and I admired the gritty Yorkshire streak he had which made him stand up to me when I would probably have preferred him to back down. He was very confident and had a mature outlook on life, characteristics which became evident in an early dealing with Robert Dunn and, later, with Ronnie.

If Robert had nothing else, he had chutzpah. We hadn't been in Jersey more than a couple of weeks when he rang up asking if he could bring a girl over to stay with us as the prize for winning a competition at his nightclub. It was typical of Robert: he'd chosen a trip to Jersey as the prize to show off that he knew me, and staying with us meant all he had to shell out for was two flights. This side of Robert was something I didn't like in him, and neither did a lot of other people.

We were renting a house from Billy Walker, the former heavyweight boxer. It had five bedrooms, so space wasn't a problem, but I didn't know how Stephen would feel about one of my ex-lovers and a girl neither of us had ever met gatecrashing what was more or less a holiday for him. Come to that, I wasn't sure how I felt about it myself. In the event, Stephen didn't have any objection, so Robert and the prize-winner, a sweet girl, got their trip to Jersey.

Back home in Swiss Cottage in the autumn, Ronnie rang, worried about the impending trial of his brothers Johnny and Jimmy, who had been charged in connection with the Security Express robbery. 'I need you to contact a good solicitor to help me prepare my defence, in case I'm brought back,' he told me.

Not wanting to go through all that again, I said: 'Can't your girlfriend do it?'

Typically, Ronnie breezed on: 'You've got more idea, Bar. You know the routine.'

I had to hand it to him: he had chutzpah, too. Another time he'd called from a hospital. 'Hello, Windsor, it's me. I've had an operation on me back. I suppose you've blown me out of your Private Patients Plan?'

'Course I haven't.'

'Oh,' said Ronnie, surprised. 'Can I have the number?'

I read out a series of figures which he repeated slowly to someone else who was obviously taking them down. I had to smile.

'Thanks, Windsor. Bye.'

As they say, more front than Brighton.

Although I didn't believe Ronnie had anything to do with the robbery, I didn't want to get involved in his legal problems and I thought he was out of order asking me. Yet I didn't feel I could completely turn my back on him. I decided to run the problem by Stephen. If he said no way, then I'd leave Ronnie to sort himself out.

Stephen, though, showed his good sense and maturity once again. 'This man obviously trusts you more than anyone else, Barbara,' he said. 'His hands are tied in Spain, and he knows you're capable of finding him a good solicitor who will do the right thing. I feel you should help him.'

So, just when I thought he was finally out of my life, I found I was taking care of Ronnie Knight yet again.

I was playing Dick Whittington in panto at the Orchard Theatre in Dartford, Kent that year, alongside a teenage heart-throb named Todd Carty, who played Tucker in the popular kids' TV series *Grange Hill*. When Todd, as Idle Jack, roared on to the stage on his motorbike, all the young girls in the audience went wild. It was just like being at a pop concert.

After the Christmas Eve show, Stephen suggested we had a quiet, candlelit dinner in Swiss Cottage. We talked about our future together. Stephen wanted us to open a restaurant where he could exercise his skills as a qualified chef and wine connoisseur. We decided that we would start looking for a suitable place in the New Year. Suddenly, Stephen took my hand and produced a fabulous heart-shaped diamond ring. 'Barbara, will you marry me, please?'

Of course, I accepted. After all those rollercoaster years with Ronnie, a quieter life helping to run a little bistro-type restaurant in, say, Covent Garden or Notting Hill, as Mrs Stephen Hollings, was just what I fancied. We would make a great team, I thought: Stephen behind the scenes, preparing magnificent meals, and me out front doing the bubbly PR bit. As it turned out, a small place in town was not what Stephen had in mind. He wanted a big pub restaurant in the country, thirty miles from the centre of London, somewhere in Berkshire or Buckinghamshire. As a London person I was a little disappointed, but if that was what he wanted, then I felt we should go for it.

My divorce was finalised in January 1985, and we started our search for the restaurant straight away, spending most mornings driving all over the place inspecting properties. It was a nightmare for me, because by the time I got to the theatre at 1 p.m., I'd be exhausted, but Stephen wanted me to go with him. We were going to be partners, after all. We still had not found anything we liked by April, when I had to switch my attention from country pubs to the trial of Ronnie's brother Johnny in connection with the Security Express robbery.

Ronnie had begged me to give evidence for Johnny and I'd given in. I didn't relish the prospect, but I didn't have it in me to let Ronnie and his brothers down. It's just the way I am. I was called on the last day of the month, and I found testifying in court every bit as nerve-wracking as it had been five years earlier. The prosecution seemed to place great significance on the fact that I'd given Ronnie £50,000 from the sale of our Stanmore house in cash.

'Why did you pay your husband in cash, not by cheque?' Mr Michael Worsley QC asked me.

'Because that's the way Ronnie does it,' I replied. 'That's one of the reasons I'm divorced from him. I didn't know him very well at the end. For the last four years I've had nothing to talk to him about.'

'This money wasn't dodgy in any way, was it?'

'Absolutely not,' I said. It was true. The money had been given to Ronnie by my accountant, Albert Fox. I'd never have had anything to do with 'dodgy' money.

The fourteen-week trial ended on 10 June. A lot of good my testimony did for Johnny: he was found guilty of the robbery and was sentenced to twenty-two years in prison. Ronnie's eldest brother, Jimmy, got eight years for receiving.

That summer, Stephen finally found a place he felt was perfect for us – a 300-year-old pub called the Plough in the picturesque village of Winchmore Hill, near Amersham in Buckinghamshire. Between us we had travelled more than 500 miles and viewed close to 100 pubs before we found our dream. The price was £400,000, and I'd have to sell the Swiss Cottage house I adored and take out a £200,000 bank loan to buy it, but I didn't mind. If it was what the man I loved wanted, if it was going to make us happy and earn us a few quid into the bargain, it was worth every penny.

Because of my work commitments and all the arrangements that needed to be made, we decided to delay opening for business until November. That summer I was doing the rounds of Butlin's holiday camps performing in *What a Carry On*, a Carry On-type farce – forgetting PC's advice – with Jack Smethurst. It was a lovely time. I was working three or four days a week, and Stephen would come with me to Minehead, where I'd have great fun doing the show in front of those wonderful Butlins audiences. On our way to the next venue in Barry Island, we'd stop overnight at somewhere like Cedar Falls in Taunton, then return home, where I'd leave Stephen to get on with plans for the pub while I went off to do the show in Bognor.

In the autumn I was busy on *The Mating Game* – yet again – with Norman Vaughan and Peggy Mount in Bradford, and working on a film, *Comrades*, with Vanessa Redgrave. Fortuitously, on 11 November, the evening we'd chosen to open the Plough Inn and Windsor Restaurant for business, I was asked to appear on Terry Wogan's TV chat show, and Terry kindly allowed me to mention the name and address of the pub. By the time Stephen and I got home at around 9.30, the place was heaving and there were more customers queueing outside, undeterred by the pouring rain.

Stephen threw himself into the Plough like a man possessed. I was so, so proud of him. I'd cry for him, seeing his hands – and even his feet – red raw and bleeding from where he had burned himself in the kitchen, as he and a small staff sweated away cooking for up to fifty people at a time. For my part, I'd come home from doing panto in Nottingham after the Saturday night performance and devote myself on the Sunday to giving the customers the Barbara Windsor smile and answering all the questions they were dying to ask. Stephen seemed to thrive on all the attention my fame attracted; he knew it would help to put our business on the map. The customers loved having a well-known face in the bar, and I loved chatting to them, I really did. I loved the whole bit – the olde-worlde English village with its little corner shop and post office and village green and cricket team. It seemed idyllic, a cosy, peaceful haven where I could switch off from all the showbiz ballyhoo. And Stephen and I felt we made a great team, both pulling in the same direction.

We decided to get married in April 1986. To be honest, although we were engaged, I was happy going along as we were: we were seriously committed to each other in the business, and we both saw ourselves staying together for ever, so I didn't feel any need for a wedding. But it meant a lot to Stephen because it was important to his parents, who put a lot of pressure on him. They had lived in a close-knit community all their lives and their friends, and people where Stephen's father worked, were, it seemed, making moralistic comments about us living together. If marriage was what Stephen wanted, that was fine by me. There was no question in my mind that it wouldn't work. Stephen was so different from Ronnie, and I believed he was good for me.

We did not want a grandiose affair, though, not one of those 'dos' where the world and his wife and the nation's tabloid press monitor your every move. So when I saw an advertisement for 'Weddings in Paradise', we both felt it was the perfect answer: a simple ceremony in the beautiful Jamaican resort of Ocho Rios which no one apart from Stephen's family and a handful of my close friends would know anything about. The Weddings in Paradise company contacted the *News of the World*'s *Sunday* magazine, which agreed to finance the trip in return for exclusive pictures, to be taken by a staff photographer, Arthur Steel, plus the story of our romance. The only other person who knew was Ronnie. I rang him just so that he would be prepared: once the magazine ran the story, I knew the other papers would be on to him.

Stephen and I were to be married by Raphael Manson, a Salvation Army minister in Ocho Rios, on Saturday 12 April. Stephen would wear an Yves St Laurent suit he had bought in Jersey, and I chose an ankle-length peach-and-white dress with a high, scalloped neckline at the front, which continued down the back in a deep V to the waist, from Rich Bitch, in Marylebone High Street. When I put it on I burst into tears, struck by the thought of how much Mummy would have liked it. After the fiasco of my wedding to Ronnie in Tottenham, I would have loved her to have been there to see me in that dress.

Everything was hunky-dory that sweltering Saturday afternoon until an hour before the ceremony, booked for 4 p.m., when I saw a side of Stephen's personality that I had not been shown before. At 3 p.m., I noticed that Stephen was still swimming in the sea with Arthur, the photographer. I ran on to the beach, my hair in rollers, and called to him to come out. 'You're due at the hairdresser's – you're going to be late,' I shouted. I might just as well not have bothered.

'Yeah, OK,' he called back, and just swam out even further.

It was as if he were trying to make a point, to assert himself, and show that, older and more experienced though I may have been, he was not going to be dictated to. I couldn't understand why he'd picked our wedding day to behave like this.

I was reminded of something Stephen's mother had said to me. 'You know, Barbara,' she'd remarked, 'I'm amazed my son is with somebody like you.'

'Oh, really?' I'd replied. 'Why? Because I'm older?'

'No, it's not that,' she'd said. 'Until now, all the women in his life have taken two steps behind him.'

Often my life seems like a cross between a Carry On and a Joe Orton play, and my wedding to Stephen was a case in point. Someone felt it appropriate to play Paul Young's 'Every Time You Go Away', and Mr Manson asked us to sing 'The Lord Is My Shepherd', a hymn more suited to funerals. To cap it all, the pale apricot cake I'd carefully ordered turned out traffic-light orange, and nobody could face eating it. Mysteriously, this monstrosity somehow came to be packed into our luggage for the journey home, and when we got to London, we discovered that the icing had melted, smothering Stephen's lovely designer suit in a horrible orange gunge. Then a customs officer, who clearly found it hard to believe that we'd had this cake made for our wedding, plunged both his hands into it, presumably in the hope of finding something sinister. But we were married, and home again, and I was happy.

For the first year of our marriage, everything was fine. Between us we had built up the business and were taking up to £10,000 a week. On the personal side, Stephen was all anyone could wish for in a husband. Unlike Ronnie, who couldn't show his love outside the bedroom, Stephen would surprise me with flowers and pay me compliments, always, it seemed, when I was in need of a loving pick-me-up. He would think nothing of turning to a customer in the pub and saying: 'Look at my little lady. Aren't I lucky? What on earth does she see in me?' Not being one to take compliments easily, I would be terribly embarrassed, but, deep down, I loved it. Who wouldn't?

He was a great support in my work, too. I was excited to be asked to perform a music-hall act of Marie Lloyd songs at Hackney Empire, but I was nervous, too. The theatre held so many special childhood memories for me that I was afraid I might try too hard and be a let-down. I felt a great sense of relief when I was sent a publicity flyer and saw Frankie Howerd's name on it. Frankie was now a cult figure among students as well as hugely popular with pensioners, and would undoubtedly top the bill, and I'd be closing Act One. But when I got to the theatre I realised with horror that I'd made a mistake: Frankie had been on the night before, and it was me who was top of the bill.

I shot round to the box office, dreading that I was going to be performing to two nuns and a dog. Happily, I had a full house and the show went sensationally well. I was treated to a two-minute standing ovation, and at the end, I took enormous pleasure in telling the audience how my dear Grandad Charlie had brought me to this theatre for the first house on Friday nights, and how proud he would have been to see me there singing the songs of the little lady he'd admired so much.

I had been so nervous about the whole thing that I'd told Stephen not to come, but now that it had gone so well I really regretted that he hadn't been there to see it.

Taking off my costume in the dressing room, I said to my dresser, 'I wish I hadn't stopped Stephen coming. He would have been proud of me tonight.' At that there was a knock at the door, and there stood Stephen, a massive bouquet of flowers in his hand and a huge smile on his handsome face. I burst into tears. It was the perfect ending to a wonderful night.

But by the following April I noticed that these sweet gestures were becoming fewer and farther between. And ominously, Stephen had begun to find fault with me over the most trivial of matters. On one occasion I arranged for a car to pick me up in Scarborough and take me home to Amersham. I'd been away doing a one-woman tour for several weeks and I was looking forward to seeing Stephen. 'Hi, darling,' I said warmly as he opened the door to our flat above the pub. He just looked straight over my shoulder at the red Toyota.

'Just look at the state of that car – it's filthy,' he said.

'And good afternoon to you, Miss Windsor,' I responded sarcastically. 'And how are you? Oh, you look absolutely wonderful.'

But Stephen just stared at me, then went upstairs to the flat and didn't speak to me for an hour.

Even more worrying, our deeply satisfying sex life was going out of the window. At first I put this down to the pressures of the business. He was very preoccupied by the pub. After all the publicity, he had a lot to live up to and I knew it was taking its toll of him.

I started thinking that maybe it was not the pressure of the business that was to blame. Then I began to wonder whether it was me. Maybe Stephen did not find me attractive any more, as simple as that. I had to face it, I would be fifty later that year, and after all those years of being a turn-on for millions of men, perhaps now I was a turn-off.

It never occurred to me to be unfaithful: I knew I wouldn't find the answer to our problems by sleeping with someone else. Instead I went out and did something I'd never done before: I bought some sexy underwear. If the old body was finally beginning to show its age, then I'd cover it up. I even changed the Shalimar perfume I'd been wearing for more than thirty years. I hoped I'd be able to make Stephen forget how exhausted he was and put him in the mood, but none of this did anything to raise his sexual temperature.

I found it a difficult subject to broach, but I had to say something; if I was to be able to put it right, I needed to know why Stephen rarely even touched me now. But every time I brought it up, he brushed me aside. I'd get hold of him and cuddle him, and ask, 'What's wrong, darling? What is it?' He would just tell me not to be so silly. 'Stephen,' I'd say, 'you hardly come near me any more.'

'Yes I do,' he would claim, then give me a kiss on the cheek and go. If he felt there was a sexual problem between us, he certainly didn't acknowledge it.

Inevitably, my next thought was that if he wasn't interested in sex with me, he must be getting it somewhere else. One day, I asked him straight out, 'Stephen, have you got another woman?' He was horrified. He glared at me as though I was the most disgusting creature on God's earth.

Over the next few days, as I watched him pour all his energy into the pub, it dawned on me that I was a fool to worry that Stephen would betray me with another woman. His mistress was the Plough. And the more I thought about that, the more I began to understand what the problem was: with me always around, Stephen had little chance to shine in his own business. He was a qualified chef, a talented, professional restaurateur, and although his customers loved him, they wanted to talk about me all the time, commenting on how wonderful I'd been in this film or that play, or asking about the Carry On days and what it had been like working with Sid James and Kenny Williams. It seemed the first thing everyone asked when they came in was 'Is Barbara Windsor around?'

To begin with, Stephen loved and valued my celebrity status: I was great for business, and the place was teeming every night. But after a year it had worn a little thin. Stephen was working all the hours God sent to consolidate the fantastic start we made, but the Plough's main function still seemed to be as a meeting place for the Barbara Windsor Appreciation Society. It did not do much for Stephen's self-esteem to be living in my shadow. He was a proud, strong-minded Yorkshire lad who desperately wanted to be a success in his own right. His attitude to me had changed, I was sure, because I was getting in the way of this. I was reminded of something else his mother had said to me early on: 'One thing about my Stephen is he's always wanted to go first class.' I started to worry I was cutting his balls off.

Before I had the opportunity to sort things out with Stephen, Ronnie Knight reared his head again, and with typical thoughtlessness did something that renewed the interest of the very people I did not want to have anything more to do with: the police.

I'd been tipped off that Ronnie and Susan Haylock were about to get married, and I rang him the night before to wish him luck. Ronnie told me that the wedding was going to be a quiet affair at Fuengirola Town Hall, with only a handful of friends present. He said he had no money for anything grander; in fact he was so short he'd had to borrow a few quid. He even had the cheek to ask if some Premium Bonds Mummy had bought him had come up. 'If they had, sweetheart, I'd have been straight on the phone to tell you,' I said, hoping he'd pick up the note of sarcasm in my voice. I was still waiting for him to keep a promise to sell our villa in Spain and give me my half of the money.

The trouble started the following Sunday morning, when I set off for Newcastle, where I was making a personal appearance. Emerging from the flat, I found the green at the front of the pub crowded with photographers and reporters. I had no idea what they were doing there and, judging by the looks on their faces, they were almost as surprised to see me done up to the nines so early in the morning.

'What do you think of Ronnie's big wedding?' one of them called out.

'What do you make of him lashing out twenty grand on fireworks?' shouted another.

I hadn't a clue what they meant, so I just got into Stephen's car, apologising that I was in a hurry to catch a plane. It was only when I got to the airport and bought the papers that I saw what all the fuss was about: there was Ronnie, pictured hosting a lavish party to celebrate his wedding, and among the guests were a good sprinkling of faces from London's underworld.

I spent the flight to Newcastle steaming at the blatant lies Ronnie had told me only four days before, and fretting about the reaction the huge media exposure would provoke at Scotland Yard. If money was so tight, why was he sending £20,000 up in smoke with a bloody firework display? OK, so newspapers do tend to exaggerate figures, but if he'd spent only a quarter of that on fireworks, it was still a fortune to a man who claimed he'd had to borrow money. And what about the food and drink for all those guests? Where had the cash come from for all that? It made my stomach knot with fury that he could splash out like that when he still hadn't sold the villa as he'd promised, and that he had the nerve to lie about it into the bargain. But much worse than that, any fool could see that inviting well-known gangsters to such a high-profile shindig would be seen as cocking an arrogant snook at authority. It was tantamount to shouting from the rooftops: 'I'm above the law and you can't touch me.' And it didn't take a crystal ball to foresee that it would upset the police who had for three years been thwarted in their efforts to have Ronnie extradited from Spain.

I knew that they would want to talk to me, and sure enough I got a phone call asking me to go to Leman Street Police Station in Whitechapel a few weeks later. There was no question of me refusing, of course, and I decided to go alone. Stephen wanted me to take a solicitor, but I didn't see why I should: I hadn't done anything wrong. I'd been asked to go in and answer some questions, that was all. I only had to tell the truth. Even so, I have to admit that I was frightened. The only time I'd ever been in a police station before was to arrange bail for Ronnie, and the mere thought of being questioned gave me the willies. I suppose it was just the feeling that you wouldn't be in a police station being interviewed at all if you hadn't done something wrong.

I was relieved that Detective Inspector Reid McGeorge tried to put my mind at rest immediately. I was the least important of the witnesses, he said, the last one to be called in. They already had so much damning evidence against Ronnie they didn't really need me, but they were keen to see my appointment diaries.

When I produced them, Mr McGeorge said the police were concerned that around the time of the Security Express robbery in 1983 there were no entries at all. I told them that although Ronnie and I had still been living together at the time we'd been leading separate lives, and I was pleased that they seemed to accept this.

I was interviewed six times in all, and Mr McGeorge very kindly saved something he knew would upset me until last. The police had some photographs taken at a villa in Estepona which showed a group of men and women sitting round a pool. Mr McGeorge wanted to know if I recognised any of them. I didn't have my glasses with me, but I was able to pick out Ronnie, Johnny and his wife, Diane, and Susan Haylock, all laughing and obviously enjoying themselves.

And I *was* upset. Very. The photographs, which had been taken long before Ronnie and I divorced, showed Diane and Susan Haylock as bosom buddies, lapping up the sun with Ronnie. Yet Diane had always told me that she'd only met Susan once and couldn't stand her. That upset me more than seeing Ronnie and Susan together. At least I had an inkling, if not cast-iron proof, that they were were an item, whereas I'd had no idea Diane was being so two-faced. I never forgave her. There was no need to lie to me. In marital break-ups, people often have to decide where their loyalties are, and if Diane had put family ties before me, I would have accepted that. Instead she played both ends against the middle and took my hospitality while laughing behind my back with a woman she claimed not to like. Not only was I bitterly upset, I was disappointed, too: I'd thought Diane was stronger and more likeable than that.

The day after my last interview with the police, the *Sun* ran a story with an inaccurate and totally misleading headline: 'BABS SHOPS RONNIE'. And the next thing I knew, Ronnie was on the phone, angrier than I'd heard him in years. 'You're a fucking grass!' he screamed. He made it sound as if I'd gone to the police and said, 'I haven't given a press interview this week, so do you mind if I come in and do some with you?' You'd have thought he might have apologised for dragging me into this mess, but all I got was foul-mouthed abuse and gangster talk. He even compared me with Bertie Smalls, a big-time police informer.

'So what should I do when the police are asking to see me?' I said when I could get a word in. 'Tell them no, too busy, sorry?'

He just carried on bellowing at me until I yelled back at him: 'I don't need this. I've got on with my life. I'm not having you talk to me like this.'

Ronnie had got it into his head that he was an innocent man. But if he was innocent, why was he worried about me being interviewed by the police? What was there for me to tell them?

I found Ronnie's behaviour and his accusations distasteful, and I felt tarnished by him. Here was a man who had already faced murder and arson charges, and now we were talking about a brutal robbery in which a man had had petrol poured over him and had been threatened with being set on fire. When I put the phone down, what tiny speck of love I may have had left for Ronnie went out of the window.

That summer of 1987 I did two shows – *The Young Ones* and *Filthy Rich and Catflap* – for BBC TV. It was a great experience to work with a new wave of comedy writers and actors. And, along with Gareth Hunt and Joss Ackland, I appeared in 'It Could Happen To You', a video with the highly successful Pet Shop Boys.

The film was being shot in Clacton on the east coast, and I got up at 4 a.m. to make sure I was there in time for the 8 a.m. start. Filming went on until the early evening and by the time I got home to Amersham at around 10.30 p.m., I was almost out on my feet – and dying to go to the loo. I got out of the car, loaded up with all my gear, praying that I could slip into the flat quietly without being seen. No such luck: half a dozen customers leaving the pub spotted me climbing out of the car and came running up.

'I told you she lived here,' said one to her friend, and to me: 'We've been waiting for you all night.'

'Can we have your autograph?' asked another.

I love the public's affection for me and I try very hard never to let them down. No matter how I'm feeling I'll always bubble and give them the Barbara Windsor they want to see, and that night was no exception. They were sweet, lovely people. As I signed the last autograph, I must have relaxed at last because my self-control went and I wet myself. When I told Stephen the next day what had happened he laughed, but the incident obviously played on his mind, because later he said: 'It's ridiculous you having to drive back here and get involved with the public when you want to switch off. Let's look for a little place away from here.'

I thought it was a brilliant idea. The first year at the Plough had been very wearing on me as well as on Stephen. I wanted to mooch around with my Lhasa Apso dog, Bonnie, with my hair screwed back and no face on, and be plain Bar, wife, not Barbara Windsor, famous personality, and I was never able to do that at the pub. In our own little place away from the business, however, I'd be able to relax completely for a few days and do all the usual housewifey things and talk and think about anything but showbusiness.

And I thought it would be great for Stephen, too. If the strong, dynamic lady that was Barbara Windsor was not around so much to pull in the punters, he would have to maintain and build up the business himself. If he did think, in a business sense, that I was cutting his balls off, then my absence would give him the chance to come out of my shadow and prove himself. And, of course, a place away from the Plough could be wonderful for us as a married couple; it could be our own little romantic hideaway where we could rekindle our love.

So I went into house-hunting mode and within days I'd arranged for various estate agents to send details of likely-sounding properties within a five-mile radius of Amersham. Stephen looked at me as though I were nuts. 'Why on earth are you looking at places around here?'

'I thought you'd want to be near the pub, in case of—'

'No,' Stephen interrupted. 'It's you I'm concerned about. You need to be away from this place.'

'So where were you thinking of?'

'London,' he said. 'The West End. You always complained that Ronnie would never let you live in the West End. Why don't we find a place there?'

I was delighted. I did love the West End and for years I'd wanted to live there. Now, with the pub doing so well, I could realise that dream. We could take out a sizeable mortgage and buy a place that suited us both. What was the point in working hard, day in and day out, if we couldn't indulge ourselves?

'I'll start looking right away,' I said.

Stephen fancied Soho. We looked at some properties there, but they were too 'in your face', if you know what I mean. I suggested Maida Vale, but Stephen pointed out that we would be for ever getting taxis to and from the West End. What made things difficult was that he insisted we had to have a garage and a garden, in that order. I did find a lovely place in NW1 that fitted the bill, but Stephen turned his nose up at it. 'It's not a good enough address,' he said. 'I want W1.'

I was beginning to despair of ever finding a place when, shortly before I was due to open in *Babes in the Wood* at the Palladium with Cannon and Ball and John Inman, we received details of a cute, three-bedroomed house in Marylebone, a five-minute drive from the A41, which leads to Amersham. It had a garage, it had a garden, and the address was W1. It sounded perfect. I went to see the house the next day and fell in love with it immediately. It was the sort of house I'd dreamed of owning all my life and, nestling in a quiet mews near Harley Street, it was in precisely the area where I wanted to live. Happily, Stephen loved it, too. The price was £312,000, more than we could afford, really, but I felt it would be worth every penny if it brought us closer together. So we went ahead and moved in during that pre-Christmas panto season.

The plan was for Stephen to leave the Plough in the hands of the bar and restaurant managers and spend at least three days in London, ideally including Sundays and Mondays. Sunday in particular was the day I wanted him there: it was the one day of the week when I would be least likely to be working, a day when I could cook a lovely roast dinner, and we could walk around Regent's Park with our little Bonnie, browse around the Bayswater Road or just curl up on the sofa and read the papers. A day when Barbara Hollings could unwind with her husband and recharge her batteries before going out to be Barbara Windsor again.

It sounds ideal, and I think it could have been if the cracks in our marriage had not widened to the point where they could not be repaired permanently. But they had: all the things that were bothering Stephen were still there.

Near the end of the panto, I was rushing around Marylebone buying a few things to take on a holiday to Barbados when I bumped into Kenny Williams. When I told him I'd moved into the area, just round the corner from his home off Great Portland Street, he said: 'Oooh, get you, darling. Got the young husband, got the restaurant in the country, now the house in town. You're doing all right for yourself, aren't you? I'll be round for the melon and lamb cutlets.'

'Lovely, darling,' I laughed. 'I'll call you when I get back from holiday.'

As he walked away I thought: oh, he looks so ill.

A few days later, in the final week of the panto, Kenny rang to ask if I would meet his milkman and his wife, who were coming to the show.

'Aren't you coming, Kenny?' I asked.

'Oooh, no,' he said. 'I wouldn't go and see that crap, would I?'

'Send your milkman round, Kenny. I'll make him welcome.'

Afterwards he wrote me a lovely letter, saying: 'You truly are a great friend. Only you, after doing two shows in the day, would entertain my milkman. Thank you.'

The day before Stephen and I were flying off, I was in Marylebone High Street picking up some last-minute bits when I saw Kenny disappearing round a corner. My first reaction was to rush after him for a chinwag, but I was too pushed for time. I'll see him when I get back, I thought. It was a decision I would regret.

At lunchtime one Thursday in mid-April 1988, a man fitting some wardrobes for me was sitting in my lounge working out an estimate. I went into the kitchen to make a cup of tea and switched on the TV. The second the picture came to life I saw a photograph of me. I wonder what I've done? I thought. Probably the Carry On producers had sold another series of compilations. But then Kenny's face appeared next to mine. I turned the sound up. To my horror, I realised that I was watching the national news and the presenter was telling me that Kenny Williams had died that morning.

I walked slowly back into the lounge and told the wardrobe man: 'I've just had a bit of bad news. I don't know what to do. Kenny Williams. They've just said he's died.'

'Oh, I liked him,' the man said. 'He was ever so funny, wasn't he?'

'Yes,' I agreed, dully. 'He was. I don't know what to do.'

'Look, I'll leave this,' he said. 'I'll come back later.'

'No, no, don't. Please stay and do the estimate.'

It was a terrible, terrible shock. I wandered around like a zombie for the next few minutes, consumed with an overpowering regret that I hadn't chased after Kenny that day before my holiday. And then the phone started ringing, of course, with newspapers and TV people wanting me to tell the country what Kenny was like and what he meant to me. It all went by in a blur, and afterwards I couldn't remember who I spoke to or what I said.

The funeral, at a church in Finchley, north-west London, was private, and only a handful of people apart from Kenny's family were invited. As well as me, Maggie Smith and Rona Anderson, with her husband, Gordon Jackson, and Stanley Baxter were there. Afterwards, when we went on to the home of the ITV producer David Bell, we all realised that although we all knew each other independently, none of us had been out together with Kenny. He liked to keep us all compartmentalised, it seemed. Stanley Baxter, for instance, was his best friend, but when Kenny walked into an Italian restaurant with Maggie Smith and saw Stanley sitting there on his own, he didn't even say hello to him. He just said: 'We can't eat here, Maggie. Let's go somewhere else.'

Kenny had once told me that Maggie wanted her bust to look right for a West End play but that when she'd heard the price of a particular bra was seven guineas, she'd said: 'I'd sooner have my tits cut off than pay that!' I had no idea whether she had actually said it or not. Everything Kenny said had a grain of truth in it, but he elaborated greatly, to put it mildly.

I do believe one story he told about Charlie Hawtrey, though. It was one of his favourites. Charlie had retired to a cottage in Deal on the Kent coast, and one weekend Kenny and some other pals visited him there and went for a walk along the seafront. Charlie was wearing orange trousers, a blue shirt and a bright silk scarf at his neck and using an umbrella as a parasol. 'Fishermen were eyeing us warily,' Kenny said. 'The rest of us were trying to look anonymous, but Charlie kept calling out, "Hello, boys." He turned to us proudly. "They all adore me here. Brings a bit of glamour into their dull lives."'

That October, five months after Kenny's death, I was honoured to be asked to sing 'The Boy I Love Is Up In The Gallery' at a memorial service for him held in St Paul's, the 'actors' church', in Covent Garden. Many showbiz stars came to celebrate his life and there was lots of laughter. I came away sad because we had lost Kenny, but happy that he had chosen me to be one of his friends.

Little more than three weeks after that service, Charlie Hawtrey died. I was terribly sad about that, too, because we'd got on well. In fact, he'd once said in an interview that his favourite people were Kenny and me. Given his reputation for being a bit antisocial, it was a particular compliment. If I'm honest, he was my favourite of the Carry On regulars. Charlie died very bitter that those Carry On TV compilations, for which he received nothing, actually cost him money. He had retired on a small pension, and when those clips brought in a different audience he had to find money he could ill afford to pay for photographs to send to the hundreds of new fans who wrote to him in Deal.

A few months before he died, one of Charlie's friends rang me, very worried that he was getting drunk all the time and going down to the docks and waving to the sailors. When I asked what I could do, the friend said I should talk to him. But as far as I was concerned, if Charlie wanted to live on the coast and smoke his Weights and wave to sailors, that's what he should be allowed to do. He may have been a bit of an oddball, Charlie, but he was a brave one. When he was dying and his doctors told him they would have to amputate his legs, he lit a fag and said: 'No. I want to die with my boots on.' And that's what he did.

I still stayed at Amersham regularly, usually for several days during the week, depending on my work schedules. However, the lovely London house did not prove the magnet to Stephen I'd hoped it would be. He came there less and less, and always arrived later than expected. I lost count of the times he said he would be there at 2 p.m. but had not even left the pub when I rang at three. Often he did not get to Marylebone until six. And even when we were together, we got on each other's nerves. Neither of us seemed to be able to do right in the other's eyes. I began to sense that a huge wall was growing up between us. If I said I liked his hair Stephen would say he hated it and was going to have it cut off. If I liked a particular outfit, he would say he didn't. If I wanted something in white, he would prefer black. We went to buy some furniture and Stephen wanted a sideboard. When I said I didn't, he said: 'No, of course you don't. You must have what you had when you were married to Ronnie.'

Once he even told me off after I sneezed. We were sitting opposite each other in the lounge and I looked up at him. He didn't say anything. I sneezed a second time, and looked at him again. 'What's the matter?' he demanded irritably. 'Haven't I jumped to order? Is it because I haven't said "Bless you"?' It was as if he were trying to put me down and assert himself. Certainly it was plain that he had fallen out of love with me.

Whatever the problem was, the atmosphere between us was not conducive to any romantic feelings whatsoever. Physical contact between us dwindled until there was none left at all, and Stephen devoted more and more time to the pub.

Alone in the house in Marylebone, I'd study myself in the mirror, imagining what Stephen thought when he looked at me. He obviously didn't find me attractive any more. What could I do about it? I wondered. I've never been vain; if I never wore make-up again, it would be too soon. And I'd never been in favour of plastic surgery. But if I was to save our crumbling marriage, I needed to do something dramatic to boost my confidence and make me feel better about myself.

20

IT WAS MY EYES. My eyelids were heavy, as if all my sadness and worry were weighing them down. Although the idea of meddling with nature still seemed scary to me, I decided to see a specialist to have a bit of fat – and, I hoped, a few years – removed. When I told Stephen, he said: 'Don't be so silly.' He knew I was against cosmetic surgery so I don't think he thought I was serious. But the next day I went to see a doctor in Harley Street. He conceded that perhaps a little fat could come out, though he didn't think it was really necessary. However, when he heard how unhappy I was, and in much need of a boost, he agreed to go ahead and give me the operation I wanted.

Stephen did not see me again until four days after the operation. I was sitting in bed in the London house, both eyes so bruised and swollen it looked like I'd gone several rounds in the ring with Mike Tyson. Stephen's face fell when he saw me. 'Oh, Barbara, what have you done to yourself?' he said. Then he just burst into tears and took me in his arms and cuddled me.

Even so, the operation did nothing to change his attitude: it seemed he was still more in love with his 'mistress' than he was with me. The eye job did nothing for me, either. The renewed confidence I'd hoped for didn't materialise because I didn't feel, or look, any different, so the surgery served no purpose, and I regretted having had it done.

I decided I would draw comfort from the people who, unlike the men in my life, had never let me down: the great British public. I began to carve out a new life for myself in London, making myself so busy, taking almost every job that came along, that I hardly had time to even think about my disintegrating marriage and non-existent sex life. I knew that being unfaithful to Stephen was not the answer, and I just got used to it. Instead I found that performing on stage gave me an even bigger high than ever. It was like a substitute for sex, and the love and adulation of audiences replaced the affection I was missing in my private life. I began to understand what Kenny Williams had meant when he told me once that he could get a non-physical orgasmic experience from listening to a marvellous piece of music.

After a show I would hang around outside the stage door chatting to fans. I wanted to know where they had come from, what they were doing, and, of course, I'd write personal messages in their autograph books. In the best showbiz tradition, I put on a happy face.

It was the weirdest lifestyle. I'd always been a good timekeeper, but now I started ruling myself by the clock: if I had to get up at 7 a.m. I'd be wide awake at 6.55. When I was not working, it became vital that I was back home in Marylebone at 5 p.m., with the TV switched on at 5.05. I even set a precise time for me to hang up my clothes, put things away and read the newspapers. I was wound up in the morning and ran my life like clockwork until I collapsed into bed at night.

One of the shows I did that year was, you've guessed it, *The Mating Game*, at Bournemouth. This time I didn't want to because it meant starring opposite Terry Scott, who had his own ideas on how the female lead should play the part, but I owed the director, Mark Furness, that favour for letting me drop out of *Rattle of a Simple Man*. It turned out OK: I played the role my way, and although Terry didn't approve, he knew that I made it work.

All the time I was able to hide behind my wall of fake contentment, I was all right. I knew that if someone saw through me and smashed that wall down, I'd be in trouble, but I didn't believe for a moment that would happen. It was a strange time, but I did feel in control of myself. And at least one of the things I'd hoped to achieve by moving to London worked out: Stephen did manage to emerge from my shadow. Over the next year, he really came into his own, proving himself not only as a top-quality chef, but as a terrific businessman, too. Weekly takings at the Plough, he was thrilled to tell me, were up to just below £12,000 a week.

In 1990 the most marvellous opportunity came along with the casting for a lavish new musical called *Gold Diggers*, which was due to open at Plymouth's Theatre Royal for the summer season before going into the West End. The star of the show was the Hollywood actress Raquel Welch, and I was recommended to play her maid, a woman in her fifties, who had been a performer herself and had seen and done it all. It was perfect for me:

not only would I be playing a character of my own age, but I would be a supporting artiste, below the first and second leads, and would have two numbers of my own. Before I could get too excited, however, I was told that I had to do an audition in the West End.

Neither the producer nor the director were the slightest bit interested that I had been in the business forty years and had sung and danced in such musicals as *Calamity Jane*, *Guys and Dolls* and *Sing a Rude Song*. They wanted to see what I could do now. Maybe it was the irritating Carry On legacy again: that very month, ten Carry Ons had been released on video, and maybe they really did think all I could do was stick out my chest and wiggle my bum. Whatever the reason, their attitude was 'You say you sing, you say you dance – let's see if you can', which, having been around for so long, I found hard to take.

I did the auditions, though – four of them. They were all quite daunting, particularly the final one, because I had to perform the two numbers, including a bit of dialogue, for the producer, the director, butcher, baker and candlestick-maker, all standing in a line in front of me, with the most enormous mirrors surrounding us on all sides. Leaving afterwards was awful. Someone offered the customary 'Thank you very much', and everything went deathly quiet. I saw my face staring back at me from the mirrors, and was acutely aware of the deafening click-click of my high heels on the wooden dance floor as I walked towards the exit, trying to make sure I wasn't looking cocky, as though I'd landed the part, or down in the mouth because I thought I had not been good enough.

I was outside crossing Oxford Street when I heard someone calling my name. It was the director, Mark Brambell. He had run out of the building after me. 'Barbara, we all think you're wonderful,' he said. 'We want you to know now that you've got the part. We didn't want you to go home thinking you hadn't. We think you'll be great.'

That was the good news. The money and terms of contract were worked out and I allowed myself a little excitement at the possibility of appearing on the West End stage again. The bad news was that, a couple of weeks later, Raquel Welch walked out after a row over her part and the show was scrapped.

I was gutted, of course, but I didn't let the disappointment drag me down for too long. 'Oh well,' I thought. 'At least I've got the satisfaction of knowing that I proved myself in those auditions, and was chosen because I showed them I could do what I'd said I could.'

It was late in the day to land a pantomime, but Paul Elliott, who produces most of the pantos in Britain, fitted me in at Wimbledon, playing Fairy Godmother to Bonnie Langford's Cinderella. 'We can't have you not doing pantomime, Barbara,' he told me. As he'd already done his billing it meant taking fourth billing behind Bonnie, Brian Conley and Gyles Brandreth, but I didn't mind.

After one matinée performance, the cast were as surprised as the audience when the company director took the stage as the final curtain was about to come down. 'Please wait a moment, ladies and gentlemen, there is someone who would like to meet you all,' he said. To everyone's delight, Benny Hill walked out from the wings. He'd been in the audience and wanted to say a few words. He rubbed his hands in that way of his and giggled: 'Thanks for a lovely show and for entertaining me. Well done.'

It was a wonderful moment for the cast because Benny was our hero and we adored him. But we were all shocked by his appearance: he'd always been plump, but now he was positively fat, and sweating profusely. And he was very hyper, agitated almost. I thought: my God, Benny, you're not at all well, darling.

It was the last time I was to see the wonderful Benny Hill: by April 1992 he was dead – followed just eight days later by another great friend and comic genius, Frankie Howerd.

While I was in *Cinderella* I was approached to play Adelaide in another production of *Guys and Dolls*. I accepted immediately: the 1991 show was to be a far more lavish production than one I'd done in 1988 and was scheduled to play all the major theatres throughout the country. Not only that, but the director was to be the renowned Michael Bogdanov, whose recent superb production of the musical in Europe had been widely acclaimed.

Straight away, I started thinking about who I'd like as leading man. On tour it is important to have good, solid, reliable, friendly people around you, and no one fitted the bill better than Gareth Hunt. He had a good voice, and the presence to make a good Nathan Detroit, the role made famous by Frank Sinatra in the movie.

'You must be joking, Bar,' was Gareth's reaction when I rang him. 'I can't do that.'

'Why not?'

'I'd have to trip the light fantastic, the twinkle steps,' he said.

'No you wouldn't. Haven't you seen the movie?'

'Yes, I have.'

'Did you see Sinatra dance?'

Silence. I could picture Gareth trying to bring the Hollywood classic into focus.

'He moves around a bit,' I reminded him, 'but there's no tap dancing in *Guys and Dolls*, you know. The girls have great choreography, but the guys do a bit of strutting, no tap dancing.'

'What about all that balletic stuff? You know, where you have to lift the girls and all that?'

'No, there's none of that, Gareth.'

There was a long pause. 'I'm not sure, Bar, I'm not a good mover. I can't put one foot in front of the other. I don't know . . .'

'I'll get the movie over to you,' I interrupted. 'Have a look at it, you'll love it. You'll be great. You can't sing as well as Sinatra, but don't tell me you can't play Nathan Detroit as well as him.'

A few days later I learned that Gareth was going to do it. I was delighted for both of us. We would have a great time: we were going on a no-expense-spared national tour with the best theatrical text in showbiz history, great choreography by Lynnda Curry, a great director, and what promised to be a wonderful supporting cast. As we headed for Plymouth to start the tour, nothing, it seemed, could go wrong.

But it did, and from the word go. When we arrived we were horrified to discover that the 'studio' where we were to rehearse was a derelict building a forty-minute drive from the theatre. Worse, there was dog's mess all over the place. I did not have time to be too upset about that, though, because something even more worrying caught my eye: dozens of pairs of tap-dancing shoes lined up against a wall. Most of the guys were looking anxious, and telling anyone who would listen that they had not been asked if they could dance, but to my surprise, Gareth did not seem bothered in the least.

When one of the production team went round asking everyone their shoe size, he gave his and happily tried on a pair of the tap shoes. I didn't know what to say to him, so I stayed out of his way. When we were told to rehearse the big tap routine which closes the show, Gareth went along with it, doing his best to pick up the steps. Even when he was instructed to lift one of the dancers, his face was a model of concentration.

I didn't dare look at him: I was terrified that he was just keeping his cool for the time being and would tear into me later for tricking him into making a fool of himself. It was not until we drove back to our hotel that I found out why he'd reacted so calmly. He thought the whole thing had been a flamboyant wind-up; that I'd hired all the tap shoes and persuaded everyone to go along with it. Once Gareth realised it was all for real, he knuckled down and did his best, and bore no hard feelings towards me. What a professional. I love him.

The next day we learned that Michael Bogdanov was now not going to direct the show; instead we were to have a Japanese man who had worked on *Guys and Dolls* in Germany as his assistant. Warning bells started to ring: it was bad enough that some of the men in the show had been cast on the basis of their looks, not their musical ability, but to put the production in the hands of someone none of us had ever heard of, and who did not know us, seemed a recipe for disaster. The director was very sweet, but he did not understand our sense of humour and had no idea what we were talking about as we kicked ideas around during those early rehearsals. Michael had also changed some of Damon Runyon's masterful dialogue, for reasons which mystified us.

Three weeks later, when we had left that dreadful building to rehearse in the Theatre Royal, I was passing the stage door with Gareth and saw someone with his back to us talking to the theatre manager. Suddenly, the man turned and looked at me. It was Thomas Powell.

'Thomas!' I exclaimed.

'Barbara.' Tears filled his eyes. He hugged me, then broke away and started walking round and round in circles, then coming back to me, saying over and over again: 'I can't believe it.'

He was shaking. 'It's all right, darling,' I said gently. 'It's lovely to see you. What are you doing here?'

Thomas said nothing. He just kept on walking round in circles. He seemed to be in shock. I introduced Gareth, but Thomas could not even say hello. He simply carried on staring at me and repeating the same words. 'I can't believe I've seen you.'

At first I assumed he had turned up in Plymouth because he knew I was appearing there. But we did not open for another four weeks and there were no posters out and the publicity had not started. 'We're due for rehearsals soon, love,' I said. 'But there's a Green Room here. Let's take you up there for a coffee.'

Poor Thomas. He was in a terrible state. His hair and his scruffy clothes looked like they had not been washed in months, and he had aged dreadfully: although he was ten years younger than me he looked ten years older. My heart went out to him.

Gareth was great. He realised there had been something between us, and that Thomas had hit a bad time. 'Can I see you?' asked Thomas. The past could never be recaptured, but I could never turn a cold shoulder. I gave him the name of the hotel where I was staying. 'We'll be there this evening, Thomas,' I said. 'Come there if you like.'

After he had left, Gareth remarked: 'He's seen a bit of life, that one, hasn't he? You have to give him some time, Bar. And I know you will.'

I still had no desire to deceive Stephen. He knew about Thomas, so that evening, I phoned the Plough and came right out with it. 'I bumped into Thomas today, Stephen. He's in a bad way and would like to see me. He's coming here this evening. You don't mind, do you?' He didn't, but to be honest, even if he had, I would not have had it in my heart to go back on my word to Thomas.

I deliberately underdressed in a tracksuit, tied my hair back and did not put on any make-up. When Thomas came up to my suite, I saw that by contrast he had made an effort to look his best. He was wearing a tan jacket and jeans, probably his only decent outfit, and had washed his hair. He seemed a lot more together.

'You're wearing pink,' he said at once. 'You always looked great in pink.'

I was worried about offering Thomas a drink in case it set him off on a bender, but he was shaking and clearly needed one. Reluctantly, I poured him a miniature brandy from the mini bar, and we started chatting. When I asked him why he had gone to the theatre that day, he said he had just arrived in Plymouth after a spell abroad and was looking for a job. He knew what I'd been doing, he said, because I was always in the papers. It was lovely sitting there talking to him after all that time. I liked him a lot, but I felt no attraction any more, just a deep, deep sadness at what a mess he was in. The sorrowful look in his eyes said it all: the little lady he had loved and who had left him had hardly changed, but he had changed almost beyond recognition.

We chatted for a couple of hours, both of us slipping back into the easy way we had shared. We discussed what was happening in our lives and I found myself being honest about Stephen. Thomas said he very much wanted to see the show and I promised I'd arrange a ticket as soon as we opened. All the time we were talking, he kept glancing at the mini bar. I told him to help himself. By the time he left, he had drunk every bottle in the mini bar. He was not shaking any more.

As we came to the end of rehearsals and the first preview approached, I was not as happy as I should have been as the star of what was undoubtedly going to be the number one touring show in the country. There was plenty of room for improvement in the production itself, but something else, something deeper, kept nagging at me, dampening my usual exuberance and drive. Call me old-fashioned, but when I started off in theatre it was second nature for newcomers to respect older, more experienced performers. As a youngster, I'd always been in awe of household names and their theatrical achievements, and went out of my way to be extra polite and friendly. I'm not toffee-nosed, la-di-da, or 'lardie', as we say in the business – when I'm working, I'm plain Bar to everyone, from the veterans who have seen and done it all to novices still coming to terms with stage fright. Having said that, I did feel it was only right that people with less experience should acknowledge that I knew my way around a stage. After all, I'd been treading the boards for more than forty years. With some of the *Guys and Dolls* cast, however, I sensed an off-hand, almost arrogant air of 'Barbara Windsor – so what?' And it saddened me, as it did Gareth.

Maybe it's me, not them, I thought. Maybe ideals and attitudes had changed. Maybe this was the way it was now. But I still found it hard to accept that these youngsters thought nothing of sitting on the dirty stage, sometimes even smoking, in their costumes, behaviour which was worlds away from the early days of my career.

And there was something else bothering me, too. Over the years, I'd loved popping into theatres when it suited me, to perfect a dance step I was not happy with or to sit in my dressing room answering fan mail. But now, new laws or staff shortages kept the stage doors locked until early evening. It was another development that fuelled my nostalgia for the days when the theatre truly was a magical world.

The show was dealt another major blow in the last week of rehearsal. I had been concerned about Gareth for several days; the pressures of learning to dance had taken their toll and he was exhausted and not looking well. We were practising our duet, 'Sue Me', one day, when I was horrified to see blood seeping through his light-coloured tracksuit bottoms. 'I think you're in a bit of trouble, darling,' I whispered.

He told me he was suffering from haemorrhoids and rushed off to his dressing room. I dashed to a chemist's to get him some sanitary towels and he was able to carry on, but he was far from well. Later that morning, he had to be taken to Plymouth General Hospital for an operation, and he had to miss the first week's performances.

I felt so sorry for Gareth, not only because of the pain he was in, but because he was so disappointed not to be able to do the early shows after he'd worked so hard at his role. And I felt bad about lumbering him with an energetic tap routine, albeit inadvertently. When he returned, every night as we started our big number, he would grumble and whisper to me: 'I *will* get you for this, Windsor.' At the end of the show, when he should have been at the front, Gareth would steadily work his way right to the back and hide behind more accomplished dancers.

Thomas was coming to see the show on the Friday of the first week. I'd arranged a good seat for him in Row K of the stalls, but when I looked, it was empty. After the final curtain, I was in my dressing room, getting changed to go out with some of the cast, when he turned up, clutching his programme. 'It was brilliant,' he told me. 'Absolutely brilliant. And so were you.'

'You weren't there,' I said.

'I was,' said Thomas. 'But I didn't want to watch you from the stalls. I went upstairs. I wanted to see you from up there.'

I could understand that: he knew I liked to sing to the gallery. He came back to watch the show again the next night and told me that seeing me had made him decide to go into a clinic to dry himself out. 'I look at you and then at myself, and I feel ashamed,' he said. I was sceptical, but the next day, a Sunday, he gave me the number of an NHS clinic in Plymouth and asked me to phone him during the three weeks he'd be there. He was allowed only one caller and he had chosen me. He was very frightened. He knew the horrors of going cold turkey.

I called the clinic several times, always as Mrs Hollings, and was delighted to hear that he was doing well. When he came out, he looked great, really clean and lovely, and I invited him to my dressing room after a matinée for tea and sandwiches. He was lively and articulate – and he didn't need a drink to stop him shaking any more.

'You know this is my last week, Thomas,' I reminded him. 'My last show is Saturday night, and I leave Sunday morning. You've got my number at the pub, so if you ever need to talk, you know how to get hold of me.'

'That's lovely, Bar,' he said. 'Thanks.'

Suddenly, he looked embarrassed.

'What's the matter, Thomas?' I asked.

'I don't know how to say this, Barbara, but some newspapers have been on to me. They want me to do a story.'

'Do you want to?'

'Well, I could do with the money.'

'Thomas, if things get really dreadful and you feel you can get yourself a few quid, then go ahead.'

'You know I'd only say the most wonderful things about you.'

'Of course I know that, darling,' I said. 'I know that.'

When he left, I felt all choked up. It didn't matter a damn what he said to any paper; what bothered me was how he would cope with a lot of money in his pocket. I wondered what on earth was going to happen to him and whether I would ever see him again.

Guys and Dolls was good, but it could have been better with more professionalism and attention to detail on the part of the production team. In all the musicals I'd done before, someone – the choreographer or the producer's assistant – had always been out front watching the performance to make sure that everyone was doing what they had rehearsed, that no one was deviating and doing their own thing; in short, that the public were getting their money's worth. On *Guys and Dolls*, no one did this, which I could not understand.

Shortly before we were due to leave Plymouth for our next venue, Sheffield, we were called in early one morning to sort out a few things. Gareth and I were on time, sitting in the front row of the stalls, but many of the cast were late. When they did stroll in, they seemed more concerned that Labour had ousted the Conservatives in a local election the day before and there was a lot of chatter and cheers of 'Got rid of the lousy Tories!' and suchlike. After waiting for what seemed an age for things to quieten down and the meeting to start, I could stand it no longer. 'Excuse me,' I said. 'Aren't we getting our priorities wrong? What *is* all this political shit? Isn't this about *Guys and Dolls* and the tour? We're going on the road and should be sorting out the show here.' You could have heard the proverbial pin drop. I don't think the group of troublemaking lefties liked it one little bit that I'd spoken out, but I was right. I'd worked with Britain's most famous politically minded actress – Vanessa Redgrave – and the only time she ever gave any of her fellow performers earache was over a cup of tea or a meal in a restaurant. When she walked through that stage door it was to work, not to pontificate. And I'm the same, always have been.

That last scene in Plymouth brought it home to me that the magic of the stage that had thrilled me since I'd walked into Wimbledon Theatre as a schoolgirl was disappearing. Fings certainly weren't wot they used t'be, and I was becoming disenchanted.

On the Sunday morning after our final night in Plymouth, my driver picked me up at the hotel to take me to Amersham. On our way out of town, we stopped at traffic lights next to a shopping precinct near the theatre. My eyes were drawn to it, almost as though they knew what they were going to see. There, amid a group of down-and-outs, was Thomas, sitting on the pavement holding a can, his back resting against a pillar. It was ten o'clock in the morning and he was drunk. Probably he had been there all night. I sat there staring at him until the lights changed and felt the sorrow sweep through me again. Poor, poor Thomas. I'd been in Plymouth just eight weeks, and in that time he had tried so hard to recapture some of the person he once had been. It had been a desperately traumatic experience for him to go into that clinic, and he had done it to make himself look good for me. I'd opened my heart to him about my problems with Stephen and, who knows, maybe he thought he could bring back our yesterdays and make me fall in love with him again. As the car pulled away, I wondered sadly once again what would become of him, and whether it really had been coincidence that had brought us together again.

I was sitting on my own in Marylebone one Saturday evening when Richard Swerrin rang to ask if I'd like to go out to dinner that night. Richard had played Prince Charming in the production of *Cinderella* I'd worked in at Stevenage over the Christmas of 1989 and was soon to have a big success with a five-year run as Joseph in *Joseph and His Amazing Technicolor Dreamcoat*. We had been out with mutual friends since then and he had even popped in for a cup of tea a couple of times. I liked him: we giggled a lot and found each other easy company. He was gorgeous-looking, with blond hair and blue eyes, but there had never been anything sexual between us; we had not even kissed. So I readily accepted his invitation. I'd had a busy day and needed to unwind, and I thought it would be lovely to have someone to talk to.

We went to the Tang Dynasty Chinese restaurant in New Cavendish Street, a five-minute walk from my home. We chatted for a while about the business and what we'd been doing and then, to my surprise, he looked at me searchingly and said: 'You're very unhappy, aren't you?'

My protective wall was firmly in place. 'Are you mental?' I replied.

Richard shook his head. 'You're *not* happy, Bar. I can tell.'

'I don't know what you're going on about,' I lied.

'I know you, Bar. I can see through you. There's something wrong between you and Stephen.'

'What do you mean?'

'I've never seen you with him. You only seem to speak on the phone.'

'Stephen's very busy,' I said defensively. 'He's got a fantastic business.' Trying to reinforce the barrier, I added: 'Anyway, who the fuck are you to ask? Mind your own business.'

Richard just smiled. 'You're such a lovely lady, Bar. You're fabulous. You shouldn't be on your own, living like a nun. It's not right.'

I tried to laugh that off by telling him how I had actually wanted to be a nun once, but he wasn't going to be deterred by flippancy.

'You need to talk about it, Bar. You need to let it all out. You'll feel better, I promise.'

I tried to change the subject by telling him about the *Mothers By Daughters* interview I'd done for TV, on which I'd been filmed crying as I talked about Mummy. Richard said he had always wanted to see it. I had a video at the house, so I suggested he came back to watch it.

Whether it was Richard's probing questions or us talking about Mummy I don't know, but something upset me and I started pouring out the story of unhappiness with Stephen. And the more I said, the more I realised that Richard was right: I'd kept those feelings bottled up for too long. I really opened my heart that night. I told Richard the lot and felt better for it. Many men had come on to me over the previous two years or so, but no one reached me the way Richard did. He saw through the facade I was presenting to the world; saw the sadness behind the happy face, and smashed my protective wall to pieces.

I knew we were going to make love when we got home; I knew, too, that once we had, my life would never be the same again.

Going to bed with Richard was wonderful, and not just because he gave me what I needed and had been missing for so long. It was almost like therapy, as if Richard were helping me through my problems. There was no 'Oh, my God, I'm madly in love with you, I want to be with you for ever' stuff. We both knew what it was about, and that was what was so good about it.

Despite everything, I wanted to stay married to Stephen, and I was still prepared to try to find a way back. But whenever we did spend time together, he continued to be irritated by the slightest thing.

Although Richard Swerrin had reawakened my interest in sex, I was still wary of men who came on strong. Most of them were younger guys who had experienced their first sexual thrill seeing me half naked in the Carry

On films, and I could easily resist them. But then Robert Dunn phoned and invited me out to dinner. After our car accident and the rows in Australia, I'd vowed never to get involved with him again, and my first instinct was to keep to that. 'Thanks, Robert,' I said. 'But I don't think so.'

Robert is difficult to sum up. People either like him or they don't, and women either fancy him like crazy or not at all. Some people think he is wonderful and others dismiss him as a lying toe-rag. But it cannot be denied that he has a way with him and can be very persuasive. On this occasion Robert would not take no for an answer. And because with Richard I had been given a little love and felt a bit more like the old Barbara, and Robert and I usually had a good laugh together, I changed my mind. He came to Marylebone, looked around my little house and said it was so right for me, and that I should have bought it long before.

We started with a couple of drinks at the Savoy, then crossed the Strand to Joe Allen's, one of my favourite restaurants. We had a lovely evening talking about the theatre and showbiz in general, and when we came back to the house I felt that was as far as I wanted it to go. Robert sat down on the sofa by the window, and I chose an armchair about five feet away, and we carried on chatting. He brought the conversation round to my unhappiness with Stephen, and asked me to join him on the sofa.

'If all you want to talk about is sex, Robert, you'll have to go,' I told him.

He kept on and on. 'Come and sit with me. Or let me come over and sit with you.' And I kept telling him I wanted him to go. We were like a couple of kids. Finally, after an hour or so of verbal tennis, Robert decided he was fighting a losing battle and held up his hands.

'All right, Bar,' he said. 'You're probably right. I think it would be better if I went.'

And that's when I changed my mind for the second time that evening. I just thought, oh, what the heck, why not?

'No, don't go, Robert. I don't want you to.'

And I went over to him and fell into his arms. It just seemed right. I'd made a bit of a fight of it, but, like Richard, he had said all the right things. The talking and the attention had done the trick, and I simply felt wanted.

21

I COULD SEE OLIVER REED'S HANDS SHAKING. It was not yet ten o'clock on a freezing February morning, but he clearly needed a drink, so someone rushed off and got him two large cans of strong beer. We were outside the Prince Charles Theatre in London's Leicester Square with the great Peter Cushing, ready to put our handprints on a pavement, Hollywood style, and Ollie wanted to steady himself before plunging his enormous mitts into the cement.

Apparently, we had been invited to this 'ceremony' as the 'cream of British films' and I raised a titter when I grinned at Ollie and Peter and quipped: 'They're scraping the barrel a bit, aren't they, with us?' You would have been hard pushed to find three people more different from one another. I'd first met Ollie at Elstree thirty-one years earlier when he was filming *The Curse of the Werewolf*, and remembered how delightful he was: so handsome, with a gentle nature behind the boisterous hell-raising image. I was thrilled to find he hadn't changed. Like millions of others, I'd admired Peter Cushing for years, but I'd never met him until that morning. I thought him a dear, sweet man. Even though he had only just lost his wife and was grieving desperately, he treated everyone with a lovely old-world charm and courtesy.

This bit of publicity – and the three music halls I had booked in the coming weeks, in Clacton, Croydon and Sheffield – were particularly welcome. The pub's takings had recently begun to show a worrying downward trend and we'd taken out another loan to give the Plough a face-lift. Depending on the size of the theatre, for the music halls I would get either £750 or £1,000 a night, which I was happy to put into the pub. More important, I would have a guaranteed income from a five-week summer season in Blackpool, with a Sundays-only spin-off through to the end of

October. This safety net enabled me to devote some time to charity work, and on Trading Places Day in March, I became a bus conductor to Bernie Bresslaw's bus driver in aid of a cancer charity. I also attended a tribute dinner to raise funds for the Royal Marsden Hospital and went round Soho with Julian Clary handing out condoms in pubs and clubs as part of a national condom campaign.

Like *Guys and Dolls*, the 1992 Blackpool revue looked perfect on paper. I would be working with my Carry On pal Bernie Bresslaw, and the director was my favourite choreographer, Tudor Davies, who had directed my *Carry On Barbara* tour in New Zealand and South Africa. The content would be a mixture of what I'd performed with Tudor and the boys in New Zealand and South Africa and other work I'd done throughout my career. The writers were the wonderful Barry Cryer and Dick Vosburgh, arguably the best in the business at the time. And the icing on the cake was that I'd be working on the famous North Pier in a town I loved.

After rehearsals and a huge publicity launch in London, I arrived in Blackpool at four o'clock on Sunday 17 May. Touring performers always arrive in town on a Sunday, and it's nearly always chilly and wet and miserable, and you're nearly always dying for a pee. This Sunday was no exception.

Before checking into my hotel a short walk from the North Pier, I asked my driver to cruise along the promenade. Even though seaside towns often have a depressing, drab air before the season gets underway, I wanted to have a look at the Irish Sea and that wonderful, never-ending Blackpool beach, and drink in the intoxicating coastal atmosphere. I was full of optimism about the show. I hoped it might even restore some of the magic the theatre had lost for me and make me fall in love with it again. I'd had reservations during rehearsals when some Carry On-type sketches crept into the scripts, but I'd made my feelings known about those. Otherwise, the format consisted of music and sketches, modelled on the traditional variety shows of the forties and fifties. As far as I was concerned, it was an untitled extravaganza and I was happy with that.

The car trundled slowly along the promenade, past the South and Central piers and up to the North. When I spotted the poster for my show I felt a knot in the pit of my stomach. 'Oh, my God,' I said. 'Stop the car.' I stared at the poster, horrified. First, I was not top billing – Bernie was. That was wrong: I'd been the first performer to be approached. Secondly, it was being promoted as *Wot a Carry On in Blackpool*. No one had mentioned any title to me, let alone one with 'Carry On' in it. All my misgivings returned. At coming up to fifty-five, I did not want to be prancing about the stage pretending to be a nubile twenty-year-old, and I didn't think the public would want that, either. But that was what they were bound to expect from the title of the show. It was the same old story. I felt physically sick. After all the battles during rehearsal, it seemed I was going to have another fight on my hands.

What made matters worse were the masses of people beginning to crowd around the car, smiling and waving at me. I gave them the customary Barbara Windsor smile and thumbs-up, but all the time I was panicking: oh my God, what am I going to do about all this? I asked the driver to take me to the hotel, fast. I needed to be on my own to work out the best way to handle what could prove an embarrassing and, more importantly, career-damaging situation.

If I had not been swayed by Stephen before I'd left the Plough, I could have slipped up to my room quietly, wearing a hat and glasses and with no face on, more Barbara Deeks than Windsor, before anyone recognised me. But Stephen had been adamant that I didn't dress down. 'You're going back to a town that's special to you, and you're a star,' he said. 'You should arrive looking like one.' I didn't usually get all dolled up to travel, and I certainly didn't want to make a grand entrance at the hotel, but for some reason I'd gone against my natural instinct and done the full monty: great outfit, hair just so and made the best I could of the face. I was glitzy Barbara Windsor in all her glory, and I had no chance.

The hotel lobby was packed with holidaymakers wondering what to do with themselves in the dreary weather, and I was spotted immediately. Within seconds I was surrounded by people wanting autographs or to be photographed with me, and it took me forty minutes to check in and get to my room.

Having thought through the problem, I confronted the show's associate producer, Martin Witts, at rehearsal the next morning. He claimed my name had been on the left of the poster, but something had gone wrong with the photograph negative and the poster had been printed back to front so that my name was on the right, a crucial difference. There was nothing that could be done now about the title, which, Martin explained, had been decided on the same basis as the inclusion of the Carry On section: because they felt that, with Bernie and me topping the bill, it would boost ticket sales. I had no choice but to accept that. However, I called my agent – I had just joined the Noel Gay agency – about the poster and asked her to check my contract: if it said my name should be on the left, I had every right not to do the show unless the poster was changed. My agent said she would look into it; in the meantime, I should go back to my hotel.

'But I need to rehearse,' I told her.

'Don't do anything,' she said. 'Just wait in your hotel till you hear from me.'

I was worried. Nothing like this had ever happened to me before. On a tour, once you have unpacked and settled in, all you want to do is get to the theatre and sort out your costumes, then spend the first few days polishing what you have been rehearsing. Now I was being told to stay in my hotel room on my own.

My absence from the rehearsal and a press conference on Tuesday hit the headlines the next morning, one of which, predictably, ran: 'BABS WON'T CARRY ON'. It made me look like a temperamental prima donna who was sulking about not getting her own way. In fact I was rehearsing like mad in my hotel room, because I was sure the contractual dispute would be sorted out one way or another and that I would be able to go ahead and do the show.

And it was, later that day. Martin Witts came to the hotel and explained that Bernie's contract stated that his billing should be on the left on all promotional material. I was not a happy bunny. I had not settled with one particular contact at Noel Gay and I felt I'd been let down, but at least the matter was settled and it had not dragged on for long. I went into the theatre and apologised to everyone. I was very emotional, but fortunately, I was performing with people I'd worked with before who understood my position and sympathised with me because they knew that the row, short-lived though it was, had been very unpleasant for me.

The following morning, the *Mirror* reported 'BABS CARRIES ON IN PEACE', but in truth, there was a distance between Bernie Bresslaw and me. Don't get me wrong: it wasn't a war, just a frosty silence. I'd known Bernie since our first movie together, *Carry On Doctor* in 1968, and had always found him such a happy person, always full of spirit and joy. But, that summer, I saw a dramatic change in him. I knew he was extremely tired, and not particularly well, but that shouldn't have stopped him joining me and the rest of the cast for a drink or two every so often. It was not only me who had noticed the difference. The Krankies, who had worked with Bernie in panto the previous year, told me that it had not been a happy show. He did not seem at all embarrassed that his agent had edged him ahead of me in the billing on *Wot a Carry On*. I didn't say anything to Bernie – it's not something one actor would discuss with another – and he said nothing when I was given the number one dressing room, though if number one had been very much grander I dare say he might have been tempted to bring it up.

However, Bernie did make a fuss over who should take the final call. The director suggested we walked on together – it was that kind of show, after all – but Bernie insisted on taking it alone. I agreed because I knew I'd get a great reception from the public when I took my call and he would then have to follow that.

To end the show we did a tribute to the Carry Ons, using props such as a nurse's hat and a doctor's stethoscope, against huge screens displaying blown-up photographs of Sid James, Hattie Jacques and Kenny Williams. We threw in all the old chestnuts and, to be fair, the audiences enjoyed it. But the whole project was ill conceived. If the billing fiasco was not an omen, the opening night should have been. Stephen had bought me some beautiful diamond heart earrings, and I lost one during that first show. I remember thinking, 'This is doomed, this stage.' To add to the misery the theatre leaked everywhere and the rain seeped into the dressing rooms. I was so fed up I told my mates: 'If you really care about me, don't come to Blackpool. If you do, I won't see you.'

One friend who rang me to say he was coming to see the show was Barry Burnett, a showbiz agent. I tried to put him off, but, because I knew he would give me good advice, I poured my heart out to him. Barry insisted on coming and, in a way, I was pleased he did: I was worried that my feelings were clouding my judgement and thought it would be helpful to have the opinion of an unbiased outsider. 'Well,' he said after the performance. 'You're doing the best you can. You sparkle, and the public love you, but you just shouldn't be in it. It's as simple as that.'

I'd known Barry since before he'd become an agent – he was the son of Al Burnett, who had run the Stork Room in the 1960s, and I'd seen him around town as a kid. He'd never held it against me that I had once thrown a bucket of ice over his father. We'd talked before about the possibility of him taking over my career, but we'd always been concerned that it might spoil our friendship. But now he felt that perhaps I wasn't getting the right advice and, seeing how depressed I was, he began to wonder whether it might be a good idea for us both if he did.

Wot a Carry On was the lowest point of my career. *Twang!* had been bad enough, but my experience in Blackpool affected me far more, probably because I was older. I knew I needed to take stock and decide what I wanted to do with my career. Far from renewing my enthusiasm for the theatre as I'd hoped, those five awful weeks deepened my disenchantment. I'd always felt that once I stopped enjoying the business, once I found myself dreading going on stage, I would say, enough's enough, quit performing and become an agent myself. I knew I would need to get experience in an office to learn how the administrative side, the nuts and bolts, of the industry worked, so I started composing a letter to send out to agents. It began: 'Ageing sex symbol, very knowledgeable about showbusiness, wishes to assist in an office.'

It was an indication of how serious my depression was that for the first time ever, I couldn't wait to get away after a show. I had moved into the Sherwood, a smaller hotel run by a couple of pals further along the promenade, and every night I had a taxi waiting at the end of the pier to take me there. There is a little tram to ferry people the 500 yards between the theatre and the pier, and I'd pray it was there when I left my dressing room. If it was I'd quickly sign some autographs and jump on. If it wasn't, I'd leg it, high heels and all, along the pier on my own. I even bought myself a pair of flat-heeled shoes so that I could make a faster escape.

The end of the run could not come soon enough: I'd always loved the northern folk, but after this trip I felt I never wanted to wake up in Blackpool ever again. I was desperate to leave immediately after the last show, but unfortunately I could not organise a van to collect all my gear from the dressing room until the following morning. I was contracted to return on 26 July for the series of *Wot a Carry On* Sunday concerts running through to October, but I couldn't think about them now. All I was thinking about was the joy I'd feel waking up in my own bed for the first time in five weeks.

By the time we hit Preston and turned south on to the M6, the cloud of depression had lifted and I was looking forward to a lazy day in Marylebone. I needed to put my feet up because, as well as the Sunday concerts, I had another eleven venues lined up for my one-woman show in various parts of the country over the coming eighteen weeks. It was a tough schedule, but by now Stephen and I needed the money.

My first decision on my return was to sign on with Barry Burnett – and it was one I have never had cause to regret. Next I needed a job that would pay a big lump sum that would take care of a sizeable chunk of the money we owed. And amazingly, what seemed like the answer arrived in the post the following Saturday morning in the form of a script for a proposed film,

Carry On Columbus. I was delighted. I hadn't made a Carry On movie for seventeen years, and the thought of pulling up at the gates at Pinewood again and being greeted by people I knew and loved really appealed to me. I made a cup of tea and settled down to see what my part was like. It didn't take me long to find out: it was not just bad, it was appalling. To me, the Carry On humour is the celluloid equivalent of a McGill postcard: naughty but nice, with rude double entendres. *Columbus*, on the other hand, was just plain obscene.

Horribly disappointed and angry, I put the script down and took Bonnie for a walk in Regent's Park to cool down. When I got back, I picked it up again: I felt I ought to go through the whole thing, not just my part; maybe it seemed so awful because I'd read it out of context. So I made another cup of tea and sat down to read it slowly from beginning to end. It left me thoroughly disgusted and depressed, and in need of a good drink, so I walked round to the Tang Dynasty and joined some friends at the bar. And I must have had a good drink, because I don't remember the local bobby escorting me home – only the hangover in the morning. When it lifted, I phoned Bernie Bresslaw, whose name was also on the script. Despite the Blackpool fiasco, we were still friends and, because he knew the movies better than me, I wanted his opinion.

'It's not a good script, Bar,' he said. '*Dick* was a good Carry On, and I loved doing it. I'd rather remember that as my last Carry On film.'

That was good enough for me. *Dick* had been my last film, too, and I was going to say no to this one as well. When I put the phone down, it rang immediately.

'Hello, Barbara, it's Joanie.' It was Joan Sims who I knew, like me, wanted to do another movie.

'I know, darling,' I said. 'It's about the film. Not very good, is it?'

'I think it's awful,' said Joan. 'I'm going to have to say no to Gerald.' I could sense a little anxiety in her voice; I think she was a bit frightened of telling him that she was not accepting the part.

Anyway, the three of us turned down the film, and a few days later, my agent rang to tell me that Peter Rogers had been on, saying that if money was the problem he was prepared to pay me more. I explained that my decision was based on not wanting to appear in a bad film rather than money, and the next thing I heard, the script was being rewritten and it was going to be biked round to me. When it was, it was still appalling, and the answer was still no.

Astonishingly, I then heard that it was being put around that I'd rejected

Columbus because I was unhappy at not getting any money from the Carry On compilations being shown on TV. Too right I was unhappy about it, but it had nothing to do with *Columbus*. To me there are more important things in life than bearing a grudge and looking for revenge.

If I'd had any doubts that I'd made the right decision, the reviews would have laid them to rest. The film was panned by every critic, with my own favourite, Barry Norman, making a particular point of saying how sensible I'd been to turn it down. But I took no pleasure from those notices. After all the popularity the Carry Ons had enjoyed, it was so sad that the last one was a flop. Thankfully, Columbus's vulgar voyage sank without trace.

As for me, I was back on the road, and the gulf between Stephen and me was getting wider and wider. When we spoke, usually on the phone, he was never affectionate or warm; he was only interested in talking about the business. When I remembered how things had drifted with Ronnie, and how we had ended up not really knowing anything about each other's lives, I had a strong feeling of déjà vu. But one night that autumn, Stephen did something quite spectacular that touched my heart and briefly made me think, 'Hold on, Bar – you've got it all wrong. He does care. We may have a chance, after all.'

I was taking my final bow at a music hall performance at the Theatre Royal in Windsor, on 16 September, when the master of ceremonies looked out at the audience of 1,500 from the side of the stage and broke in: 'Ladies and gentlemen, the evening is far from over. Because I now ask you to welcome an extraordinary eclectic delineator of diverse delights with scintillating surprises. Ladies and gentlemen, Mr Michael Aspel.'

I was standing in line with my six fellow performers, completely bewildered. I had no idea what he was talking about and I presumed they didn't, either. The two-hour show was over, and there was no more to come. Well, there hadn't been on the two previous nights, but tonight, unknown to me, Michael Aspel, tracked by a TV camera, had been smuggled through the front door as we took our bows and was now hiding in the wings. When the MC finished his flowery speech, Michael emerged, holding the famous Big Red Book. The audience applauded wildly. They were in for an unexpected treat: they were going to witness a celebrity being surprised for that magical TV experience, *This is Your Life*. I stood there grinning and clapping along with everyone else – until Michael stopped a few feet from me and said: 'Thank you, sir. May I congratulate you on your cornucopia of comedy and to add, if I may, that I am indeed here to say that tonight, Barbara Windsor, This is Your Life.'

My grin vanished. My jaw dropped. All I was aware of was the applause rising to a crescendo and Michael looking at me, patiently waiting for me to say something. After a few seconds, I'd recovered enough to exclaim: 'Darling, you *can't* do my life. It's so . . . naughty!' But the cheers were so deafening that I don't think he heard me. 'I don't know what to say,' I began again. '*Me* speechless? I can't believe this . . . It's a joke.' And then I repeated: 'How *can* you do my life, Michael? There are so many naughty bits!'

'I know the naughty bits, but they don't,' Michael said, turning to the audience.

Trying to get over the shock, I told him: 'I know everyone says this, but I would like to say that I wish Mummy was here. She always said, "They haven't done *your* life, Babs."'

Michael took my arm. 'Now, if you'll come with me and slip into something less comfortable . . .'

Mild panic set in. 'God, I don't know what I've got here,' I said. The audience's cheers turned to laughter: they love it when a star has been caught unawares. My hand went to my chin as I tried to remember what clothes I had in my dressing room: I wanted to look my best when I went in front of the cameras. 'What have I got here? I don't know what I've got here,' I kept repeating. And then Michael was gently leading me off the stage as I muttered, 'I can't believe this,' to the continuing applause of the audience and the rest of the cast.

I was taken to a hotel a mile or so away, where I got the second huge surprise of the evening: waiting for me in a suite were two sets of clothes: dresses, underwear, tights, shoes, even wigs. There was only one person who could have arranged that: Stephen. And an hour or so later, when I arrived back at the Theatre Royal, one of the show's researchers told me about everything he had done, with the help of my friend Graham Roberts. Stephen had even bought me an elegant, black two-piece costume he knew I wanted, and taken it to my dressmaker in Golders Green to have it altered to fit me.

Many cynics refer to the people who have appeared on *This is Your Life* as victims. I prefer subjects. I considered it an honour and a privilege, and I was thrilled to be chosen. Quite honestly, I'd always felt that the shadow of notoriety Ronnie Knight had cast on my career had ruled me out of TV's most endearing accolade. My joy must have been obvious to everyone as I walked in front of the cameras to the famous, nerve-tingling, *This is Your Life* signature tune. It was one of those very rare times when I enjoyed making an entrance and wasn't embarrassed to be the sole centre of attention. I waved at Stephen's family and friends and other familiar faces on either side of the stage; then, not too sure what to do next, I turned my back to the audience and wiggled my bottom in cheeky Carry On style.

'Thank you for that,' said Michael. 'We all enjoyed that.'

I sat down, excited as a little girl on Christmas Day, and waited for my life, and some of the people who had featured in it, to be presented to the nation. I expected Stephen to be there, but when Michael Aspel opened the programme with a film clip of Stephen at the Plough, surrounded by our staff, I wasn't sure, especially when the camera zoomed in on Stephen and he said: 'You always said they'd never catch you, but I told you they would one day. It's business as usual here, but everyone wants to say they hope you have a lovely evening.' The camera picked up my gorgeous dog, and Stephen added: 'Including Bonnie.'

But then Michael said: 'He's not really there, of course. He's done the washing up and is here tonight. Your husband, Stephen.' And there, walking towards me, immaculately groomed, with the broadest grin on his handsome face, was my old man. I jumped up and we hugged. 'I love you,' I said, squeezing him. 'I love you. I *love* you.'

When we sat down, I told the audience how I'd panicked about my clothes, and how Stephen had arranged everything behind my back. 'The Irish, the shoes, the dress, the tights – they're all here!' I said. 'We look after our guests on this show,' laughed Michael, but neither he nor the audience could have had any idea how much it meant to me. From someone who had not shown me any affection for three years, it was a kind, loving gesture and I was deeply touched by it.

The show got off to a hilarious start when Michael innocently left me an opening to make a joke about Ronnie Knight. Referring to the headlines in which Stephen was cast as my toyboy lover, Michael asked if anyone, apart from the press, had shown any interest in the age gap. 'No one,' I said. 'Apart from you know who. But I'd better not mention him.' I waited for the laughter to die down, then giggled: 'I suppose he's coming on later, Michael. I bet he's the surprise guest at the end.'

'I like to live dangerously,' replied Michael, 'but not that dangerously.' Everyone fell about.

I was thrilled by the pre-recorded messages from Jeannie Carson and

June Whitfield, which brought back warm memories of *Love From Judy*, and from Joan Littlewood, speaking from France. That was a worrying moment, though, because Victor Spinetti had just told the story of how I'd stood up to her on his behalf in New York, and I'd broken in with: 'Yeah, she could be a right cow!' When Michael said: 'And now we can go to Joan Littlewood at her home in France,' my face fell.

'Oh, dear, did she hear me?' I asked anxiously.

That got another laugh, but thankfully Joan did not hear Victor's anecdote or my careless quip.

One remark that did go down well concerned three wonderful actors and friends who'd been my leading men over the years: Dennis Quilley from *Sing a Rude Song*, Jack Smethurst from *The Mating Game* and, of course, old Nathan Detroit himself, Gareth Hunt.

'Look at them all sitting there, grinning like fools,' said Michael.

'That's because they've worked with me, dear,' I giggled. 'I make them all very happy in my shows, Michael!'

'Well, the night *is* young,' he grinned.

Everyone was laughing – including Stephen, I was happy to see.

My wonderful evening ended with a parade of some of my closest friends from the Water Rats and Lady Ratlings: Ronnie Hilton, John Inman, Anna Karen, Davy Kaye, Rose Marie, Toni Palmer, Jack Douglas, Bert Weedon and Paul and Debbie Daniels. And then Michael was holding out the Red Book and saying those time-honoured words, 'Barbara Windsor – This is Your Life' and suddenly everyone was smiling and clapping and converging on me from all sides. As we all moved towards the studio audience for the traditional end-of-show applause, I was aware that Stephen was not there. I looked around in the mêlée and spotted him standing on his own behind everyone, near Michael Aspel, who always retreats out of shot. Clutching the Big Red Book to my chest with my left hand, I turned and motioned to him to come through to me. He took my right hand and we moved to the front of the stage and drank in the acclaim.

When everything had quietened down, I looked into his eyes and said: 'I love you so much.' And I meant it. I remember thinking later: 'I've been so stupid. I must not have any more affairs. Stephen *does* love me. Maybe he has lost the desire to demonstrate it in bed, but what he did with *This is Your Life* was his way of showing that he does care about me.'

But what happened the next morning in Marylebone brought me crashing down to earth and convinced me that I was living in a fool's paradise. Still high from the show, I went into the bathroom and sat on the loo seat to talk to Stephen while he was having a bath. 'I don't know what to say to you, darling,' I told him. 'I just thank you. *Thank you. This is Your Life*! I can't believe it has happened to me.'

'Yeah,' he said matter-of-factly. 'Great, wasn't it?'

I felt deflated. On the night, and at the after-show party, with his family and friends around him, he had been wonderfully warm. But now, on his own with me, he was cold and offhand about it all. He got out of the bath and dressed, then left for Amersham with the briefest of goodbyes. He didn't want to spend another minute with me. He seemed more interested in getting back to his 'mistress' and telling his staff all about the programme.

After I watched him drive off, I went upstairs to the bedroom, fighting back tears.

22

ONE EVENING IN DECEMBER 1992, I ARRIVED AT THE THEATRE ROYAL IN BRIGHTON FOR ANOTHER PERFORMANCE OF *CINDERELLA* AND FOUND A BOUQUET OF FLOWERS FROM RITA MITCHELL, AN OLD SCHOOL FRIEND FROM THE CONVENT AND A FELLOW JUVENILE JOLLITY FROM MADAME BEHENNA'S SOME FORTY-FIVE YEARS BEFORE – I STILL HAVE THE PROGRAMME TO PROVE IT! She now lived in nearby Hove. I really must call her, I thought: it would be nice to meet and catch up with what had been happening with her and her husband, Ronnie, one of those Jewish boys who had hung around outside the E and A salt beef bar in Stamford Hill when we were all teenagers. Early in January, with one week left of the run, I rang and asked Rita if we could meet up the following Monday.

'Why don't you come to dinner?' she suggested.

I said yes immediately, although a bit of me felt it might not be a good idea: I hadn't seen Rita or Ronnie for about twenty years and I wondered if we'd have anything in common to talk about after such a long gap. I was also concerned that she might invite a lot of people I didn't know who would want to talk about showbiz all evening. I wasn't sure I'd be good company. I wasn't feeling up to much: Stephen had brought down a coachload of his customers the previous Sunday and had waltzed off afterwards having hardly bothered to say hello. I didn't have time to change my mind, however, because Rita, all enthusiastic, was saying how lovely it would be to see me. I told her I was staying at Victor Spinetti's house in Kemp Town, and she said her son would drive over and pick me up at 7 p.m.

It's amazing when you look back and consider how such apparently small decisions can alter the course of your entire life. If I'd decided to cry off that dinner, I would probably never have met someone who was to change mine dramatically.

I decided to dress down, choosing a high-necked black and white top and black skirt, and was just putting my coat on when the doorbell rang. Standing in the porch was a shortish, slightly built young man with dark, medium-length hair in an extremely smart full-length waisted overcoat. He looked sort of continental and I'd have said he was about eighteen.

'Hello,' he said, in a cultured voice. 'I'm Scott. Ronnie and Rita's son.'

Although I was ready, I invited him in on the pretext of showing him part of the house: he seemed nice, and I wanted a closer look at him. We made idle conversation for five minutes, then climbed into Scott's green Range Rover and headed towards the Mitchell house in Hove.

'You're a very smart young man,' I told him, just to make conversation.

Scott laughed. 'This is a Cecil Gee coat. I used to work there.'

'Oh, really?' I said. 'My husband's very, very smart. He's tall and slim, and he likes Cecil Gee.' I can't think why I was building Stephen up into some Brad Pitt character.

I tried another tack. 'What do you do now?'

'I'm an actor,' said Scott.

'You don't look like an actor.'

'What are actors supposed to look like?' he asked, and immediately I felt stupid for having made such a ridiculous comment.

'I came in late,' he went on.

I was confused. 'How old are you, then?'

'Twenty-nine.'

I was shocked. He looked so much younger. At virtually the same moment a naughty thought flashed through my mind: Mmm, I may be in with a chance here.

Scott told me how much he loved acting, and how excited he was about playing the Dauphin in Shakespeare's *Henry V* at the Tabard, a fringe theatre in Chiswick. We chatted easily, almost like old friends, and before we knew it, we were pulling up outside a lovely semi-detached house and Scott was hurrying round to open the car door for me. Rita, looking as pretty as I remembered her, greeted me with a warm smile. 'We've got some people here,' she said. I groaned inwardly. Oh, God, I thought. It's all the neighbours.

I could not have been more wrong. Rita and Ronnie had sprung the most wonderful surprise: waiting for me in the lounge were two more dear pals I hadn't seen for many years: Brian Hall, who played the chef in *Fawlty Towers*, and his wife Marlene. Apart from being a marvellous actor, Brian was a great raconteur and my misgivings quickly vanished: I knew the six of us were in for a joyful and interesting evening.

Over dinner the conversation flowed as fast as the wine, and by the time Rita – the only one who had not been drinking – offered to drive me back to Kemp Town I was pleasantly tipsy. Scott came with us and saw me to Victor's door. I gave him a peck on the cheek, promising to arrange panto tickets for the Mitchells and the Halls the following Friday, and went inside.

That, as they say, should have been that. But it wasn't.

That Friday the five of them came to see the show and we had champagne in my dressing room afterwards. When I arrived at the theatre on the Saturday afternoon, I was handed a package. It contained a book – *Seven Ages*, *Poetry for Life*, chosen by David Owen – with a thank you card which read: 'This is a token of appreciation for an absolutely wonderful evening.' It was signed Scott Mitchell. I was touched: the Mitchells were a lovely couple and their son was the most endearing young man.

A couple of days later I was in the Colonnade pub next to the theatre when two strangers approached me. One of them said he had seen me before, in Plymouth, talking to Thomas Powell.

'Oh, really?' I said, surprised but pleased. 'You know Thomas? How is he?'

'Not too good,' the man said. 'He's in Brighton right now, actually.'

An image of Thomas in that precinct in Plymouth, out of his brains, flashed into my mind.

'We'll try and keep him away,' the man said. 'If he knows you're here, he'll be hanging around outside the stage door.'

There were only a couple of days of the panto left, and I did not see Thomas. I knew he was going to do a story for the *Star*, because an assistant editor there, Nigel Blundell, had phoned to tell me. Nigel wanted it to be with my blessing, and had taken me to Rules restaurant in Covent Garden to talk it over. He bought me an expensive lunch, and I soon realised why: he wanted me to do the voice-over for a radio commercial plugging the paper's exclusive story. I couldn't blame him for trying, but of course, I said no. Stephen was going to be embarrassed enough as it was, and he wouldn't want me to play any part in Thomas making money out of me.

But that decision blew up in my face. I was in the kitchen at the pub when the most salacious advertisement came on the air, urging people to buy the *Star* and read about 'my sex with Carry On actress Barbara Windsor'. I could handle it – I'd had worse than this – but Stephen was mortified. We had the most awful row.

Four weeks later, I was back in Brighton, this time with my one-woman show, when Thomas turned up asking for me. I was stunned by his appearance. He had shaved, his clothes were clean and he was not drunk, but his hair was dyed a bizarre mixture of red and brown and blond, and his face was ravaged from binges on the booze, his hands swollen and scarred from falling over when drunk or from fighting. He was a mess, a man without a life who had lost everything, and I was consumed with a familiar overpowering sadness.

We chatted about this and that for a bit, but I had to get ready to go on stage. I knew that whatever he had got for his story, it would not have been put away for a rainy day, so I took out some money from my handbag.

'I haven't come for that,' said Thomas.

'I know you haven't, darling,' I said gently. 'But I want you to have it. It's just a little something to help you out.'

He took it, promising to pay it back, and I opened the dressing-room door for him. 'Take it easy,' I told him.

For a while after he left, I couldn't get Thomas out of my mind. I wondered whether in some way I might have been responsible for his tragic decline. I'm aware of what kind of lady I am. I embrace the man in my life and I'll do anything for him and make him feel good. I had breezed into Thomas's life, a bouncy, confident film star, and made him fall in love with me when the relationship was quite clearly doomed. Had I been selfish and irresponsible in not recognising that? *Was* I to blame for turning upside down the emotions, the entire world, of such a fragile and insecure person? In a way, it was a relief that I was in Brighton for only one night. Who knows, my guilt may have got the better of me. I still had a strong affection for Thomas and I might have been tempted to spend more time with him than was good for either of us.

The following week, Barry Burnett and I went to Smith's restaurant in Covent Garden with two other agents, Shane Collins and George Heathcote, to see a performance by the *Phantom of the Opera* cast to raise money for an AIDS charity. Some people at a table next to us made a lot of noise during the show, particularly when the former pop star Mark Wynter came on to sing one of his numbers from *Phantom* and they kept shouting for him to sing his 1962 hit 'Venus in Blue Jeans'.

Later, as we were leaving, a woman rushed up to me angrily, screeching: 'Who the hell do you think you are, making a noise while people are performing?'

She was a biggish woman and very intimidating, and seemed out of control. She was screaming abuse at me and I was frightened. I was sure she was going to hit me. Ronnie had always told me to pick up the nearest weapon and go on the attack if ever I felt in danger, so I hurled a fist into the woman's face and, as she fell back, I picked up a chair, ready to whack her with it if she came for me. It was so heavy that I dropped it. At that point someone grabbed me and bundled me out of the restaurant and into a taxi. The next morning I was woken by a phone call from Stephen, who wanted to know what I'd been up to.

'What do you mean?' I asked sleepily.

'You were in a fight last night,' he said. 'You're on the front page of the *Sun*.'

I'm sure that anyone who read that story, printed under the headline 'BUSTY BABS IN PUNCH-UP', must have thought that both the other woman and I were drunk. I can't speak for her, but I wasn't; I only had two drinks all night. If I had been drunk, what was merely a storm in a wine glass could have been a lot worse. And I did get lots of messages saying that the woman had been out of order, which was nice.

Scott Mitchell had said he'd like to see me in a music hall, so I rang him on the first Saturday in February to tell him I'd got him a ticket for my performance at Brick Lane in Hackney the following week. It was 1.30 p.m., but Scott was still in bed, nursing a hangover, and at first seemed less than thrilled to hear from me. He thanked me for the invitation, however, and said he would be there. As I didn't want him to have to come on his own, and, more importantly, thought it might be useful for him to meet some people in showbusiness, I arranged for him to go with Barry and a couple of other agents.

On the night, I came through the main doors of the theatre and ran among the tables, kissing bald heads and complimenting all the people who had dressed in period clothes for the occasion. Scott didn't have a bald head, but I gave him a kiss, too – by accident, honest.

For once Stephen was at the show, and during a question-and-answer session afterwards, I introduced him to the audience. With all the chit-chat and autograph-signing that followed I didn't have a chance to speak to Scott, but as Stephen drove me home to Marylebone that night, I felt a strong desire to see him again.

The next Monday Barry asked to see me to discuss my career. He said he felt I should be tackling a serious acting role, playing someone nearer my own age. I could see the logic of that, but nothing sprang to mind.

'*Entertaining Mr Sloane* is going on a national tour,' Barry said. 'I'd like you to consider playing Kath.'

I adored that play and had enjoyed playing Kath in Kenny Williams' production in 1981, but I didn't think it was the right move now. Barry had a point, though: I did need to be playing someone closer to my fifty-five years, and at least Kath was in her forties. I was still wondering whether my best years were behind me as far as the theatre was concerned and whether I should become an agent. I was sure I'd be good at it: I'm not good at pushing myself, but I'm unsurpassable at pushing other people. And, vitally important in a flaky business, I am 100 per cent reliable.

But Barry wouldn't let it go. '*Sloane*'s on at the Greenwich Theatre, Bar,' he said. 'Let's go and see it next Saturday. Nothing's lost.'

I wasn't sure, but it would be good to see the play again anyway, so I went and thoroughly enjoyed the production. Barry was certain that *Sloane* was the perfect vehicle for me. A four-month tour covering sixteen venues was being planned, and he believed it could kick-start my career again and restore my flagging confidence. The producer, Lee Dean, was keen for me to play Kath, he said; all I had to do was say yes. It was a huge decision, and I wanted time to think it through. But I was going to Barbados with Stephen the following week and *Sloane*'s producer needed a yes or no before I left. Over the next few days I did a lot of heart-searching, and in the end I decided to play safe: I would do the play, but at the same time, I would do something positive about becoming an agent. Then if I found I could not cut the mustard any more, at least I'd have made some headway in a new direction.

So, before Stephen and I left for the Caribbean, I phoned Barry. 'I'll do it,' I said. And the moment I heard myself say those words, I was filled with dread. My confidence was so low that I was doubting myself before I'd even picked up the script.

The Barbados trip was confirmation, if any were needed, of just how bad a state our marriage was in. At the airport, before we had even got on the plane, I told Stephen I was going to W.H. Smith's to get some paperbacks, but he said we didn't have time. 'You can get them at the other end,' he snapped, hurrying me along to the boarding gate. I'm an avid reader, and for me one of the great luxuries of a holiday is having the time to enjoy a few good books, so I always pick up a pile of them at the airport. But this time, not only did I not have a book on that long flight, but of course when we got to Barbados there were none to be found anywhere, neither at the airport nor in the hotel, and all I had to read for two weeks were the newspapers or a small version of *Sloane* I'd packed.

It was a sad holiday. Stephen was at his most contrary, always wanting to do precisely the opposite of what I suggested, and time dragged. It was probably not the right atmosphere for reacquainting myself with Joe Orton's little gem, but it was either that or the newspapers, and there was only so much news I wanted to read. So I took *Sloane* on to the balcony one morning and, within minutes, I had got myself into a right state: I'd forgotten just how much dialogue there was in the play. Suddenly it hit me what I'd agreed to do, and I became extremely nervous, and I mean *extremely*. The more I read, the less confident I became that I could do it. What on earth had possessed me to think I could?

Kath is the pivotal role in *Sloane*, but the part of her bisexual brother, Ed, is vital, too, and on my return to England I convinced the producers and director that Peter Dean, who had recently left *EastEnders*, was perfect for the role. They decided to take a chance with him because according to his CV he had done some stage work.

One morning Barry and I went to the Players' Theatre on London's Victoria Embankment, where we sat at the back while the producer and the director auditioned six actors for the part of Sloane. Over lunch, the producer and director decided that Chris Villiers was the perfect choice.

Walking along the Strand with Barry afterwards, I bumped into someone I had not seen since I was in Nottingham playing Calamity Jane. We exchanged pleasantries, and then he told me excitedly: 'I think I've finally cracked TV, Bar.'

'Lovely,' I said. 'What is it?'

'A quiz show. It's about a supermarket. I ask questions and the contestants rush round picking up as many groceries as they can.'

I stared at him in disbelief. A quiz in a supermarket? He sounded off his trolley. But not wishing to be unkind, I said: 'Good luck, dear. I hope it takes off for you.'

'Oh, I'm sure it will, Bar,' said Dale Winton.

I wanted to see Scott Mitchell again. Towards the end of April, I phoned him at Hampstead Garden Suburb, where he was now living, to invite him to Wimbledon Theatre with me and three other mates, to see a musical version of *Sherlock Holmes*. I was keen to see dear Roy Barraclough, who was playing the legendary detective, but I was also curious about the production itself because I'd been offered a part in it. I satisfied myself that I'd been right not to get involved in the show, and then we all went on to Joe Allen's for dinner afterwards and had a lovely time. Scott really enjoyed himself: he had not laughed so much in a long time, he said. He told me there was no one special in his life, and, as I took a taxi home, I found myself wondering why.

Early in May, with rehearsals for *Sloane* due to start in a month, I rang Anna Karen in a bit of a panic. 'I can't get my head round all this dialogue!' I wailed.

'Why don't you do what I do?' she suggested, trying to calming me down. 'Get someone to read the other lines with you, then tape them.'

It sounded a great idea, but who did I know with that sort of time to spare? Ideally, I needed an actor who was sitting around waiting for work. Scott came to mind. He was perfect for Sloane, and he could read the other parts as well. So I called him and he was delighted. A few days later he arrived at Marylebone, looking very much like Sloane, in black leather trousers and biker boots. We read the parts of the play where Sloane and Kath are together, then did them again and recorded them. I was overjoyed. Anna was right: suddenly all those words that had frightened me so much were leaping off the page and into my brain, and I was feeling less intimidated by the minute. Afterwards, as a thank you, I offered to buy Scott dinner, but he had a party to go to and settled for a glass of wine. Waving goodbye to him, I thought again what a pleasant and friendly person he was.

Two days later, Scott rang, unable to contain his excitement. 'I'm going for an audition, Barbara,' he said. 'You'll never guess what for.'

I couldn't, so he told me: 'The part is Joe Orton himself, in a new version of his own *Ruffian on the Stair*!'

It was an amazing coincidence. My prayers for him to get the part were answered, and we found we had the same amount of time – three weeks – before we began our respective rehearsals. In those three weeks, our friendship grew steadily: Scott was fascinated that I had known Orton, and we started to talk on the phone most days. I found I was more at ease with him than with most of the men I had seen since meeting Stephen, but at that stage he was still no more than a friend; a charming, intelligent and very attractive friend, admittedly, but nothing more than that.

On Wednesday 2 June, Scott came round again to go over my lines before joining me and some other friends for dinner at an Italian restaurant in Marylebone Lane. By now we were familiar with the lines and rattled through them so fast I had no option but to open a bottle of Sancerre to kill a bit of time before dinner. We laughed and joked as easily as usual, and then we got round to talking about relationships. I had not spoken much about Stephen, but Scott did not have to be Einstein to work out that it was not the closest of marriages. I made light of it with a rather obvious sexual innuendo about brushing the cobwebs away every now and again. 'Well, it's no big deal, is it?' I added quickly, in case Scott was embarrassed. 'When it comes down to it, it's only sex, after all.'

We liked each other and our friendship had grown into a mutual attraction. We were both on a high: me because at last I'd cracked the *Sloane* lines; Scott because he was opening soon at a theatre in Chelsea. It was a wonderfully warm summer night, the sort of night that promised much, and we both felt it.

The evening at the restaurant enhanced our mood: everyone was in a gregarious, positive frame of mind, with all sorts of good news to report, and, of course, the constant flow of Chianti helped things along splendidly. By the time we left, just after midnight, we were all very tipsy and I was happier than I'd been for ages. We were all standing outside the restaurant saying our goodbyes when I suddenly grabbed Scott's hand and started running along Marylebone Lane and down Wimpole Street, giggling like a naughty schoolgirl. 'Let's get away from 'em. Let's get away from 'em,' I kept saying, pulling Scott along. I did eventually slow down to a walk, and we turned into Wimpole Street and strolled along the mews, holding hands and still laughing. The evening had been an intoxicating aphrodisiac and we were both high on it, both eager to get behind closed doors and release the passion that had grown so suprisingly swiftly from our unlikely friendship.

I awoke with a jolt, as usual. And the second I realised where I was and what had happened, I reacted quickly. Nudging Scott, I said: 'Excuse me, sweetheart, but you'll have to go. I've got my cleaner coming.' It was only six o'clock, and obviously my cleaner was not due; she was probably asleep herself. But I wanted Scott out of the house before the rest of the mews woke up, and the cleaner was the first excuse I could think of. He got dressed and we went downstairs. Although we both had hangovers and there was a faint awkwardness in the harsh light of morning, we were also both a bit giggly, which was nice. I thought nothing of offering Scott a £20 note for a taxi, but he felt insulted and refused it, saying he would get the tube from Regent's Park.

I went back to bed and dropped off immediately. Half an hour later the phone rang. It was Scott.

'Hello, love,' I mumbled. 'What is it?'

'I just want you to know I respect you, Barbara,' he said. 'I like spending time with you, and I don't want you to be embarrassed and feel you aren't able to pick the phone up again.'

'All right, love,' I said. 'That's very sweet of you. Take care. Bye bye,' and I went back to sleep.

We didn't speak over the weekend, but I left a message on Scott's answerphone on the Monday evening to say I hoped that everything had gone well with his rehearsal. Later, he rang back, thrilled I'd called: he said he was afraid he'd seen the last of me.

Even at that early stage, we both knew that deep feelings were stirring in both of us and that the friendship was turning into love. I sensed it was becoming very serious when I did something out of character a few days later: I rang Scott and told him how much I missed him. It was the first time I'd said anything like that. Scott wrote in his diary: 'Oh, dear, we could be getting into trouble here.'

I arrived typically early, at 9.30 a.m., at the Churchill Theatre in Bromley to start rehearsals for *Sloane*. I was surprised to find Peter Dean already at the theatre, looking very confused. He said he had been there an hour. 'Nobody phoned me last night telling me when to be here,' he said.

'It's not *EastEnders*, Pete. We were all told when rehearsals would start. That's it. We don't get call sheets the night before. That's TV. This is theatre.'

He just looked at me glumly, and I began to wonder how much theatre he had actually done. When we started rehearsing, it was clear he did not know the piece at all. He kept fluffing his lines, particularly when he had to speak while using one of the props. He seemed very unsure of himself, and after three days he had not improved at all. He was not seeing eye to eye with the director, who was by now concerned that he was not up to the job and never would be. By the end of the week, Peter seemed to have come to the conclusion that the director just didn't like him. He was in a right state. Although I never travelled by train, that Friday evening I took one to London with Peter because I wanted to talk to him and try to put his mind at rest. I talked about his role for most of the journey, and as the train was pulling into Victoria, I said: 'What you should do is go home, have a nice hot bath and a drink. Then give your missus a kiss and cuddle and try to put all this out of your mind until Monday. We've got another ten days to wrap it all up and you'll be great. You're perfect for the part.'

That evening I put Peter's problems out of my mind to turn my attention to a repeat performance of the previous week: dinner with Scott and another group of friends, then bed. Scott left at around 4 a.m.

Peter failed to turn up that Monday, or any day after that. His agent would only say that he had gone away somewhere, possibly Scotland, and could not be contacted. I never got to the bottom of what happened, but it was clear that he was unable to overcome his differences with the director and his own concerns about his suitability for the role. He did not pull out of the show, preferring to stay away until he was sacked, because that was a crucial factor as regards financial compensation. He was a nice enough man, but none of us thought that was fair on the production.

The important thing now, though, was to find a replacement, and fast. In the meantime, rehearsals had to go on. In *Sloane*, every part is in itself a lead role, and going through such a demanding script without one of the major players there, with just a week to first night, was terrifying.

On the Wednesday afternoon, Dean's replacement walked into the Churchill: it was John Challis, famous for his role as Boycie in the TV comedy *Only Fools and Horses*. John had been drinking in his local pub near Richmond, when his agent had phoned. 'How do you fancy touring *Entertaining Mr Sloane* with Barbara Windsor?'

'I'd love it,' said John.

'Can you get to rehearsal this afternoon?' his agent asked.

'I'll be there,' promised John.

John played Kath's brother brilliantly, and no one would have suspected that he had stepped into the role at such short notice. He was very professional, a joy to work with, and saved the day for all of us. He also became a very close friend.

That Friday evening, Scott and I saw a musical at the Churchill and on Sunday we went for a leisurely stroll around Hampstead and Golders Green. I could have gone to the Plough, but I desperately wanted to see Scott. And to be honest, I would rather have been spending my time off with someone who liked me for myself than to be surrounded by people who wanted to talk to me only because I was Barbara Windsor. I was so happy with Scott that lovely, lazy Sunday. I suggested we dropped in on an old teenage pal of mine, Frankie Stevens, who knew Scott's father really well. When he saw us, Frankie burst out laughing. 'Look at you, walking in here with a handsome young man, like you're sixteen years old. And, I can't believe it: he turns out to be Ronnie Mitchell's son!'

But by the end of the day I started to feel guilty. Maybe it was too nice, and I shouldn't have been enjoying myself so much. When I felt it was time to be heading home, around 5 p.m., and I couldn't find my door keys, I got panicky and rounded on Scott. 'It's all your fault I've lost them,' I snapped. 'I shouldn't be here. I really shouldn't be here. Now look what's happening to me!' I finally found the keys, but I was in a state, and Scott saw another side of me. Not that it seemed to put him off. That night he wrote in his diary: 'I think I'm getting involved. I can't help it.'

Before we'd met, there had been so little going on in Scott's life that he could cover six days in just two pages in that diary. Now he was doing so much he needed a whole page for each day. It was turning into a chronicle of the beginning of our affair.

23

Every June, the Conservative MP Sir Fergus Montgomery and his wife, Joyce, invited me, along with dozens of other showbiz 'faces', to the House of Commons for a party. In 1993, when Stephen said he was too busy to go, I invited Scott.

He was so sweet. He arrived at the house in a suit and tie, with his long dark hair gelled neatly into place, and gave me a present: a very pretty diamond bracelet. 'Thank you so much for inviting me, Bar,' he said. 'I'm so thrilled to be going.' He was very concerned about his appearance and asked: 'Do I look all right? Is this OK?' He seemed anxious to look right for me as much as for himself, and I found that endearing: so many men don't give a monkey's. I felt a bit like Mrs Robinson in *The Graduate*.

We had a fabulous time. Loads of stars were there – people like Shirley Bassey, Jim Davidson and Elaine Paige – and afterwards Scott and I were in such high spirits that we ran up Whitehall to Trafalgar Square, holding hands, then walked all the way back to Marylebone like a couple of love-struck teenagers wrapped up in each other and in the warm, summer night.

Scott had been dreadfully nervous, not only about mixing with MPs, but also about meeting my showbiz friends who might be wondering what the nature of our relationship was. If anyone did, no one showed it. Everyone was kind and respectful to Scott, and just accepted him.

I was relieved as much as pleased about that, because I'd discovered that beneath Scott's strong, confident exterior lay an extremely sensitive, self-doubting person, who, like me, had an unquenchable desire to please and to be liked. As a kid, he'd been small, skinny and very nervous, a soft and easy target for the bullies at junior school in Brighton who had knocked what little confidence he had out of him by the age of seven. My heart went out to him when he related several incidents in which he was pushed to the ground and kicked by a group of bullies. It had a deep, long-lasting effect on Scott, causing him to carry forward certain fears, not only about being picked on physically, but verbally as well.

His self-belief was not helped by having a father who, in his younger days, had been a fearless tough nut who never walked away from a fight. Ronnie had been mates with the actor Steven Berkoff, and Steven described in his autobiography the pride Ronnie's pals took in the battle scars Ronnie got from taking on the Kray twins. It was inevitable, I suppose, that, growing up with all these stories about his dad's legendary courage, Scott would want to be like him. But it was a different time and a different environment: the Brighton of the early seventies was as far removed from the East End of London as you could imagine. And Scott was a vastly different boy from the father who had been forced to fend for himself in a rough area where violence was a way of life.

It did not help that Scott was small. He told me how, in his early teens, his parents' friends had taunted him about his size. 'Aren't you small!' they would say. 'Our boy is nearly as big as his dad.' No wonder Scott felt he did not measure up. At drama school he had huge expectations of himself, but was filled with self-doubt. He worked hard and was told that what he did was good, but he never believed he was as good as he thought he should be. And with that self-doubt came a deeper, more damaging fear: that he was not liked as a person. 'Why are you so hard on yourself?' his friends would say. 'Why don't you like yourself? You're a nice person.' I could understand that, because there have been times in my life when I've felt exactly the same about myself.

Happily, Ronnie and Rita felt that I was good for Scott. When he had decided to break the news to them, it had come as no surprise to Rita. 'Mum, I've got something to tell you,' he began.

'Don't worry, I know what you're going to say,' she replied. 'You've fallen in love with Barbara, haven't you? That's great. I've known her since she was a little girl, and she's wonderful.'

On the day after the Commons bash, a Sunday, I gave the Plough a miss again, preferring to go to a party at John Inman's house and then on to Scott's flat, to give him some moral support during a painful procedure. He had asked an ex-girlfriend, Sarah, to remove the hairs from his chest for his role as Joe Orton, because he had to undress on stage, and Joe had had no hairs on his chest. It was just as well I went: Sarah put wax on Scott's chest without cutting the hair first, and when she ripped it off, Scott cried out in agony. I'd already been impressed by his love of the theatre, and now I was seeing how dedicated he was to his profession. He lay there squeezing my hand, feeling sick. Later he told me he hadn't treated Sarah that well when they'd been out together as nineteen-year-olds, so maybe she was getting her own back!

As we both went into our last week of rehearsal, we were both in a state of mild panic. Normal opening-night nerves were partly to blame, but what was happening to us emotionally was undoubtedly another factor. I'd been so stressed about whether I was doing the right thing getting involved with Scott that I'd lost more than a stone since the affair had begun. I was terrified that someone would spot him leaving the house in the early hours and ring the papers. And I had another worry, too: I was in love with the idea that such a desirable man was attracted to me, but how did I know whether it was the cheeky film star with lots of front that he loved, or Barbara Deeks, the quiet, thoughtful lady with all those insecurities.

As our respective productions opened, we were nervous as much for each other as for ourselves. I got in such a state the day before my opening night that I actually forgot my lines. I had gone in word-perfect; now I was falling apart. I calmed down after the opening night and got through the rest of the week, but when Sunday came, and I had a chance to see Scott in his play, I started feeling shaky all over again. I'd never seen him on stage and I didn't know if he could cut the mustard. I shouldn't have worried: he was great, absolutely terrific, and he got some smashing reviews, especially the London *Evening Standard*'s, which he posted to me in Malvern, where *Sloane* was starting its tour. The paper's critic wrote that Scott Harvey – his stage name – was 'full of cocky, cockney charm – an irresistible young thug'.

I longed for Scott to see me in *Sloane*, but he was working seven days a week. I wanted Stephen to see me, too, but he showed no interest. It probably said everything about our marriage that I had no interest in his business and he had none in mine. But I was a little hurt, all the same. For all his faults and selfishness, Ronnie had always turned up to see me perform.

Someone who did make the effort, in Bath, was Robert Dunn. He had been playing golf with a friend in the area and came backstage to say hello, then joined me and the rest of the cast for dinner. It was lovely seeing Robert again, but Scott was not pleased when I told him: it was not the fact that Robert was a former lover that bothered him; it was that I'd told Scott Robert had not been a good influence on me, and Scott couldn't understand why I would want to see him again.

With my fifty-sixth birthday coming up in August, while *Sloane* was playing Hornchurch in Essex, I decided to throw a party for twenty or so friends and Stephen's family, who wanted to come and see the play. I knew I would be apprehensive performing in front of so many people who knew me so well, particularly the ones in the business themselves, but I thought, what the hell, it's my birthday – let's all have a good time. To make things easy I arranged for a coach to pick up my guests in the West End and take them to the Queen's Theatre, which had a bar-cum-restaurant that was ideal for the intimate party I had in mind. The manager willingly agreed to lay on an after-show buffet.

Scott and I had a tough decision to make. He was dying to see *Sloane*; I wanted him to come to the party and he wanted to be there. It might sound shocking that I should consider entertaining my lover in the same room as my husband and his family, and I must admit it did bother me, greatly. But Scott and I consoled ourselves with the argument that it was precisely because Stephen was never with me and rarely phoned that we had been able to spend so much time together in the first place. Scott was more a part of my life than Stephen, so why shouldn't he be at the party? As long as no one knew the truth, no one was going to be hurt.

The moment we decided that he would be there, I knew that, come what may, I was going to tell Stephen the next day that we had to talk; we had to decide whether or not we wanted to try to get our marriage back on course. My marriage to Ronnie had broken down because we had not talked our problems through, and I did not want to repeat the same scenario with Stephen. Yes, I was in love with Scott, but even so, I was not prepared to throw myself wholeheartedly into the affair unless I knew for certain that Stephen and I did not have a future together.

On the night of the party, Stephen came to my dressing room half an hour before curtain-up. He knew I did not like having anyone in my dressing room before any show, let alone such an emotionally draining one as *Sloane*, but he popped in anyway. I thought he would just say: 'Everyone's settled. Have a good one,' and leave me to prepare myself. Instead he astounded me by asking: 'Have you got anything to eat? A sandwich, maybe? I'm starving.'

A sandwich? I thought. In my dressing room? I'm not a bloody pub!

Nevertheless, as I was trying to concentrate on transforming myself into Kath, I rang the management to arrange something.

After the performance, I was doing my hair and wondering what shoes to put on when Stephen walked in with Barry Burnett and his partner, Richard Wellington, and a couple of other friends. Stephen had not seen the play before and I was keen to hear what he thought of it. As I put the finishing touches to my face on, I was waiting for him to say something. But he barely even glanced at me. Finally, I had to ask: 'What did you think?'

'Oh, you were brilliant – as usual,' he said.

His voice had a sour, almost sarcastic tone to it. It was as if he was muttering under his breath to someone behind my back.

Richard came over. 'What's wrong with Stephen?' he asked quietly.

'I don't know,' I whispered tearfully. 'I don't know.'

Stephen is normally very sociable and enjoys a drink, but that night he did not touch a drop of alcohol and spent most of the time sitting in a corner on his own. Friends who were fond of him kept asking me what was wrong with him, but I couldn't tell them. Instead I made excuses. 'I think it must be the shock of seeing me in the part for the first time,' I said. 'No make-up, and that gumshield making it look like I've got no teeth. Seeing me run around with hardly anything on and being beaten up.' But I knew it was much more than that. I asked his sister Jane. 'Oh, we've had murders with him,' she said. 'He's been in a bad mood all evening.' But she didn't say why.

At first I was too upset to face a drink, but as the evening wore on and everyone apart from Stephen seemed to be having a good time, I tried to put him out of my mind and enjoy myself. By the time we all got on to the coach, I was in a happier frame of mind and moving around trying to talk to everybody. Stephen just sat in his seat sullenly throughout the journey, not talking to anyone.

When we got home to Marylebone, I was steaming. 'Stephen, I really want to talk to you,' I told him. 'Please can we talk?'

'It's late, Barbara. Let's go to bed.'

So we went to bed, but not surprisingly, I didn't sleep well. I finally gave up trying at 6 a.m. and went downstairs to make some tea. I took a cup up to Stephen. 'I need to talk to you,' I said again. 'I mean it.'

Later, when he had dressed and was sitting in the lounge, I came right out with it. 'So what was wrong with you last night?' He did not want to talk, but I couldn't let it go; I had to know what it was all about.

'It wasn't me, it was you,' he said. 'You were all emotional because it was your birthday and you had a lot to drink.' And then, out of nowhere, he asked: 'Barbara, have you met someone else?'

'Don't be silly,' I said. 'Of course not.'

I didn't like telling a lie, but what was the alternative? 'Well, actually, Stephen, I have. His name is Scott Mitchell. He's the most wonderful, charming, considerate, romantic man, and when I'm with him, I feel the most interesting, desirable and wanted woman in the world. I can talk to him. I can't with you.'

Instead I tried to get to the core of the problem. 'We don't seem to be really having a marriage. We don't talk. We don't see each other. We—'

'Oh, don't be silly, Barbara,' Stephen interrupted, laughing. 'You're busy, I'm busy. We've both so much to do.' He paused. 'Anyway, I've got to get back to the Plough.'

As he drove off, I remember thinking, I just can't get through to this man. And that confused me. Stephen was an intelligent person and I couldn't believe he didn't realise what was happening to us. I felt he must know, but did not want to confront it.

As soon as he'd gone, I phoned Scott, who said he'd drive me to Hornchurch for that evening's performance. All the way there and back, we talked about how serious my marriage breakdown was. It might sound a strange thing to say – after all, I was so discontented that I had happily gone to bed with Scott and had inveigled him into that intimate party – but until now, I hadn't realised just how desperately miserable I was. And until now, I hadn't met anyone I wanted to be with as much as I wanted to be with Scott. I still needed to have a heart-to-heart with Stephen, but with the *Sloane* tour continuing in Stevenage, Croydon and Crewe in September, and Plymouth and Brighton in October, plus music-hall performances in Guernsey and Scarborough to be fitted in, I couldn't see when we were going to find the time – if, indeed, my husband even wanted to find it.

I was agonising over whether or not to seek a legal separation from Stephen, and so frustrated by his offhandedness that I relied on Scott even more. It got to a point where Scott and I wanted to be with each other whenever we possibly could. Neither of us knew where the relationship was leading, but we were both absolutely certain now that it was far more than a fling. We did discuss the age gap, but agreed that it would be more of a problem for other people than for us. What concerned me more was that being involved with someone so famous might adversely affect Scott's career. We spoke on the phone virtually every night while I was on tour and, during one call, I brought this up. Scott was very clear on the matter. He said: 'If I have the choice of taking that gamble, and my career goes out the window, then I'll take that gamble, because I'd rather be with you and not have an acting career than have it without you.'

In September I did a personal appearance just outside Gloucester and was booked into a nearby hotel. On such evenings I would usually have a drink in the bar and eat in the restaurant, but on this occasion I was missing Scott so much I just wanted to be on my own. I had a long bath, then ordered dinner from room service. After I'd eaten, Scott phoned for a chat. I was so pleased. We talked for a few minutes about what we'd both been doing, and when I rang off I was wishing he was there with me.

I settled down in my dressing gown to watch TV. There was a knock on the door.

'Who is it?' I called out.

'Room service.'

'I didn't order anything else, darling.'

'I have something for you,' the voice called back.

Mystified, I opened the door slightly and peeped round it. Standing there was Scott, wearing a cap. He looked about fourteen and was so nervous he was breaking into a sweat.

'Scott!' I said. 'What are you doing here?'

When I'd thought Scott was ringing from London, he'd actually been downstairs. He had told Reception that he was my godson and was in the area and wanted to see me. He had said he understood they could not take his word for that, so he'd asked to speak to me on the phone to prove he knew me. After our conversation they'd happily given him my room number.

Scott had wanted to surprise me after a personal appearance in Hereford the day before, but had missed me. He had taken a three-hour train ride and a half-hour taxi journey to spring the surprise in Gloucester instead. I'd told Scott many times I loved surprises like that, so he was confident of a good reaction, but he was scared nonetheless. As he said, he took a chance knocking on that hotel-room door: he had no way of knowing if Stephen had decided to drop by, or anyone else for that matter. The effort he had made meant so much to me and it strengthened the bond between us.

The night *Sloane* opened in Croydon, I got another surprise. In the audience was someone I hadn't seen for thirty years: Charlie Kray. The years had robbed him of the Steve McQueen image that had been so attractive to me in the sixties, but he had lost none of the charm. And he looked fantastic, too, in a smartly tailored grey suit that set off his year-round sunbed tan. He gave me a hug and a kiss, then proudly rolled back his jacket sleeves to reveal the most stunning cufflinks.

'Bet you don't recognise these, Bar,' he said, grinning.

'Oh, yes, I bloody do. They're the cufflinks I bought you as a farewell present when you said you were leaving your wife for me!'

When I was with Scott I felt fabulous, but the nagging fear of what lay ahead with Stephen was always there. I knew I was going to have to tell Stephen that our marriage was over, that I was in love with somebody else, but I did not know when to do it, or how.

Under the pressure of it all I started to drink heavily. Not during the day, and never, ever before a performance, but as soon as a show finished I would pour the vodkas down me as though there were no tomorrow to block out the unhappiness that was tarnishing the joy of being with Scott. By October it was becoming something of a problem because I'd lost so much weight that I would get drunk very quickly and pass out. It was not unknown for Scott to have to virtually carry me out of a theatre bar or restaurant. He would get dreadfully upset and plead with me to go easy, to remember who I was, but I didn't care: it was as if I were trying to prove that it is actually possible to drown your sorrows. Scott, bless his heart, quickly learned to spot when I was nearing the point of no return, and would slow down himself so that he was in control and able to get me out before I made a prat of myself.

And then, just to add to it all, I went into hospital for tests and was told I was going through the change of life. I would wake in the middle of the night with hot flushes to find the whole bed saturated with perspiration, and I started having panic attacks and irrational outbursts when I'd flare up over the least little thing. Scott didn't know what to expect from one day to the next: one minute I'd be calm, the next I'd be shouting like a lunatic.

One Tuesday in October was particularly bad. Scott and I took the train home from a *Sloane* performance in Swindon and I stayed overnight at his flat in Hampstead Garden Suburb. In the morning, he went off for an audition, leaving me in the flat. Everything was peaceful when Scott left, but when he returned, he was greeted by this she-devil screaming at him: '*I don't want to be here! I've got to get out of here!*'

I was told that sooner or later I would have to have a hysterectomy. And, of course, that preyed on my mind terribly. There I was, with this lovely, young man, enjoying a satisfying sex life, and I was going to have all my bits and pieces mucked around with. Was that fair on him? For someone whose own emotional state was far from steady, Scott was unbelievably understanding of my mood swings and tetchiness. We talked through what was happening to my body, and whenever I flared up over nothing, he knew it was my hormones, not me.

Since our affair had begun, I'd avoided high-profile functions with Scott because of the risk of the press discovering the truth. I always read the *News of the World* to see who was being exposed as a liar and a cheat, and I didn't want to open it one week and find that it was me. But that autumn, I wanted to be seen out with Scott, so we started taking the odd risk. It was easy: people never asked who he was, just accepted that he was a best mate or my chauffeur, anything I cared to tell them, actually. Sometimes Scott would offer the explanation that I'd been a friend of his family for most of my life, which was of course perfectly true. It was well known that I had gay friends who had escorted me to premières, first nights and club openings when Stephen did not want to leave the business, and I'm sure that, in those early days of our romance, many people wrongly believed that Scott was gay.

In October, I went back to Brighton with *Sloane*. It was an ideal opportunity for Scott and I to spend some time with his family, so we travelled down together. On opening night, about half an hour before I was due on, I got a call to say that Thomas Powell was at the stage door wanting to see me. My immediate reaction was to let him come in, but Scott would not hear of it.

'You can't see anyone, Bar, let alone Thomas,' he said. 'You can't be doing with all that – you've got to get out there and perform.'

Sensing that I didn't want to hurt Thomas, he added: 'I'll go and see him. I'll explain.'

'Be nice to him, Scott,' I said. 'Please be nice to him.'

When Scott came back a few minutes later, he had tears in his eyes.

'What did he say?' I asked.

'He was in a state, Bar. Very drunk. It would have upset you if you'd seen him. I told him you were getting ready to go on stage and he grabbed me and hugged me and said. "That's all right, man. I don't want to upset her. Give her all my love. Make sure she's all right, man."'

And Thomas had walked away.

The encounter had obviously distressed Scott. 'God,' he said to me. 'I hope I never end up like that.'

By the beginning of November, the *Sloane* tour over, I knew I had to make the decision I'd been dreading. I thought, Christ I'm getting old, and I've met someone who may be right for me. I wanted to take the gamble and be with Scott. I loved him, and I didn't want to be involved with Stephen any more. We were no nearer even examining the gaping holes in our marriage, much less repairing them, and I was now certain that we never would. Very sadly, I had to acknowledge that it was too late.

I had not been to the Plough for months, but the one day I knew I had to be there was Thursday 11 November, for a party to celebrate our eighth year at the pub. I decided I had to tell Stephen then. At first I planned to talk to him before the party, but I decided that would not be fair. It would have to be the next day. That, of course, compounded the agony – I'd have to play the contented wife in front of dozens of guests and local newspaper photographers, while all the time I knew what was going to happen in the morning.

At midday that Thursday, Scott came to Marylebone and, over coffee, I told him what I intended to do. He said he would stay in all night, waiting by the phone, in case anything unforeseen happened and he needed to pick me up.

The one thing I didn't need was a personal appearance, but I was committed to switching on the Christmas lights in Milton Keynes. So I pulled myself up to my full four feet ten and a half inches, put on a big smile and got on with it.

For someone who had spent a lifetime putting on a front, it was a piece of cake. And so, in the end, was the birthday party at the Plough. I put on one of the most convincing performances of my life, serving good old cockney pie and mash, and fooling the hundred or so guests that I was the usual bubbly Babs while my mind was elsewhere. I did not touch a drop of alcohol all night. Stephen behaved as though we were a happy couple in a normal marriage and strangely, as we cut the cake, with our arms round each other, I felt more resolute about what I had to do in the morning. The charade somehow made me realise how wrong it all was and that there was no going back, no matter how nervous or apprehensive I was.

That party, like my birthday, could have been a happy, fun-filled event, but for me it was sad, tragic almost. As I made my excuses and went to bed at around midnight, it struck me that, as far as I was concerned, the evening had been less of a celebration than a wake for the death of a marriage. I could not get to sleep and was still awake when Stephen came to bed at around 2 a.m. I couldn't remember the last time he had touched me in bed, so I was amazed when he reached out and tried to cuddle me. 'Don't do that,' I snapped. 'Go away. It's too late.'

'What's wrong?' he asked.

'Please, Stephen. Don't.' And I pulled away from him and pretended to drop off. Within seconds, he was asleep.

The next morning I got out of bed quietly, just after 8.30, and crept downstairs in my dressing gown to ring Scott to let him know that I was all right. Then I went upstairs, got dressed, and woke Stephen. 'I want to talk to you,' I said firmly, feeling strong for the first time.

'What?' he said.

'I've tried to talk to you so many times, Stephen, and I'm not going back to London until I've talked to you properly. I'll wait for you in the lounge.'

He got up and came into the lounge. 'What is it?'

'To me it's pretty obvious what it is. We're married, but we don't have a marriage. There is nothing between us, and you just won't discuss it.'

'Everything is all right,' he said.

'No it isn't.'

He kept trying to make light of what I was trying to say until I got so exasperated that I came out with it. 'Stephen, it's over between us. Finished.'

He stared at me, totally bewildered. 'Why? Why, Barbara?'

'Why? Because, next month, it will be five years since you last came near me.'

'I tried to touch you last night.'

'I think that's a bit late, don't you?'

'Why didn't you sit me down and tell me all this before, you fool?'

I shook my head sadly at the irony of his question. 'I did try, sweetheart. But you weren't hearing me.'

'Have you found somebody else? Is there someone else?'

I hadn't planned to tell Stephen about Scott. I was just going to say I was leaving. But suddenly I felt there had already been too much dishonesty. Stephen needed to hear the truth.

'Yes,' I said.

Stephen went berserk. You would have thought from his reaction that I was leaving the most wonderful, loving marriage. He screeched and screamed and demanded to know who the other man was.

'No one you know,' I said. 'But I'm in love with him and want to be with him.'

'Who is he? How old is he?'

'That doesn't matter,' I told him. 'That's not the issue. I don't want to be with you, I want to be with him.'

'How old is he?' Stephen persisted.

'He's younger than me,' was all I wanted to reveal.

'Much younger?'

'Well, he is younger than you,' I said.

'Oh, Barbara, how could you do that? Barbara, Barbara, *how old is he?*'

'He's thirty,' I said.

Stephen's face tensed. Suddenly, his accent thickened into a broad, heavy Yorkshire. 'Go,' he said. 'Go now. I don't want to look at you. I don't want to talk to you. *Go now!*'

I was more than happy to comply. I was out of that lounge in seconds and on the phone to my driver, telling him to pick me up as soon as possible. Then I phoned Scott. 'I'm on my way, darling.'

The debts were still there, so the show had to go on. Later that month, I did a Friday and Saturday night of my music hall in Wolverhampton, then travelled down to Clacton for two performances on the Sunday. It was bitterly cold and snowing when we arrived in the seaside resort on the east coast. I was dreadfully tired and wished I had only one show, not a 2 p.m. matinée as well. And before that I had to sort out my lighting and sit down and write a few gags. As always I got through the early performance without anyone noticing how shattered I was, but the moment I came off stage at around five, I staggered into the tiny, dingy dressing room and fell into a chair, exhausted and starving.

Scott was there, looking concerned. 'I'm going to go and get us something to eat, Bar,' he said. 'Anything you fancy?'

'I don't mind, darling,' I replied wearily. 'I'll have what you're having.'

After Scott left, I got some towels, made them into a pillow on the floor, lay down and pulled my heavy fur coat over me. I had two hours before I was due on stage again, more than enough time to close my eyes and try to restore some energy.

When Scott arrived with some fish and chips about half an hour later, he was not so much shocked as angry. 'I can't believe what I'm seeing,' he scolded me. 'You're a famous lady, a household name. And here you are, lying on a cold, dirty floor like some tramp.'

It made me sound a bit like poor Marie Lloyd at the end. Popular, but not playing number one theatres.

'What's wrong with it?' I said, defensively. 'I'm waiting to go on and do another show. This is the way theatre is. It doesn't come with all mod cons, Scott. Anyway, I didn't take the place because it was luxury, I took it to earn money.'

It was true. I felt I was lucky to have a job and to be able to do it. But Scott didn't see those one-night stands that way at all. To him they were a relentless treadmill I should not be on at my age, and the poignant picture I made, curled up like a child on that hard floor on a bleak, snowswept Sunday afternoon, touched him deeply. Dear, dear Scott: this was not what he wanted for the woman he had fallen in love with.

24

I KEPT MY MARRIAGE BREAK-UP SECRET FROM ALL BUT MY CLOSEST FRIENDS FOR TWO MONTHS. It was bound to leak out, however, and when I heard that a national newspaper reporter was hanging round the Plough, asking leading questions of customers and staff alike, I decided to go into print myself. If the story of our split was going to be told, I wanted it to be the real version, not a load of half-truths cobbled together by someone I didn't know. So I confided in Robin McGibbon, a journalist I'd known since the early seventies. Between us we explained in the *News of the World* precisely why I'd fallen out of love with Stephen and in love with Scott.

As Scott was younger than Stephen, the headline writers predictably went for the 'toyboy' angle in the Monday papers. Early the same morning reporters and photographers besieged my mews cottage, eager to see and hear from the young man who had stolen my heart. We stayed indoors, with the phone off the hook, until it was time to leave for the Gordon Craig Theatre in Stevenage, where I was playing Aladdin again.

We rushed out to Scott's Mercedes, fending off reporters' questions with the apology: 'Sorry, can't stop, I'm appearing in panto.'

The next day the *Sun* used a picture of us running to the car under the headline: 'SORRY, MUST DASH – I'VE GOT A-LAD-IN TONIGHT'. It was a witty double entendre, and full marks to Fergus Shanahan, the sub-editor who wrote it. What I was going through during that panto, however, particularly the matinée performances, was far from funny.

Emotionally I was on a high, but physically, I was a wreck. I was still having the most terrible hot flushes and my periods were going on for ever. My work was beginning to be affected. In the previous two years I'd had three D&Cs, but my gynaecologist had warned me I could have only a limited number of these.

What made up my mind that I needed to go ahead and have a hysterectomy were those matinée performances. There I was, playing an eighteen-year-old boy, bouncing around on stage with my hot flushes. I thought, Bar, this is all wrong. This isn't good for you. Not at fifty-six.

When I revealed on TV that I was to have the operation, I put a positive slant on it, saying that over the previous three years I'd spoken to many women who'd had it, and that the general view was that it would make a new woman of me. I got a stack of letters and, of course, the tabloids picked up on it, claiming I was having the hysterectomy solely to pep up my sex drive because I had a new 'toyboy' in my life. That, of course, was not the case. My sexual appetite was quite strong enough, thank you. But it was true that, now I was ready for a long-lasting relationship, I wanted to get myself sorted out, not only for me, but for Scott, too. However, when I read an article which reported that while 60 per cent of women felt the operation made them want sex more often, 40 per cent admitted that it turned them off, I began to have second thoughts.

My gynaecologist calmed my fears. 'No chance, Barbara,' he said. 'The kind of woman who loses interest did not have much before. In fact, many use a hysterectomy as an excuse not to have sex, because it has become a chore.' Reassured, I arranged to go into the Wellington Hospital in St John's Wood as a private patient on Monday 31 January 1994, the day after I finished *Aladdin*.

Without wishing to sound melodramatic, the thought that I might die under the knife did cross my mind, as it must most people's, and I thought I should perhaps have a look at my will. I remembered my mother and grandmother both saying to me: 'Don't forget, Barbara, when you think it might be time for you to go, leave your house in order.' To be honest, I didn't have a lot to leave, but as things stood, all I did possess went to Stephen for him to dish out to whoever I named. Now I felt I should amend that document to leave half of everything I owned to Scott.

Having altered my will, I was tidying up a few other loose ends before leaving for the hospital when Stephen rang. He wanted me to speak to our accountant about something to do with the pub. I did not need the hassle just then. 'Can't it wait, Stephen?' I asked. 'I'm going into hospital today.'

'I know, but we've got to get this sorted before you go in.'

I was exasperated. If it was so important for me to sort out something with our accountant, why had he left it until a few hours before I was due at the hospital to ask me about it? If not, why the hurry? Did he, too, think I might die under the anaesthetic? Whatever, he would just have to wait.

The hospital staff were very protective. They very thoughtfully put a notice on the door of my room which read: 'DO NOT ENTER – ASK SISTER'. Even so, word obviously got round the hospital that I was there, and throughout the afternoon various people working at the hospital popped in for a chat. It was nice: it took my mind off the impending operation.

That evening Scott sat with me while I had dinner and a glass of wine. Then I kissed him goodbye, promising to call him the next morning before I went down to the operating theatre. I spoke to him for a few minutes around 7 a.m., feeling deeply in love and wonderfully woozy from my pre-med jab, and remember nothing more until I saw a hazy image of Scott at my bedside later that morning. Apparently, I said: 'Hello, I love you.' But, a little while later, in my delirium, I asked him: 'Who are you? What am I doing with you? Are you a toyboy?' Even in dreamland I was sending Scott up.

Stephen rang me that evening. 'I love you, you know that,' he said. 'Is there anything I can do?'

'No,' I told him. 'I'm fine.'

Again, I felt his timing was off. If he cared about me and wanted to show it, I thought he should have done so the previous day, not when I was coming round from an operation and away with the fairies.

What a difference the next morning. I woke up feeling I could conquer the world. The doctor and gynaecologist were surprised: they said I was twenty-four hours ahead of the usual recovery time. But it did not surprise me: I was desperate to get well and get out of there.

I was told that the sooner I got up, the better, so when Scott arrived, a nurse disconnected the two drips attached to me and asked him to hold the bottle collecting my urine from the catheter. Anxious to stretch and get rid of my stiffness, I eased myself off the bed and toddled off for a walk round the room, with Scott behind me, clutching the bottle. Suddenly, the ridiculousness of the scene struck me and I became terribly embarrassed. Sensing myself blushing, I started walking faster, not wanting to look at Scott, who was now almost having to run to keep up with me so that the catheter didn't come out and spill my pee on to the floor. 'You do realise I'm one of the country's biggest sex symbols, don't you?' I remarked, and gave one of my Carry On giggles.

My room was filled with cards and flowers and Scott had bought me Shalimar and a white rose. Stephen had not sent anything, but he phoned again, and again told me he loved me and asked if I wanted him to do anything. Then he mentioned the accountant, and I told him I would ring once I got home. 'Don't worry about it,' he said. 'Just get well.' I felt angry. He knew I was the sort of lady who'd get on the phone and sort things out straight away. If it was not that urgent to talk to the accountant, why bring it up now?

That Wednesday afternoon I was put on an extra dose of antibiotics because of an infection in my urinary tract and was in a lot of pain. Scott was very annoyed with me when he heard me tell a nurse I was all right.

'You're in terrible pain, Bar, you've got to tell them,' he said.

'They've got enough to do, Scott. They don't need—'

'Bar,' he interrupted. 'You're in one of the best hospitals in the country. You're in a £500-a-day room. The nurses are here for *you*.'

I don't know why I spend so much time apologising for this, that and the other, and trying to make things easier for people, but I do, and I always have. Even when I go to the dentist, I always say I don't need an injection, to save him the trouble. I would probably have gone without painkillers if Scott hadn't talked to the nurses. After that they came in and said: 'Barbara, it's not doing you any good putting up with all this pain. It's not going to make it any better.' That made it easier for me to admit that I did need the drugs.

The next morning I woke up feeling slightly better, especially when a nurse took the drips away. But she said that she was concerned about my blood pressure. Later a doctor came in and asked me why I hadn't told him that I suffered from high blood pressure. 'Because I don't,' I said, puzzled. So he phoned my GP, who confirmed that it had always been normal.

On Saturday I was thrilled to be told I could have a bath. It was just what I needed. I turned down a nurse's offer of help because I wanted to be on my own, take my time and relax. I was so preoccupied with easing myself into the bath that I didn't notice my reflection in the big bathroom mirror until I got out. It was the most sickening shock: looking back at me was a lady I didn't recognise; a lady with an angry wound, vivid red against the pale skin of a stomach so bloated it looked as if a cushion had been squeezed inside it. I'd been warned that the after-effects of the operation could make me weepy. I hadn't cried yet, but when I saw myself like that the tears began to flow and just wouldn't stop. I stood there for a long time wondering where on earth it was all coming from.

When my gynaecologist took my stitches out, he assured me that I was recovering faster than most people, but my blood pressure was still causing concern. I was not given time to dwell on this because the physiotherapist arrived and got me to tackle the staircase. Once I was back in bed, however, I started asking every nurse I saw about blood pressure. They all told me I had nothing to worry about, but they all seemed to say something different, which made me wonder whether there was something very seriously wrong and no one wanted to tell me.

That Sunday Stephen phoned for the first time in four days. He told me he had been clay-pigeon shooting and that he had a migraine. Whether the two were related he didn't say, and I didn't ask. I was more concerned about my own health.

I convinced myself that my blood pressure was high as a result of the operation and that I'd be given a pill to take it down. What I didn't know was that arrangements were being made for me to see a heart specialist the following day, and that he wanted me to have an ECG beforehand. I didn't know what an ECG – an electrocardiogram – was, and when I was told it was to check for any irregularities in the function of the heart, I relaxed. There was nothing wrong with *my* heart; it was as strong as a lion's. How could I have performed on stage the way I did if it wasn't?

That Monday was Valentine's Day, and Scott sent me the most beautiful card, with wonderful words. We had agreed to have dinner together in my room, and when he arrived at six o'clock, looking handsome in a dark blue suit and maroon tie, he was carrying a huge bunch of white roses with a red one in the middle. I had dressed for the occasion, too, in a white negligée I'd bought specially for hospital, and we settled down to make the evening as romantic as possible in the circumstances. We had melon to start, then Scott had roast duck, and I had roast lamb, with fruit salad for dessert, and we shared a bottle of mineral water. It was a lovely evening, given the less than cosy environment, and after Scott had left, I wrote in the diary I was keeping of my stay at the Wellington: 'I love this man more than life itself. Why did I have to wait so long for him to come into my life?'

That wonderful, loving feeling made me wake with a warm glow the next morning. Now I felt on top of the world, and when Barry Burnett arrived, very excited, that afternoon, I felt even better. There was a lot of work coming in for me, he said: a marvellous offer had been made for me to appear in an episode of *One Foot in the Grave*; I was wanted by Melvyn Bragg for a *South Bank Show* on Kenneth Williams, and the producer of *Sloane* was keen to bring the new tour forward to April. There was even a request from *Penthouse* magazine to pose for a spread of glamour photographs. All in all, it was a bright and busy outlook. Barry stayed for an hour or so, chatting cheerily about the good year that lay ahead.

And then Dr Roweth Spurrell, the heart specialist, came to see me, and everything changed.

Dr Spurrell had been at the Tamarind Cove Hotel in Barbados at the same time as Stephen and me the previous year, and that coincidence got us off to a friendly start. We chatted about our holidays for a few minutes before he started asking questions about heart problems in my family. All I could tell him was that my father had had heart trouble in his fifties, but that he had recovered and was still alive in his eighties.

'Well,' said Dr Spurrell, 'I have looked at your ECG and it is abnormal, I'm afraid.'

I stared at him, dumbfounded. Abnormal? I always thought of myself as Superwoman. OK, I've had health problems over the years, but a dodgy heart was something else. I just couldn't understand it. As Dr Spurrell went on about my heart muscle, and the arteries behind my eyes thickening slightly, and explained that I would need to have some blood tests the next day, I was beginning to feel very scared.

My cholesterol level was too high, the doctor continued, and I needed to get it down, pronto. He would arrange for me to see a dietician, who would explain the problems of high cholesterol and tell me what I could and could not eat. I was not too bothered about that: my cholesterol was almost certainly up because of all the junk food I ate during the panto season. I knew that once I was out of hospital and looking after myself, I would be eating balanced meals and that my cholesterol level would drop.

When Scott came in I tried to make light of it, saying no more than that the doctor wasn't happy with the ECG. If I was going to have a good bawl, I thought, I'd do it when I was on my own. But then, for some reason I'm unable to explain, I went for him. 'If I've got a heart problem, it's because of aggravation,' I said. 'And that's down to you. *You've* given me it.'

Scott gazed at me in amazement. Nothing could have been further from the truth: he did everything he could to make life easier for me. I just needed to let my feelings out, and he was the one in the firing line. Scott was the last person, the very last person, I wanted to upset. But they say you always hurt the one you love, don't they?

For the next two hours, Scott and I sat staring at the TV while a nurse came in every fifteen minutes to take my blood pressure. I think the Brit Awards were on, but I can remember little about it: I was too busy thinking about what I was going to do. Never once had I thought about physical disability or illness stopping me bounding on stage and kicking my legs in the air.

Now it seemed I had a heart condition. OK, I still had to have the blood tests that might show it was nothing much to worry about, but the fact remained that my heart was not functioning properly. And, to my mind, that meant I was not in good working order.

If my career as a high-energy performer, which I loved with a passion, had to end, my whole life would have to change. I was going to have to slow down, stop tearing around, working here, there and everywhere at 100 miles an hour, trying to please everyone. I was going to have to act my age. That, to me, meant becoming a different person. And I would not be the same Barbara Scott had fallen in love with.

I loved him so much I started thinking about his future before considering mine. Scott was young and ambitious, with an uncertain acting career ahead of him. It wasn't fair that he should be saddled with someone who was not the woman she had once been.

The following evening I had an ultrasound heart scan, and I was so relieved when Dr Spurrell came in the next day and said that it had not revealed anything untoward. But he was still far from satisfied, and told me he would be doing other tests. He particularly wanted to see how my heart reacted when I ran on a treadmill, but of course that was out of the question because of my operation. So instead, he was going to give me an angiogram, which meant injecting a blue dye into one of my veins which would highlight any blocked or damaged blood vessels around the heart. He said this was the ultimate test, the big one that should tell him all he needed to know.

I was worried about what the angiogram would show. My big concern, apart from Scott, was money. I was still committed to paying back huge loans taken out for the Plough at high interest rates. So it wasn't just that I loved to work, I had to.

When I brought this up with Scott, he said: 'Your health's far more important than money, Bar. You should just be thinking about getting yourself better.'

'But I'm worried I might lose the house,' I said.

Scott knew how much I adored the house, but he told me: 'Well, if you do, we'll live in my flat.'

It was the sort of comment I had come to expect from Scott. He was always trying to solve my problems rather than add to them.

All I wanted was to be ready to start the new tour of *Sloane* in April, but when I mentioned this to Dr Spurrell he just looked at me and said quietly: 'No, Barbara. Working that soon is a non-starter. You will have to put it back.'

I was already in a dilemma about who to confide in, apart from Scott, but now I knew I had to speak to Barry, not only as a friend, but as my agent. He needed to know that my career was going to have to be put on hold. I decided in the end to tell only one other person, Anna Karen. Not only was she a very close friend but her husband, Terry, had had a heart operation himself and so she knew a lot about it all.

Scott had an audition for a play which, if he got the part, would take him to the Far East for three months. I had mixed feelings about it. I wanted him to get it for his sake, of course, but the thought of us being apart for so long was depressing. But Scott was only just starting out as an actor. The play was important to him, and might well lead on to other things. It crossed my mind that this might be the perfect excuse to end our relationship if the results of my angiogram were not good news.

When Scott breezed in, he was grinning broadly. 'The audition went brilliantly. They want to see me again on Sunday. It looks like I'm in with a chance.'

I gave him the smile. 'That's wonderful, darling. That's great.'

Just a minute later, I suddenly felt sick. My pulse rate dropped, I turned deathly white and what strength I had oozed out of me. Looking at Scott's worried face, I felt guilty: he had come in on such a high, bursting to tell me his good news, and I had brought him down with a bump.

'Darling, I'm so sorry, I'm so, so sorry,' I kept saying. 'I don't know what it is . . . I feel awful.'

I think Scott was well aware of my anxieties about the play, even though I had not breathed a word. 'Bar,' he said, gently. 'Don't worry about the play. I'm not going anywhere with you like this.'

After he left, and I'd recovered, I settled down to try to read a book. Suddenly I felt a weird sensation, a sort of numbness, down the right side of my face. I didn't want to make an unnecessary fuss, so I put my book down and lay still, waiting for the strange feeling to pass. Ten minutes later it was still there, and I began to worry. After another five minutes it seemed to be getting stronger. My mind went haywire. Fucking hell, I thought, I'm having a stroke! I waited another five minutes before total blind panic took over and I plucked up the courage to buzz for a nurse.

My blood pressure was up again. A night doctor tested my face with a needle and cotton wool, then spoke to Dr Spurrell, who prescribed Valium. I was petrified. And, once I was on my own again, I began to cry. I rang Scott and he was at my bedside twenty-five minutes later. He sat there, holding my hand, waiting for the extra sleeping tablet to take effect. I kept dropping off, then coming round and going off again and, eventually, was aware of a hazy impression of Scott tiptoeing towards the door, then closing it quietly.

Thankfully, I awoke with none of the facial numbness, but that evening, shortly after Scott arrived, it came back. Dr Spurrell was not unduly concerned: he put it down to anxiety. I certainly could not argue with that: apart from worrying about myself and what the all-knowing angiogram would tell me, I was now very concerned about Scott. Unlike me, he is unable to hide his feelings and that evening he was, for him, quite depressed. Whether it was the dilemma of the play, or feelings of guilt that he might be to blame for my poor physical state, I didn't know, because he didn't seem to want to talk about it, but something was certainly preying on his mind that night and it was not a happy evening. I'm sure we were both relieved when it was time for him to go.

Trying to get to sleep, I found myself wishing, yet again, that I had not had the bloody operation. But then, I consoled myself, it was probably fortuitous that I had: at least it had brought to light the heart problem. Had I not come into hospital, it could have gone undetected for goodness knows how long. I might even have gone out on stage one night, thrown everything into a strenuous routine, and collapsed in a heap like poor Sid.

Next Dr Spurrell sent a neurologist to see me. He made me march around the room with my eyes closed and my arm outstretched, and announced that my high blood pressure had bruised the back of my brain, causing a blood vessel to go into spasm. I would have to have a brain scan in the morning.

Less than half an hour after the neurologist left, I had another spasm, this time down my right arm to my hand. I buzzed the nurse, who called the doctor back. Again, I was told there was nothing to worry about. I dozed for a couple of hours or so, trying to keep my anxiety under control. When I woke, around midnight, I phoned Scott and told him what had happened. Later Anna called. She had been speaking to Scott, who had been in a dreadful state, terrified that there was something deadly serious wrong with me.

Scott insisted on being with me for the brain scan. I was more than a little apprehensive and was glad that it was scheduled for 10 a.m.; the sooner it was over, the better. Scott and I had got ourselves all geared up when we were told the machine had broken down. By the time it was fixed, six whole hours later, our nerves were shot to pieces.

Thankfully the scan showed nothing sinister, and Dr Spurrell put the icing on the cake when he said he felt that being in hospital was adding to my anxiety and that I would be better off at home. He was going to discharge me the next day, and I could come back in two weeks for the angiogram.

Scott was relieved that I was coming home, but the strain of the previous two weeks was taking its toll and we had a bit of a blow-up. He was now convinced

▲ *My first day on set: a scene from* Carry On Spying, *the first of my nine Carry Ons, with Charles Hawtrey, Kenny Williams and Bernard Cribbins.*

▼ *Backstage on the same film: Dilys Laye joins me and the others.*

▲ ▶ *The famous Windsor boobs:* that *scene from* Carry On Camping *and in the shower in* Carry On Abroad.

▲ *Kenny Williams and I always got on really well – so much so that he ended up coming on my honeymoon!*

▲ Carry On Dick: *rehearsing with Sid. He found it increasingly difficult to hide his feelings for me on set.*

▲ *Rear and front view: Sid and I on the pier at Brighton during the filming of* Carry On Girls.

▼ *Sid and I were heavily involved when we appeared in* Carry On London *at the Victoria Palace, in 1973. Clockwise from left to right: me, Jack Douglas, Sid, Bernie Bresslaw, Peter Butterworth, Kenny Connor and producer Peter Rogers.*

PANTO SEASON . . .

▲ *As Aladdin in Chichester with Aubrey Woods.*

▲ *With fellow Ugly Sister, Ann Emery (sister of Dick) at the Royal Court, Liverpool.*

▲ *With Scott, as Dandini, in Cinderella at Basingstoke.*

◀ *In* Babes in the Wood *with John Inman at the London Palladium.*

FRAZER ASHFORD

▶ *Playing the lead in Dick*
Whittington alongside my
favourite cat, aka Terry Doogan.

◀ *In the Thames TV Christmas*
Carry On Special in 1969, with
Frankie Howerd, Hattie Jacques
and Peter Butterworth.

▼ *Visiting Great Ormond Street*
Hospital as the Fairy Godmother,
while appearing in panto in
Stevenage.

▼ ▲ *On Russell Harty's chat show in 1977 with the reigning queen of* Coronation Street, *Julie Goodyear, and with chat show king Michael Parkinson as his guest in 1999.*

▸ Surrounded by family and friends on This Is Your Life *in 1992.*

THAMES TELEVISION

▾ It was a great honour to be the first person inducted into the BBC's Hall of Fame. My dear friends, Dale Winton and Ross Kemp, shared the moment with me in March 2000.

◀ Cor Blimey! *was a marvellous look behind the scenes of Carry On, recreating the story of my love affair with Sid James. All the actors bore an uncanny resemblance to their characters: Samantha Spiro as me, Adam Godley as Kenny Williams and Geoffrey Hutchings as Sid.*

▼ *Scott with Samantha and Hugh Walters, who played Charles Hawtrey.*

that whatever was wrong with me was caused by stress, created by the big age gap between us. I did my best to console him, saying that I would rather spend ten years with him than twenty without him.

But the next night I sparked another row, and Scott stormed off into the spare bedroom, saying he wanted to sleep on his own. I lay in my bed cursing the operation for making me so moody and irritable, and then, in the middle of the night, crept into the other room and said I was sorry. Scott was as understanding as ever, but when the next day it was clear that I was very depressed, he said it might be best if he went to his flat for a few hours to give us both a break from each other. It was a sensible idea. By the time he came home in the evening, I had done my exercises, made lots of phone calls and shaken off the blues. We sat in bed eating a Chinese takeaway and watching TV, happy again.

I had the angiogram at last, and it showed that there was no immediate cause for concern. But Dr Spurrell warned that I would have to have three-monthly checks and eventually surgery to clear the blocked arteries.

It took me another three or four weeks to recover from the hysterectomy and everything that came in its wake. I knew I was finally getting back to normal when Scott and I got a fit of the giggles one day and nothing, it seemed, could make us stop. Don't ask me what we found so funny; I don't know. I had been told it could be dangerous to my insides if I laughed or coughed too vigorously, and I had been very restrained. But this particular afternoon we were sitting on the bed chatting when something tickled me and set me off. I got an excruciating pain in my stomach and desperately tried to stop, but the more I tried, the more I laughed, and, of course, this set Scott off as well. Knowing how much it hurt, he left the room to give us both a chance to compose ourselves. When he came back we were all right for twenty seconds or so, then we looked at each other and started all over again. He kept going out, but every time he came back the same thing happened. What he found so amusing was that, because of the pain and my attempts not to damage my insides, I couldn't let myself go with the famous Windsor giggle. Instead I had to force myself to laugh softly, in a very low pitch, and it sounded so weird. I was holding a pillow close to my stomach to try to ease the pain, and I dubbed it the Laughter Pillow. It made us carry on laughing for over half an hour, bringing to life the old gag 'It only hurts when I laugh.'

25

SHORTLY AFTER I CAME OUT OF HOSPITAL, I HAD THE MOST ASTON-
ISHING PHONE CALL FROM RONNIE. His wife was obviously not in the
villa, because he was at his most relaxed, and opened his heart to me in
a way he'd never done in all the years I'd been with him. For an hour
and a half, I sat on the stairs holding the phone away from my ear so
that Scott could hear as Ronnie went on and on about how desperately
unhappy he was. Things weren't too clever in the marriage, he said. All
the money he'd had was gone, and with business bad at the bar he
owned in Fuengirola, he was on his uppers. He started to get nostalgic.
Although he'd read about my relationship with Scott, he seemed to think
he and I could somehow get back together again. Now that our respective
second marriages were over, he felt we were destined to be with each
other. He told me how he would like to cook me a Sunday roast, and
laughed about how I'd have to make the gravy because he couldn't. He
said he was missing England and would come home and give himself
up if only he could get a few quid out of it. *The Sunday Times* had
apparently offered him £80,000 for his story, but the deal had fallen
through. He asked me whether I knew of anyone else who might be
interested.

As luck would have it, Robin McGibbon, the journalist I'd co-operated
with to break the news of my break-up with Stephen, rang the next night
to see how I was after my operation. I told him I was going to Spain to
recuperate and might be seeing my ex-husband. 'He's desperately unhappy,'
I said. 'He wants to come home.' I told him about Ronnie's collapsed deal
with *The Sunday Times*. 'I'd love to set up a deal with a paper and do the
story,' Robin said. 'How much would Ronnie want?'

'*The Sunday Times* offered him £80,000. Could you get more than that?'

'I'm sure I could. But I'm not sure how much higher any other paper would go.'

'Do you want to see what you can do?'

'I'd need to speak to Ronnie first to make sure he's serious,' Robin said.

I gave him Ronnie's number, but asked him to give me a couple of minutes so that I could warn Ronnie to expect a call.

Fifteen minutes later, Robin rang back to say that he was as satisfied as he could be over the phone that Ronnie was up for it and had arranged to see the *News of the World* editor, Piers Morgan, and his deputy, Phil Hall, in the morning. They were delighted with the prospect of landing one of the biggest crime stories of modern times, and agreed to pay £150,000 for it, subject to the customary guarantees of exclusivity. On 7 February 1995 Rob flew to Spain at the paper's expense with a contract in his briefcase.

From what Robin told me later, what happened over the next three days says more about Ronnie Knight's greed, stupidity, naïveté and misplaced judgement than anything I can. He was shown the contract, then prevaricated for thirty-six hours before saying that £150,000 for himself was fine, but what was his wife going to get? Robin told him that the newspaper was unlikely to increase its offer, but asked him what sum he had in mind. After more stalling, Ronnie said that he felt another £30,000 was fair. Ronnie had always been a chancer, but asking for £180,000 to come home to face criminal charges was cheeky, even by his standards.

Yet amazingly, the *News of the World* agreed to stump up the extra cash. All Ronnie had to do was to behave sensibly and honourably and do what he had said he would do, and everything would have been fine. Unfortunately, that was all too simple, it seemed. The following day, when Robin went to the villa with another contract, Ronnie brought up the subject of expenses.

'What expenses?' Robin wanted to know.

'I'm going to have a lot of legal costs, you know,' said Ronnie. 'I don't want to have to dip into the hundred and fifty for them, do I?'

'You want the *News of the World* to give you £180,000 *and* pay your legal costs on top?'

'Well, yeah.'

Robin laughed. 'No newspaper in the country will pay your legal costs, Ron.'

'Well, in that case, I don't know,' said Ronnie.

Of course, there had to be more to it: even Ronnie, dense as he can be at times, knew that £180,000 was a better payday than he could possibly have imagined. I learned later that another journalist was pursuing him for his story. Ronnie put his trust in the wrong man, because the *News of the World* pulled out of the proposed deal, taking the promise of £180,000 with them, and Ronnie had to settle for far less.

At 7 a.m. one morning in early May the phone woke me from a deep sleep. It was a reporter from the *Daily Mail*, ringing to ask me if I knew that the *Sun* were bringing Ronnie home from Spain that afternoon. I didn't, and, no, I had no comment to make about how I felt. Half an hour later, the phone rang again and I recognised the slight West Country burr of the *Sun*'s editor, Stuart Higgins, who told me what I already knew.

'We have to get you out of the house, Barbara,' he said. 'You have to be protected, because everyone will want to speak to you. I'm sending a reporter to take you and Scott to a hotel for a couple of days.'

I went along with it because I was in a panic and didn't know what else to do. We didn't discuss doing a story at that point. Less than an hour later, a woman dressed like a prim-and-proper schoolmarm arrived and to our surprise introduced herself as Sue Crawford from the *Sun*. She drove Scott and me off in her car, heading south out of London to Sussex, where we wound around endless country lanes till we finally arrived at a secluded little hotel, where she checked us into a room. Sue was extremely nice to us and very sympathetic, and soon her tape-recorder was on and I was collaborating with a story about how I felt about my ex-husband coming home to face the music. Sue was extremely capable. She never took her eyes off me and didn't allow me to leave the room, but someone at the paper must have felt that a mere woman wouldn't be able to cope, because later that morning a couple of *Sun* heavyweights in the shape of Paul Hooper, a reporter, and photographer Arthur Edwards turned up.

Shortly after 2 p.m., the paper rang to say that Ronnie had boarded a plane in Granada and was on his way home. I burst into tears. 'Why are you crying?' Scott wanted to know, all concerned.

'This is all going to cause me a load of aggravation,' I sobbed.

'Are you sure it's not something else?' Poor Scott. He sounded so insecure.

'No, sweetheart,' I said. 'I'm just worried it's all going to start all over again.'

We'd been cooped up in the hotel room for ages and were hungry. Sue, concerned about security, thought we should stay there and have some lunch sent up, but Paul said it wouldn't hurt for us all to go down to the restaurant. As we all chatted over lunch about Ronnie's return, I mentioned a cartoon featuring my ex-husband that I'd seen in the *Star*, and which had amused me.

As we finished our meal a woman came towards us from a table out of our line of vision. She was obviously known to the *Sun* contingent, and clearly they were not overjoyed to see her, because their faces all fell in astonishment and alarm. She came over and said she was from the *Star* and had been taping our conversation. 'Thank you very much,' she said. 'Oh, and Barbara – it *was* a good cartoon, wasn't it?' Needless to say, the *Star* ran the reporter's story the next day to spoil the *Sun*'s exclusive.

At 4.12 p.m. that afternoon, a LearJet carrying my ex-husband, a couple of *Sun* reporters and a Sky Television camera crew touched down at Luton Airport. According to the *Sun* the next morning, Ronnie celebrated his homecoming with champagne and roast beef sandwiches, and his first words on seeing English soil were: 'Look, the sun's shining. It's lovely, innit? I feel like dancing.'

Unfortunately for Ronnie, dancing was not on the agenda. A few minutes after the jet taxied to a stop, Reid McGeorge, the detective inspector who had pursued Ronnie and the Security Express robbers for more than ten years, arrested him. Before being taken to Leman Street Police Station, Ronnie, asked by a customs official if he had anything to declare, quipped: 'Only my innocence.' He could prove that, no problem, he had told the reporters during the flight. His only fear was being locked up on remand until his trial. As he discovered the next morning, it was well founded. At a fifteen-minute hearing at Bow Street, the prosecuting barrister, Reginald Mays, objected to bail. 'Ronald Knight does not realise the full extent of the evidence against him and when he does, he will leave the country again,' he argued. Two sureties, 'well into six figures', put up by two unnamed people in court cut no ice with the magistrate, who remanded Ronnie in custody for a week, accused of robbery and handling stolen money. As he left the court, Ronnie apparently winked at reporters, but that would have been an act of bravado. Ronnie dreaded prison, and the humiliating regime that went with it.

One Saturday, in April, Scott and I had gone to a party thrown by my old mate Mike Reid, the comedian and actor, at his home in Essex, and met a lovely young woman, Jane Deitch, who was a casting director on *EastEnders*. During our conversation, I had revealed my desire to play a character of my own age for once. It was only a passing comment, but it was one Jane filed away for future reference.

Although the doctors had forbidden me from returning to the exhausting *Sloane* tour after my health problems, I was later able to resume my one-woman show, with some small changes to the format to minimise the physical demands it made of me. Three weeks after Ronnie's return, I'd just finished a performance in Brick Lane when I was told that Jane was out front and wanted me to have a drink with her and the friends who had brought her there. Jane was surprised by my stage act. She said she had had no idea I did all the singing and dancing and chatting to the audience at the end, and she'd loved it.

One warm July afternoon, Scott was driving me to Swiss Cottage to do some shopping when Barry rang his mobile phone, looking for me.

'Hello, darling,' I said.

'I need to see you, Bar,' Barry said. 'Can you come to the office?'

Barry's office was in Golden Square, off Regent Street. We had just come from there, and I didn't want to go straight back again.

'Can't you tell me what it is over the phone?'

'No,' said Barry firmly. 'It's better if I see you. It's important.'

'It's one of two things,' I told Scott as we reluctantly headed back towards the West End. 'I've either got *What's My Line?*, or he's going to drop me.'

The more I thought about it, the more I felt that it had to be the elbow. Getting *What's My Line?* would be great – it would provide a quick and much-needed cash boost – but it was after all only a panel game for a limited audience on cable TV. Surely Barry wouldn't drag me all the way back into town to tell me that. If he'd decided he didn't want to represent me any more, it was understandable. His phone had hardly been red hot with offers of late and I'd heard he was offloading several other clients. And being a friend, Barry would want to let me down face to face, not over the phone or by letter.

Scott knew I would be upset if this did turn out to be the case, so he offered to wait for me. But that hardly seemed fair, since I had no idea how long I was going to be. 'No, darling,' I said. 'You go home and I'll get a cab back.'

I took the lift to Barry's offices on the fifth floor and walked through the large, open-plan office, saying hello to the girls I'd come to know, to a smaller office in the far corner. Barry was sitting in a swivel chair, his back to me. I didn't want business to ruin our friendship, and I was preparing a little speech in my head to make it all as easy as possible for him: 'That's all right, sweetheart. I understand. I haven't been happy with the way things have been going, either . . .'

As I sat down, Barry swung round theatrically in his chair. He leaned forward, looking at me closely, and said: 'What do you want first? The good news or the bad news?'

Good news? I was confused. 'Give me the bad news,' I replied.

Barry's expression was grave. 'I'm sorry. You didn't get *What's My Line*? They've gone for June Whitfield.'

Bollocks, I thought, seeing thirty-six grand going out the window.

I love June. You can't not love her – she is a nice, sweet lady – and she's a mate. She had been part of my life, on and off, for more than forty years. But she didn't need the work – she never stopped as it was. She had *Absolutely Fabulous*, for God's sake. And I was scratching around to pay my mortgage and my debts. 'Oh, that's wonderful, that's lovely for her,' I said through gritted teeth.

'Now, do you want the good news?' Barry asked.

'Yes,' I said listlessly, though I couldn't imagine what good news there could be.

'How would you like to be in *EastEnders*?'

'Are you kidding? Would I like to be in *EastEnders*?' I said. 'I'd love it. I'd give my right arm to be in *EastEnders*.'

'Well, they've been on,' Barry told me.

'What do you mean, they've been on?'

'The call has come through. They want you in *EastEnders*.'

I felt a hot flush spreading across my face and a tiny knot of excitement in the pit of my stomach. 'They want *me* in *EastEnders*?'

'Yes. But there's a problem.'

'Well, yes,' I said, 'there's got to be a problem.'

'They don't think you'll want to play the part.'

'What part is it?'

'The mother of the Mitchell boys.'

'You're joking,' I said. 'That's *the* part.'

'I knew that's what your reaction would be.'

'But the Mitchells have already got a mum,' I said. She was an actress named Jo Warne, and I thought she was very good. I'd worked with Jo myself, along with Martine McCutcheon, who was also in *EastEnders*, on the TV series *Bluebirds*, a few years before.

'It hasn't worked out with Jo,' Barry told me. 'They've tried out somebody else, but she hasn't made it. They want you.'

I didn't know what to say. It sounded too good to be true. Working regular hours in one place, playing a woman close to my own age in a straight, dramatic role that would stretch me ... if it was for real, it was the answer to all my prayers. Of course, I would miss my one-woman shows, but at coming up to fifty-seven, I was getting too old to go schlepping all over the country kicking my legs in the air. And although I was prepared to carve out a new career as an agent if need be, nothing could be more perfect than a dream part in a soap opera with millions of viewers.

Barry was looking at me, waiting for me to say something, but I was in shock.

'Let me tell them you're interested and see what happens,' he said.

'Yes,' I replied. 'Do that. See what they say.'

I didn't dare get too excited: getting a phone call and being offered the role were light years apart and I always felt it was tempting fate to celebrate too soon. A picture of one of Bruce's cakes at Winston's came to mind. I wanted to see a contract. Then there'd be no stopping me.

'What did Barry want?' Scott asked me the second I got through the door.

'They want me in *EastEnders*,' I said.

'*What?*' Scott almost jumped for joy. 'That's it! That's what you want!'

When I told him what the part was he was even more excited. 'You'll be perfect as Peggy.'

But no phone call came. Not that week, or during the next two. I was disappointed, but also puzzled. Having got a positive reaction from an initial approach, I would have thought their next step would have been to sort out the contract. The only reason I could see for the lack of communication was that *EastEnders* had changed their minds. And I had a feeling I knew why. A series of half-hour Carry On clips was being shown on television at the time. Oh, dear, I thought, someone is going to see that half-naked bird giggling again, and think, no, no, no – how did we ever think she could do Peggy Mitchell?

And then, on the last Friday in August, Barry phoned me at home: someone from *EastEnders* had been on, asking if I would mind going to the studios at Elstree in Hertfordshire, the following Monday, a Bank Holiday, to do some tests for clothes and make-up. They were sorry for asking me to give up a Bank Holiday at such short notice, but it couldn't be helped. I wasn't bothered about that, but something else Barry said set off an alarm bell in my head. 'They'd like you to act out a couple of scenes for the camera,' he said. 'One is strong and dramatic, the other a bit softer. They're biking over a couple of scripts for you.'

Uh-oh, I thought: that sounds like an audition. That sounds as though someone has suddenly got scared and thought, can she do it? Can the Carry On girl carry it off?

It was a bit of a blow to my pride. I felt like I had with *Gold Diggers*: surely I'd been around long enough and done enough for people to know my capabilities? You could hardly blame *EastEnders*, though: those Carry On compilations must have made it seem as if sexy comedy roles were all I'd ever done.

When the scripts arrived, my heart sank. There were so many lines I couldn't see any way I could learn them by Monday. Seeing my forlorn face, Scott said: 'You *can* do it, Bar. And you will.'

I started to panic. 'I don't think so, darling.'

I spent most of that weekend in tears, from a mixture of frustration that the lines wouldn't sink in, and fear, that even if they did, I'd blow my chances by performing them badly. The role was too important to me. I wanted it so much that I felt I had to be better at that audition than I'd ever been in my life. So, instead of keeping cool and allowing the lines to sink in and my natural acting ability to take over, I was weighed down by a crushing compulsion to give an Oscar-winning performance. And the harder I tried, the more convinced I became that I was not up to it. My lowest point came on the Sunday, when I watched the ninety-minute omnibus edition of *EastEnders*. I'd been an avid follower of the programme but now I was watching it for a different reason. I leaned forward, studying the delivery and movements of all those famous faces as though, by some form of osmosis, I could absorb the secret of soap success. I couldn't believe what I was seeing.

'They don't seem to be *doing* anything,' I said. 'These actors, they don't work at it, they just do it. And it's great.'

That worried the life out of me, because in the theatre I was loud and boisterous – over the top and larger than life, if you like – and always used my hands a lot.

'So why not keep your hands out of the way?' Scott suggested. 'Sit on them while you're saying your lines.'

It was good advice – the very same thing Joan Littlewood had made me do for my solo number in *Fings*. Later that day, I sat on my hands and went over and over the lines I'd been learning since Friday, and when I fell into bed, I slept like a baby, too exhausted to feel nervous about what lay ahead in the morning.

My nerves went straight to my stomach the moment I woke up. Opening nights in the theatre have always been traumatic for me, but I'd never experienced such anxiety as I did that morning. The moment I got into the car to set off for Elstree I felt sick, and I had to ask Scott to stop several times during the first fifteen minutes because I felt I was going to throw up. Finally, all the tension bubbled to the surface, and this time there was nothing I could do to prevent it.

'Stop the car,' I said, putting a hand to my mouth. *'Now!'*

Scott pulled over and I scrambled out as quickly as I could and spewed up on a grass verge. I looked up, embarrassed, wondering if anyone was watching, and I realised that my surroundings were familiar. The place I'd chosen to be sick was right outside Hendon Hall Court, where I'd lived with Ronnie.

'I'll tell you something, Scott,' I said. 'If I do ever get this part, we're going to have to find a different route to Elstree. I don't want to be passing this place all the time.'

We were due at the studios at 11 a.m. and were politely early. Waiting for me were three lady producers and Jane Deitch. I did not know whether to feel relieved or worried to see that she looked as nervous as I felt.

Every decent wig in the BBC's Costume Department, it seemed, was being used for a big period drama, and the make-up girl, Martine Randall, had only been able to find some old, dark ones. I was keen to get away from the Barbara Windsor image, but I didn't want to wear something that made me look like Whistler's Mother. We were wondering what to do when Martine opened a drawer and spotted a tatty blonde wig that Letitia Dean had worn for a scene where, as Sharon, she had had to run through the rain. It was a short-haired wig that aged me, which was what they wanted. Then we rummaged around in Wardrobe and found an old tracksuit that Barbara Windsor would never wear. By now it was clear that I'd been brought in for a fully fledged audition, but I didn't mind. I was as ready as I'd ever be.

My prospective sons, Ross Kemp and Steve McFadden, were there. They were very sweet and respectful, but it must have been a drag having to come in early on a Bank Holiday to help someone else try to prove herself.

The audition was very strange. We were supposed to be in the Queen Vic pub, but we played the scenes in the Arches garage, using china mugs for glasses. The first of the two scenes was the dramatic one. I didn't fluff a line, although my stomach was in my mouth all the way through. The second was lighter, a little more frivolous, but I was even more nervous in that because I didn't want to giggle and offer even a glimpse of the Carry On lady. What made it more difficult was that Ross and Steve, not having seen the script, didn't know the dialogue so they were reading their lines, and kept their heads down all the time.

Afterwards I went back to the dressing room relieved it was over, but afraid that I hadn't done well and had not proved to be what they were looking for. But the three producers, who had been watching my performance on a TV monitor, were all smiles. 'That was wonderful, Barbara, absolutely fantastic,' they said. Jane, meanwhile, had tears in her eyes. 'The one thing we all thought Barbara Windsor wouldn't have was vulnerability,' she said. 'Good God, vulnerability oozed out of you.'

Thrilled, but embarrassed, I said: 'With what I've gone through in my life, I'm good on vulnerability, darlings.'

They all laughed.

After I changed and turned into Barbara Windsor again, Ross Kemp came and found me and asked if he could show me round the set. I was touched by that: he could easily have shot off to enjoy what was left of the day. As we walked around the famous square, he smiled at me. 'I know this is going to become home for you, Barbara.'

The next day Barry rang with confirmation that I'd been offered the job, and the news that he was about to negotiate the contract. Scott and I allowed ourselves a small celebration, but by the following Monday I was wondering, with a sense of dread, whether even that had been jumping the gun.

On his *Big Breakfast* show that morning, Chris Evans was discussing *EastEnders*. 'Did you see that omnibus yesterday?' he asked his viewers. 'What's happened to *EastEnders*? It's gone, hasn't it?' And he urged them to phone or fax him suggesting ways to perk up the show. 'I know what I'd do,' he went on. 'I'd get Barbara Windsor behind the bar of the Queen Vic, pronto.'

When I was told what had happened, I was horrified – and terrified I'd lose the part. I didn't know Chris, but I was sure that the BBC would think it was a leak and maybe even that I was behind it – that I was using a mate to put pressure on them to hurry up and sign the contract. I phoned Barry in a state. 'Don't worry,' he said. 'The BBC have confirmed they want you. No way will they change their minds.' And he assured me that no one would think I had

had anything to do with what Chris had said. In the event, his harmless plug did speed up things: *EastEnders'* bosses had planned to keep my debut secret until a week before filming, but as the secret was out they simply brought it forward to capitalise on the publicity Chris had generated.

The producers of Noel Edmonds' Saturday night TV show *House Party* would probably never have thought of setting me up for one of Noel's famous 'Gotcha Oscars' if I hadn't been given the part in *EastEnders*. But once it was revealed that I'd be moving into Albert Square, I became a prime target, especially as the screening of the 'Gotcha' could be timed to coincide with my first appearance as Peggy.

The idea of the 'Gotcha' is, of course, to set up a well-known personality by pulling a stunt on them in the hope that they will lose their rag or react in some other way that will amuse the viewers. Unfortunately, the programme's researchers didn't do their homework well enough on me. Anyone who knows me is aware that the one thing guaranteed to make me 'go' is unprofessionalism. But the programme chose the scenario of a personal appearance in Basingstoke to promote the forthcoming panto, *Cinderella*, in which Scott and I were appearing. The PA had been organised by local people who were raising money for charity. In those situations I'm especially aware that everyone is trying their best to make things run smoothly, and I'm well known for coping well if they don't.

So when the *House Party* 'plants' tried to wind me up with daft tricks – for example, making me put my hand into runny cement which went on to my clothes, giving me a tiny penknife instead of scissors to cut a ribbon, scheduling me with more than twenty bogus press interviews in under an hour, and leaving me stranded without a car with the excuse that it had run out of petrol on its way to collect me – I was hardly likely to go into one and provide the kind of entertainment they were looking for. In fact Scott, who was appearing in panto with me for the first time that year, said that the resulting 'Gotcha' was incredibly boring because I didn't react badly. The only time I did pull a face and look a bit agitated was when the 'interviews' looked like making me late for a meeting with *EastEnders* executives that evening. What the programme-makers should have done was set me up to do a 'professional' show where everything that could go wrong did. Now that *would* have provoked a reaction.

I felt sick again as I set off in a taxi for my first day on *EastEnders*. All I wanted to do was sit there quietly, rereading my lines and trying to calm my butterflies, but the taxi driver kept talking about his favourite Carry On films. I just sat there, nodding, saying yes and no in the right places. The driver hardly shut up all the way to Elstree.

My call was not until midday, but I was early, as usual, because I wanted to arrange things in my dressing room. I assumed that the other actors and crew would be around, but when I arrived at 10 a.m., the huge studio and outside set were deserted: it was a midday start for everyone. I was walking up and down, feeling a bit silly, when I spotted Joan Harsant, who plays the sweet-stall owner. I knew her slightly, so I asked her if she knew where my dressing room was. She didn't. As we were talking, Sid Owen, who played Ricky Butcher, came tearing round in his car, on his way to a rehearsal on another part of the studio. Joan introduced us and suggested that Sid took me for a coffee. He drove to where he was rehearsing and we chatted for a while, but at 10.30 he had to go, and I had to find my own way back.

There was still no one around to tell me where my dressing room was. When Peter Halston, the head of Wardrobe, arrived, he discovered I hadn't even been allocated a dressing room. He found me one: it was small, dark and depressing, but I had other things on my mind, like what I was going to wear. Series producer Barbara Emile had already looked over the clothes Peter had got for me and wasn't happy with them, so I'd gone round the charity shops for clothes and had brought in some of my own that were out of fashion. The one item Peter had found that Barbara liked I most definitely didn't want to wear. It was a leopardskin jacket. Julie Goodyear of *Coronation Street* had made a brilliant job of establishing leopardskin as the trademark of her character, Bet Lynch, and I did not want to invite unfavourable comparisons. But that's what I wore in my first scene, with Ross Kemp. Naturally, I kept my mouth shut.

I was waiting in the foyer when Ross came along and asked if I wanted to walk with him to the location. We'd only gone a few yards before he remarked: 'God, you're in a state.'

'Yes, I bloody am,' I said. 'This is far worse than the audition.'

'Let's walk round a bit,' he said. 'It'll help to calm you down.'

Ross, bless him, meant well, and I was very, very grateful. But we had walked only fifty yards or so into Albert Square when I felt sick again. 'Excuse me,' I managed to say apologetically, before throwing up outside Deals on Wheels.

Ross said he found it very endearing that such a well-known lady should be so nervous, and was sympathetic and understanding.

The director of that first scene was kind to me, too. My first word was simply my son's name, 'Grant', but I couldn't seem to say it the right way. All those hours battling to quieten my over-the-top stage voice seemed to have been wasted once the cameras started rolling. The director was so, so patient as I delivered that one word too loudly time and again. 'Take it easy, Barbara. Take it easy, Keep it down,' he kept saying gently.

So much for 'One-Take Windsor'. It took me five takes to get the tone right on my first word on *EastEnders*! It was embarrassing, but that's what nerves and fear can do to you, no matter how many times you've performed in front of an audience. With me that day, it was more than just forgetting my lines or discovering that I wasn't as good as I thought I was. It was the Barbara Windsor thing of wanting to please. I knew that everyone was taking a chance on me, trusting that this tiny lady with the sexy, dumb-blonde image could convince the nation that she was a powerful, dominating matriarch. And it was all-important to me to live up to their expectations and not let anyone down.

I would love to be able to say that my first day was a roaring success, that I set the whole place alight. But that just wasn't the case. I arrived home at seven o'clock that night shattered and very depressed.

'I don't know if I'm going to get the hang of this,' I said to Scott.

'It's your first day, Bar, don't worry about it,' he reassured me. 'It's all new to you. You're bound to feel a bit down.'

Thankfully, that one day was all I had to do until the following Tuesday. In the meantime, I was booked for two one-nighters, in Epsom and Leeds, which I hoped would take my mind off my disappointing debut. The next Tuesday, when I went back to Elstree for some scenes in a hospital, where my other TV son, Phil – played by Steve McFadden – was recovering after a fight with Grant over Grant's wife, Sharon. In an example of how soaps mirror real life, Steve was in fact nursing a knife wound after being attacked himself. I must have been feeling more confident, because I suggested a change to one of my lines. I didn't think Peggy Mitchell would repeat 'What am I doing here?' in response to a question. I felt that 'What do you think I'm doing, waiting for a number thirteen bus?' was more like it.

The fact that that minor adjustment was made did a lot for my self-esteem. But the rest of the day was as difficult, unrewarding and unenjoyable as the first, and when I got home, I poured out all my misgivings to Scott once again.

'Maybe it's playing your age,' he said. 'Maybe you don't want to do that after playing someone younger all your life.'

I didn't think that was it. It was a great relief to be playing a part where I didn't have to give a monkey's how I looked, and where the focus of attention was on my expressions and what I said, not on my boobs and bottom. No, it was more to do with my lack of self-belief. Although I was older, and had been in showbusiness longer than anyone else on the show, I was a novice as far as soaps were concerned, and I truly felt I could never be as good as the others. I was also used to being in command, the fount of all knowledge; to people asking my opinion because I knew what I was talking about. On *EastEnders*, though, I didn't have a clue what I was talking about, so nobody asked my advice about anything. I was not given a lot to do, and on the odd days I was required, I felt like a spare part, a dinosaur making a brief noise before vanishing into TV extinction.

Happily, I had the opportunity to do two more one-woman shows, in Ipswich and Chipping Norton. Scott still loathed the thought of the travelling and the cold dressing rooms, but the stage was my saviour – a sanctuary where I could throw off my depression, grab the audience, breathe and be me. And, of course, I needed the money.

Over the next three weeks or so, my depression deepened. I had ideas about what to do with Peggy Mitchell, and I felt I could bring some depth to the part, but I was not allowed any input. I just went in, did as I was told, and went home. If I had another scene later, I would go to my dressing room and worry. That wouldn't have been so bad if my dressing room had been a cosy home-from-home, but it wasn't, and I spent as little time there as possible.

To add to my gloom, I would hear other actors moaning about their time schedules and workload, and generally whinging about what a tough time they had. I kept my mouth shut but it annoyed me that certain actors didn't appreciate how fortunate they were to have such well-paid and enviable jobs.

I continued to come home and pour it all out to Scott. He never fed my insecurities or allowed me to wallow in self-pity. He just told me to hang on in there and things would get better. But when I saw myself on the programme for the first time I thought, who am I kidding? To make matters worse, my *EastEnders* debut was not confined to the TV pages – it was splashed all over the papers as a news story as well, and the *Evening Standard* insisted on photographing me watching myself on TV. The press didn't slaughter me, thank God: the reviewers seemed to agree that I'd made an OK debut, and that cute, cuddly Barbara Windsor needed time to develop into the no-nonsense, domineering Peggy Mitchell. But I thought, 'Oh, God, this is not good. No way are they going to keep me on once my four-month contract comes up for renewal at the end of the year.'

I consoled myself that playing the Fairy Godmother in *Cinderella* in Basingstoke would see me through financially until the end of January. I was also booked to do a music hall in Darlington and the guest appearance in *One Foot in the Grave* on my days off from the panto, so I was by no means at panic stations when I got the call I expected from Corinne Hollingworth, who had just taken over as *EastEnders* executive producer. I walked to her office determined to take the knock-back graciously, as I pictured the new boss letting me down lightly, telling me it had been lovely having me on the show, but that I hadn't been her choice, it wasn't working and she was going to have to let me go. When I went in I found myself confronted by a striking woman with long, flowing hair.

'God, aren't you pretty?' I heard myself say. The words just slipped out, and the moment they did, I was horrified: it sounded as if I were buttering Corinne up to make her extend my contract. But she just laughed and motioned to me to sit down. 'It's lovely to meet you at last, Barbara,' she said. 'I'm sure your agent has told you your contract is being renewed for another four months.'

I just stared at her blankly. Was I hearing things? I usually spoke to Barry a couple of times a day, but I'd been filming all morning and hadn't yet had a chance to talk to him. Corinne went on: 'I want you to know, Barbara, that whoever chose you for Peggy deserves a medal. I think you're absolutely right. Why you have never come into *EastEnders* before, I don't know.'

Feeling the familiar compulsion to put myself down, I said: 'I haven't really scored, or done anything exciting. I haven't been that great.'

'You have done what has been asked of you,' she told me. 'You have slipped Peggy in and done enough for us to know you are right for the show. You were brought in by my predecessor, and I owe a lot to her. But now we have to do something with you.'

I opened my mouth to speak, but Corinne carried on: 'I want you to sort out her clothes. You're not happy, are you?'

'No, I'm not,' I replied. 'I want Peggy to look at magazines, then get it a bit wrong. She shops at Walthamstow Market for her version of what she has seen, and it's never quite right. And I'd like her to wear earrings and old-fashioned court shoes.' Sensing that Corinne was in agreement with me, I added: 'Please believe me, Peggy will never, ever look like Barbara Windsor. But I would like to change the wig. Can I do that, please?'

'Yes, that's fine. Now, what I want you to do is go off and enjoy your pantomime and think about how you want to play Peggy.'

'Thank you so much,' I said. 'I'm absolutely thrilled, I can't tell you. I'll really come up, I promise you.'

As I stood to leave the office, Corinne said: 'By the way, I'm going to make you landlady of the Queen Vic when you get back.'

For the rest of the day I was walking on air. But I found it so impossible to believe that I didn't tell a soul for four days. Not even Scott.

26

From the minute I stepped into the Vic, in February 1995, I felt I *was* Peggy. I had got the outfits right and the wig was perfect – just a little over the top. And to make me feel even more at home, I was allowed to put photographs of my real-life relatives on the walls upstairs in the pub. There was a lovely picture of Mummy in her bridal gown on the day she married my dad in 1935, a group picture taken when Auntie Mae married in 1931, one of Auntie Dolly and Uncle Charlie Windsor in the 1920s, plus a beautiful photo of Mummy and Len on holiday in Capri. I also wore Mummy's locket containing a picture of her and Len. I felt great, very secure.

On my first day as landlady, filming was due to start at 8.30 a.m., but I made sure I got there early because I wanted to work out a way of reaching the shelf behind the bar. Ross and Letitia Dean had only to lift an arm to get a glass but, being so tiny, I knew I'd have a problem. Before anyone else arrived that morning, I'd solved it: I found a little ledge from which I could balance to add the necessary inches to my reach. It worked, but it did prompt some letters from people wanting to know why I seemed to be hopping every time I went to pick up a glass!

One of my first scenes behind the bar was with Letitia Dean, Gilly Taylforth and Pam St Clement, all of whom I admired and respected. I was shaking at the prospect of acting with the best, but I don't suppose they were aware of that. In fact, I quickly learned that, despite their experience in the show, a lot of the stars were actually nervous about working with me.

Michael French, who played David Wicks, for example, was ultra-professional, but he tripped over his lines the first time we did a scene together. As I was thanking my lucky stars it was him and not me, he said:

'I'm so sorry, Barbara. I just can't believe I'm working opposite you – Barbara Windsor, who I've watched for ever.'

Afterwards, he told me: 'I'm glad that's over. I was so scared of meeting you.' If only you knew! I thought.

In those first nerve-wracking months on *EastEnders*, the Plough was losing money faster than ever, but the loans still had to be repaid. Stephen's only source of income was the pub, so whatever I earned from my shows or personal appearances went towards paying them off. Although I'd signed for all the loans, I had no idea how much we owed; I just went to my accountants in Camden Town and deposited whatever cheques I had with them. Scott was most concerned that every time I crossed their threshold I was told I had to find yet more money, and suggested I asked another firm to look into my whole financial situation. You can imagine my horror when I was told that my liabilities were close to £1 million. It completely freaked me out. There was no way I could ever repay that: I hadn't earned that kind of money in all the years I'd been in showbusiness put together.

The debts were more than the business was worth, but selling it would at least make a huge dent in them. I could understand why Stephen was reluctant to let it go, of course: the Plough was his baby; he had nurtured it and turned it into a healthy money-earner, and he passionately wanted to nurse it back to health. He had built a kiddies' playground in the garden, invested in a new interior design and tried all sorts of different menus. But by 1995, the baby was getting sicker and it was only my money that was keeping the bailiffs at bay.

It was the thought of losing my Marylebone house that terrified me, but as the debts mounted, it became a realistic possibility. In one of my rare phone calls to Stephen, I said: 'I don't care what I have to pay – don't make me lose my little house.'

'That definitely won't happen, Barbara,' he promised.

Scott couldn't understand how I managed to be so nice to Stephen after the financial mess he had got me into, but I saw no point in shouting and swearing at him. I suppose I still had a lot of respect for the way he had worked so hard to try to make a success of the Plough.

The joy I felt at being valued so highly at *EastEnders* after what I'd felt was a difficult start was marred by my anxiety about Scott, who was going through a lean time. If the phone rang, I'd pray it was a job offer for him, but it never was. He had coped with it well after moving in with me, but now the inactivity was getting to him. When I returned from the studio, one evening, he said: 'I'm going to have to get a job, Bar.'

'What sort of job?' I asked.

'Any job. Maybe I could work in a clothes shop, like I've always done.'

'What? Somewhere down Oxford Street?'

'Why not?' he said.

'No, darling,' I told him. 'I don't want you working in a jeans shop.'

But it was a problem, I knew that. Far from being a help to him in his career, it seemed that his relationship with me put him at a disadvantage. Scott's life was now revolving around me twenty-four hours a day. He had no identity of his own, and because he refused to go on the dole, he was living on his dwindling savings. His already low self-esteem was not helped by having no work; now, he was beginning to feel like a ponce as well.

A day or two later, I came up with an idea.

'Why don't I employ you as my driver?' I suggested. 'You're already taking me to and from the studios. If you weren't, I'd have to pay goodness knows what for taxis, so why not drive me and get paid for it?'

It seemed the perfect solution, and for a while it was. Scott would drop me at Elstree early in the morning, do his own thing during the day, then pick me up in the evening. He knew the cast and crew, so if he arrived early he was always welcome to sit in the Green Room and watch the show on a monitor as we were filming. But it was hardly an enriching experience. Here was someone who had spent three years at drama school having to sit and watch people doing what he wanted to do. No one knowingly put Scott down, but, to make conversation, someone might ask, 'Are you working?', and that would embarrass him. He felt it was obvious he wasn't, otherwise he wouldn't have been at the studio waiting to pick me up. He could have waited in the car like the other drivers, but that would not have done his self-esteem much good either.

At the other end of the scale, he had to cope with the spotlight as well – and not in his own right, but as Barbara Windsor's lover. That turned Scott's life upside down. Our age difference gave the gossips a field day. Scott could have handled it if people in showbusiness – including some I'd counted as friends – had been kind and supportive, but many were positively cruel, openly ridiculing him, which, for someone so sensitive and vulnerable to criticism, was not only devastating, but humiliating as well. They threw it all at him. Either he was homosexual and with me because I was a so-called gay icon, or a heterosexual 'front', a young man I paraded about on my arm, or he was simply using me to help him get a job in showbusiness. No one had the guts to insult Scott to his face, but such is the nasty, gossipy side of the world of showbusiness that the taunts and put-downs were delivered in loud stage whispers that he couldn't help but hear.

When people weren't sniggering behind Scott's back, they were dismissive, pointedly cutting him dead as if he didn't exist. And it wasn't just the showbiz gossips. I was appalled at how rude people could be. If we were in a club, or I was doing a personal appearance, men would flock round me, wanting to have a chat, or simply to tell me that they loved me in this movie or that TV show, and I remember a man once asking me something about a Carry On film that I couldn't remember. When Scott helpfully supplied the answer the man gave him an icy stare and snapped: 'I wasn't talking to you.'

Wherever we went, Scott would find himself being blanked – even by shop assistants. It was terribly rude, of course, but I don't think people can help it. Suddenly, standing in front of them is this woman they feel they've known all their lives, not only as the silly bird in soppy movies, but now as the East End mum in a TV soap, and they don't want to know about anyone else. If I'd been with Ross Kemp or Steve McFadden it would have been different, but usually people had no idea who Scott was, and would probably have had no interest in him even if they had. Of course, he never said anything. He just had this crestfallen look, one that was to become all too familiar as *EastEnders* made my face even more famous than it had been when we met.

Being with me was magnifying Scott's insecurities a millionfold. He'd never thought he was anything special; now, he felt that more than ever. And when he wasn't being ignored, he was being asked the questions he dreaded most: 'Who are you? What are you? What are you doing?' He just swallowed it, week in, week out, month after month.

But inside he was very angry as well as embarrassed, and, that summer of 1995, he got to a point where, if we were going out to an official function, he felt he needed a drink before we left. If he went in sober, he was acutely aware of people judging him, perhaps laughing at him. So he would have a glass of champagne or wine to give him some Dutch courage and make him less self-conscious.

Meanwhile, the financial pressure on me became so intense that Peter Jay, my lawyer at the West End solicitors Finers, said we needed to sit down with Stephen and his lawyers to determine the extent of the mess and decide what to do about it. At that meeting, my accountant, Mark Gold, left no one in any doubt that the picture was very bleak, and getting bleaker by the day.

The Plough had been losing money for the last five years, Mark said: takings were going down and losses accelerating. I sat there in shock, listening to Mark reveal that, from January to December the previous year, I'd put £79,000 into the pub, and £49,000 in the first five months of the current year. Obviously, I'd signed the cheques, but hearing those figures made me wince: £128,000 of my hard-earned income, yet still the pub was losing money. It was heartbreaking.

Peter Jay made it clear that I was not in a position to finance the losses any longer, and that if action wasn't taken soon, the bank would move in to recover its £203,000 debt. An ideal solution, he said, would be for Stephen to take over the pub's liabilities himself. Stephen produced a list of his own ideas, but they began and ended with me taking over the Plough's overdraft, which, Peter quickly pointed out, was essentially what I was already doing. Stephen put his list away.

The problem was not only a loss-making pub; it was the size of our general debts. The outstanding mortgage on the London house was £178,000, which, with the £475,000 brewery and building society loans, bank overdraft and other debts, meant we owed £922,000 in total. It was all so distressing after the high hopes Stephen and I had had for the pub, and for each other. No wonder we were so upset that we both broke down and cried in front of everyone.

It was Stephen's wish to keep the Plough and to try to make a success of it. I wanted that too – the pub was his dream, his baby, and I hated the thought of him losing it. Maybe I had a guilty conscience abut Scott, I don't know, but I was prepared to write off all the thousands I'd put into the pub and let Stephen have it – anything to save my home. The harsh truth, however, was that Stephen was the only one in the room who believed the pub could make money. I admired him for his faith, but the big question was why it hadn't worked up to now. He blamed the problems we'd had over the previous eighteen months, but as we'd just been told the pub had been losing money for five years, it didn't add up.

Peter felt that, if Stephen was not going to take on all the liabilities, the pub should be put on the market as soon as possible, allowing a short period of grace to give Stephen a chance to refinance it himself. Stephen had assured me the house was safe no matter what, but it was still a relief to hear Peter confirm that only the Plough and my endowment policy would go towards reducing the debts. The amount outstanding would be a colossal financial millstone, but I'd make sure I found the money to pay that off. All I wanted now was to see the back of the Plough and of the never-ending drain it was on my income.

Apparently Stephen was shocked by what he had learned at the meeting, but his lawyer said he would co-operate with plans to put the pub up for sale should he fail to refinance it. However, he said, Stephen would not be steamrollered into anything and must walk away with 'no onward indebted mess'.

I was willing to accept all that for Stephen's sake, but what I didn't expect, and didn't consider for a moment, was that walking away with no debts was only part of my husband's legal plan. In the divorce settlement, to be negotiated once the pub was up for sale, he would claim many thousands of pounds for himself as a 'kiss-off'. That was what really hurt. I paid it – and I had to take out another loan to do so – but it was a real kick in the teeth, especially when you consider how much younger than me Stephen was and all the years he had ahead of him to make a success of a new venture.

One evening shortly after our crisis meeting I was watching TV with Scott when the phone rang. A cultured woman's voice slurred: 'Hello, Barbara, this is Jane.'

'Hello, Jane,' I said, recognising Stephen's sister and realising that she had had a drink or three.

'Now, about this pub,' she said. 'Can't you let Stephen have it? Why don't you give it to him?'

'Because we owe masses of money,' I told her calmly. 'I can't. Haven't you talked to Stephen? Hasn't he told you what the accountants said?'

Either she had spoken to Stephen and he hadn't told her, or she had spoken to him and hadn't understood – or maybe she hadn't spoken to him at all. Whatever the case, she had no idea what she was on about and was only ringing in the way that people often pick up the phone late at night, feeling brave after a few drinks, thinking, I'll sort this out.

It was hardly surprising that Jane and I had a row, because I could not get it across to her that it was me, not her brother, who had to get us out of debt, and that it was not legally feasible to hand over the pub for nothing, much as I would have liked to do so. Although the whole business was nothing to do with Jane, I asked her: 'Do you want to buy the pub? Do you want to have a go at making it work? That would be fine by me. You take on the debts and I'll walk away. I won't ask for a penny.' That shut her up. Jane was a secretary: I doubt she could afford to pay off even her own debts.

While all the wrangling over the pub was going on, I received a phone call one day from the *News of the World* to say that a Robert Dunn had offered them a story. They wanted to know whether I'd like to put my side of it to them first. I was wise to this ploy, which the papers use to try to make you get your retaliation in first, so to speak, in the hope that you will give them something more controversial than what they have already. I told them that I would wait until the piece came out to see what he had to say. Whatever it was – presumably his account of his relationship with me over the years – I never found out, because, thankfully, they never ran the article.

In what seemed like no time at all, what had started out as Dutch courage got a hold on Scott and changed our lives. Soon, one glass of wine before we went out was not enough; he would have two, and often more than that. And he was never content to enjoy himself for a couple of hours at functions, then head for home, as we always had. Instead he would linger on, getting more and more drunk, until the bitter end. Of course, this worried me – apart from anything else, more often than not I'd have to be up around 5 a.m. to get to the studios and was relying on Scott to drive me there.

Gone were the nights when we would nip out to a local Italian restaurant for spaghetti Bolognese and a glass of red wine, then go home to bed. Now Scott would drink before we left the house even when we were going out on our own, drink in the restaurant and still want more when we got home. If we were spending an evening with friends, he seemed to want to get pie-eyed as quickly as possible and I would be on edge all the time, afraid of what he might say or do. Eventually, I starting making excuses not to go out at all, but when we stayed in, Scott was more interested in pouring drink down his neck than in talking to me. I would go to bed, leaving him alone with a bottle, and come down in the morning to find him on the kitchen floor, or slumped across the dining table.

I think I could have stopped Scott's spiral of self-destruction had it not been for another craving that transformed him from the smart, happy-go-lucky, wonderful guy I loved into a sad, pathetic creature I hardly recognised. It was drugs: cocaine, to be precise. I didn't know it at the time, but Scott was into coke in a big way.

By the end of the year it had got to the stage where he was constantly preoccupied with where his next drink was coming from. We were at a great party one Saturday night when a friend of ours suggested going on to a West End club. I didn't see the point: the party was still in full swing, and it would be rude to leave our hosts simply to go on to do the same thing somewhere else. But when I looked at Scott, I knew exactly what he was thinking. I could see his brain working it all out: this party will probably finish in an hour or so and I won't be able to have another drink; much better to be in a club, where the booze – and probably drugs, too – will be available for several more hours. Against my better judgement, I went with him on that occasion. At least that way I knew he was safe.

I had been thinking about making my peace with my father. I had not spoken to him since that awful day in 1984 when he had so cruelly rejected my cry for help, but I hated the thought of him dying without us having talked and, I hoped, made things better between us. So when I was asked to do a personal appearance in November in Lowestoft, where Daddy was now living with Julie, it seemed the perfect opportunity. This is meant to be, I thought.

I got a good reaction from them and we were invited round for tea and sandwiches on the day before my personal appearance. We hadn't seen each other for thirty years – not since my father had thrown those Christmas presents in my face – and although I was excited about seeing him again, I was understandably nervous, too. What were we going to talk about? I wondered. Would I say something to provoke that terrible temper? When I saw my dad waiting outside his block of flats, he was all smiles. I thought that was really sweet. I gave him a kiss on the cheek, asked how he was, and we all went into his little flat on the ground floor. It was going to be all right, I was sure.

It was. The four of us spent a lovely, relaxed couple of hours, chatting about this and that, and Scott took a picture of me in an armchair, with Daddy and Julie on either side, all smiling happily. When Scott and I left for our hotel, I was thrilled to bits: everything had been calm and friendly, with not one hint of the bitterness that had blighted our relationship. I honestly felt that the rift had been healed.

I had told Daddy about my job the next day, which was for the spectacles company Vision Express, and when I spotted him in the crowd, watching me sign autographs, I called him over and made a fuss of him. He liked that, I think. I felt so much better for having built that bridge, even if I wouldn't be able to see that much of him. I got a real buzz out of sending flowers, chocolates and champagne, with 'Happy Birthday' balloons to my dad: it was wonderful to be able to spoil him at last knowing there was no longer any bad feeling.

In January 1996, after Scott and I appeared in *Cinderella* in Dartford – I played the Fairy Godmother and Scott was Dandini – we went to Henlow Grange health farm for a much-needed rest. It was there that I got the good news, from my new accountant, Mark Gold, that the Plough had finally been sold.

What a relief. At last I was able to stop pouring all that hard-earned money into a bottomless pit.

However, I had other problems by now. Scott's drinking was getting worse and worse. If we were out somewhere and I wanted to leave early, he would look at me imploringly and say: 'You don't mind, do you, Bar? As long as I always come home.' And he'd put me in a taxi, tell the driver to make sure I was safely through my front door before driving off, then go on to get well and truly smashed.

Did I mind? Yes, I minded a lot. But I stomached it because I did not want to come over as the archetypal, over-protective, nagging older woman. I am a worrier, though, and a bad sleeper, and I'd lie awake for hours, which defeated the object of coming home early, my concern turning to anxiety, anxiety to fury, wondering where he was, who he was with and what he was doing. Eventually I'd hear the taxi pull up, the key in the door and take him in my arms, the anger melting into blessed relief that he was home safely. Other times I felt I was being taken for granted and would lash out to remind him not to treat me like a doormat. All the screaming and shouting and punching never got me anywhere, though, because Scott was so out of it that he hardly knew where he was.

What would infuriate me was that Scott would stay on at a club getting higher and higher on drink and coke when he knew I had to leave for Elstree at 5.30 a.m. The drugs would make him lose all track of time, and all thought of me. Having finally arrived home in a drunken stupor, he would be like a zombie for the rest of the day, oblivious of the worry and inconvenience he had caused. Only when I came home in the evening after filming on *EastEnders* would he be sober at last. He'd be full of remorse then. I'd force him to face himself in the mirror to see how dreadful he looked, and he would sob: 'How can I do this to you, the woman I love so much?'

I didn't have the answer. In fact I was feeling the same about him. I would look at him, so pathetically sad, and think: 'I've done nothing wrong, and yet I've managed to ruin this man's life.' I cast my mind back to what Scott had said when Thomas Powell had turned up in Brighton: 'God, I hope I never end up like that.' And now it seemed as if he was heading down the same path. Then Scott would look at me and see the tears and the hurt and the worry in my eyes, and promise to go on the wagon. And he would, but it never lasted for more than three or four days, and then he would be off on another bender.

In March, Corinne Hollingworth left *EastEnders*, and the new producer, Jane Harris, asked any actors who had ideas for their own storylines to let her know. Peggy had now settled in at the Vic, and I was loving every minute of a wonderful part, but I didn't have my own storyline as such: I was always on the periphery of plots centred on more established characters. I told Barry Burnett what Jane had said, and we agreed to keep our eyes open for a possible 'hook'.

Public awareness of breast cancer was growing at this time, and one morning Barry told me about a piece he'd seen on breast cancer in one of the tabloids. After reading it, I felt that a story involving Peggy Mitchell getting the disease, and perhaps having to have her breasts removed, would touch the viewers' hearts. More important, what better person could there be than an actress celebrated for her bosom to highlight the trauma of the condition?

I told Jane about the idea, explaining why I thought it could work, and she took it on board, promising to let me know in due course. A few months later she called me to her office and said that they were going to go with the cancer story – which had apparently already been considered – but that although Peggy would discover a lump in her breast, she would only need a lumpectomy. Other actors and actresses, especially June Brown, thought I was brave to want such a storyline, but I was pleased the powers-that-be felt it had merit.

Like other soaps, *EastEnders* does its homework when it tackles serious issues, and I was sent masses of bumph to read. Arrangements were also made for me to talk to a Macmillan nurse who had had direct experience of counselling breast-cancer sufferers.

It was a great opportunity to show what I could do as an actress. Peggy had been involved in dramatic scenes, but she had never had a long-running storyline that required pathos and poignancy. But no matter how I played the role, I knew that some people with first-hand experience of the disease were bound to say: 'That's not the way it is at all.' I consoled myself with the knowledge that no two cases are the same – I would simply portray how it affected Peggy. I was fortunate to have a sympathetic director and a lovely fictional fiancé, George, played by Paul Moriarty, who helped me get through a traumatic yet exciting time.

My pleasure at Peggy's impending high profile was put into perspective shortly before filming when Wendy Richard, who plays Pauline Fowler, developed breast cancer herself. I went to the script department expecting to hear that Peggy's storyline was being dropped, but I was told it was too far advanced to be pulled.

The public reaction was astounding: I got thousands of letters thanking me for drawing attention to the dangers of breast cancer, and was invited to dozens of functions in aid of the illness. I attended as many as I could. It made me much more aware of the dangers of breast cancer, too. I had never been worried about lumps before, but swotting up on the subject made me realise how vital it is to do regular checks.

Scott and I were having dinner with my old friend John Reid in the Ivy restaurant in Covent Garden when I mentioned that we were going on holiday to New York for a couple of weeks in July. John was flying there himself for a couple of days around the same time and was disappointed to learn we'd be arriving on the day he was leaving. 'Tell you what,' he said. 'Why don't you fly out with me on Concorde? You can stay at my apartment and we can spend a couple of days together.'

'That's so sweet of you, darling, but we can't. It's all arranged.'

'Don't be silly,' John insisted. 'You can change it and fly Concorde.'

On our way home, I was in a tizz. 'John's very wealthy and most likely thinks I am, too,' I said to Scott. 'But I can't afford two tickets on Concorde.' I spent the night worrying about how we were going to get out of it without losing face. In the morning, you could have knocked me down with a feather when two Concorde tickets were delivered to the house with a note from John saying that they were his treat for my birthday.

Flying Concorde was a wonderful experience for both of us, but particularly for Scott, because he had always said it was an ambition he never thought he would fulfil. The beauty of the flight, of course, is that you touch down in under four hours, so when we arrived we had the rest of the day to enjoy. *Rent* was the hot show in town, but John was able to just pick up the phone and arrange two tickets for that afternoon's matinée. Then Scott and I went back to his spectacular apartment on the twenty-seventh floor of the Millennium Tower and watched *The Lion King* on video while John went off to meet Disney executives for early production talks on the Elton John–Tim Rice musical *Aida*.

The next day, John arranged for us to see *How to Succeed in Business Without Really Trying*, which was a real treat because I'd seen the original in New York in 1963 when I was promoting *Sparrows Can't Sing*, and Scott had performed in a drama school production of the play. Then we saw *The King and I*. It was a hectic, but wonderful, three days.

Before John flew back to London, I told him that two friends of mine, John Addy and Nicky Marsh, had invited us to spend a few days with them at a house they were renting on Fire Island, off New York, a retreat that attracted wealthy gays from all over the world. John shook his head. 'You won't like it,

Bar,' he said. 'You're great with gays, but that's not the place for you. They're very much into their own thing there.'

How right he was. Scott and I knew the place wasn't our cup of tea within minutes of arriving, shortly after dark. Marc Almond, from the band Soft Cell, and his manager, who had also been invited by John and Nicky, were at the dock to meet the ferry that had brought us from Manhattan. The fixed grins on their faces clearly said: 'You're going to hate this, too.'

John and Nicky are the sweetest people, and they tried to make our stay enjoyable, but Fire Island was very 'In the Navy' – full of guys with moustaches and cropped hair, and very hedonistic. And apart from the odd lesbian, I was the only woman there. Marc and his manager had had enough by the next day and moved on, and after four days we left ourselves, and went back to bask in the luxury of John Reid's sumptuous apartment. We had the most fabulous time seeing Manhattan's wonderful sights and, of course, we did not forget to drink a special toast to John, whose generosity put the icing on the cake of a memorable holiday.

Back in England, I went to the Regent's Park Open-Air Theatre with Joan Collins to see our mutual friend Christopher Biggins in *The Tempest*. I'd introduced Joan and Christopher the previous year when we had all gone to see Joan's ex-husband, Anthony Newley, in his one-man show at the Langan Hilton, and they had got on brilliantly. A few weeks later, I'd bumped into Joan at a book launch, and she'd said: 'Tell me, that delightful man I met, Christopher Biggins – is he really as lovely as he seems?'

'Oh, yes,' I told her. 'He's an absolute joy. He is lovely for ladies like us, especially if you haven't got a gentleman to escort you to a première, or if you want to go to the movies – or even if you fancy fish and chips. He's that kind of person. Every actress should have Biggins in the small print of their contract as an essential.'

'Oh, really?' said Joan. And that was the beginning of a great friendship. After that, they were seen everywhere together.

That night after *The Tempest* we went to dinner at the Ivy, where Joan taught me a lesson I've never forgotten. She looked amazing, given that it was a chilly night and we'd been sitting in the open air for a couple of hours, but even so she asked the press photographers waiting outside the restaurant not to take her picture until she came out.

After dinner Joan checked her lipstick to make sure she was looking her best, whereas I didn't bother. As we left we were photographed together. While I grinned broadly, waving my hands all over the place, the immaculate Joan smiled sweetly and kept hers discreetly behind her back – which, for ladies of our years, is essential, because if you show your hands, you show your age. When I saw some of the photographs, the difference was clear – at least, it was to me! I take my hat off to her.

All the time we had been in New York, Scott had controlled his drinking; being 3,000 miles from London and all the Barbara Windsor razzmatazz had relaxed him, and he seemed to enjoy himself without feeling the need to get smashed every night. Now that we were back home, however, he started hitting the bottle harder than ever, night after night, and it frightened the life out of me. I had to face the fact that I was living with an alcoholic. But I was at a loss as to what to do – until September, when he hit a new low and it became clear that I had to take drastic action.

I had an important lunchtime personal appearance in Trafalgar Square, and had arranged for Scott to drive me there and then on to Elstree, where I would be working until 8 p.m. Even in his worst state, he had never arrived home later than 6 a.m., but this morning he did not turn up at all, and I panicked. I didn't know who he had been out with, and had no phone numbers for any likely candidates anyway. In desperation, I rang his brother-in-law, Laurence, but he had no idea where Scott was. I left for the PA in a taxi, my mind a whirl of confusion, worry and anger. At last, at midday, Scott called me on my mobile phone. He was very quiet, very hung over and very, very sorry, and he was sobbing so much that we could not have a proper conversation. I said we would talk that night.

When I got back to Marylebone both Scott and Laurence were waiting for me. Scott was sitting on the couch, embarrassed and forlorn. His stomach had been churning with panic attacks and he was deathly pale and dreadfully thin, thinner than he'd been even one day earlier. He hadn't shaved, and his normally bright brown eyes stared at me blankly from deep, dark sockets. I went over to him and took him in my arms. He buried his face in my shoulder and began to sob uncontrollably.

'I'll take him back to his family in Brighton,' Laurence said. 'You get on with the rest of your week.'

I looked at my dear Scott. 'This is not good, my darling,' I said. 'We have to sort you out. We've got to.'

The following Sunday, while Scott was on his way back from Brighton, I phoned John Reid.

'I need your help badly, sweetheart,' I said.

27

I TOLD JOHN THE WHOLE STORY AND HE ARRANGED FOR SCOTT TO SEE BEECHY COLCLOUGH, A RENOWNED COUNSELLOR WHO HAD HELPED MANY SHOWBIZ CELEBRITIES, INCLUDING ELTON JOHN AND MICHAEL JACKSON, THROUGH THEIR ADDICTION PROBLEMS. Two days later, Scott was having his first session at Beechy's practice, a five-minute walk away in Harley Street, and our lives were about to be transformed in a way I would never have foreseen.

Scott went on the wagon, and I found I was living with a guy I didn't know. I'd fallen in love with an amusing, chatty and interesting young man who had turned into a boring, selfish, self-obsessed madman hell bent on destroying himself. Now, I met a third Scott: a quiet, introverted, sullen individual with none of the infectious *joie de vivre* of the first.

During the crucial first two months, when he was seeing Beechy twice a week, the change in Scott was extraordinary. He had gone from one extreme to the other. Having wanted to stay out wasting himself until his body could take no more, now he didn't want to go out at all. If I was invited to a theatre first night or film première, he'd say: 'Can't you take Barry?' Sometimes I did, but mostly I didn't go at all. If there was something I particularly wanted to attend – a charity dinner, for example – Scott would go with me, but naturally people around us would be drinking and he would be on edge all the time. He developed what he called the Cinderella Syndrome: the need to leave a social gathering at midnight because by then the alcohol was making everyone else talk a language he didn't understand. As that hour approached, and I could see other people getting merry, I'd be toying with my own glass, knowing that Scott was not enjoying himself and wanted to go home.

As Christmas approached, the number of invitations increased, and I'd make sure I got to the post first to sort through it and dump some so that Scott didn't feel guilty that I might be missing out. One event I particularly wanted to attend was the National TV Soap Awards. My boss, Jane Harris, had said that if *EastEnders* should win anything, she wanted me to receive the award on behalf of the show. Of course I asked Scott to accompany me, but he refused, which was such a shame, because the previous year, we had won an award, and we'd had a great time with Ross Kemp and Steve McFadden and the rest of the *EastEnders* gang. Reluctantly, I told Jane I couldn't make it, but she's a very persuasive lady and, in the event, I did go, though on my own. I was pleased I made the effort because *EastEnders* won the major award again. But I didn't hang around afterwards, much as I felt like celebrating. After posing for photographs I left, and was back home with Scott by eleven.

The big test for Scott was when he went to Bristol in December to appear as Bosun Cringe in *Dick Whittington* with Jim Davidson. All the time he was driving me to work and I could keep an eye on him, he was OK, but I knew the pitfalls of panto: the adrenaline runs through you so fast on stage that the moment you are off and start to come down, there is a great temptation to have a drink. Happily, Scott resisted it, and even on Christmas Day at home with me, he didn't touch a drop. That Christmas was lovely: it was the first time I hadn't worked over the festive season, and Scott seemed to be less depressed. It was wonderful to wake up on Boxing Day knowing I didn't have to go out and do three shows. Instead I watched TV in Scott's hotel room in Bristol while he did a matinée performance, then went to the theatre to see him in the evening show. After everything he had been through, it was fantastic to see him enjoying himself again.

Few people on *EastEnders* had a clue about Scott's problem: it was my secret. And I had another secret to keep as I went to work on the last Monday in January 1997. Happily, this one was a cause for celebration: I was the only person on the set who knew that Michael Aspel would be arriving later to surprise Ross Kemp with the big, red *This is Your Life* book. I had to perform a long scene with Ross by the stairs at the back of the Vic, and I was nervous about giving the game away. All I had to say, walking down the stairs, was, 'Now, look, Grant, I don't care what you say . . .' but every time I opened my mouth to speak, all I could hear was that dramatic *This is Your Life* signature tune. I kept stumbling over my line and it took me nine takes to get it right. I was so embarrassed I felt like slashing my wrists, but of course I couldn't tell a soul what the matter was.

After the fourth or fifth take, Ross realised that something was wrong.

'Are you OK, Bar?' he asked, most concerned. 'Have you had a row with Scott?'

'No, sweetheart,' I said. 'I'm all right. It's just that I've got a lot on my mind at the moment.'

Just how much became apparent shortly after 6 p.m. when Michael walked on to the set and gave my TV son the surprise of his life. Ross looked at me and grinned. Suddenly everything had clicked into place for him.

Scott had not seen Beechy while he'd been in panto, and when he returned to London felt he had progressed enough to do without counselling for a while. When a great friend of someone at *EastEnders* told him about Alcoholics Anonymous, he decided to go with him to a meeting.

I was horrified, and tried to talk him out of it. To me, AA was for people who found it hard to survive without drinking – you know, the poor people you see on the street – and I didn't think Scott fell into that category. Sure, he had a problem, but he hadn't touched a drop since 10 October, and showed no sign of weakening. But he went to that meeting, somewhere over in South Kensington – and came home elated. He'd expected to meet like-minded people, but he was amazed at how many people from different walks of life, including some celebrities, did suffer from alcohol addiction.

I wasn't happy when he said he wanted to go to more meetings, but consoled myself that, if he came away feeling better, they must be doing him good.

I realised I'd been wrong to put people into categories when we saw three very drunk down-and-outs at a soup kitchen in Marylebone High Street one day. Without thinking, I said: 'How awful. I wonder how they got like that?' I bit my tongue. I realised I'd seen Scott in almost as bad a way at home. Those unfortunate souls hadn't had the strength to go to AA. Thank God Scott had.

On Wednesday 2 April, I came home late after a long day in Elstree to find among that morning's mail a letter from the manager of the Davigdor Rest Home in Hove. And when I read it, a familiar sadness swept through my body.

Dear Miss Windsor,
RE Thomas Powell
I write in connection with the above person.

From various conversations with Thomas, it came to my attention that he had known you very well in his not too distant past, and he indicated that there may have been a close friendship between the two of you. He always expressed his strong desire to renew his acquaintanceship with you. Therefore the purpose of this letter is to inform you of his unfortunate decline. Sadly Thomas passed away at the Royal Sussex County Hospital in Brighton on the 11th March 1997.

Myself and the staff here have all read your autobiography where you spoke very highly of Thomas so I felt it was my duty to inform you of this very sad event.

Should you wish to attend his funeral, or to make any form of floral contribution, the details of the funeral directors are as follows.

The funeral had taken place that morning. The letter had been written on Thursday 27 March, but it had been forwarded to me from the Plough – the only address Thomas had for me – arriving just too late. Of all the people I'd encountered in my life, Thomas was the one whose funeral I wouldn't have wanted to miss. If I had received that letter in time I would most certainly have been there. I was terribly upset to learn later that only six people had been at his pauper's burial. Even in death, it seemed, poor Thomas got kicked in the teeth.

That evening Scott and I raised our glasses – his filled with mineral water, mine with white wine – and drank a toast to a dear, sweet man who had battled against the odds all his life and tragically lost.

The following week, I was called to the Publicity Department at *EastEnders* to be shown an advance copy of a now-defunct showbiz magazine called *Here!* Staring at me from the front cover was my father's face, alongside my own, under the headline, 'BARBARA WINDSOR'S FATHER PLEADS: "LET'S END OUR 30-YEAR FEUD".' It completely knocked me for six. As far as I was concerned, everything was fine between us: bridges had been built on that peace-making visit to Lowestoft eighteen months earlier, and since then I'd kept in touch with phone calls and acknowledged Daddy and Julie's wedding anniversary with champagne, chocolates and flowers. Yet now here they were complaining that I didn't have time for the likes of them. It was true that I hadn't yet gone up to see them again, but clearly they didn't appreciate the fact that Lowestoft was hardly round the corner, or the demands of my *EastEnders* schedule.

Whatever they felt, I was at a complete loss to understand why they had done such a terrible thing. What really upset me was that this article came out of nowhere. Daddy had not even warned me that he was being interviewed, let alone what he was going to say. It was later followed by an even nastier piece in the *News of the World*, in which Julie said she hated me and made some horrible remarks about my mother.

I was so badly hurt that I could not bring myself to contact Daddy and Julie again. Julie later started to write to me, usually claiming that my father was ill and asking me to get in touch, but neither of them ever offered any kind of explanation or apology for those articles, and that was just one kick in the teeth too many for me. I felt that I had given Daddy my best shot, but it seems that wasn't good enough.

Thanks to our friendship with John Reid, we had been invited to Elton John's fiftieth birthday party at Hammersmith Palais the following Sunday. Elton's parties are legendary, and this huge, star-studded event was to be a fancy-dress affair. For weeks leading up to it many of the people invited had been racking their brains over what to wear. Paul O'Grady – alias the comic Lily Savage – rang seeking inspiration, but I had none; we were at a loss as well. Scott and I had already been to Berman's, the West End theatrical costumiers, but everybody, it seemed, had got there before us.

Scott saved the day. He said we shouldn't try to compete with the elaborate and outrageous costumes most of the guests would be wearing, and go instead for something relevant to my cockney image. So we went as a Pearly King and Queen. With the additional *EastEnders* connection, it was the perfect choice, and we got a fantastic response when we arrived.

Even by Elton's standards the party was sensational, the most phenomenally lavish do I'd ever been to. Even though there was a huge band playing, the acoustics were so good you could have a good chat without having to bellow in people's ears. Elton looked amazing in a spectacular curly Louis XIV gold wig that came down to his chest and a white satin outfit. Others were dressed equally flamboyantly. Someone who wasn't, however, was the famous showbiz photographer Terry O'Neill, who was not dressed up at all.

'Why have you come as yourself?' I asked him.

'I haven't,' he grinned. 'I've come as one of James Bond's deadliest rivals.'

I frowned. 'What do you mean?'

'Well, I'm Goldfinger, aren't I?' He lifted his hand and showed me a forefinger painted gold. Clever, eh?

There was food from all around the world, and, naturally, the champagne – pink – flowed from start to finish. I had not intended to drink much because I wanted to keep an eye on Scott, but I got caught up in the heady atmosphere and splendour of the occasion and got tiddly very quickly. By the time the 'Cinderella' clock in Scott's head told him we should be leaving, I was totally out of it. On the way out, we bumped into Beechy Colclough, who was as sober as Scott, and I vaguely remember Scott looking at me, then shrugging his shoulders to Beechy as if to say, 'What can you do?'

Scott was still going to AA meetings, often with Lionel Bart, whom he knew through me. They became friends and often had a coffee together afterwards in a little café in the Fulham Road. One night, Scott came home very depressed because Lionel had not turned up and he was worried that he might have fallen off the wagon. Sadly, Scott's fears proved justified, and Scott didn't see Lionel any more. It upset him greatly.

One of the rare events Scott did agree to attend was a charity night for children with cancer, organised by Bill Wyman, the former Rolling Stone, at his restaurant, Sticky Fingers, every July. I'd first been invited shortly after I met Scott and we'd gone every year since. Bill is such a good man. He couldn't do enough to make it a special evening for the charity, giving over the entire restaurant, organising all the food and laying on everything. It was always a really wonderful night and Scott and I had always made an occasion of it by having an exotic cocktail at the Ritz or Dorchester beforehand. But that was out of the question now. Instead we left the house after a cup of tea and headed straight for the restaurant.

I'd be lying if I said those nine months when Scott was not drinking were easy for me. Like many people, I love coming home after a stressful day and unwinding with a glass or two of wine, but I knocked that on the head because I didn't think it was fair on Scott. And I have to admit that some evenings were strained and tense.

I wasn't crazy about celebrating my sixtieth birthday that August, but the *Sunday Mirror* wanted to throw a big bash for me the Sunday before, and my good friend Paul Bennett, the paper's picture editor, persuaded me that it would be a great idea. The omens were not good. I couldn't find anything to wear, and when I did it was altered so badly that I had to scrap the outfit and run around on the Saturday looking for something else. I bought a green suit which, unfortunately, was exactly the same shade as the jacket Scott planned to wear. Oh well, I thought, people will think we are wearing matching clothes on purpose. It was not until the night before that I began to relax and look forward to the party: it was a great excuse to meet up with lots of old friends I hadn't seen for years, and if the *Sunday Mirror* were happy to pay for it all in return for a story and a spread of celebrity photos, so much the better.

But when I woke up the next morning and picked up the *Sunday Mirror*'s rival tabloid, the *People*, I was so devastated I wanted to cancel the party immediately and hide myself away. Staring me in the face was a most humiliating and embarrassing double-page article by my ex-husband, Stephen, which reduced me to tears. He had 'told all' about our relationship in the *Sun* soon after I left him, but this was far more personal and hurtful. He had never told me why he found sex with me such a turn-off, yet he confided in a reporter. 'It didn't take long for the novelty of bedding a woman the same age as my mum to wear off,' he said.

> I loved her, but I just didn't fancy her, even though she spent a fortune on sets of sexy lingerie ... it wasn't long before she was happy for me to see her taking off her make-up ... and hanging up one of her many wigs on the row of polystyrene heads she kept on the wardrobe. Before then I'd always thought what a cute little body she had, but once the designer clothes, hair and face came off, I just wasn't interested in the sex side: Barbara spends a fortune on trying to look young, but without the designer clothes, make-up and wigs, she's unrecognisable.
>
> I'm sure most men still think of her as the busty little sex bomb, but if they saw her like I used to, trying to pose seductively on the end of the bed with saggy boobs, straggly clumps of grey hair and no eyelashes, they'd run a mile. It got to the stage where I used to turn over and pretend to be asleep, or go through the motions just to get it over with ... I used to make excuses about working hard and being tired because I dreaded having to perform in bed.

Stephen twisted the knife even deeper at the end of the piece, predicting that I'd dump Scott like I'd dumped him and end up a sad, lonely old lady.

I just couldn't believe that he was so eaten up with bitterness he could come out with such nasty things – and on the day of my sixtieth birthday party as well. Many of my friends were equally shocked, and rang to say how dreadfully they felt Stephen had behaved. Some even commented that his rantings made him sound like a bitter old queen.

I was heartbroken, of course, and far too embarrassed to face anyone. I told

Scott he'd have to cancel the party. But, quite rightly, he pointed out that there were so many people coming it would be impossible to let everyone know in time.

So we went ahead with it. To be honest, although I knew some people would have seen the piece, I didn't expect everyone to have read it. But they had. And from the minute we arrived at Johnny Gold's Belvedere restaurant in Holland Park, everyone was sympathetic and said I should just ignore the whole thing and have a good time. Steve McFadden, bless him, flew back from Spain specially for the party. His first words to me were: 'I read that rubbish. The bastard!'

And do you know, I did have a good time after all. Buzzing about in the warm, comforting atmosphere created by people who genuinely liked me made me forget about Stephen's vicious diatribe, and whatever the *People*'s motive for printing it was, and I really enjoyed myself.

Naturally, most of the *EastEnders* gang were there, including the new-comer Nadia Sawalha, and her sweet husband, Justin. Scott spent some time talking to Justin, who seemed to be going through a bad time coping with Nadia's fame. This was something Scott knew all about, of course, and he did his best to give Justin the benefit of his experience.

I was thrilled with the turn-out: Gaby Roslin; John Challis; John Inman; Danny La Rue; the two Lionels, Bart and Blair; Dale Winton and Christopher Biggins, of course; Ned Sherrin; dear Brian Hall, who came even though he was desperately ill with cancer, and John Reid, who gave me a bracelet set with sixty diamonds and made a lovely speech. There were many infamous faces, too, from the early days, including Freddie Foreman and Tony Lambrianou – both jailed for their part in the Krays' notorious murder of Jack 'the Hat' McVitie – and 'Mad' Frankie Fraser. Tara, the daughter of Joan Collins and Tony Newley, found mixing with them terribly exciting. 'I'm having a great time,' she told me in a voice just like her mother's. 'I've been talking to bank robbers and serial killers – it's amazing!'

By the end of the evening, the nasty double-page spread that had upset me so much had become a distant memory, and that was down to all the people who turned up and made me feel so special. I'll always be grateful to them.

For me, there's nothing better than leaving the Barbara Windsor persona outside the front door and loafing about with no make-up on and hair screwed back, in comfy clothes. But now Scott resumed his counselling sessions with Beechy, and became more withdrawn than ever, and I found it harder and harder to relax. Instead of coming home and being myself, I was walking on eggshells. First I'd ask: 'Are you all right, sweetheart? Is everything OK, darling?' If I got no response, which was usually the case, I'd go into an act and tell him about my day, being careful not to sound too bubbly while he was feeling so flat. At times it was like performing a monologue to an unresponsive audience.

But if Scott was finding it hard to communicate, he had lost none of his sensitivity. I'd catch him looking at me, as if he were about to say something important, but he never voiced his thoughts. I believed that as long as I was there for him, we would get through this. It was just a matter of time. And I had plenty of that for Scott.

On a wet Tuesday in October, I arrived home shattered after a hectic day on *EastEnders*, but looking forward to hearing how Scott had got on with Beechy that afternoon. I scurried in out of the rain. Scott was sitting on the couch. Not watching TV or reading, just sitting there, as though he was waiting for me. If he was tense, I didn't notice.

'Hello, darling,' I said, throwing my jacket over a chair. 'How are you?'

'I'm all right. How did it go today?'

I bent down and kissed him on the cheek. 'Busy. I'm glad to be home. To you.' Then I went out into the kitchen. 'Fancy a cup of tea?'

'No, thanks,' he said. Then, a few seconds later: 'Bar, we need to talk.' It was an odd thing for Scott to say, but I was not unduly alarmed. I made my tea, brought it into the lounge and sat down in an armchair opposite Scott, ready to hear what he had to say.

He talked about how unhappy he was, and how miserable that was making me; about how he had been trying to come to terms with what our relationship was doing to him. And then he stopped and looked at me, a deep sadness in his eyes. 'Bar,' he said. 'I'm going to have to leave.'

I stared at him, unable to take it in. A heavy silence hung in the air. All I could think was, this is awful.

Finally I asked gently: 'But why, Scott? We love each other.'

'Yes, I know, Bar. But I've got to go. I've decided I have to go.'

I imagine I tried to say something – I can't remember. Scott's words were like a hammer blow in my head, words I never wanted to hear in my life, and inside me a little voice was screaming: *'No! No! No!'* My eyes filling, I grabbed my jacket and ran out of the front door and into the rain, my head spinning with a horrible mixed bag of emotions: sadness, anger, fear. And blind panic. I ran out of the mews into Harley Street, oblivious of traffic lights and cars, sobbing my heart out. That little voice came again: 'Why? Why? I'm such a good lady.'

I kept running, my high heels clattering on the rainswept streets, my mind focused on the need to go on running. Yes, run and run. You're sixty years old and you've got a dodgy heart. Run and that little heart is going to say, enough is enough, and then you'll drop dead and it won't matter any more.

I don't know how long I kept running. I don't know where I went. I just kept going, wildly, until I found myself back at the house about an hour later, drenched and still crying. Scott wasn't there: he had been running round the streets, too, checking pubs, looking for me. I was upstairs in the bathroom drying myself when he came back, soaked to the skin.

'I can't believe you're doing this to me,' I said.

'Do this to *you*?' he yelled. 'How could you do that to *me*? I was so fucking worried! I thought you were going to do something stupid!'

'It's me, isn't it? You're going because of me. It's because I'm too old, isn't it?' It was the first time I'd ever said that in all the time we had been together, and it upset Scott, because it wasn't true.

'No, it isn't, Bar,' he said. 'I know I'm hurting you so much. But this is how it's got to be. It's for the best.'

And then he broke down and started to cry, and that set me off again.

I couldn't remember ever feeling so unhappy and let down in my whole life.

It took some time for the tears to stop, and when they did, we talked. I knew Scott was hurting badly, not just because of his own pain, but because of mine, too. The knowledge that he was tearing me apart was agony for him. He admitted to me that he felt that life was just not worth living and that he was worried about being a burden to me. He believed it would be better all round if he were dead; better for him, because he wouldn't have to face all the pain he was going to cause, and better for me because, with him out of the way, I would be able to get on with my life.

I awoke in the morning dreading going to the studios. I felt awful, totally drained from all the crying and emotional tension, and when I saw myself in the mirror, I looked awful, too. I had a long scene to do with Ross, and I wondered how on earth I was going to manage it.

Until then I'd never taken my personal life with me to work: the Soho stabbing, the subsequent murder charge and all the other unsavoury stuff with Ronnie had always been left at home when I went out to perform. When it all hit the papers, friends would ring up wondering why I hadn't said anything.

That's just me, I suppose. But that Wednesday morning was different: I was in such a terrible state that I took my heartbreak with me out of the front door and through the gates of Elstree.

The scene Ross and I had to do was outside, in Albert Square, and we had to rehearse it for camera angles and lighting. I'd come in bright and breezy enough, and no one had a clue that anything was wrong, but the second I opened my mouth to speak, the tears started to trickle down my cheeks.

Ross frowned. 'Are you OK?'

'Yeah, yeah, I'm fine,' I lied. 'My eyes are watering. I must have a speck of dust under one of my contact lenses.'

We tried again, but Ross knew something was wrong. He asked the director, Geoff Feld (who, incidentally, had been in the same class as me at Church Street School) to stop filming and took me to the alleyway at the back of the Vic. He asked me what was the matter and I told him. And then I burst into tears.

Ross adored Scott. 'Oh, God,' he said, and put his arms round me.

Fighting back the tears, I said: 'Let's get through the scene, darling.' Now I was worried that I was holding up filming, letting everyone down.

'Hold on a minute.' Ross went back and spoke to Geoff. 'Geoff's willing to do the scene later,' he told me when he came back.

'No, no,' I said. 'Let's do it now, Ross.'

'OK,' he agreed. 'We'll talk later.'

He gave me a gentle pat of reassurance and we went back to the set. I was glad he didn't hug me again, or I'd have lost control. I was still feeling bad for delaying the shooting and felt the need to cover my embarrassment with an excuse. 'I'm ever so sorry, Geoff,' I apologised. 'I haven't been feeling too good and I don't like filming outside.'

'Don't you ever apologise, Barbara Windsor,' said Geoff. 'You always give us your best.'

'I'm sorry,' I repeated. 'I was having a moment.'

When we had finished the scene, Ross came to my dressing room and sat there listening as I sobbed my heart out, crying over and over again: 'I don't know why, Ross. I don't know why.'

28

THAT FRIDAY I ARRIVED HOME FROM WORK TO FIND SCOTT IN A TERRIBLE STATE. He had woken from a brief nap and was in the middle of one of his panic attacks. He was shaking and having to run to the loo every few minutes to be sick. I managed to talk him into going to Henlow Grange immediately to relax and unwind on his own for a week. I phoned Stephen Purdew, the owner, booked Scott in and helped him pack. As I watched him drive off, I was shaking myself. Scott was so disorientated that I was afraid he had gone over the edge, and I was worried sick about him. It was a great relief when he rang from the health club that evening to tell me that he had arrived safely and was going to eat in his room and then go to bed.

For the next seven days, I was the only person Scott spoke to outside the health farm, and even there, he kept himself to himself. He spent virtually every day on his own, reading and swimming and dozing, and in the evening he had a massage to help him get a restful nine hours' sleep. It was not a miracle cure – he told me that he didn't step from black and white into colour like Dorothy in the *Wizard of Oz* – but the soothing atmosphere definitely helped, and when he came home the following Friday he seemed calmer and less mentally exhausted.

That evening I persuaded Scott to come with me to a farewell party for an *EastEnders* producer, which was a mistake. He tried to enjoy himself, but it was clear he didn't give a monkey's about most of the people there and couldn't wait to get away, though no one, apart from Ross, had an inkling that behind the party smiles our hearts were aching.

We went through a similar charade the next Sunday. I was committed to attending a Lady Ratlings Ball at the Hilton Hotel and, despite being in a deep depression, Scott agreed to go with me. He was doing a brilliant job convincing fellow guests that he was having a good time until the lovely Welsh actress Ruth Madoc made him the centre of attention by asking him to join her on stage to take part in a comedy song-and-dance routine with half a dozen celebrities. Ruth, bless her heart, was simply looking for a smart, good-looking young man to help the evening along. Unfortunately, when Scott politely declined, she assumed he was just being modest and refused to take no for an answer. But Scott kept saying no, and she kept trying to persuade him, and soon everyone in the room, it seemed, was straining their necks to see who the miserable party-pooper was.

Poor Ruth! In the mood Scott was in, nothing could have forced him on to that stage, and if she had had any idea of the torment raging inside his head, she certainly wouldn't have tried.

The appointments in our diaries for the following Wednesday just about summed up the strange lives we were leading. I was meeting the Queen and Scott was seeing two faith-healers! My encounter with Her Majesty took place at the BBC's Broadcasting House, where she had been invited to see how broadcasting had developed since the early days of radio. Someone thought it would be a good idea for her to meet some of the *EastEnders* cast, and I was there with Gilly Taylforth, Patsy Palmer and Adam Woodyatt. I was at the head of the line, and when I was introduced, I could not resist asking Her Majesty if she had ever seen *EastEnders*. 'No,' she admitted. 'It comes on at the wrong time for me.'

The press photographers were not likely to pass up the opportunity to snap two Windsor ladies together, and having my picture taken with the Queen was a wonderful moment for me – even if I was a little embarrassed at having chosen to wear the same colour dress as Her Majesty (burgundy, for the record).

The faith-healers Scott visited in Ingrave, Essex were a husband and wife recommended by our friend Paul Bennett, who felt they might be able to cure his depression. When Scott described what had happened there, I could hardly believe my ears. He was asked to lie on a table while the couple laid their 'healing hands' on him. He was silent for fifteen minutes or so, but then a woeful cry rose from deep within him and he broke down and sobbed, letting out all the pain and grief he was suffering at the prospect of losing me. He cried solidly for half an hour and, afterwards, the wife told Scott that the spirit guiding him had been in the room and wanted him to know that he must never again think the thoughts that had been on his mind.

That night we cuddled up in bed, telling each other how much we loved each other and admitting how scared we were of the future.

We staggered on for the rest of that week and the next, hardly mentioning what had been said on that terrible Tuesday. I hoped that if we left it alone Scott might sort himself out and change his mind about going away. Deep down, though, I knew he wouldn't, even though the mere thought of walking out on all we had built between us terrified him. No matter how tormented he was, he genuinely believed that the only way to save his sanity was to break away from me and the relentless, dazzling glare of that spotlight.

And yet never in my wildest nightmares did I ever think he would actually do it. I knew he was unhappy – he complained about it all the time – but at least we talked about the problem and tried to deal with it. Call me naïve – stupid, even – but I always felt that our love for each other would eventually conquer the fears and insecurities that were making Scott so miserable.

But that weekend he told me that he had taken up an offer from John Addy – the friend we'd visited on Fire Island during our New York trip – to housesit John's London house in Notting Hill. He would be moving in the following Wednesday, he said. At last it hit me that I had been living in a fool's paradise. I had not appreciated the depth of Scott's despair, and I had been dreadfully wrong in imagining that we would come through it. With the end of our love affair staring me in the face, the prospect of a future without Scott was simply unbearable.

Over the next few days, we sometimes talked about Scott going; at other times we ignored it totally, as if somehow that might make the problem disappear. One day we'd be chatting normally and rationally, and the next one of us would say the wrong thing and we'd have a bit of a row. It was extremely peculiar. I don't think either of us had much idea what was going on.

Even though Scott was preparing to leave me to fend for myself, he lectured me about how I should behave when he had gone. He was particularly concerned about me going off the rails, getting smashed and bringing home a stranger. 'It's your life, and you can do what you want with it, Bar,' he said. 'But remember, it's a different world now, with AIDS and everything else. People wear condoms.'

I laughed. I'd never liked condoms; in fact, I'd never once slept with anybody using one.

'I don't want any other men,' I told him.

'You may feel like that now,' he said, 'but, who knows, a little way down the line, you might meet someone attractive, have a few drinks and go for it.'

Scott was also terrified that, if I got blind drunk, someone could take advantage of me or beat me up. Anything could happen, he said. He had a point, but I couldn't envisage going out and getting into that sort of state. All I was concerned with was how I was going to get through each day and night without the man I loved.

He was anxious about my safety at home as well, and wanted me to have CCTV video cameras fitted outside the house so that I could see who was at the front door before opening it.

'I don't want all that, sweetheart,' I said.

'You *must*, Bar,' he insisted. 'You're going to be by yourself now.'

I'm sure Scott would have forgiven me for saying, 'If you're that worried about me, why are you going?', but that never crossed my mind. He was simply being protective because he knew how vulnerable I'd be without him around. For the same reason, he also warned me not to let certain people back into my life.

One of them was Robert Dunn. 'Be careful about him, Bar,' Scott cautioned. 'Once he hears I'm off the scene, he'll pick his moment to make contact, I promise you.'

It was a warning I did not take seriously. I hadn't seen Robert for several years. If he'd wanted to speak to me, he would have done so long before now.

Only a handful of people knew we were splitting up, so when we took Scott's two nieces, Abbie and Charlie, to *An Audience With the Spice Girls* that Sunday, we had to put on the phoney front again. We really weren't feeling up to it, but Scott had promised to take the girls and the delight on their faces as they watched the show made the effort worthwhile.

On the Monday evening, Scott had some news for me. He had got himself a job, in a clothes shop in a shopping centre off the Bayswater Road, until he started in panto in Manchester with Jim Davidson the following month. He would be working from 10 a.m. to 8 p.m., tagging merchandise, packing boxes and generally helping the sales staff, for less than £100 a week. Far from feeling embarrassed about taking such modest employment, he was thrilled. He was walking out on a woman he adored, a beautiful home and an enviable lifestyle for a job many sixteen-year-olds would scoff at, but it was a move towards restoring the sense of identity and self-esteem he had lost as a result of being with me.

It could only be a matter of time before the press got wind that he was leaving, so I was hardly surprised when I had a phone call the following evening from a *Sun* journalist, Sue Carroll, a great friend who I'd known for ten years. She said she had heard about the split and was so sorry, because she felt we made a good couple. But there was a professional reason for her call as well: she wanted to write the story for the next day's paper. Would we talk to her exclusively? She was so sympathetic that I went to pieces and dropped the phone. Scott picked it up and asked her to give us a few minutes to decide whether we wanted to talk publicly about why he was going. In the end he rang Sue back and told her he was getting out of my life because he felt he was making me unhappy. Half an hour or so later I was walking across the mews to put out some rubbish when a paparazzo moved out of the shadows, making me jump. 'Oooh, darling, you scared me,' I said. He was so embarrassed at having frightened me that he respected my request not to take any pictures.

Scott and I were both hyper, knowing that the next day would be his last in the house, and that the whole country would be buzzing with his walk-out when the *Sun* story was picked up by other papers and by the TV. Tired and too strung out to eat, we went to bed around 10 p.m. and lay there crying in the dark.

In the morning, Scott walked down to Marylebone High Street to buy the *Sun*. Sue's story was on the front page. The article itself was fine – she had written it accurately and sympathetically, for which we were very grateful – but it had been published under a huge, inaccurate and infuriating headline: 'TV BABS DUMPS TOYBOY'. Not only was it a total misrepresentation of the facts, but it would be what stuck in the reader's mind. I felt sick for Scott, but, typically, he was more concerned about my dignity than his own. 'It doesn't matter, Bar,' he said. 'It would have been awful for you if it had been the other way round.'

When Scott drove me to work I knew he would not be there when I got back, but nothing could have prepared me for the utter desolation that swamped me when I came home that night and went upstairs. The empty wardrobes in the bedroom and the bare shelves in his bathroom broke my heart. It was as if someone had died. And, in a way, that was what had happened. I'd lost a dear loved one and was already in deep mourning.

Scott popped back the next evening to check that I was OK. He was concerned I'd think he didn't care if he didn't make contact, but all it did was confuse me, and we parted on a sour note. I was hoping that his job would take his mind off things, but late on Saturday night, unable to sleep, he rang me saying he hated it. Worse, he was in such a nervous state and so worried about me that he had been violently sick.

As usual, I started to blame myself. I reproached myself for not having got on top of the situation earlier, and letting it drag on and on until Scott felt he was going off his head. But I'd honestly believed everything would sort itself out once he got himself together. I didn't care about why he was with me; I just wanted him there. I loved him, and as far as I was concerned, even if he had been using me, he was safe if he stayed with me. OK, there had been times of late when he had not been much fun and didn't want to go anywhere, but if you love someone, you put up with a lot, don't you?

In those last two depressing weeks of November, I thought, as I had done when my marriage to Stephen was running out of steam, that all I could do to keep my sanity was throw myself into my work. Fortunately, there was plenty of it, because at that time I was being written into every *EastEnders* episode.

Normally, I chat about all sorts of things when a cabbie drives me to the studios, but during those two weeks I sat in silence, lost in my own thoughts, still trying to come to terms with why it had all happened. When I got to the studios, I'd hurry to my dressing room and stay there until I was called. I'd go over my lines, but all the time my mind was on Scott and what he had done to me. I could not shake off the overwhelming shock of being abandoned. I had not seen it coming and felt so dreadfully let down. I'd been there, like a rock, through all Scott's drunken binges and when he was out of his skull on coke. I felt I didn't deserve all this pain when I'd done nothing wrong; didn't deserve to be deserted and left on my own at sixty when I thought I had found happiness at last. And what made it even more excruciating was that I knew that Scott was riddled with guilt and hurting every bit as much as I was.

By the following Tuesday he'd chucked in his job and started to cut himself off from people, a self-imposed loneliness he felt he needed to get me out of his system. He had made this big step to break free from the pressure my life put on him, but all he was doing with this freedom was isolating himself in a house, not wanting to talk to anyone except me and his parents. It was dangerous, and he knew it. He told me he was becoming incredibly frightened.

I urged him to get out of the house, and that Friday he went to Brighton. His parents were dreadfully upset by the break-up: looking in from the outside, they felt I'd been good for Scott; they had never seen him so happy or contented. But he had cleverly hidden his true feelings from his loved ones to save them from worrying about him.

Watching *Children in Need* with his parents that evening, the emotional torment Scott had been suffering all week became too much when Lisa Stansfield came on and sang a sad song about two people splitting up. He broke down. Rita and Ronnie were distraught, and did their best to comfort him, but there was little they could say or do to help.

That Scott and I were still talking a lot on the phone was a blessing. After the hurt and guilt I'd suffered over Sid James, I felt it was vitally important that we kept in touch and remained friends. But then, on Saturday, Scott said we were speaking to each other too much – we were not letting go – and that he thought it best if we did not have any contact for a while. I could see his point, of course I could, but I was so low, so miserable, that it was the last thing I wanted to hear.

The silence lasted just three days. It did not solve a thing: we needed each other, craved the contact, even if it was only a few minutes on the end of a phone line. I clung to the hope that all this anguish would convince Scott that being apart from me was not what he really wanted, and that he would change his mind. But the timing was bad. The next week he was leaving for Manchester to begin rehearsals for *Dick Whittington*, and the distance that would put between us would be the real test.

We'd been invited to spend Christmas with John Addy and Nicky Marsh at their home in Huddersfield. They'd been planning to take a small party to see Scott's panto. But this had all been arranged before Scott and I had broken up, and I wondered now whether it would be wise to cancel the visit and do something else for Christmas. I didn't know what to do for the best. My heart told me that a reunion with Scott at this most emotional time of the year could bring us back together again, make him realise he had made a mistake, but my head argued that going north could just as easily prove to be a disaster.

In the end I let the arrangements stand, and Paul Bennett drove me up north. I knew I'd made the wrong decision the moment Scott arrived at the Huddersfield house just before midday on Christmas Eve. John and Nicky are warm, hospitable people, and they could not have made him more welcome, but he was uncomfortable and on edge, and I could see he did not want to be there. On Christmas Day John took over a restaurant to entertain his family and friends. At any other time it would have been wonderful, but as it was it was miserable for Scott and me and totally confusing for everyone else. People had seen the papers, and must have been wondering why we were here together, apparently happy. No one knew that it was Scott who had left me, not the other way round, and we did not enlighten anybody. We just steered clear of the subject and chatted about general things, making sure no one picked up on any underlying tension between us. In turn, nobody embarrassed us by mentioning our relationship, which I thought was lovely.

On Boxing Night, a crowd of us went to see the panto. I get myself into a terrible tizz worrying that everything is going to be all right for other people, and I didn't want to pull out after John and Nicky had arranged things. But I had a sneaking feeling it would end in tears, and I really should not have gone.

Jim Davidson and I are good pals and, in his dressing room afterwards, he was his usual ebullient self. 'Hello, Bar, 'ow yer going, girl?'

'Fine,' I said.

'Now, listen,' he said. 'What's all this soppy nonsense about old Scotty and you?'

I burst into tears.

Jim's face fell. He put an arm round me. 'Oh, Windsor, I'm ever so sorry. I didn't think it was serious. I thought it was just paper talk.'

'Oh, no,' I told Jim. 'He's gone.'

Jim turned to his girlfriend, Debbie. 'Have you seen Scotty with any birds, Deb?'

She shook her head. 'I haven't seen him with anyone.'

'Oh, fucking hell,' said Jim. 'The bloke's bloody mad. He's mental. I honestly didn't think it was that serious.'

Jim kindly invited my friends and me to the Midland Hotel, where he was throwing a small party for the cast. Knowing Jim, he was thinking that if he could get Scott and me together in a happy, relaxed atmosphere, we might patch things up and maybe spend the night together. To be honest, I didn't want to go, but it was Jim's night and I felt it would be rude to refuse. It was another mistake – not because of anything Scott did there, but because of what happened as I left. When I said I had to be going, he came outside with me and Paul, who was driving me back to Huddersfield. I so much wanted to be with Scott that night; we hadn't talked much since he'd started the panto, and I felt we needed to, particularly with New Year's Eve coming up. I was hoping he would suggest that I came back to his hotel and booked a room there, but he just stood there, not speaking at all, just waiting for me to get into the car. We looked at each other for a second or two, then I said: 'All right, then.' As we drove off, Scott went back into the Midland Hotel. If he had said, 'I'm going, too, can you drop me off at my hotel?' it would have helped, but he just gave me a little wave, then strolled back to join the party as though he didn't have a care in the world.

It was the first time since I'd met Scott nearly five years before that I felt he hadn't been nice to me. He knew I had only gone to the panto for him, that I'd put myself out, and he must have realised that it had taken me a lot of courage to walk into that hotel knowing that everyone was aware of our break-up. If he hadn't wanted me there he could have said. I just thought that once I *was* there he should have considered me, and not packed me off like some distant relative or business contact. I felt hurt and let down.

The following afternoon Paul and I drove over to Bradford to see the panto at the Alhambra before returning to London.

During the performance one of the box office staff came down and whispered to me: 'Miss Windsor, are you with a Mr Bennett? There is an urgent message for him.' It was from Jo Lockwood, Paul's assistant at the *Sunday Mirror*, who had tracked us down via Scott. When Paul called her back, he was told that the *Sun* had carried a front-page story that morning reporting that Justin Mildwater, the husband of *EastEnders* actress Nadia Sawalha, had been found hanged at his north London home.

It was dreadful news, and my heart went out to Nadia. The shock was heightened because I knew that Justin, who had recently split from Nadia, had been suffering from his own traumas, and the thought that perhaps it could have been Scott flashed through my mind and sent a shiver down my spine.

That terrible tragedy, and my own huge disappointment in Scott, combined to make Christmas 1997 the worst Christmas of my life. I travelled back to London very depressed, and at a loss to know what I was going to do with myself during the quiet days leading up to the New Year. Don't ask me what I did do, because I can't remember, but I got through them somehow, and then New Year's Eve was upon me.

New Year's Eve is for many people the most exciting night of the year, but for me, and for most people in showbusiness, it is just another working day. Personally, even when I have the night off, I have never minded whether

I went out or not, and this year I cared even less. I had lots of personal invitations – Anna Karen had tried to persuade me to go to see her panto and join in the celebrations afterwards, and another friend, Yvonne I'Anson, who helps me with my fan letters, had asked me to come up to York – and there were plenty of big bashes to choose from, too: a party at Morton's club in Berkeley Square and another do at the Dorchester. But I turned them all down. The only person I wanted to be with at midnight was Scott, and he didn't want to be with me, so what was the point?

My lovely mate Dale Winton popped round at about 9.30 on his way to seeing in the New Year with his twin godsons in Stoke Newington. He didn't want to leave me and tried very hard to get me to go with him, but I just didn't feel like it. All I wanted was to be at home on my own with my self-pity.

So I said goodbye to 1997 watching TV in my little lounge, feeling tearful, very sad and lonely and, if I'm honest, my age. My mind, my entire being, was consumed by Scott and by what he was doing and who he was with. A few minutes after Big Ben chimed in 1998, the phone rang and it was him.

Scott had been with the rest of the panto cast at a party in the Piccadilly Hotel, and watching everyone hugging and kissing at midnight had made him feel very lonely. The only voice he wanted to hear was mine, so he had gone to his room and called me. Listening to him breaking his heart on the other end of the line set me off too, and we cried together for ages, neither of us wanting to get off the phone. It had been a dreadfully upsetting year for Scott: as well as his relationship with me, he had lost a much-loved grandmother, Lil, and dear Brian Hall. I was still weeping for him, and for myself, when I went to bed.

29

THE FIRST FOUR DAYS OF 1998 ARE AS MUCH A BLUR TO ME AS THE LAST FIVE OF 1997. Anna, Dale and Paul Bennett rang, trying to coax me out on the town, but I was just not in the mood to be sociable. And it was the same when I went back to *EastEnders* on 5 January: all I wanted to do was think about Peggy's problems, not my own, then go home and shut myself away until the next day. Martine McCutcheon, Sid Owen, Marc Bannerman and some of the others had persuaded Nadia Sawalha to come out for a drink in the Atlantic Bar in Piccadilly the following Friday night, and invited me to join them.

'Come on, Bar,' they said. 'It'll be a laugh. You need to get out.'

'Thanks, sweethearts,' I said. 'But I'm not in the mood. Honestly, darlings.'

I was appearing on the Chris Evans show *TFI Friday* that night and planned to go straight home afterwards. In the make-up room at Riverside Studios in Hammersmith, Chris Evans asked if I'd had a good New Year's Eve.

'No, I didn't, actually.'

'Why was that?' he asked.

'Well, you know my fella, Scott. He left me. So I was on my own.'

'Fuck that, Babs,' he said. 'You shouldn't have been on your own. You should have come out with us. When things like that happen, you can't be on your own. You've got to get out there.'

'Funnily enough, some of the kids on *EastEnders* have asked me out tonight,' I told him.

'So are you going?'

'No,' I said. 'I'm going home.'

'To be on your own again?' Chris said.

I didn't reply.

'Now, look. There's no excuse. You're going to be all dressed up for this show, so go out afterwards. You'll pull someone, you see.'

It did not thrill me to get 'all dressed up': I was totally unconcerned about whether I looked attractive or not. And I certainly was not up for 'pulling' anyone, that's for sure. I was feeling far too sorry for myself, wondering whether I would ever again find that wonderful home life Scott and I had enjoyed: you know, that lovely, warm feeling you get when you close the front door and relax with someone you love within your own four walls, doing silly things and having a giggle together.

Scott had never once said anything nasty about me, but all those cracks about me being old enough to be his mother were spinning endlessly in my head, making me think that maybe he had, after all, taken a close look at me and thought, my God, she *is* old. And, yes, she *has* lost her looks. I couldn't help but remember what Stephen had told the *People* about me taking off my wig to reveal thinning grey hair. It wasn't true, but people believe what they read in the papers, and I was paranoid that everyone was looking at me, thinking I was mutton dressed up as lamb.

But there was something in what Chris had said that struck a chord. OK, I didn't feel sociable, didn't want to force a smile when I felt like howling, but at the same time, sitting at home alone was only dragging me deeper into depression. Maybe I shouldn't be on my own. Maybe I should get out there, as Chris said. And then I thought of Nadia, and I knew I ought to go. With the unimaginable anguish she must have been suffering, she would be the last person to feel like a carefree night out. Her marriage had been over, but to have a husband you had adored hang himself over the Christmas holiday must be one of the most horrendous shocks a woman could experience. If she could put on a brave front so that people didn't feel awkward about her personal trauma, then so could I.

So I tried to throw myself into the spirit of the evening, but I just couldn't, and spent most of it regretting being there. Around midnight, I was given the perfect opportunity to leave, and I seized it with both hands. One of the young studio runners from *EastEnders* lived in Kenton, on the outskirts of west London, and was worried he could not afford a cab home. So I told him that if he could flag down a taxi and see me safely to my door, I would pay his fare. The look on the kid's face. He couldn't believe it.

I woke the next morning depressed. Once the heart of the West End had been a glittering stage and I had been one of its liveliest players, but the innocent fun I'd enjoyed as a youngster was gone. I didn't want to go back any more. I wanted to hold on to the treasured memories of the West End I had loved.

It was the East End, and the Brick Lane Music Hall in particular, that came to my rescue later that month. I was invited to the annual pantomime and took a dear friend, Laurie O'Leary, and his wife, Iris, for company. My mood was reflected in what I chose to wear: a beige jacket, brown skirt and long brown boots. I hate brown, and hardly ever wear it, but I always keep a couple of brown bits just in case I need them. I usually find myself putting them on when I'm feeling low. During the interval, I was asked to draw a raffle and I remember thinking, I bet people are saying to each other, 'Doesn't she look awful in beige and brown?'

After the show, Brick Lane's owner, Vince Hayes, came to our table and introduced one of his best friends, Nigel Wildman, a smartly dressed man in his early fifties. Iris leaned over to me and said, 'God, isn't he attractive?' I had to agree.

The next couple of hours are something of a blur. As I'd lost more than a stone in weight, the drink went straight to my head. What I do vaguely remember is Nigel telling me he'd seen me at Brick Lane before, that he'd queued to get me to sign a copy of my book and that I'd been nice to him. That made me feel good. And Iris was right, he *was* an attractive man.

Nigel offered to take me home in his van. Laurie, ever-protective, was concerned. 'I don't know, mate,' he said. 'I'm not sure I want her getting in a van.'

'Whatsamatter, Lol, love?' I slurred. 'I'm not precious. I don't care what I get in.'

In the end we trundled in the van to Marylebone. Nigel hadn't told me much about himself, what he did for a living and so on, but I was in no state to care. He obviously fancied me. And, drunk as I was, the feeling was mutual. Since Scott had gone I hadn't thought about sex, but it must have been in the back of my mind, and I tumbled into bed willingly.

My head spinning from an intoxicating cocktail of drink and intense sexual anticipation, I was in no position to say no to anything. But suddenly my brain cleared and in that split-second of clarity two thoughts filled my mind simultaneously. One was Scott's warning to be careful, and the other was that, for supporting the Terrence Higgins Trust, for AIDS victims, I'd been given a packet of condoms, and they had been in a bedside drawer ever since.

'Hold on a minute, darling,' I said. Then, with no shame at all, I reached into the drawer and took out the packet.

Scott had been right, of course, and it would not have looked good for me to support charities advocating the use of condoms and not practise what I preached. I had to face the fact that times had changed dramatically since I'd first discovered sex. I had been extremely lucky not to have contracted some disease or other in a free-and-easy lifestyle involving God knows how many partners over more than forty years, and nowadays, the dangers were far greater.

In the morning, I thought: 'Oh, no, I bet Nigel thinks I'm some old tart who has done that all her life.' On the stairs, however, I found a sweet note with Nigel's telephone number on it, which told me that he hadn't thought that for a moment. In the cold light of day I didn't know what to make of it. My mind now was full of Scott, and I didn't want another man in my life as long as there was a chance of us getting back together. And there *was* a chance: one of his panto pals, the impressionist Roger Kitter, had phoned a couple of times to tell me how unhappy Scott was, and Scott himself called regularly indicating that he wanted a reconciliation. I was not going to risk spoiling that by sleeping around; in fact, I felt dreadful that, just three weeks after leaving Scott in Manchester, I'd let someone else into our bed. I consoled myself that it was just a pleasurable and reassuring one-night stand. But I felt so guilty, I chucked out all my underwear and lingerie.

When I didn't phone Nigel, he phoned me. My friend Yvonne I'Anson said that if I really was hoping to get back with Scott, I should call Nigel and be straight with him. I took her advice. 'Nigel, I don't want you ringing here again until I contact you,' I said.

'How long will that be?'

'I've no idea, sweetheart. It's not completely over with Scott. We might get back together.'

Nigel seemed to accept that, but three weeks later Vince Hayes called me, saying that Nigel really wanted to see me and was upset that I hadn't phoned. Vince assured me that his friend was a good bloke, a man to be trusted. He was a policeman, and liked by all his colleagues at Police Headquarters, who had nicknamed him Dapper of the Yard because of his stylish clothes. Vince told me that he'd advised Nigel to send me flowers, and on Valentine's Day, a huge bouquet arrived from Nigel. Here was a man who had seen me at my worst, unglamorous in brown and very drunk, but who, despite what I'd been thinking about myself, obviously found me attractive and wanted to see me again. A man who was not going to take no for an answer.

I didn't know what to do. Much as I wanted Scott back in my life, I couldn't be sure that that was what he wanted. And no matter how much I believed there would never be anyone but him, I knew I was not the type to go on crying behind closed doors for ever. And now there was Nigel waiting in the wings, kind, attractive and unattached, eager to take me out and spoil me.

Well, I succumbed. Whether it was the flattery or the timely romantic gesture I don't know, but I agreed to go out with Nigel again. After that we carried on seeing each other from time to time, and I'm pleased we did. When we'd met that January night in Brick Lane, I was wandering forlornly down a long, dark road with no end in sight, and Nigel helped me to take a side turning and start feeling better about myself. For that, I shall always be grateful.

In February I went to see my old pal Anthony Newley in cabaret at the Café Royal's Green Room. I've seen many cabaret acts over the years, but none to compare with Tony's: he could work a room like no one else. He was sheer magic that night and, a few days later, I had an idea. I went to see Matthew Robinson, the executive producer, and told him I thought Tony could be a great addition to *EastEnders*: not only did he still look fabulous, but he was a good actor, too. And, of course, he'd been born in the East End.

It is impossible for *EastEnders* actors to persuade the powers-that-be to give their mates a job just because they are mates, but, naturally, we are listened to if we have what sounds like a good suggestion. Martin Kemp, for example, was recommended by Michelle Collins. I kept my fingers crossed that Matthew would find a spot for Tony because we went back a long way and it would be lovely to have him around – and if we could actually be on screen together, even better.

One morning the following week I had a call at Elstree to say that a writer named Terry Johnson was sending me part of a script he had written and would like to know what I thought of it. I assumed it was a play he had me in mind for if I ever left *EastEnders*, and I was intrigued. But when I saw the title – *Carry On Cleo, Camping, Emmanuelle and Dick* – I groaned. Surely no one was seriously intending to put a Carry On comedy on the stage? But when I read the script I realised that the play was not a Carry On at all: although it did feature characters from those comedies, it was essentially about my love affair with Sid James. Terry Johnson said he hoped to take it to the West End, but that if I had any objections – I was the only real-life character in the play still living – he would scrap it.

The script was funny, moving and hugely enjoyable and, as my affair with Sid was now out in the open, I had no problem with Terry going ahead. I made a few minor suggestions and wished him every success. However, I couldn't imagine for a moment who would want to go and see a play about Kenny Williams, Sid James and me, so I expected to hear no more about it.

How wrong can you be? Six weeks later Barry called me to tell me that the play had been chosen to start the season at the National Theatre in October, a great accolade. Even more amazingly, one of Britain's finest actors, Anthony Sher, had been signed to play Sid. I could hardly believe it. I was more than happy to discuss the Barbara Windsor role, and when Terry rang me, I said it didn't matter a toss if the girl didn't look like me, wasn't blonde and didn't have big boobs, because make-up and props could fix that. But it *was* important that she was petite. And a bloody good actress.

On Saturday 21 February, Scott invited me out to lunch. When we returned to the mews, there was a *News of the World* reporter waiting outside my front door. It was something to do with Ronnie, he said: a rival paper was running a story the next day about money from the Security Express robbery being laundered. Did I know anything about it? I'd heard that Ronnie had written a book which was being serialised in the *People*, but that was all. Money-laundering? Why would I know anything about that? I was intrigued, though, and looked forward, with a strange fascination, to reading the *People* in the morning.

Just as Scott was about to go home, I had a phone call from the same reporter which marked the start of one of the most terrifying nights of my life. The first edition of the *People*, he said, was carrying a story on its front page and on two pages inside about £250,000 cash from the Security Express robbery being paid into my bank account. And the person who had paid in £55,835 of it, according to the paper, was me.

My mouth went dry. I started to tremble. I turned to Scott: 'We've got to get the *People*, darling,' I said. 'They're saying I had something to do with that robbery.' Within seconds, Scott was on his way to King's Cross Station, where the first editions of the Sunday papers go on sale at around 9.30 p.m. I sat down in the lounge, trying to relax. I couldn't. I got up and walked around then went into the kitchen and switched on the telly. Maybe the news would be on. It wasn't. I went back into the lounge and paced up and down anxiously, willing Scott to hurry up. Ten minutes or so later, he came back with a bundle of papers. One look at his face told me it was bad. He handed me the *People*.

An icy terror took over my whole body. On the front page, next to a photograph of me looking like someone else, a huge headline screamed: 'BABS AND £250,000 GANGLAND CASH'. Underneath was the sub-heading: 'Used Notes Funnelled Through EastEnders Star's Bank Account'. My eyes flashed over the beginning of the story, which continued on page 4. I flipped the paper open. Another big headline: 'BABS CLATTERED INTO HER ACCOUNTANTS ON HIGH HEELS CLUTCHING A BAG CONTAINING £25,000 IN USED NOTES'. And another sub-heading: 'Husband Ron in £6M Raid Days Earlier'. The 'investigation' ran over two pages, dramatically dressed up with a picture of an open briefcase showing dozens of packets of £10 notes. I tried to speed-read the story but I was shaking so much I couldn't take it in. The terrible headlines were enough: they told the nation that I'd paid money into my bank account knowing it had been stolen in one of Britain's most wicked robberies.

I became hysterical. I ran round the kitchen screaming, holding my head in my hands and stamping my feet like some madwoman. 'Why? Why? *Why* has he done this?' I started thumping the table: 'Why would he do this? What have I done to him?'

Scott just stood there, helpless. He had seen me lose my temper, but he'd never seen me out of control. I paced round the kitchen, still stamping my feet, shouting: 'I didn't do it! I didn't do it, Scott! I never touched his stinking money!'

'Bar, you don't have to tell *me*,' Scott said. 'I *know* you. But you've got to calm down.'

'Calm down?' I screeched. 'You know what's next. The police will be here. I could go to jail!' And I started to shout and scream even louder. 'I DON'T NEED THIS. I COULD GO TO FUCKING *JAIL*.'

'Bar!' yelled Scott, drowning my screams. 'Now, stop it. *Stop it!* You're going to give yourself a heart attack.'

I did calm down – a bit. And when I did, I was able to read and absorb what had been written. I kept shaking my head in disbelief: my name was in the story, but it seemed as if they were writing about a different person. It was there in black and white that, on 15 April 1983, I deposited £25,000 in cash with my accountants, Fox Associates. But, as I'd told the police years ago, I'd never seen such a large sum of money in my life. The rest of the story, as far as I was concerned, was fiction, but the fact remained that it would without the shadow of a doubt bring the police to my door, I was convinced of that. I needed to do something, but I didn't know what. Neither did Scott. What could we do at nearly 11 p.m. on a Saturday night?

In the end I decided to ring Scotland Yard. I had nothing to hide, after all. I wanted to speak to the one detective who would reassure me that I had nothing to worry about: Reid McGeorge, the detective inspector who had arrested Ronnie at Luton Airport and interviewed me at Leman Street. I could not stop myself breaking down when a female voice answered: 'Good evening, Scotland Yard.'

'Good evening,' I said through my tears. 'My name is Barbara Windsor . . .'

'What's the matter, Barbara?' she asked, very concerned.

'I need to contact the officer who worked on the case of my ex-husband, Ronnie Knight,' I said. 'Mr McGeorge, it was. Could you possibly get hold of him for me, sweetheart? And get him to phone me back?'

The lady said she would. But a few minutes later she rang herself, saying that Mr McGeorge had retired and they could not contact him.

For some odd reason, the only other person I could think of to call was Freddie Foreman, who I'd known, through Ronnie, for several years. He was not going to help me with the police, but he might be able to explain why Ronnie had lied and dropped me in it when I'd never said or done anything to harm him. What I couldn't get out of my head was that if I had done what the *People* claimed, it would have been in Ronnie's interest to keep quiet, not to grass me up, as they say in his world. It didn't make any sense at all.

I started to cry again when I heard Freddie's voice. I read him the story and all he kept saying was, 'Oh, what a silly bugger. What a silly boy.' Like me, he had no idea why Ronnie would have done this to me.

Scott stayed with me that night. We sat up, dressed, ready to leave when the police arrived. I kept thinking about my mother, wondering what she would have made of it all. She was ashamed of me answering the door in a dressing gown. What on earth would she have thought of me being carted off to prison?

Well, the police did not come that night, or the next day. We didn't leave the house – we just sat there all day, waiting for the knock on the door, and dreading what people all over the country were thinking about me. I tried to console myself that the *People* was the only paper running the story, but of course the other papers picked it up from the first edition and ran their own versions, giving the *People*'s so-called investigation a wider audience.

Scott said he'd stay with me for the next few days and went home to get some clothes. It was the most horrendous Sunday of my life, and when I fell into bed at 11 p.m., physically exhausted and mentally drained from not having slept for more than thirty-six hours, I still lay there with my eyes open, waiting for the police to come. At 5.30 a.m., I was roused from a fitful sleep by the sound of a vehicle in the mews; right outside the bedroom window, or so it seemed. I lay there in the dark, holding my breath. Seconds later, the doorbell rang.

'It's the police,' I said to Scott, who was only half asleep himself. He put on his dressing gown and went downstairs.

'Who is it?' he asked brusquely.

'Is that you, Freddie?' a quiet London accent whispered.

'No,' Scott said. 'This is Barbara's partner. Who is it?'

'I'm a friend of Ronnie's,' the voice said. 'Jim Lumley.'

Hearing Scott open the front door on its chain, I got out of bed, slipped on my dressing gown and tiptoed halfway down the stairs. I saw a man showing Scott a badge. 'This is my identification,' he said. 'I'm a taxi driver. Ronnie has asked me to come and see Barbara about the story.'

'Wait a minute,' Scott said, and closed the door again. Seeing me on the stairs, he told me: 'He reckons he's a friend of Ronnie's. A taxi driver. He seems genuine.'

I was immensely relieved that it wasn't the police, but angry that Ronnie had sent someone to speak to me at 5.30 in the morning. I thought I had heard the name Jim Lumley before, though, and was curious to know why he had come. 'All right,' I said. 'You'd better let him in.'

When the man came in and I switched on a light, I was shocked by his appearance. I had never seen anyone look so ill: his face was deathly white, he was literally foaming at the corners of his mouth and he was trembling with nerves, or possibly fear.

'I thought Freddie would be here,' he said, sitting down in the lounge.

'Freddie who?' I asked him.

'Freddie Foreman.'

I had no idea why he would think an infamous villain would be sleeping in my house, and nor did I care. 'What do you want?' I demanded.

'Ronnie wants you to know how sorry he is about what's gone in the paper. He feels terrible.'

'So he bloody well should,' I said.

'He's sorry about the things he said, Barbara,' Lumley told me. 'He was writing a book to make some money. He was trying to make it sensational.'

'I don't give a damn about him making money, sweetheart,' I said, raising my voice. 'He has pointed the finger at me for something I haven't done. He's accused me of laundering money. That's against the law.'

Lumley just sat there, on the edge of the seat, saliva on his lips, still shaking.

'I could go to prison,' I went on. 'I want my name cleared.'

'That's what Ronnie wants,' Lumley said quickly. 'He's going to put it right.'

'Oh, yeah? How is he going to do that? How can he put it right from inside a prison cell?'

'I've known Ron all my life. I'm his best friend. He trusts me. I'm going to do everything I can to get those things about you taken out of the book.'

Lumley sounded so upset, so worried, that my heart went out to him. The poor man was not a villain, he was a taxi driver who looked like someone's grandad – a loyal friend of Ronnie's who had been sent round to clean up the mess. A man so full of fear he looked as though he might have a heart attack any second. So I made him a cup of tea and calmed him down, and he started telling me about the Ronnie Knight he knew. What shocked me most was the drug-taking. In all the time I knew Ronnie, he had been strongly anti-drugs, but Jim and his wife, Joy, had apparently seen a different side of him when they'd stayed with Ronnie and Sue Haylock at the villa. 'He'd start on cocaine on Friday night and take it all weekend through to Sunday night,' Lumley told me.

A couple of hours later, after listening to a stranger talking about my ex-husband, all I could say was: 'Jim, you know this man. I spent twenty years with him and thought I knew him, too. But I don't know the man you're talking about. He sounds like someone else. Anyway, what is he going to do to clear my name?'

'He's going to make a statement through me, today, which I'll give to the *Sun* reporter who brought Ronnie back from Spain.'

'You do realise that I may have to get an injunction to stop the book coming out?'

This seemed to make Lumley even more scared: he fidgeted on the edge of the seat nervously. 'I'm going to speak to the publishers to get all the lies taken out,' he said.

'How will we know if they're going to?' I asked.

'I'll be in touch later today.'

We exchanged phone numbers. What happened next turned the whole terrifying scenario into something out of an awful B-movie, or perhaps *Carry On Spying*, or maybe a mixture of the two.

'We need to be very, very careful,' Lumley said, lowering his voice.

As Scott and I stared at him blankly, he went on: 'What I mean is, we need to know who we're talking to. We need a code word. So we know it's us.'

He looked anxiously round the room. Scott and I found ourselves doing the same thing without really knowing why. Then we looked at each other again.

Finally, Lumley said: 'Well, we're all drinking out of pink cups. Every time we speak, we must say three pink cups.'

If I had not been so strung out, I would have found it funny. There I was, splashed over the Sunday papers like some criminal mastermind, and now I was talking to a stranger who looked like he might die on me, and we couldn't speak on the phone unless one of us said: 'Three pink cups.' You have to laugh, don't you?

Later that day, I went out to do some shopping and returned to find a message on my answering machine. 'Three pink cups,' it said. 'Please call Jim Lumley.'

I rang his number. 'Hello. Is that Jim?'

'Yes,' he said. 'Who is that?'

'It's Barbara,' I said.

'Who?'

'Barbara,' I repeated. 'Barbara Windsor.'

'I don't know her. Never met her.'

'This morning, when you called on me,' I reminded him.

There was silence for a few seconds. Then I remembered. 'Oh, three pink cups.' This relaxed him and we began our conversation, but I did feel an idiot.

Lumley confirmed that the *Sun* was interested in what Ronnie planned to say from prison; he also said that Ronnie's publisher was worried that the book libelled me and was considering delaying publication and deleting the defamatory passages. This was comforting. But then Lumley said he wanted to see me early the next morning to show me some documents from Ronnie's trial. I was bemused. What on earth had any documents to do with me? Why would I want to see them?

At 7.30 a.m. on the Tuesday, Lumley arrived with the fifty-five-page statement I'd given to the detectives investigating the Security Express robbery. And he spent the next hour going through it, picking out phrases and sentences he felt incriminated Ronnie. From being terrified I'd been wrongly accused, he now seemed to be insinuating that I was a guilty party. Scott and I went through the statement carefully and, of course, there was not one word that incriminated Ronnie, or suggested I'd played any part in laundering stolen cash. I was now dubious of Lumley's motives and decided to give him and his three pink cups a wide berth.

The person I needed to see, and quickly, was my lawyer. Surely, I had a cast-iron case for libel against the *People*, if not Blake Publishing, the publishers of Ronnie's book, particularly since Scott had taped a telephone conversation with my former accountant the previous evening which proved my innocence indisputably. The legal position, my lawyer said, was clear: yes, I did have a good case, and I would almost certainly win a libel action. But the effect it would have on me, as a high-profile personality, was a different matter. The case would not come to court for about three years. Did I want to be embroiled in a costly, mentally exhausting high-court battle when I would be getting on for sixty-five? The defending newspaper and/or book publisher would send out their investigators to drag up any muck they could find. Was I prepared for my personal life, and any skeletons I might have in the cupboard, to be put under the microscope as all the other newspapers rubbed their hands at every salacious word spoken in court?

I was tempted, sorely tempted, to sue the *People*, even though I knew its editor, Neil Wallis, quite well. The reason I didn't was because I'd seen the catastrophic effect of an unsuccessful libel action on my *EastEnders* mate, Gilly Taylforth, and I was not prepared to risk a similar fate. Gilly had been advised that she stood a good chance of winning substantial damages against the *Sun* after it ran a story about her indulging in a sex act with her boyfriend in a car. By the time the *Sun*'s lawyer, the eminent George Carman QC, had finished with her, however, poor Gilly had not only lost her case, but she was ordered to pay the *Sun*'s costs. She was left virtually penniless. If I'd had hundreds and thousands of pounds in the bank doing nothing, I probably would have sued, but I didn't. I swallowed it, but it was a bitter pill. The *People* and Blake Publishing can count themselves lucky they got away with it.

As for Ronnie – well, like most East End villains, he had an odd view of loyalty. Each time he was arrested it would have been easy for me to have walked away and let him fend for himself, particularly on the murder charge, because our marriage was on the rocks in any case. But good old reliable Babs rallied round and stuck by him, and this was how he repaid me.

Ronnie claims that if it were not for my fame, no one would have known anything about him, but what he chooses to ignore is that if he had earned a living like millions of hard-working people, he would not have become a notorious criminal in the first place. And what about the effect his villainy had on my career? I used to love bouncing into theatres and having a chinwag with the stage doormen, no worries on my mind except that evening's performance. But after his activities dragged me into the headlines, those stage doors were often besieged by journalists wanting my reaction to his latest misdemeanour. There is no doubt that Ronnie screwed up my working life and the pleasure I got from it, but I doubt he ever gave that a thought.

By Wednesday, my nerves were shot to pieces. I still thought I knew Ronnie, but the terrible lies in a book going out under his name had rattled me and I was terrified of what might happen next. I jumped every time someone came to the door because I thought it would be the police (they never came, of course). It was a great relief to have Scott there. On top of everything else, I thought I might be going down with bronchitis, and quite honestly, I wouldn't have been able to cope on my own.

That night, I went to bed early: apart from feeling ill, I wanted to have a look through my script for the next day. Scott said he would bring me up a cup of tea in half an hour. I'd had a bath and was reading in bed when there were two very loud knocks on the door. 'Who's there?' I answered, knowing it was a joke.

The door opened slightly and two hands appeared, holding three cups.

'Three pink cups,' said Scott in a serious, theatrical voice from behind the door.

We laughed and laughed until the tears rolled down our cheeks. It was the first laugh we'd had in four terrible days and it released a lot of pent-up tension.

For the rest of that week, I had a lot of work on *EastEnders*: I was featured heavily in a big musical storyline, and then I was starting a dramatic episode in which Grant hit me. I was enthusiastic about it all but I still felt rough: I was coughing a lot, and my energy drained away as the day wore on. Towards the end of the week I was going downhill fast. I had Sunday and Monday off,

▲ *Elton John's ex-manager John Reid celebrates his 40th birthday.*

▲ *With my wonderful agent Barry Burnett.*

▼ *My 60th birthday party: Patsy Palmer, Lionel Bart, Scott, Danny La Rue, me, Dale Winton, Pam St Clement, Steve McFadden and Eric Hall.*

▲ *With Martine McCutcheon at the National Television Awards in 1997.* EastEnders *won the award for Best Drama.*

▲ *My best friend Anna Karen – who became famous as Olive in* On the Buses – *joined* EastEnders *as Aunt Sal in 1996. This picture was taken on her first day.*

◀ *Peggy's breast cancer scare was one of the most difficult storylines I've ever tackled. Here fiancé George (Paul Moriarty) comforts me in hospital.*

▶ *With Ross Kemp on his last day on the* EastEnders *set in August 1999. I was devastated to see him go.*

▼ *My* EastEnders *wedding: held aloft by 'sons' Phil (Steve McFadden) and Grant (Ross Kemp) as groom Frank Butcher (Mike Reid) toasts his bride.*

▲ *My Madame Tussaud's waxwork model was unveiled in April 2000.*

▼ *On my first proper date with Scott Mitchell, the son of dear friends of mine, at the Houses of Parliament in June 1993. At the next table Shirley Bassey can't resist a peek...*

◀ *Togged up for Elton John's 50th birthday fancy dress party held at Hammersmith Palais.*

▼ OK! *magazine ran a feature to mark my engagement to Scott in 1999. Here is one of the beautiful photos they took of us relaxing in Marbella.*

▲ ▶ *Scott and I married secretly at London's Dorchester Hotel in April 2000. The only people there, apart from two registrars, were Scott's mother Rita, his father Ronnie and sister Marsha, and the wedding co-ordinator and her husband.*

▶ *At Buckingham Palace in July 2000. My spontaneous curtsey to Dame Shirley Bassey is the picture that seemed most to capture the public imagination.*

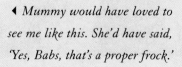

◀ *Mummy would have loved to see me like this. She'd have said, 'Yes, Babs, that's a proper frock.'*

I told myself; if I could just last out till then, I'd rest and be OK. I made it through to the weekend, but by the Sunday, I had started having trouble breathing in the middle of the night, and Scott made me promise to see my doctor first thing in the morning.

Conveniently, the doctor's practice is close by the mews and I was there at 9 a.m. He was concerned that I might have pneumonia and wanted to send me to hospital immediately. I refused, but less than an hour later I felt so dreadful that I went back and held my hands up. 'I think you're right,' I said. 'I should be in hospital.'

By lunchtime, I was having tests at the University College Hospital in nearby Bloomsbury. I didn't have pneumonia, I was relieved to hear, but I did have a severe chest infection and my asthma had worsened. By the next day I was having so much trouble breathing, I needed an oxygen mask.

Judging by the media coverage, everyone else could have been forgiven for thinking the worst, too. There were reporters and photographers and TV cameras outside the hospital the following morning, all wanting Scott to tell them why I was there. He said I had been run down with a virus anyway and the anxiety over the allegations about the stolen money had sent me over the edge. He was right. Everybody who knows me knows I'm a battler who never succumbs to ill health without a fight. For me to give in and go into hospital, I must have been at my lowest ebb as well as medically sick. And for that, I blame all those responsible for that insidious allegation that unjustly blackened my name – Ronnie, his pals, Blake Publishing and the *People*.

Physically, I gradually got better over the next three days; mentally, too, I started feeling a lot brighter, and for this I have to thank all those lovely people who sent me bouquets of flowers and cards wishing me a speedy recovery. By Thursday afternoon, ninety-two bouquets had arrived and I was beginning to feel embarrassed at the extra work I was causing the nurses, not to mention, how much space I was taking up.

The next day, six more bouquets arrived. Scott came in shortly afterwards and noticed a message on one of them signed 'Nigel'. 'Who's Nigel?' he asked.

'Paul Bradley,' I lied. Scott knew Paul, who played Nigel in *EastEnders*, but if it struck him as odd that Paul would send me flowers under his screen name, he didn't show it.

We'd been talking for half an hour or so when a nurse came in with another bunch of flowers. She handed them to Scott, who read out the message on the card. 'Sorry to hear you're not well. Please phone me if there's anything I can do. Robert Dunn.'

Scott went apeshit. 'You don't want that man back in your life, Bar,' he said. 'You've always said he wasn't good for you.'

'Scott, it's not my fault if the man sent me flowers,' I reasoned.

'I wondered when he would. He couldn't resist it, could he? He's read that I'm not with you and knows this is a way of getting back in with you. He did it with Ronnie, he did it with Stephen and now, he's doing it with me.'

'What are you going on about?' I said, angry myself now. I was lying in bed in hospital, not feeling too clever, and I didn't need this aggravation.

'Have you been in touch with him?' Scott snapped.

'No, I haven't.'

'And you're not going to,' he said, putting the card, with Robert's phone number on it, into his pocket.

That's where Scott, in his fury, made a huge mistake. If he hadn't made such a big deal of it, Robert would have received the same thank-you note as the other ninety-seven people who sent flowers, and that would have been the end of it. I hadn't wanted to speak to Robert, but Scott's unreasonable attitude made me want to; after all, Scott had left me. And what happened later that afternoon and in the evening made me even more inclined to contact Robert.

Scott went home, and returned to the hospital in the afternoon, saying he had rung Robert's pub-restaurant in Wiltshire, and told a waitress to tell him that Miss Windsor did not need his flowers.

That upset me. 'You shouldn't have done that, Scott,' I said.

'Why not?'

'You could say that to Robert – he was the one who sent the flowers – but you shouldn't have said it to a waitress.'

Scott went home again, and when he came back in the evening he told me he had rung the restaurant again: he was worried Robert might not have received the message, and he wanted to make sure he did.

'So what happened?' I asked.

'I asked to speak to Robert Ramsay-Dunn personally.'

'Robert who?'

'That's the name he goes by,' Scott said.

I was mystified. It was the first time I'd heard the Ramsay bit. Another time, I would probably have found it intriguing, but just then I wasn't in the mood.

'So what did you say to him?' I asked.

'I said, "This is a friend of Barbara's. She doesn't need your help. Don't even think about it."'

Robert had explained that he'd sent the flowers in good faith and Scott had told him: 'I don't care what they were sent in, Mr Dunn. Just keep out of her life. Don't go near her. Don't get in touch again.' And then he'd put the phone down.

As Scott left me that night, the last thing he said was: 'Good night, darling. And I'm never going to give you that number.'

That's where he made his second, even bigger, mistake. He was making Robert seem like some long-lost, wonderful lover I was pining for. And it made me devious. I started thinking: I'll find that phone number, even if I have to call in Dapper of the Yard to help me. Scott was not going to get the better of me.

I was lying in bed wondering how to go about it, when I saw the black bin-liner containing all the wrapping paper from my bouquets: the name of the florist Robert had used was bound to be there. I rummaged through, looking for paper with a yellow ribbon. I found it easily, then phoned Yvonne at home. 'Hello, darling,' I said. 'I wonder if you'd do me a favour in the morning. I've been sent some lovely flowers, but don't know who sent them. If I give you the name of the florist, would you mind ringing them to find out?'

Of course, I could have done it myself, but I didn't want to risk Scott seeing my hospital phone bill and asking questions. The next day, Yvonne rang and confirmed she had Robert's address and phone number. I told her to hang on to it until she came to the house to help me write my thank-you notes.

I had no plans at that moment to ring Robert Ramsay-Dunn, but there might come a time when I might want to, I thought.

Poor Scott. He had made the break, and was trying to sort out his life, but now he was stuck in the house feeling he couldn't leave me until I was better. He never moaned about being trapped, but I sensed that's how he felt. He was quieter than usual the week I came out of hospital. And then on the Friday, when I was more or less back to normal, he broke the news.

'I've just got to get away, Bar,' he said. 'I'm going to go to America.'

I was shocked. 'Where in America? What'll you do?'

'California,' he said. 'I've got a cousin who lives just outside LA.'

'What'll you do?' I asked again.

'I don't know, Bar. Just chill out, I guess. But I've got to get away. Put some distance between us.'

I didn't like the thought of him going, but I could understand why he wanted to. At least 6,000 miles away he would not open a paper, or switch on the telly, and see Barbara Windsor's face every day. 'If that's what you want, darling,' I said. 'If you feel that's what you really want to do, then that is what you have to do.'

Having made the decision, he felt he had to move quickly, not drag it out, so he booked a flight for Saturday 28 March and arranged to leave the house the Wednesday before.

It was an unbearably emotional couple of weeks. When two people split up because they don't get on, it is much easier to walk away; if they are still in love and breaking up for different reasons, it is heartbreaking. Scott and I spent most of those nights in tears, dreading that awful Wednesday. We didn't go out, preferring to savour every precious second of each other's company without having to share it with anybody else. Every so often I'd ask Scott if he was sure about going. He'd say he had to, and I'd say, 'Yeah, I know you have, darling,' and always the tears would stream down our faces.

When Tuesday night came we fell into each other's arms in bed. 'I will always love you, Bar,' Scott kept saying.

'And I will always love you, darling,' I told him, and we cuddled together, tight, and cried ourselves to sleep.

I woke up still crying and suddenly scared. Later that morning, I broke down and begged Scott not to go. He put his arms round me, his head on my shoulder, and sobbed like a baby. He did not want to go himself.

I thought that maybe if Scott went away and sorted himself out properly we could get back together. I wanted him to know that he could always come back. So, when he had collected himself, I said: 'Scott, I want you to make me a promise. I don't care how long it might take, but if you ever feel you made a mistake leaving, I want you tell me.' He said that he would.

A few minutes before two o'clock, we said a final goodbye and he went to the car. I watched him drive out of the mews and saw that he was crying again. Then I went into the lounge and howled myself. I didn't have a clue what I was going to do with my life. And at that moment, I didn't care.

I was the first person Scott rang when he landed in California. He was anxious that I should know he had arrived safely. Over the next few weeks, we spoke a couple of times a week, at least, and he sounded happy: he was unable to get a green card, a work permit, but had wangled himself an off-the-record mornings-only job answering the phone for a new company still being set up, and was hoping to be able to rent his own apartment. He had bought a 1970s English car, and his cousin and her husband had allowed him to install his own phone line in their house. He was getting himself together. The distance he had put between us, it seemed, was working for him. He had flown into a new life without all that Barbara Windsor baggage that had been weighing him down. He could walk into a bar, a restaurant, and relax and enjoy himself without wondering what snide comments the gossips were making behind his back.

I loved Scott so much, I was pleased for him: it had broken me up to see him miserable and lacking in confidence, and I wanted him to be happy, doing something he really wanted, being his own man. I just hoped that America, and all the freedom it offered, would not turn out to be a novelty that wore off; that the blue skies, warm sun and intoxicating, if unreal, holiday atmosphere, would not merely mask what was really going on in his head.

30

It was Saturday 18 April, and I was feeling better about myself. I'd had a good, if exhausting, week on *EastEnders* and was now preparing to go to Kent for a party to celebrate Tony Lambrianou's sixty-first birthday. I didn't know Tony that well, but the party was being thrown by John Corbett, one of Charlie Kray's pals, and out of friendship for Charlie – for old times' sake, if you like – I decided to go. It promised to be a night when I could switch off and enjoy myself as me, and I was looking forward to it.

Sitting in my bedroom, contemplating what to wear, I put on Erroll Garner's *Concert by the Sea* CD and poured myself one of the miniature bottles of champagne I'd bought for times such as this. A few weeks before, I'd decided that, if I was going out socially, I would give the evening a sense of occasion and spend half an hour or so getting in the mood. I put on a chic black dress, then picked up my champagne and went downstairs. When I caught sight of myself in the full-length mirror at the foot of the stairs, I thought, 'Bar, old girl, you look your best tonight.'

And then, on the spur of the moment, I decided to make a phone call. I went into the kitchen, took a small piece of paper from my letter rack and dialled the number written on it.

A young woman answered.

'I'd like to speak to Robert Dunn, please,' I said in a voice she would not have recognised.

'May I say who's calling?' she asked.

'Just say, a friend of his, if you don't mind.'

Robert came on the line.

'Hello, Robert.'

He knew who it was immediately. 'My God – Bar!' he said, shocked.

'Listen, I—'

'What the hell did I do?' he interrupted. 'That guy – Scott? – went mental on me. What did I do? All I did was send you flowers.'

'I know, Robert,' I said. 'I'm phoning you because, to be honest, I didn't like it. But you have to understand you were never Scott's favourite person.'

We had a brief chit-chat about what we were both doing, and then he brought up Scott again. 'We're not together any more, Robert,' I told him. 'He only came back to look after me. He's living in America.'

'I see,' he said. 'Well, let's keep in touch. Let's meet up.'

'That would be nice.'

'I'll phone you.'

'OK,' I said.

Robert didn't ring. So, two weeks later, just before midnight and quite tipsy after a couple of cocktails, I called him. Scott had put it into my brain that Robert was looking for an opportunity to get back into my life and I was curious, disappointed maybe, that he hadn't seized it. Any inhibitions I may have had were calmed by the drink. I came straight out with it: 'Why haven't you phoned me?'

'I was going to,' Robert said. 'But I've been tied up with the business here, and I didn't want to call until I knew we could meet up.'

We chatted for a bit, then he said: 'You know, it's funny. Whenever we talk, things seem to happen to me, things connected with you.'

'What do you mean?'

'Two days after you rang me, the secretary of my golf club came to the restaurant and offered me tickets for the Lady Ratlings' ball next month.'

'Are you going?'

'Yes,' he said. 'You know me. I love all those Ratling dos.'

'Well, I'll see you there, then.'

Over the next couple of weeks, he phoned late several times at night for a chat. He told me that his friend had let him down with the tickets, so I arranged a couple for him. I told him I was having a drink with the singer Rose Marie and June Brown before the ball, but that he and his friend were welcome to come to Marylebone to change into their dinner suits and to join us. I suggested they arrived around 4.30 p.m. 'We'll be there,' Robert said.

Although Nigel Wildman's interest had restored some of my confidence, I was still nagged by doubts that Scott had left me because I was not desirable any more.

Robert and I had not spent any time together since he had come to see me in *Sloane* in Bath five years before, and I can't tell you the state I got myself into on the day of the ball. Suddenly it seemed terribly important to look extra special. It would not be enough just to look good; I would have to be take-your-breath-away stunning. And not just the face and hair, but what I was wearing, too. Robert had been in and out of my life for over twenty years and, more than anyone – Ronnie Knight included – had seen me at my very best, with all sorts of looks: he'd seen me with my hair down, with it swept back, with feathers in it; in posh hats, dresses to the floor, short skirts up to my bum – the lot.

We can't turn back the clock, of course, but when Robert walked through the door, I wanted him to think: 'My God, she's hardly changed.' And to tell me how great I looked. I'd always enjoyed wearing clothes that the man in my life liked, and recently, with no one around to please, I'd been missing that. I'm not vain, but we all like to be told we look nice, don't we? And Robert had always been very good with compliments.

I had two great outfits that fitted the bill: one was new and I had never worn it, but the other, which I preferred, had been out a few times and had been seen. I decided to make up my mind after I'd had a bath and put my face on. In the meantime, I had to go to Marks for hors d'oeuvres, which I would heat up and serve with the champagne I had on ice. I wanted everything just so. I wanted to impress Robert.

I'd had my bath and was about to put on my make-up when I suddenly thought, shit! The champagne I'd bought was Moët. That would not do for him. Robert had always been one for insisting on the best of everything. I put the face on hold, threw on some clothes and dashed round to Oddbins for a bottle of Dom Perignon. Sixty quid, it cost me, but it was worth it, I reasoned: Robert knew his bubbly, and you could hardly do better than Dom Perignon.

I hurried home again and started getting ready. I slipped into one dress, then the other. I couldn't make up my mind. The new one was OK, but it was not enough for the impression I wanted to make. The other was perfect, but it bothered me that my *OK!* magazine friends would have seen it. I looked at the clock. It was 3 p.m. There was no need to panic, but I did. I picked up the phone and rang Yvonne.

'Darling, I don't know what to do,' I said, trying to keep the anxiety out of my voice. 'I've got to look great. I've got to look stunning. But I don't know what to wear. And I've got no one here. I can't do up the frocks. I can't fasten my necklace. I don't know what—'

'I'm coming round,' Yvonne said.

She was in Vauxhall, but quickly got a taxi and was outside my door in less than half an hour. I posed in both dresses and she convinced me that the new one was the one to wear. Now I started getting worked up about how to greet Robert. I didn't want to show how desperately anxious I was to see him. I was putting the finishing touches to my make-up, knowing I had plenty of time to think about how I should play it, when the phone rang. It was Robert.

'I'm round the corner,' he said.

I looked at the clock: 3.45 p.m.

Round the bloody corner? Three quarters of an hour early?

'Oh, lovely,' I said. 'Where exactly are you?'

He told me and I gave him directions. I turned to Yvonne. 'What should I do?' I asked. 'Do I open the door and stand there, waiting? Shall I leave it open and be on the stairs? Do I just wait for him to knock or ring the bell?'

Yvonne looked at me blankly as if she couldn't believe what she was hearing. 'I don't know, Bar. I don't know what you should do.'

I felt a trickle of sweat on my forehead.

'Anyway you shouldn't be here,' I said, in a state again. I almost pushed her out of the door, then forced myself to sit down and compose myself. A couple of minutes after she left, I heard a car pull up and Robert's voice. 'You'd have thought she'd be waiting at the door to greet me, wouldn't you?'

I waited for the bell to ring, then sauntered as slowly as I could to the front door, an image of the swarthy, dark-haired, bearded Al Pacino lookalike filling my mind. I opened the door, a friendly, welcoming smile already in place, and looked for Mr Pacino. He wasn't there. In his place was a man I barely recognised; a clean-shaven man with pallid skin and dyed fair hair who looked as nervous as I felt. Robert's rugged looks had vanished, and he looked older than his fifty-four years.

He introduced his friend, Terry, and I led them into the lounge, remembering suddenly that I'd forgotten to heat up the hors d'oeuvres. Ah, well, not to worry: on to the champagne. 'What can I offer you, Robert?' I asked.

'A cup of tea would be lovely, Bar.'

'A cup of tea?' I couldn't believe it. 'That's nice! I've bought Dom Perignon.'

Robert laughed.

I poured three glasses and we started chatting.

'My God, Bar,' said Robert. 'You look fantastic. Have you had a boob job?'

'Don't be daft!' I was seven stone ten pounds, my best possible weight, and the panic getting ready had been worth it: I knew I looked stunning. Thank you, Yvonne.

'You don't look so bad yourself,' I said.

Robert smiled. 'That's kind of you, Bar. But I've aged, I know that. Three years ago, I had peritonitis and nearly died. I was nervous about seeing you again because I don't look like the guy you knew.'

'Don't worry about it, you look fine,' I said, noticing that the chin that had always been hidden behind a beard before seemed weak. His lovely smile was still there, though.

I took Robert and Terry to Rose Marie's flat near the Royal Lancaster to meet her and June, and by the time we arrived at the hotel, I was buzzing. Immediately after dinner, I arranged for Robert and Terry to sit at my table and proceeded to let my hair down. The early-evening champagne, the warm atmosphere and the general excitement of being with a familiar lover quickly went to my head and the last thing I remember is wildly outbidding everybody for a TV in a charity auction.

Fortunately, my mate Anna knew I needed to be at the studios at 7 a.m. the next morning, and a good friend of ours, David Thomas, offered to run me home. I woke up at 5 a.m. wondering what I'd got up to the night before. I felt something unfamiliar next to me in bed. It was the TV I'd bid £500 for.

I travelled to Elstree subdued and hung over. For once, I wouldn't have minded filming a scene in Albert Square, but I was in the Vic, and spent the morning surrounded on all sides by booze, or so it seemed. My feelings of nausea were tempered, however, by warm thoughts of Robert the day before. Despite the rocky path of our on-off relationship over the years, it felt good to have seen him again.

A week or so later, Robert rang to say he had heard I was doing a personal appearance in the West Country and to invite me to call into his pub, the Charlton Cat in Pewsey, on my way back. It wasn't really convenient because

I was going to a party Patsy Palmer was giving that evening, and afterwards I'd promised to see Nigel at an anniversary do at Brick Lane. But Robert was insistent and I was quite curious to see his pub.

Robert took me upstairs to show me the living area above the pub, and I met his two fabulous-looking sons, Asa and Jem. Outside their bedroom was a glass case. I saw something move inside it.

'What's that?' I asked.

'It's the boys' pet snake,' Robert said. I've been terrified of snakes since I was a child. I was too frightened to say anything; I just made an excuse to go back downstairs as fast as possible. Robert followed me down into the pub, chatting about what we were going to have for lunch, but I could think of nothing but that snake.

'I'm sorry, Robert,' I said eventually. 'I won't ever be able to come here again. I don't like snakes.'

'Don't worry,' he reassured me. 'Next time, I'll take it outside.'

'No, no, you don't understand. I'm absolutely petrified of them. It would be enough just knowing it was somewhere in the grounds.'

Poor Robert didn't know what to say: Well, he could hardly get rid of his sons' pet snake just to keep me happy, could he?

Robert cooked a meal for me, Roger Burnett, who had set up my PA, and our driver. Just before we sat down, he motioned towards a man standing alone by the bar. 'The local photographer found out you were coming,' he said. 'Would you do me a favour and let him take your picture?'

I was a bit annoyed. It was obvious that Robert must have rung the man and told him I was going to be there. I didn't mind being photographed to plug the pub, but I did feel Robert could have asked me first. Anyway, I went into the garden and the photographer took some shots of me with Robert and his boys, some of which, of course, appeared in the local paper.

Over the next three weeks Robert and I went out to dinner twice, but never to bed: he travelled up from Wiltshire and went back the same night on both occasions. I fancied him as much as ever, though, and dropped a hint that he was welcome to stay at Marylebone any time, provided it did not interfere with my *EastEnders* schedule. We made a date to go to Langan's in Mayfair the following Monday. Up to then, we'd been careful to keep our distance from each other, so that no one seeing us together would jump to conclusions, but that night, Robert forgot himself and leaned across the table, put a hand to my cheek and kissed my hand. Someone must have spotted us and rung the newspapers, because the moment we walked out into Stratton

Street the paparazzi pounced. Robert and I were too tiddly to give a monkey's and happily posed for photographs, embracing each other like the lovers we had been. The press interest in me took Robert by surprise because of course I hadn't been a TV soap star when we'd been together before.

The next morning I had to do a photo shoot for a TV magazine with Mike Reid on a golf course in Essex. As Robert and I left the house, two photographers were waiting in the mews. I'm sure neither of them could believe they'd caught us bang to rights. Asked if I had anything to say, I shook my head. 'Not really, darlings.'

'We just want to know his name,' one of them called out.

'His name's Robert,' I told them. 'Robert Dunn.'

They looked at him and one asked: 'How are you?'

'I'm wonderful,' replied Robert with an impish grin. 'Wouldn't you be?'

We got into his car and drove off, laughing.

I was thrilled when Peter Charlesworth phoned me to say that he was coming to the *EastEnders* studios with Tony Newley to talk about a possible part for Tony as a dodgy car dealer. I was filming when they arrived, but the minute I finished, I sought them out.

Tony was all smiles. 'Oh, Bar, thank you, little blonde lady,' he said.

'Don't be silly. I just hope everything goes well for you.'

I went off and got three cups of tea for PC, Tony and Tony's girlfriend, the designer Gina Frattini. 'Now, listen, Tone,' I said. 'If there's anything I can do, let me know.' Tony just kept thanking me. But whether or not he got the part wasn't down to me – all I'd done was tell my boss I thought he'd be great for the show.

The following week, Robert and I were driving into the *EastEnders* studio when one of Robert's employees called him on his mobile to tell him that a reporter and photographer from the *People* were making a nuisance of themselves at Robert's pub, wanting to know about his association with me. I was caught off guard: I hadn't realised how newsworthy it was that Barbara Windsor, having had her heart broken, was now openly dating another man. What I did know was that the people of Pewsey were not used to dealing with national newspaper reporters, and that Robert's staff were quite clearly upset.

I rang the paper's editor, Neil Wallis.

'What's going on, Neil?' I demanded. 'You've got someone at Robert's pub. Why are you doing this?'

'Because I wanted to talk to you,' he said. 'And now you've phoned me, haven't you?' He was trying to be funny, not nasty.

'Why didn't you phone me at home?' I asked.

'You would probably have ignored my call. No, I wanted you to phone me. And now I've got your attention, I want to talk about this man in your life.'

'Why?'

He laughed. 'I just think it's wonderful that, at your age – you rascal – you're getting it. I think it's fabulous.'

'Really.'

'Yeah, really. It's great. You look great. The pictures of you are good. I think it's lovely. I want to do a story. I'd just like you to talk to Sue.'

He was referring to Sue Crawford, the *Sun* journalist who had taken Scott and me to the hotel in Sussex when Ronnie came home from Spain, who was now, Neil told me, his deputy.

I wasn't mad about co-operating with the *People* after the misery some of their previous stories had caused me, but it was clear they were going to do a piece anyway. Obviously it was going to be safer if we were involved than if we left them to their own devices. And in any case I am not one to bear grudges. I think you have to forget about what has happened in the past and move on.

'Let me talk to Robert about it, Neil,' I said. 'If he's happy to talk, so am I.'

He was, so we did the story. On 21 June, Neil ran a photo of me on the front page above a headline announcing that I'd found the love of my life. Then there were two pages inside which told the story of the *EastEnders* star who had 'rekindled her passion with an old flame who had put the buzz back into her shattered life'. Colourful, emotive words – and at the time, they were absolutely spot-on. Robert was like an old glove, warm and comfortable, and I meant it when I said I'd never been really out of love with him for eighteen years. But as I threw myself into the affair that summer, I was still aching for Scott. And I wondered what he was going to say when he found out that I'd proclaimed my love for a man he felt should have no place in my life.

As it happened, he found out the day the story was published, because it was reported on the Internet. Scott rang me immediately from Los Angeles, steaming. 'What the hell have you done, Bar?'

'Darling, it's all right,' I said. 'He's changed.'

'Why didn't you tell me?'

'I couldn't,' I said. 'I knew you'd have a go at me.'

I didn't think Scott had any right to have a go at me, but he was still protective towards me and feeling guilty that he'd left me alone and vulnerable. I couldn't lie to him. I told him Robert hadn't been to blame; I'd contacted him, not the other way round. I said we'd been on a few dates, and then the press had found out so we had been more or less thrown together. Not very convincing, I have to admit, but there you go.

Three weeks later, another Sunday, Scott phoned again and said he had something to tell me.

'What is it?' I asked, intrigued.

'I've decided to come home,' he said.

I didn't know what to say. Of all the things I might have expected him to come out with, that wasn't one of them.

'Are you sure?'

'Yes.'

'But why, Scott? I thought you loved it out there.'

'I just feel it's pointless me being here. Don't worry, I'm not coming back to get in your way. I realise you've made your own life now and there's nothing I can do about that. As long as we'll always be friends, that's the main thing.'

I was totally confused. I'd been trying to force Scott out of my mind and build a life without him because he didn't want to be with me, and I was feeling comfortable with Robert. Whatever Scott said, he was bound to complicate things.

'I do hope you're doing the right thing,' I told him, for want of something more positive to say.

In the last week of July Scott phoned to tell me he'd arrived home the previous day – and had got stinking drunk on the plane. 'Did you, love?' I said sympathetically. But inwardly I sighed, oh, dear, this doesn't bode well.

When the *EastEnders* producer, Jane Harris, moved on, the executive producer, Matthew Robinson, came to Elstree to talk to us about our roles. He was familiar with the notes for my storyline, and felt we should move it forward by acting on the suggestion that Peggy should now start to worry that she was going to lose one of her breasts. 'Are you still willing to go along with that, Barbara?' he asked me. I said that he was the boss: if he thought that was the way Peggy's life should go, it was OK by me. He said he would think about it.

My sixty-first birthday was coming up. I had no particular plans for a celebration, but it's odd, isn't it, how sometimes you can do something on the spur of the moment and it turns out better than a special evening you might have spent months arranging. The week before, I was asked to reopen Heaven, the gay club near Trafalgar Square, and went along there with Robert, Ross Kemp and Ross's girlfriend Rebekah Wade, then deputy editor of the *Sun*. Afterwards we were having a drink at Soho House and Ross asked what I'd got planned for my birthday.

'She doesn't want a party,' Robert said. 'She had a big one last year.'

Ross looked at me. 'You should do something, Bar.'

On the spur of the moment I decided I would throw a party after all and by the end of the evening I had booked a room at the top of Soho House with a spectacular view over London. I then made a few phone calls and suddenly I was having another big birthday bash. Most of my mates came, including Jim Davidson, John Inman, Lionel Bart, Dale and Martine and Sid from *EastEnders*. Les Dennis, who happened to be having a drink in a downstairs bar that night, came up to join us, and the pop star Robbie Williams made my night complete by turning up unexpectedly with his All Saints girlfriend, Nicole Appleton.

Scott was staying with his parents in Brighton, and we were talking on the phone a lot. He wanted to see me, but we hadn't yet managed to meet: it was a busy time, and I was either working flat out, or seeing Robert or Nigel. I was just happy that, despite everything, we were still great friends. Then, one evening soon after my birthday, I rang Scott in a bit of a state.

I was due to go to the Bahamas with Robert in October on a holiday arranged by *OK!* magazine. I was dreading it. I had only ten days off and didn't want to travel that far – and I didn't really want to go away with Robert. I'd said publicly that he was the love of my life but already, just two months on, I knew that wasn't right. We had little in common: he was a country person and I was a townie, and we didn't really have a relationship beyond going out to dinner and to bed. Scott had never been out of my life, even when he'd been 6,000 miles away, and, deep down, I knew that he, not Robert or Nigel, was the man I'd been searching for all my life.

Hearing me so strung out, Scott said he would drive up the following Saturday to spend the afternoon with me. We were both shocked at the sight of each other. Scott had put on weight and had had his lovely long hair cropped to a number 2 and I'd lost a stone. I'd put on a long, blue summer dress, but Scott said it was practically hanging off my skinny frame. He said it was the look of a lady in turmoil. And he was right: seeing two other men, while the man I really wanted to be with was back in my life, was doing my brain in.

Scott and I talked in the garden, then shared a couple of vodkas in the evening sunshine in a bar on Marylebone High Street. We talked as we had always done, and when he drove off to Brighton at 7 p.m., I could not stop myself wishing – hoping – that in time we could get back together. What I didn't know was that Scott had no hope for that, none at all. He was the one in real turmoil. He was heading for a terrifying suicidal depression, brought on by the guilt he felt at having hurt the woman he now knew really was the love of his life.

That summer I'd been leafing through a magazine one day and seen an ad for extensions that made your hair thicker. I decided they might be just the thing for my fine, unmanageable hair and decided to give them a go. I went to an address in Maida Vale where I was greeted by a tall, exotic-looking woman with long, dark hair – she looked like a model from the seventies – who showed me some examples of her work.

I was impressed, and when she said the hair would be made up for me within two weeks, I willingly wrote out a cheque for the full cost, £1,200. I didn't hear anything over the next two weeks, however, or during the two after that. And every time I rang the woman's number, the answerphone was on. I became suspicious. In the end I left a message to say that if she didn't get in touch with me, I would call on her personally the next time I was passing to arrange for the return of my £1,200.

Finally she rang me back, and when I told her that I was going to the Bahamas for a photographic shoot for *OK!* magazine, the hair suddenly arrived. Unfortunately, it was yellow, whereas I'm ash blonde.

'Not to worry,' said the woman. 'I've got this wonderful hairdresser. Let's see if she can dye it up. Can you take it in?'

I was very busy with *EastEnders*, but having waited so long already I agreed to take the hair extensions to her hairdresser. However, there was nothing she could do: the hair, she said, had already been dyed 'to buggery'.

I went back to Maida Vale and got a bit bolshy. 'Deliver what you promised, and what I paid for, or I'm going to a solicitor,' I said. That seemed to frighten the hair lady and she promised to fix everything before the Bahamas trip.

Meanwhile, I learned that I was to be given an *EastEnders* two-hander with Pam St Clement, who plays Frank Butcher's ex-wife, Pat. I was thrilled to bits because a two-hander – in which a whole episode is devoted to just two characters – is considered a great compliment. It was only when I stopped to consider the realities of acting with only one other person for half an hour that the nerves set in.

Pam and I were as nervous as each other, and whenever we met we would pull faces and groan, 'Oh, God.' When the scripts arrived a few weeks before filming, I booked myself into Henlow Grange for three days: the two-hander was my most important episode to date and I wanted to be on my own, in tranquil surroundings, to make sure I was word perfect. When I left, I was.

On the night we were to start shooting the episode, Matthew Robinson came to watch. As we walked to the set, he told me he had visited the little church where Peggy would later marry Frank Butcher. 'It's a lovely old-fashioned church in Harrow,' he said.

'Oh, lovely,' I enthused. 'I'm going to have a church wedding.'

As Pam and I got ready for action, he called out: 'Oh, by the way, Barbara, we're going with the cancer storyline. Peggy's going to lose her breast.'

'Yeah? But not before she gets married, though!' I joked.

'Yes,' he said. 'Two weeks before.'

'Only one? That's clever. That means you can have another cancer storyline in a couple of years, can't you?'

It was true: Peggy might indeed have to go through it all again one day.

As the director prepared to go for a take of a car whizzing round Albert Square before Peggy and Pat began their row, I could think of nothing but how the public was going to react to Peggy having a breast off, then walking down the aisle two weeks later.

That two-hander was one of the most explosive *EastEnders* episodes for years. We had a great director, Paul Annett, and the script department excelled themselves: one minute Pat and Peggy weren't talking, then they were; one minute they were having a row, the next they weren't. For nearly thirty minutes it was all light and shade, ups and downs. Breathtaking stuff. And thrilling to perform, particularly the memorable finale, in which Pat and Peggy hurl vicious insults at each other. At one point Peggy screamed at Pat: 'No wonder Roy can't get it up.' I thought this was a good, supremely nasty line, because Peggy was having a great sex life with Pat's ex-husband Frank, while the new man in Pat's life, Roy Evans, was impotent. But Mal

Young, the BBC's head of drama series, felt that although the remark was OK on paper, the way I said it was too strong. I pleaded with him to leave it in but he wouldn't have it, and when I watched a private screening, a new line – 'No wonder Roy can't do it' – had been dubbed in. I could see Mal's point, but still thought the original line was better. It was something an angry, vindictive woman would say to wound a rival.

Acting in that episode was one of my best times on the show and I know Pam enjoyed it, too. Before the cameras started rolling we sent each other good luck notes, and after it was all over, we exchanged presents: I bought her pink orchids and she gave me a bottle of pink champagne. That sort of thing isn't usual, but it was a monster episode for both of us and we both knew how nervous the other was. Although I'd known Pam for many years, we'd hardly ever worked together, and I couldn't have wished for a better actress to share the screen with.

Someone else I wanted to share the screen with was Tony Newley. When I discovered that he was indeed coming to *EastEnders* to play that dodgy car dealer, Vince Watson, I looked through the scripts for the forthcoming shoots to see if I was in any of his scenes. I wasn't. So on the day Tony made his debut, I went up to the script office and asked if he was in any scenes at the Vic. He was, but I wasn't. I knew I'd regret it in my old age if there wasn't a video of us on screen together to look back on, so I found out who the director was and asked him: 'While you're filming Tony, would you mind if I casually wandered through in the background?' He agreed, and that's how two old East End pals came to be on TV together for the first time since they'd met more than forty years before.

I was so pleased to have been proved right about Tony. He worked so well as a rival to Mike Reid's car dealer, Frank Butcher, that the producers were intending to beef up his part. Tony could have been in *EastEnders* for years, but, tragically, the cancer he thought he had seen off returned and he became too unwell to work.

For six weeks after leaving me on that August afternoon, Scott did not move from his bedroom in Brighton. He didn't shave; he let his hair grow long and unkempt. He stared at the walls and ceiling for hours on end. And he became so isolated and into himself that he started to mumble his words, unable to get them out.

Typically, he did not let on to me just how bad he was feeling, and, in the last week of September, I thought nothing of ringing him when I got myself in a state while packing to go to the Bahamas. I have a phobia about packing at the best of times – I'm always terrified I will forget something vital – but on this occasion it was more than the suitcases that was bothering me. Whether it was because Scott was back in my life – albeit just on the end of a phone – I don't know, but I now realised that he had been right all along: it had been a mistake for me to get back with Robert.

The holiday seemed doomed on all counts. The right-colour hair extensions I'd been waiting for from the woman in Maida Vale did not arrive until the day before we flew, but I wanted to get the whole business sorted out before I went away, so I dashed off at the last minute to have them woven in. An assistant to the exotic-looking woman did the job, and it was so painful it felt as if she was sewing the hair straight into my scalp. She assured me that everything was fine, though, and off I went. My bad luck continued at the airport: we were warned that hurricanes were threatening the islands and that we might have to stop over in Miami for a day or two. In the event we didn't, but then, when we touched down in Nassau, my luggage had gone on somewhere else and didn't turn up until three days later. To cap it all, I had an uncomfortable time because I kept getting a burning sensation in my scalp from the hair treatment.

The hotel was fabulous and the holiday itself was nice, but it was apparent early on that I was not going to gel in the same way with Robert on holiday as I had with Scott. He liked to go off and play golf, though I didn't mind that because it left me on my own to read. One of the hotel waiters recognised me from a Carry On film and insisted on looking after me personally. He called me Lady Windsor and took great delight in fussing over me. I enjoyed doing the shoot for *OK!*, but I wasn't sorry when it was time to leave. On the flight home I promised myself that I would end the relationship with Robert before Christmas.

Two days after the holiday I was due to attend a ball at the Park Lane Hotel in Piccadilly in aid of breast cancer research, at which Cherie Blair, the prime minister's wife, was to be guest of honour. *EastEnders* ran over time and I was running forty-five minutes late. I'd had no time to go to the hairdressers or to comb out a curly wig, so I plonked on a short, straight one I'd chosen for the Bahamas picture shoot for *OK!* magazine and flew out of the door and into a taxi with Robert. When we arrived, the photographers could not believe their luck: Barbara Windsor with the premier's wife, *and* a new hairstyle, was news.

As we hurried to our table a woman I'd never seen before came up to me.

'In case you need any help on the breast cancer storyline, Barbara, I'll give you my phone number and you can call me.' I looked at her blankly. *EastEnders* storylines are closely guarded secrets and actors are forbidden to give them away. 'I'm sorry, darling,' I said. 'I don't know what you're talking about.'

But I did, obviously. We were to start filming the breast cancer episodes early in the New Year. To my relief, the lady at the dinner turned out to be a Macmillan nurse who had been called in to advise on the script!

I hadn't been sure about my new wig – I'd intended to wait until I saw it in *OK!* before I wore it in public – but the picture made the papers the next day and seemed to capture the media's imagination. A day later, I bumped into the hairdresser Nicky Clarke in Marylebone High Street as he was rushing to the *Richard and Judy* TV show to talk about my hairstyle, and several newspaper columnists followed up the picture with their own views. Most of them seemed to think the reason for the new look was the new man in my life. It just shows how wrong people can be.

The next day I went to film a Christmas edition of *Ready, Steady, Cook* with Lily Savage and master chefs Ainsley Harriott and Antony Worrall Thompson. *EastEnders* had overrun, and I was still carrying £30,000 worth of jewellery, hired by *OK!* for the Bahamas shoot, in my handbag, because I'd not yet had a chance to return it. By the time I got to the studio in Wembley, everyone was panicking about the time. Lily's alter ego Paul O'Grady was in the worst state, pacing up and down and drawing heavily on a fag, but his anxiety had nothing to do with my late arrival.

'What on earth's the matter, darling?' I asked.

'It's for real, Bar!' he said. 'They want us to fucking well cook!'

'Don't be so daft,' I told him. 'It's pretend.'

I thought it was. I'd seen the regular show, of course, and knew that the guest celebrities did some cooking, but this was a Christmas show, with me dressed up as the Christmas Fairy and Paul as the Wicked Witch, and I assumed we were only there for the fun. But we quickly got the message when we were given a bag of food to cook and some huge, lethal-looking chef's knives. Oh, yes, and a tin of plasters, in case we cut ourselves.

I don't know about Paul, because I was too busy concentrating to look at him, but I was totally useless: when I had to cut an onion and then some butter, for instance, I forgot to change knives and Ainsley and I had onion-tasting butter. Nobody was more surprised than me when the audience voted us the winners.

Paul and I get on really well; so well that whenever we go out socially, we always seem to end up the worse for wear, and that night was no exception. After the show, a group of us went to Wiz, Antony's restaurant in Holland Park. I don't remember anything about it, other than that I woke up with a terrible hangover at 4.30 in the morning and immediately turned my thoughts towards getting myself together to leave for *EastEnders* at 6 a.m. When I went to get something from my handbag, I froze in horror. It wasn't mine. Someone was walking around with my handbag and thirty grand's worth of jewellery I'd promised to return to the international jeweller Theo Fennel.

Before the show, *Ready, Steady, Cook* had sent me a load of information, which I still had. I was so hysterical that at five in the morning, I started ringing all the contact numbers I could lay my hands on. But no one I managed to raise had a clue where my bag could be, and by the time my car arrived to take me to Elstree I was ready to slash my wrists. Thank God, when I got to my dressing room there was a message from the *Ready, Steady, Cook* producer, Mary Ramsay, telling me not to worry: she had discovered when she got home that she had my bag by mistake and was sending it over by courier. I returned hers and promised myself never to get drunk with Paul O'Grady again.

Three weeks after I returned from the Bahamas, I was still having trouble with my scalp and it got worse and worse until it got to the stage where it felt as if my head was on fire. I was about to seek medical help when I read an article about a trichological practice called Attention X, run by Mark and Lucinda Ellery-Sharpe, which treats people with this kind of problem. The Ellery-Sharpes came to my rescue. The damage turned out to be horrendous: at my first appointment it took them and their son Chris four hours to unpick what that woman in Maida Vale had done to me, and the pain was excruciating. My scalp was just red raw. And after that I had to go for treatment for nine months to get my hair back to what it had been. It was a huge trauma for me, and I was very grateful to Mark and Lucinda, who have since become dear friends.

While I'd been away Scott had become even more depressed, and I was now one of only a handful of people he would speak to. Realising that his problem was not something that was going to blow over quickly, I phoned him a couple of times a day, urging him to get out of the house and to talk to his friends. But all he said was that he didn't want to face people and that he'd lost the will to do anything.

Rita and Ronnie were wonderfully understanding, particularly when Scott refused to leave his room to go to a surprise party for his mum's sixtieth birthday. They were very anxious about him, but never nagged him. Once, they asked him, 'Is it Bar? Are you still in love with her?' Scott said: 'Of course I still love her.' But he refused to admit even to himself that he wanted to come back to me.

He began to worry that in all this misery he hadn't cried once, so he went to see a doctor, someone he had known for twenty years. The doctor asked him if he felt suicidal. Scott said he did, because he would never be with me again, and that he hated himself for hurting me and destroying our relationship. The doctor told him he was in a deep depression and was having a breakdown. And Scott broke down in tears.

He was put on a course of antidepressant tablets which lifted him through the first part of October, but whenever I spoke to him on the phone, he still sounded dreadfully unhappy. He said something once that I'd have found funny if I hadn't been so worried: he said he was thinking of becoming a postman. For someone who hates early mornings and walking it was hardly the ideal job. But that was Scott's shaky frame of mind at that time.

That October, Scott's favourite aunt, a warm-hearted, eighty-four-year-old East Ender named Bessie, had a heart attack and unwittingly helped Scott snap out of his introspective ramblings. Suddenly he had to stop thinking about himself and care for someone else again. At one point, in the hospital, Bessie had a convulsion and, because of staff shortages, Scott had to help a nurse administer emergency treatment. Later, Bessie told him: 'If you hadn't been here, I'd have been gone.' They chatted for a while, then she surprised Scott by saying: 'You still love her, don't you?'

Scott said that he did.

'I understand why she loves you,' Bessie said. 'You're a good man. You make people feel safe.' She looked deep into his eyes and added: 'Be happy, Scott. Just be happy. Don't worry about what people think, it doesn't matter. Do what you have to do with your life.'

Four days before the first night of Terry Johnson's *Carry On Cleo, Camping, Emmanuelle and Dick*, Barry went to a preview performance. In the event Anthony Sher had not worked out as Sid, and he had been replaced early on in rehearsals by Geoffrey Hutchings. I was being played by a young actress called Samantha Spiro. Barry was very impressed. 'It's an amazing bit of theatre,' he told me. 'Terry obviously adores you. You come over as this wonderful little lady. There's only one thing wrong. In the last scene, Sam has a look that's all wrong. You've got to get it changed before the play opens.'

'I'm not doing that, Barry,' I said. 'I can't go in at this late stage.'

'But I've *never* seen you look like that in all the time I've known you,' he insisted.

'Well, maybe I did look like it once,' I said, and left it at that. No way was I going to rock the boat three days before the play opened. Everyone would have enough on their plates. I wouldn't have had a chance in any case: apart from *EastEnders* and various other commitments, I was also co-operating with a TV documentary about me for a series called *The Best of British*, which would include coverage of me arriving at the National on the first night and meeting the cast backstage.

Two days before the big event I got in a panic over what to wear. I'd decided on a colourful little number, but suddenly I felt it was the wrong choice. I didn't want to steal Samantha Spiro's night. I needed to wear something nondescript that would draw as little attention as possible. I dashed into my favourite shop and said: 'I need something in grey. What have you got in grey?' I settled on a beaded grey cashmere twinset and grey trousers and shoes.

As opening night loomed I began to feel apprehensive about having given Terry permission to portray me the way I was in one of the most emotional, painful relationships of my life. I wished I'd had Kenny there to talk to, him more than Sid. Kenny could have gone one way or the other. He'd either have said haughtily, 'Aaaah, yes, dear, about time we were fêted. We were so good,' or, 'No way is anyone doing my fucking life.' You never knew what to expect with him. But whatever view he would have taken, it would have been lovely to have been able to talk it through with him.

In keeping with my wish to keep a low profile, I took a black cab to Waterloo. I arrived at the theatre with Barry and Robert and was amazed to find a swarm of die-hard Carry On fans, with all their memorabilia, rubbing shoulders with the National's regulars.

As the curtain went up, I felt a lot of sympathy for Sam: not only did she have to conquer her first-night nerves, but the character she was portraying was sitting only a few yards away watching her every movement, listening to every nuance. How nerve-wracking that must have been for a young actress. I found the first act very funny, but made an effort to hold back my famous laugh because I didn't want to attract attention to myself. The second half, in which Sid collapses and dies, was so moving that I spent a lot of the time sobbing into a hanky, oblivious of whether or not people were looking at me.

Naturally, I was waiting with interest to see this 'look' of Sam's that Barry had wanted me to change. But when she came out at the end with her hair up and off the face, I couldn't understand why he'd been so concerned: it was the young Barbara Windsor's 'posh' look, the one I wore for funerals or when I gave evidence in court, and it was perfect: the truest look in the whole play, in my opinion. I'm so pleased I didn't try to make them change it.

The cast took their bows to tumultuous applause; but, as the lights came up and I stood to leave, the audience got to their feet and started clapping me. As usual, I didn't take it very well; I just kept putting up my hand, as if to say: 'Not for me, not for me – it's not my night.' It was all very moving, and I knew it wouldn't take much to set me off when I went backstage to meet Sam.

The *Best of British* documentary cameraman followed me to Sam's dressing-room door. She was waiting for me, and we hugged each other. 'It's *so* lovely to meet you,' she said warmly. Forgetting the cameras, I told her: 'It was absolutely fucking wonderful, darling.' Sam was less interested in what I thought about her performance than in getting the cameras to film the good luck presents I'd sent her. 'Come in here,' she said, motioning the cameraman into her dressing room, 'See what Barbara sent.' She pointed everything out: 'There's flowers, fruit, champagne . . .'

Then she smiled at me and took my left hand. 'Did you enjoy it?' I was too choked to think of anything to say except: 'Thank you, thank you,' and then we were hugging and kissing each other again, and I felt the tears coming.

On Saturday 8 November I went to what turned out to be one of the best charity nights I'd ever attended: a masquerade ball in aid of the Princess of Wales Memorial Fund, organised by Diana's former butler, Paul Burrell. Since the Princess died, Paul and I had become friends: he has been to my home and I've been to his in Kensington Palace, and met his wife, Maria, and his sons. I'd promised Paul I would attend the ball, but I only just made it. I'd been working on Noel Edmonds' *House Party*, which went out live in the evening, and rushed into the Dorchester with Robert in the nick of time as everyone was taking their seats after the pre-dinner cocktails.

It was one of those fabulous nights when everything worked. I caught up with countless friends I hadn't seen in ages, such as Twiggy, and danced with Vinnie Jones, the former footballer who was carving out an acting career, and generally had a fabulous, carefree evening.

I still intended to end my relationship with Robert before Christmas, but less than fifteen minutes after leaving the hotel, the most dreadful thing happened, and I knew immediately that this was not the time to do it. We had been with *OK!* magazine's owner, Richard Desmond, and his lovely wife, Janet, all evening and Richard offered to run us home. On the way we stopped off in Soho to pick up the first editions of the Sunday papers.

Robert came back from the vendor, staggering under the weight of newsprint, and plonked them on the back seat of the car next to me. Before he had even got back in, I was shuffling through the papers, looking for the *News of the World*. 'Let's see who they've nailed this week,' I said, grinning mischievously.

I looked at the front page and let out a loud scream. 'I don't believe this. *I don't believe this. It's you! It's me!*'

They were all smiling: they thought I was having a laugh.

'Don't be wicked, Barbara,' said Janet. 'Don't be so—'

'No, no,' I interrupted. 'Honestly. Look. It's us.'

I held up the paper for everyone to see. There, in huge type on the front page, was the most horrible headline I'd ever seen: 'SOAP STAR BARBARA WINDSOR'S BOYFRIEND BEATS UP CHILD'.

Robert snatched the paper from me. His eyes scanned the report alongside a picture of him with me, then he turned to the inside of the paper: there was a double-page spread with a photograph of his daughter, Lorraine, who had given the paper the story.

Robert dropped the paper and started to cry. 'My kids ... my kids,' he kept saying. 'What are they going to think? These are lies. Terrible lies.'

Richard asked me to pass him the paper and he, too, got upset. 'This is strange,' he said. 'The editor rang me this morning. He said he didn't have a story for the front page. He asked me if I had anything.'

None of us knew what to make of it. We just sat there, not knowing what to say. Finally, I put my arms round Robert and hugged him. 'We'll sort something out, darling,' I said. 'There'll be something we can do to get it put right.'

Robert just sat there, breaking his heart. Then he said: 'I'll nick the bastards. I'll get them. It'll cost me everything, my business, everything I've got – but I'll nick those bastards.'

Richard dropped us at home. As we got out of the car, Richard shook Robert's hand. 'If I can help you, mate, if you want a lawyer, give me a buzz,' he said.

Robert and I sat down in the lounge at the mews and read the story slowly and carefully. It was now getting on for 3 a.m., but Robert said he must ring his ex-wife, Sue, to warn her about what was in the paper. To give myself something to do, I went into the kitchen and made some tea, trying not to listen to Robert's tears as he spoke to Sue about his relationship with Lorraine. Afterwards, I sat with him and let him talk his heart out. All he wanted to do was get in his car, drive to Wiltshire, hold Asa and Jem and tell them he loved them, but he had been drinking all night and would not risk getting behind a wheel. Finally, at around 5 a.m., I suggested that we tried to get some sleep. We went upstairs to bed, but within minutes Robert had got up again and gone downstairs. I heard him moving about, sobbing. My heart went out to him: here he was, in this little house in the middle of London, not knowing what to do with himself. But there was nothing anyone could do.

At 7 a.m., Robert rang his two sons and I listened as he told them he loved them and tried to explain what people were going to read that morning. Shortly after he left, it struck me that, throughout the agony of that long night, Robert had never once complained about the effect the story would have on him personally, or on his business. His thoughts were only for those young boys.

Two days after the publication of that appalling *News of the World* story, Scott's Aunt Bessie died. I knew how deeply her death would affect Scott, but what I didn't know was that her advice had made Scott think that maybe all was not lost between us; that maybe he could win me back.

If the *News of the World* had not run that story, I would have ended my affair with Robert. But I understood better than most what he was going through, and I just didn't have the heart to do it. We continued to talk on the phone, but my passion had cooled and I was happy to see him only now and again, usually when I was going to an official function and needed an escort, a role in which Robert excelled.

I was pleased that the cast of *Carry On Cleo, Camping, Emmanuelle and Dick* got wonderful reviews and delighted when I was asked to spring a surprise on them as they prepared to go on tour. Unknown to everyone connected with the play – including Terry Johnson – the play had won the Olivier Award for the Best New Comedy and I was asked to present it. They were all asked to get together for a rehearsal at the Playhouse Theatre on Victoria Embankment, and I was to turn up, pretending I'd popped in to watch them as I happened to be in the area.

I stood in the wings until Sam had delivered one particular funny line, then I said loudly: 'Oh, no, it was longer than that, dear. It was eight inches.'

Sam looked into the wings, puzzled. 'Barbara? Hi, how are you?'

No one suspected it was a set-up until I walked on to the stage and someone passed me the statuette. 'Actually I'm not here to watch you rehearse,' I said. 'I'm here to present you with this: the Olivier Award.'

They were thrilled to bits. And they had every right to be: they had done Terry Johnson and his brilliant script proud.

I was working all the hours God sent, but I desperately wanted to see the play again while it was on tour. The only date I could manage was during the run at the Theatre Royal in Bath, so I arranged for a car to take me there and bring me back.

Robert asked me: 'Why don't you come to my pub? Then we can go together.' I said I wouldn't have time, so he suggested I went to his manager's house, which was nearer the theatre, and said he would meet me there. I got there in plenty of time and was enjoying a cup of tea with Robert and the manager when a limousine pulled up and a local newspaper reporter knocked at the door, saying she had come to interview me. It took a second or two, but then it clicked: Robert had set this up to publicise his pub. He denied it, but how else would the journalist have known I would be at that house? I was in a difficult position: the woman was at the door with a photographer, expecting to speak to me, but I didn't want to speak to her. Not the way it had been done.

'I'm sorry, darling, I can't talk to you,' I said as sweetly as I could.

'Why not?' she asked. 'It's all been arranged.'

'Not with me, it hasn't,' I told her. 'I'm under contract to the BBC. I have to get permission from the *EastEnders* press office before I speak to newspapers.'

'Robert said you would do it.'

'I'm so sorry, love, but I can't.'

I looked out of the window at the limousine and the sweet little man standing by it. Robert had obviously arranged for the limo to take us to the theatre free of charge in return for getting publicity for the company. I felt sorry for the poor man: it wasn't his fault Robert had gone behind my back.

'Look,' I said to the journalist. 'I'll have a picture taken with the limo and you can say that I've come to see the play and I'm thrilled to be in Bath. End of story.'

She went along with that. She didn't have much choice.

I was furious with Robert. It wasn't the first time he had embarrassed me like that and I warned him never to do it again. I left him in the restaurant where we had had dinner along with the cast and returned to London. On the way home I told myself: 'I really must end this relationship.'

31

I WAS SEEING SCOTT MORE REGULARLY AND LOOKED FORWARD TO HIM COMING TO THE HOUSE FOR DINNER. It was a platonic relationship now: we simply enjoyed each other's company and wanted to be together. If either of us was feeling the familiar surges of physical attraction, we did not show them. Whenever Robert phoned and suggested coming up for the evening, I would find all sorts of excuses to put him off. The best and most convenient, of course, was *EastEnders*. 'Sorry, sweetheart,' I'd say. 'It's not on at the moment. I'm up to my neck in some huge storylines.' I know it wasn't really fair, and I should have been honest, but Robert was still reeling from the *News of the World* story and I was reluctant to add to his problems. He did once ask if I was seeing Scott, and I admitted I was. 'Of course, I see him, you know I do,' I told him, implying that we were merely mates, not lovers. Which was true, then.

Over the years I'd turned down several requests to record an album, but when the flamboyant soccer agent Eric Hall heard me singing 'You Made Me Love You' with Terry Venables in a west London club, he persuaded Ray Levy of Telstar Records to make me an offer I couldn't refuse. But I must admit it was the concept of an album of classic songs that clinched it for me. I love all those wonderful old standards like 'My Foolish Heart', 'You'll Never Know' and 'Little Things Mean a Lot', and I was sure there was a market for them that was being overlooked.

Coming up to Christmas, Scott arrived at the house one evening bubbling with excitement: he had been offered a job as a recruitment consultant. I was shocked and a little disappointed. Scott is a fine actor, and I felt sure that now he didn't have all that Barbara Windsor baggage to hold him back he could get somewhere in the business. I thought he should take a part-time job, selling advertising on the phone or serving in a bar, while he waited for a role to come along. But Scott was now determined to turn his back on acting and throw everything into learning the recruitment business.

A friend of a friend had introduced him to Lee Panayiotou, a dynamic lady who ran a recruitment agency in Holborn, central London. Lee explained what the business was all about, and Scott was hooked. He told her: 'I have no A-levels, no degrees. I know nothing about the business world, but I'm willing to learn.' That suited Lee fine. Good consultants, she said, were hard to find; she was looking for someone to train from scratch and Scott was perfect. I could see that: he is a sincere, genuine person and a good listener who cares about people. And he would be sympathetic as an interviewer because he had been on the other side of the desk himself so many times and knew how soul-destroying the process could be. To me, the role of a recruitment consultant was not dissimilar to that of a casting director and, like Scott's new boss, I realised that he was well suited to the job.

He was due to start in the New Year, so the job was like a surprise Christmas present for Scott. I got one myself that year, too: the *Manchester Evening News* award for Best Soap Actress. At the time Peggy was going off with Grant to scatter the ashes of his dead wife, Tiffany, and we were acting out long scenes up and down the A1 when I was called back to Albert Square to be filmed receiving the award, which had been sent down from Manchester that afternoon. I quickly got together a little speech, in which I said I was particularly honoured and touched that northern viewers had voted for a southerner, considering the brilliance of the stars on *Coronation Street*. And I joked: 'I've had awards for my eyes, my bosoms, my bottom, even my feet. They say actors are only as good as their parts. Well, my parts have served me pretty well, thank you.' My dear friend Roy Barraclough told me that that went down well at the awards ceremony that night.

At the end of November, after months of legal negotiations, the *News of the World* caved in and admitted that it had been wrong to publish the allegations it had made against Robert. The newspaper apologised to him in the High Court and agreed to pay him substantial damages. I was relieved for his sake that his name had been cleared at last, but with that matter resolved, my relationship with Robert was fizzling out by the day, and now, with Christmas approaching, I felt trapped. I'd arranged to go to Henlow Grange with Paul Bennett over the New Year but I was in a quandary about Christmas. I talked it over with Scott, who asked if I'd like to spend some of the holiday with him and his parents in Brighton and some with Robert. It was the perfect solution, and I seized it.

I sensed the most wonderful change in Scott: even though he had yet to start his new job, it was evident that he was bursting with optimism and raring to go. 'I'm going to make you really proud of me, Bar,' he suddenly said one day.

'I've always been proud of you, you know that,' I told him.

'No, I'm going to get myself together and really make something of myself. I want you to see how strong I can be.' He paused. 'And I'll tell you something else.'

I waited, wondering what on earth was coming next.

'I'm going to woo you back.'

'Are you going to be my knight in shining armour? Are you going to come riding through the mist to rescue me?'

'Yes,' he said. 'You may laugh, but you watch. I will.'

I decided to spend 23 December in an hotel in Southampton with Robert and his sons, then go on to Brighton for Christmas Eve and Christmas Day, and rejoin Robert on Boxing Day. As it turned out we had a lovely time in Southampton: we went to see Frank Bruno and Karl Howman in *Goldilocks and the Three Bears*, and I took Robert and his sons and some of their friends backstage to have their photos taken and to get some autographs.

Scott picked me up the next morning and drove me to Brighton, where I had the most relaxing couple of days: I felt totally at home lounging around with no make-up on and it was wonderful not to be expected to lift a finger. Scott's sister Marsha, her husband Laurence and their children, Abbie, Charlie and Harry, also came to stay. Not having wanted to upset the children, Scott had never told them we'd split up, so they were as delightfully loving and full of questions for me as usual. The whole family made a fuss of me, and I lapped it up. The next day, when Scott drove me back to Southampton, I thought, this is ridiculous. There he was, the man I wanted to be with, carrying my luggage into the hotel and driving off again, leaving me with another man.

Back on *EastEnders* in the New Year, I was about to film the crucial scenes in which Peggy loses a breast, and I was also due to record my album. First, though, I'd promised Robert I'd go to Belfast with him to see his pal Bobby Ball in panto with Tommy Cannon. It was freezing there, and I came back with a terrible cold which left me hoarse and croaky. Not being well myself helped me to make Peggy's suffering convincing, but of course my sore throat and unpredictable voice were a bit of a strain, particularly as I got more tired as the night wore on.

Obviously work on the album couldn't interfere with my *EastEnders* schedule, so I had to fit it in after filming. I'd get up at 5.30 a.m., do a twelve-hour day at Elstree, then work on the album at a recording studio in Wood Green in north London until around midnight. While the technicians were listening to the tracks or when we stopped for a break I'd go into a corner with my script and start brushing up on my next day's lines. At home, no sooner had my head hit the pillow, it seemed, than I was up again, ready to become an emotionally wrecked publican facing the most traumatic time of her life. It sounds gruelling, but in fact it was very therapeutic to go off afterwards and sing my heart out: it got the tension out of my system.

I felt awful after I'd rehearsed the first song on the album, 'You Made Me Love You'. I'd been singing it my own way for nearly fifty years, but musical director Peter Murray and his team gave the song a totally different, more laid-back arrangement that was difficult for me, and I walked out of the recording booth to the sound of my own footsteps, thinking, oh, dear, that wasn't very good. Over the following weeks, Peter was very tough with me, forcing me to do things with my voice I'd never done before. At one point, I yelled at him in frustration: 'I've heard that you guys can piddle around with a couple of knobs and make someone sound like you want them to sound!'

Peter laughed. 'Yes, but we're not doing that with you, Miss Windsor.'

Mike Reid came in to sing a duet with me, 'The More I See You', but we had to record our own parts separately because we were laughing so much. We tried desperately hard to sing them together, but it was hopeless: we just kept cracking up.

On set in the Vic, chatting to me over the bar between takes, Steve McFadden said: 'You know, I'd like to sing something with you on your album, Bar.'

'You're joking.'

'No, I'm not. I'm deadly serious.'

I knew Steve could sing, because his mother, Barbara, had told me he'd sung in a church choir as a kid, and I'd heard him singing informally at a couple of parties. When I ran the idea by Telstar, they were thrilled, so Steve came to the studios to record the lovely James Taylor number, 'You've Got a Friend'. As he'd never made a record before, Peter arranged to get his part done first, then mix mine in later. It was more difficult than it sounds: Steve has a most unusual voice and he sang the number in a key I wasn't used to. I had to match my voice to his, which wasn't easy, but Peter made me do it the hard way. And he was right, because the end product was lovely, particularly Steve's rendition: it was brilliant.

I really wanted the great Joe Longthorne on the album, even though he is an unpredictable rascal. As it turned out Joe arrived early, on terrific form, and performed ten versions of 'They Can't Take That Away From Me', each of which was fantastic.

For personal reasons, I also wanted to do a Lionel Bart number, and I felt it had to be 'As Long As He Needs Me'. I knew I could never sing it like the great Miss Bassey or the late, much-lamented Georgia Brown, but I gave it a go. I thought a club-mix version would appeal to Lionel's offbeat sense of humour, so I rang Boy George, who had carved out an additional career for himself as one of Britain's most accomplished and popular disc jockeys, to ask him, more in hope than anticipation, if he would provide a backing track. To my surprise he thought it was a great idea, and suggested I went along to a charity evening at the Dorchester Hotel, where he was appearing that evening, to talk it through. As it happened I was going anyway, and as luck would have it we found ourselves on the same table. As a result of our chat that night a club-mix version of 'As Long As He Needs Me' was released as a single. I found it very difficult to sing, not only because I'd forgotten how hard Lionel's songs were to follow but also because it brought a lump to my throat to be recording the great man's big hit as the last track on my album.

Another track with a personal significance for me was the lovely song 'Little Things Mean a Lot' – because I'd never forgotten the words Florence North wrote in the note I brought home from Blackpool: 'Barbara is only a little thing, but she means a lot to us.' Actually, I wanted to call the album *Little Things Mean a Lot*, but I was outvoted. Instead Telstar chose the title *You've Got a Friend*.

A week before the release of the album, scheduled for Thursday 18 March, I was invited to appear on the *Parkinson* show. The timing could not have been better – the programme was to be recorded on the day of the launch and broadcast the following night – so of course I agreed. But it didn't take long for sheer terror at appearing on such a prestigious show to set in, and I spent the previous weekend throwing up through nerves. I kept telling myself that all I'd be expected to talk about was the album and my *EastEnders* breast cancer scenes, but then, the day before the recording, I had a call to say that Michael Parkinson wanted me to sing as well.

I spent most of that week promoting my album on TV – I did Vanessa Feltz's show, Gaby Roslin's *Whatever You Want, The Good Stuff* and a recording for *TFI Friday* – as well as talking to goodness knows how many newspapers and magazines. It was thanks to Telstar's PR consultant, Jackie Gill, that we managed to cram in so many interviews, and she was a dream to work with. However, the hectic schedule left me no time to rehearse my number with *Parkinson*'s musical director, Laurie Holloway, so he took the arrangement off the album. For some reason, I had chosen 'You Made Me Love You', the song I'd found most difficult to do, but I had every faith in Laurie, who is one of Britain's most gifted musical directors and arrangers. Sure enough, when I had a quick run-through with him a few hours before the show, I performed the song perfectly, but then of course I started to worry – you know the old adage, 'Great rehearsal, lousy performance'.

I'd bought a grey suit for the show, but on my way back to the dressing room after some publicity shots, I noticed that Parky's two other guests, the actor Simon Callow and the comedian Jack Dee, were both wearing grey suits. The lavender suit I'd chosen for the album launch had been lucky for me all day, so I decided to wear that again.

I went to my dressing room with Barry to relax for an hour or so before I was called. But I was so jittery that I had to keep going to the toilet – I must have gone more than a dozen times in an hour. When I wasn't in the loo, I was pacing up and down, not only from the nerves, but also because I didn't want to sit down in case I creased my newly pressed suit. I was desperate to know what the running order was, but the researcher I asked couldn't tell me. So I just kept saying my Hail Marys, praying that I'd be on first so that I could get it over with and then sit back and listen to Simon and Jack, who are both great raconteurs. But then I'd remember that I was going to have to sing at the end anyway. I was in a no-win situation whenever I went on. Barry had never come with me for a chat-show appearance, but on this occasion, because it was *Parkinson*, he had especially asked to accompany me to the studio. He'd thought it would be an exhilarating experience, but seeing me so hyper made him feel ill and he told me he'd never put himself through it again.

Seeing the state I was in, the researcher remarked: 'At least you're still here, Barbara. Warren Beatty was so frightened he ran off, and one of us had to bring him back and reassure him that everything would be all right.'

In the end Jack went first, and got the programme off to a good start; Simon followed him and was wonderfully entertaining. Then it was me. Although I'd never been so wound up about an interview, Michael quickly put me at ease and away we went.

Maybe it was because the researcher had put the idea in my head, I don't know, but for some reason I suddenly found myself mentioning the fact that I'd met Warren Beatty. 'Oh, God,' I said. 'Maybe I'm digging a hole for myself here.'

That, of course, was music to Michael's ears. 'Go on,' he urged. 'Dig it deeper.'

So I told him all about Broadway, and how Warren had rung me three times for a date, and how I regretted not taking him up on it. All in all, it was a simple enough interview which did me no harm at all and allowed me to plug both my album and *EastEnders*. There was one other even more embarrassing moment, though. Earlier in the week, the education minister, David Blunkett, had taken fourteen seconds on a radio programme to do three simple sums – seven-times-eight, nine eights and twelve nines. Afterwards, *The Times* newspaper had phoned me, another politician and a university professor to see how long it took us.

I'd been the quickest, giving the answer to each one in under two seconds, and I was boasting about this to Parky when suddenly he broke in and asked me what four sixes were. And do you know what? My nerves suddenly rushed back and my mind went blank. I just couldn't tell him. What made me even more embarrassed was the fact that *The Times* had quoted me as saying: 'Well, you don't want to look a berk, do you?' Now here I was doing precisely that on national television.

By the time we got to the end of my interview, the relief on my face was visible. Michael turned to Simon again, and I tried to listen to the conversation and join in, but all the time I was panicking that I still had to sing. I was running through the words of 'You Made Me Love You' in my head, kicking myself for having picked it.

But as it turned out, I gave the best rendition of that marvellous love song I'd ever given, finishing with an unplanned, 'You Made Me Love You – and You and You', first to the audience, then to Michael. He loved it and hurried on to the stage at the end to say: 'That was wonderful.'

All in all it was a very successful day, and I'll always remember the *TFI Friday* appearance I recorded earlier because it was the one time I managed to put one over on Chris Evans. He'd been sent a copy of my album, but refused to plug it unless I dressed up in a nurse's uniform. I knew he meant it, because a designer from the programme had rung me to arrange a fitting. At first I'd said I couldn't care less if Chris didn't promote the album, I wasn't going to dress up for him. But then I thought, well, it's only a giggle, so I agreed to have the fitting on condition that Chris wasn't told.

I came on to do the show, and we'd been chatting for a while on the show when I said to Chris, 'Do you know, I think it's rotten you wouldn't play a bit from my album unless I wore a nurse's uniform.'

I don't know whether I embarrassed Chris, but for whatever reason he relented and played a bit of one of the tracks and then gave it a nice plug.

'Thank you so much, darling,' I said. 'And now I've got a surprise for you. I *am* going to dress up for you.'

'You're not!' he exclaimed.

'Yeah, I am. I'll be back.'

And off I went, leaving Chris talking to the former *Starsky and Hutch* stars David Soul and Paul Michael Glaser. When I came back in the nurse's gear, everyone gave me a cheer and Chris said: 'You're such a sport, Babs.'

I did the *Richard and Judy* show that day too, and gave them a particularly candid interview. Neither they nor the technicians ever knew the reason for that. What happened was that, minutes before I was due on, I suddenly needed to go to the loo. Usually I have the microphone fitted after I've sorted myself out, but on this occasion I had been miked up early. In my haste I forgot all about it and the mike slipped out of my tights into the toilet. I quickly pulled it out, dried it as best I could, and stuffed it into my knickers. Someone was calling, 'You're on, Barbara. You're on,' but I was more concerned that I might have ruined the damn thing. If I had, quite apart from costing the company a lot of money, it wouldn't work during the interview. So I came out sheepishly and owned up to the sound man: 'I've got the mike a bit wet, darling,' I said. He tested it and it was working fine, but I hadn't dried it properly and I did the whole interview sitting on a soggy spot. It was great for Richard and Judy because I was so distracted that I answered all their questions – particularly Richard's about my sex life – on autopilot. They were amazed at how frank I was being. When Richard asked if my libido was as strong as it used to be, Judy said: 'You mustn't ask her questions like that,' but I said: 'It's OK, darling. I don't mind.'

'So what do you put it down to?' Richard went on.

'Well, I've got this great new HRT which I rub in . . .'

*　　*　　*

I have to admit that I was dreadfully concerned about Peggy losing a breast. If the public reaction to the episodes in which she'd discovered a lump had been huge imagine what this was going to provoke. If I were in Peggy's shoes I'd have a breast removed, no problem, if that's what the doctors felt needed to be done. But Peggy didn't want to go through all that trauma unless the doctors could guarantee that they could cure the cancer, which they couldn't. There was an added complication, too: Peggy was due to marry Frank Butcher two weeks after losing the breast, and I had to convince the viewers that she would go ahead and do that so soon after such a harrowing experience. It worried me greatly.

What was easy, though, was playing touchy-feely, sexy scenes with Mike Reid: we've known each other thirty-odd years and have always been close. Neither of us wanted to be seen in bed on screen, however. We felt the viewers would prefer to see young people getting it together, not a couple of wrinklies.

Every actor needs a good director for the big scenes, and I was lucky to have one. Her name was Susan Tully, and she had played Michelle Fowler in *EastEnders* for years before embarking on a career the other side of the camera. Susan directed two emotional scenes after Peggy's breast was removed, the first when Peggy left hospital, and the other when she was alone upstairs in the Vic. She gave me two marvellous notes to help me get them both just right.

In the first she told me: 'When you're getting dressed to leave the hospital and you're doing your cardigan up, don't look down when you get to the buttons by your breast, as one would normally. Look away.' I did as she said and it worked brilliantly.

The second scene was the most tearful, and Sue was desperate to get it right in one take because she felt I'd be too emotionally drained to do it again. This was the moment when Peggy opened her dressing gown in front of the mirror to look, for the first time, at where her breast had been removed. It would have been easy to break down and sob, but Sue didn't want that: she wanted Peggy's pain to come out gradually and the tears to trickle down her face slowly. For an actor that is much harder to do, but with Sue's help, I managed it. Infuriatingly, at the vital moment there was a technical hitch and we had to do what everybody on the set hoped we wouldn't have to do – shoot the entire scene again.

Mike, bless him, said to Sue: 'You can't ask the poor girl to go again on that.'

Sue, as much as anyone, knew how deep I'd had to dig for that scene and the last thing she wanted to do was to put me through it again, but she had no choice.

My exhaustion finally caught up with me as we were due to film the end of the episode, and I faced the moment all actors dread: I forgot my lines. To be fair, four or five lines had been rewritten and I hadn't seen them until shortly before filming began, by which time I'd absorbed the original script so well that my brain wouldn't take in anything different. I had a go, but every time I came to the new lines, I made a mistake. After several attempts Mike said: 'Can we stop, please?'

He took me to one side and said gently, 'Now, Bar, how can we help you?'

What I had to say was something like: 'I can't get up there,' but for some reason I couldn't remember 'up there'.

Shaun Williamson, who plays Barry, suggested: 'When you're coming to that line, why not actually look up?'

Happy to try anything, I agreed to give it a go. It sounds daft, but that little tip helped unblock my brain and I got through the scene with no more hiccups.

On the day of the big *EastEnders* wedding I travelled to the church with Mike, Steve, Ross and Sid Owen listening to my real-life album playing on the car's stereo system. The laughter between the five of us as we sang along all the way from Elstree to the beautiful little church in Harrow contrasted sharply with the solemnity of the service as Peggy married Frank.

A few days after the filming of the TV wedding, the *EastEnders* hierarchy held a press launch at the studios. It was organised like a proper wedding reception, with Mike and I arriving in Albert Square in a Roller, all dressed up in our wedding gear. Fact blended with fiction as Mike made a 'bridegroom's' speech to assembled guests, the press included, and then our duet, 'The More I See You', which had been released as a single, got the party going.

It had been a very tiring three months, and Mike, more than anyone, knew how much it had taken out of me. He pulled me to one side at the party and said, 'My little lady, this is all wonderful, doing *EastEnders*, making albums and doing these charity things, but sometimes I think you forget your age. We all know you don't look it, but you've got to rest as much as you can.' Later, he saw me running somewhere and called out: 'There you go again, Windsor. What are your favourite flowers? I must get that wreath made up!'

I couldn't deny that Mike had a point: no sooner had the music stopped than he and I were on our way to Manchester to perform 'The More I See You' at the midweek Lottery draw. I was all for singing live, but when we were given the chance to mime, Mike seized it. 'Why make it hard on ourselves, darling?' he said. Afterwards people said they loved it, but I didn't think we were very good; we weren't in synch, for a start. I was disappointed that neither Mike nor I had had time to do our homework, and for such a big show, we should have done.

One TV programme for which there isn't any homework to do is *Blankety Blank*, and it made a welcome change for me to appear on the show as myself after all those dramatic scenes as Peggy. Paul O'Grady, as the wonderful hostess Lily Savage, was on great form as usual, and gave my album a plug when he introduced me. But he couldn't resist adding: 'I went to a car-boot sale the other day and was going through some records and found some 1930s ones of yours.' As always, we had a terrific time on camera, and off it.

Meanwhile, Scott was doing so well at work that he had been given a pay rise. He was keen to get a mortgage and buy a place of his own. 'Would it upset you if I looked for a flat in Marylebone?' he asked. 'I'd like to be close to you, should anything go wrong, or if you weren't well or needed help.'

I thought that was very sweet. We started flat-hunting in the area, and when I had time off from *EastEnders* I had a look at a few places on my own, but we couldn't find anything suitable in Scott's price range.

I was amazed when I heard that the Variety Club of Great Britain were organising a tribute lunch for me, on 14 April. Only two months before, they had voted me BBC TV Personality of the Year, and it didn't seem possible that they could now want to honour me for services to entertainment. Scott, Robert and Nigel all wanted to come. Nigel was by now no more than just an extremely good friend, but I'd promised to invite him to my next big function; wild horses wouldn't have kept Scott away and I wanted him there. In the event, Robert didn't come because he was upset that he couldn't be with me on the top table, which wasn't possible, but Scott and Nigel were there, and they loved it all as much as I did.

Although it was a memorable day it had a most unhappy start. I was at home being made up at 8 a.m., when a friend phoned to tell me that Tony Newley had died. Although I'd known he was desperately ill, I hadn't expected the cancer to claim him so soon, and I felt terrible.

I made some notes to help me say a few words about him at my lunch.

I had to say something special, too, about another dear friend, Lionel Bart, who had died eleven days earlier. That was easier in a way: I just had to state the simple fact that I'd still be a little-known performer if he hadn't written that little song for me in *Fings*. It gave me great pleasure to tell that huge gathering at the Hilton Hotel just what a fabulous man Lionel had been, and how grateful I was to him.

I had all the time in the world to mention, and thank, others who had played a part in my life, too, and I took full advantage of it. Famous directors, producers, actors – I reeled them all off, and for good measure I threw in a few backstage names no one else would know to appeal to the theatrical people.

Some great film footage of me was shown, and then Ross Kemp and Steve McFadden did a superb job introducing the celebrity guests, one of whom was dear Jim Davidson, who had flown down from Scotland. His speech had everyone in hysterics. He did a perfect impersonation of me on the phone, adding: 'She makes you die. She's so nosy. She wants to know everything – usually who's shagging who.'

Although my relationship with Scott was still platonic, we were becoming closer again. For both of us, familiar feelings were beginning to bubble under the surface, and it was hard for me, at times, to keep my hands off him! All the fame and success in the world means little if you don't have someone you love to share it with. This was brought home to me that May, when I went to two major awards ceremonies and returned home alone after both of them, my sense of pride deflated a little by feelings of emptiness and anticlimax.

The first was the prestigious British Film and Television Awards at the Grosvenor House Hotel. I was hoping that Scott and I would get back together properly, and I decided not to take him because I was concerned that if I did my private life would overshadow the occasion. I didn't want headlines screaming 'BARBARA WINDSOR BACK WITH TOYBOY' when the reason I was there was to pick up an award for Best Soap on behalf of the whole *EastEnders* team. I wore what Mummy would have called a 'proper evening dress' – a beautiful black taffeta gown. Being very old-fashioned, I was scared of showing myself up in front of my bosses, so I didn't have a drop to drink. I just collected the award and was back indoors by 10 p.m., wishing that Scott was there to crack a bottle and help me to celebrate *EastEnders*' success.

Six days later I was on my way to a studio in Wembley for the *Television Soap Awards*, a new show being hosted by Richard Madeley and Judy Finnigan. Again I was prepared to go alone, but Dale Winton was presenting an award, so we went together.

It was a thrilling night for me because I was up for not one but two, awards: Best Actress in a Soap and Best Dramatic Performance. I thought that the breast cancer episodes would put me in with a chance for best performance, but I was sure Patsy Palmer would walk it for best actress. I hoped to win something, of course, but I felt I'd had my fair share, really, with the *Manchester Evening News* and Variety Club awards, so I was pleased simply to have been nominated. When the Best Dramatic Performance went to a young man, Kevin Fletcher, a sixteen-year-old actor in *Emmerdale*, I was disappointed, obviously. I thought, that's it, that was my best chance. Jimmy Nail went up to present the best actress award, and suddenly I heard Julie Goodyear, who was sitting near me, saying, 'Well done, Bar. Well done.' I was in a daze: I'd sat there listening to Jimmy reading out the nominations, fully expecting him to say, '... and the winner is: Patsy Palmer,' and it took a second or two for it to sink in that in fact it was my name he'd read out.

Not having thought about a speech for that award, I just said how lovely it was that people watching *EastEnders* thought I'd been good and should be rewarded. Then I sat down, wishing once again that Scott was there, to give my hand a little squeeze.

Afterwards I said a quick hello to lots of people I hadn't seen for ages, and then I told Dale I was leaving. He said he'd get a taxi home later. When I got into my car, the driver was surprised that I wasn't going out on the town with some mates to celebrate. But that was the last thing on my mind. I just wanted to get home. But I wished, more than anything in the world, that Scott had been there waiting for me.

For the public, awards ceremonies and other televised tributes can be a boring turn-off, with too much banal chatter and not enough razzmatazz. It shouldn't be the case, because Britain has the finest technicians and some of the best performers and musicians in the world, but somehow we do not bring to them a sense of the grand occasion, as the Americans do with the Oscars, for example. Not many people get bored watching that, do they? So I wasn't exactly rushing around in a state of high excitement when the BBC approached me about an hour-long programme to usher in its first-ever *Hall of Fame*. *Hall of Fame*? What's that? I asked. It's a show where your peers in the business come and pay homage to you, I was told. Forget it, I said: I'm lucky to be doing something I love and being paid for it, thank you. Why would I want people

I consider my friends kneeling at my feet paying homage, for God's sake?

Well, it's not exactly 'paying homage', more a cross between *This is Your Life* and *An Audience With*, they said. That was even more of a non-starter: I'd been surprised by *This is Your Life* already, and I didn't consider myself an appropriate candidate for *An Audience With*.

It wasn't until Peter Salmon, the BBC's controller of programmes, compared his concept with the hit American TV show *The Roast* that Barry and I became interested. In that programme, although a famous person is given all sorts of accolades by his peers, what makes it less sycophantic, and more interesting and fun, is that equally famous people come on and perform highlights of the subject's work. So with that sort of format in mind, Barry and I gave Peter the go-ahead to start planning a programme for the following spring to install me in the BBC's *Hall of Fame*.

That May of 1999, I was invited to sit on the judging panel for a new talent show called *Star For a Night*. I wasn't sure I wanted to do it, because I didn't feel equipped to pass judgement, but Peter Salmon thought I'd be perfect because I'd been in the business so long. The pilot went out on a Saturday night and got great viewing figures, and on the strength of that I was asked to appear in a series of six shows to be recorded in Nottingham.

Later that month, John Addy decided to sell the Notting Hill house where Scott was living, so Scott had to move out. He was all for staying with his parents in Brighton and commuting to London until he found somewhere he could afford, but I thought that was crazy when I had a spare bedroom. Scott was not sure about moving into the mews again because he was afraid he might be slipping back into the situation from which he'd run away. But in the end he did move in, and from the word go, it was just right, terrific. He was anxious to keep things light and casual, though, so I paid attention to little details, putting a rail in the office for his clothes, for example: I knew he wouldn't feel comfortable putting them back in the wardrobe as though normal service was being resumed. But he didn't sleep in the spare room, of course; he came into my bed and slept with me. And, yes, we did make love. At first, we would both say, 'This doesn't mean anything. It doesn't mean we're back together,' but I suppose we both knew that we were falling very, very deeply in love all over again. And we were happy to go wherever our hearts led us.

The change in Scott was remarkable. He was eager to get to work every morning, and the paranoia and self-doubt that had stifled him before were replaced by a confidence and strength that were a joy to see. He would talk about his job and his clients with such infectious enthusiasm that I'd get caught up in it, too, always wanting to know if he had managed to get so-and-so fixed up, and who else he had seen. This, in turn, made me comfortable talking about showbiz and *EastEnders*, whereas in the past, I'd felt that was all we ever talked about because Scott had had little of his own to discuss.

When Scott and I started to go out together, it was quite strange. Nobody said: 'Oh, you're back together again.' It just seemed as if he'd never been away. Some people were concerned that I might get hurt again, but I told them that everything was different now because Scott had something in his life that he loved doing and what he did for a living was no longer an issue.

In fact now the phone rang far more often for him than it did for me. One evening, he had five calls in the space of half an hour and I got upset. 'Scott, sweetheart, this is not your business hours, this is *our* time,' I complained. It was ironic when you remember the days when every time I heard the phone I prayed it would be for him.

The change in Scott's drinking habits was particularly welcome. He was back in control. He no longer felt it necessary either to forgo alcohol altogether or to go to the other extreme and drink on and on into the early hours until he was smashed, and it was lovely to be able to enjoy a couple of glasses of wine together again.

32

On Friday 6 August, it would be my sixty-second birthday. Scott kept on about wanting to buy me something, but he didn't know what.

'You know me, love,' I'd say. 'A drop of Shalimar will be fine. That's all I want.'

'But I want to buy you something special,' he'd say.

'Don't worry about it, darling. Whatever you buy will be great. But I'd rather you didn't waste your money.'

The night before my birthday we were sitting up in bed, laughing about something on TV. On the stroke of midnight, Scott took out a card from his bedside drawer and seemed to be covering something with it.

'What are you doing?' I asked.

He didn't reply, just came to my side of the bed, in his boxer shorts, singing, 'Happy birthday, dear Barbara ...' Then he said: 'I've got you a present.'

He obviously wasn't hiding a parcel behind his back, so I joked: 'It can't be very big, then.'

He dropped the card on the bed and opened a small box he had been concealing underneath it: inside was a solitaire diamond ring. Then he went down on one knee and asked: 'My darling Barbara. Will you marry me?'

I didn't know what to say. Scott would never have let my birthday pass without buying me something, but I hadn't expected this. Suddenly I felt very shy. And tearful.

'Oh, darling, yes,' I said.

We hugged and kissed. Then Scott went back to his side of the bed. We were both full of excitement and relief, along with a sense of wondering why we had had to go through all the pain of our break-up when this was so obviously the way our lives were meant to be. Together. As I examined my lovely diamong ring, Scott said: 'I hope you like it, Bar. It's not the best, but it's all I could afford at this time in my life.'

I told him not to be so silly and said I loved it, but he obviously had a thing about it. Although I was Bar to him, and he knew I wasn't big-time, he was still worried that I should have the best. As he put it: 'You may be good old Bar to most people, but never forget that you're a star, and people will expect to see the Rock of Gibraltar hanging off your finger.' He meant it in the nicest way; he didn't want me to be embarrassed by the ring. I reassured him. We both fell into a sound and contented sleep.

The only people we told were Scott's parents. It was hard for us, keeping such lovely news from close friends like Dale, Paul and Barry, but we didn't want it leaking out and the papers going mad. I couldn't wear the ring until it had been cut to size, but then, very proudly, I put it on when I joined Lucy Benjamin, Danniella Westbrook, Lucy Speed and a couple of others from *EastEnders* for dinner at Joe Allen's one night. Halfway through the evening, we were chatting about nothing in particular when Lucy Benjamin suddenly touched the ring. 'That's nice,' she said. I was tempted to tell them, but Scott and I had agreed that Barry would put out an official statement the following Monday, so I passed it off as a family heirloom.

The next day, a Saturday, Scott and I were returning home after some shopping when a photographer almost literally jumped out on us as we turned into the mews. He was very polite and asked if he could take a picture. 'Of course you can, darling,' I said. 'I hope you earn a few quid.'

He was quick to notice my ring, 'Ooh, are you engaged, Bar?'

I just laughed. 'Yeah.'

We got home and said: 'Well, that's it now.'

That evening, Paul rang from his office at the *Sunday Mirror* to say that he had been offered a picture of me wearing the ring. The paper ran the engagement story in their first edition and, of course, that night the others came on too, catching up for their own later editions. The *News of the World* editor, Phil Hall, sent a photographer round with a bottle of champagne to persuade us to talk to them, then changed his front page and two pages inside to accommodate the story of Scott's romantic birthday proposal. Scott and I were amazed: we could not take it in that our engagement was front-page news. I've had a few front pages in my time, but that one was special.

About 2,000 people in Great Yarmouth didn't have to wait for the Sunday papers. The same evening Scott phoned his pal Roger Kitter, who was appearing with Jim Davidson at the Wellington Pier. Roger took the call on his mobile as he watched Jim from the wings. When Scott told him we were getting married, Roger went on stage and relayed the news to Jim.

The next thing, Jim was on the phone, talking to me in front of the audience. 'Hello, Babs, how are ya?'

'I'm OK, darling,' I said.

'Roger's just told me you're going to get married. Is that right?'

I said that it was, and heard him tell the audience: 'Ladies and gentlemen, Barbara Windsor's got engaged!' Then he said to me: 'Oh, blimey, does that mean a blow job's out of the question?'

'Oh, yeah,' I replied. 'That's it, you've had it now. I can't do that any more.'

He turned back to the audience. 'Now come on, everyone, say, "Congratulations, Barbara."'

I heard them yell: '*Congratulations, Barbara!*'

Jim said to me: 'Is it to my mate Scotty?'

'Yeah.'

'Oh, well done. Anyway, I've got to go now, but hold on just a minute.'

It all went quiet and muffled for a few seconds. Jim had obviously put his hand over the mouthpiece. Then he was back, and asking the audience: 'Now, what are you going to say to Barbara?'

I thought they were going to shout 'Good luck, Bar,' or something like that, but down the line came a deafening: '*FUCK OFF!*'

I was still roaring with laughter long after I rang off.

The reaction on Sunday and throughout the week was staggering. We received cards, phone calls and messages on the answerphone from people we knew and congratulations in the street from people we didn't. Everyone, it seemed, was happy for us. What a difference, I thought, from those troublesome early days when nasty-minded gossips jealous of our happiness did their damnedest to break us up.

Everybody wanted to know when the wedding would be, but in my own mind, I hadn't got that far. We told some friends we might just pop round the corner to Marylebone Register Office. They were shocked. 'Oh, you can't do that,' they said. 'The public wouldn't like it. You should have a big wedding.' I must admit that part of me did want to make it a big occasion, maybe a huge, typical East End wedding, with all my mates invited. After all, my two previous weddings had not been much to write home about: at the first it had rained, I'd cried and we ended up in a pub afterwards; the Caribbean setting for the second had been magical, but the ceremony had been a small, impersonal affair with strangers as witnesses. But there was no rush. For now Scott and I were more than happy to just enjoy being an engaged couple and to bask in the warmth our love had generated among my friends and fans.

The following month, *OK!* boss Richard Desmond set up a holiday in Marbella as an engagement present for Scott and me – and I ended up being fined by *EastEnders* and reprimanded for the first time in my career. It was all because *OK!* used the names of some commercial products and a particular dress designer in the story that accompanied photographs of Scott and me. My *EastEnders* contract forbids me from advertising, but of course I'd had no idea that anything was going to be plugged in the piece. When I found out I went to see Matthew Robinson and apologised. I thought that would be the end of the matter, but the next day I received a letter telling me I was being fined £3,000. If I hadn't apologised, I'm sure the fine would have been £5,000. Richard was very upset at having embarrassed me and, being an honourable gentleman, arranged for the magazine to pay the fine.

I'd never wanted anyone to make a dummy out of me until Madame Tussaud's wrote that September asking if they could immortalise me in wax. Of course I said yes – who wouldn't? I was deeply honoured and flattered to have been chosen as Tussaud's first soap actress. Living near Baker Street, I see the long queues for the the waxworks nearly every day, and it gave me a huge thrill to think I'd be standing there alongside many of the famous names I'd worked with over fifty years.

I took the whole thing very seriously. When I went for my first sitting in October, I sorted out some red satin shoes and bought a matching dress made of red jersey and a fine fishnet gauze. 'I'm not your normal shape,' I told them. 'You won't be able to buy a dress for me, and shoes will be hard to find, because I'm only size two.' I took along some photographs, too, but I needn't have bothered, because the sculptor, a lovely man named Stephen Mansfield, took 150 pictures himself, from every conceivable angle.

They asked me to strike a pose that I felt was 'me', so I did a sort of showbizzy, one arm up, one down pose as though I was greeting a friend I was pleased to see. What they didn't tell me was that I would have to hold that pose for the next two hours while stuck on a wheel that went round and round so that they could measure every part of me and take all the photographs. It was all very painstaking and I was very pleased when they said I was one of the more patient and professional personalities they had worked with. Apparently a lot of people get fed up with sitting or standing around for so long, and simply send in a photo and let them get on with it. But Tussaud's has been special to me since I was a kid, and I was prepared to go through anything to help make my figure as lifelike as possible. My patience was put to the test a week later, though, when I got a call asking me to go through the whole procedure again because Stephen wasn't satisfied with his pictures. After that I went back for two more sessions, for eyes and hands, and then it was just a question of waiting for the Great Unveiling. I was told it would take six months to complete the figure, and judging by the meticulous care everyone took over the tiniest detail, I could well believe it. I was told I would be placed at a cocktail party with other celebs like the actress Joanna Lumley and model Naomi Campbell. I was to be glad I put in that time, and grateful for the hard work of everyone at Madame Tussaud's, when I saw the result, which was wonderful. Yet again, I found myself wishing Mummy could have been alive to share the experience. My Babs in Madame Tussaud's! Now that is something she would have wanted to tell her friends.

One morning towards the end of October, I developed severe pains in my stomach. I'd had bad pains most of the year, particularly during the stressful cancer scenes for *EastEnders*. It felt as if I'd eaten the sourest apples ever. Sometimes I'd make an excuse that nature called and go and sit in my dressing room, hugging myself until it went away. But this time the pain wasn't just bad, it was excruciating. I was doubled over in the kitchen, and it frightened the life out of me, because uppermost in my mind was an image of poor Len, doubled up in the same way at Stanmore, and what the cause of that had turned out to be. My doctor arranged for me to see a specialist, Dr Ackle, a top bowel man. He said I would have to go into hospital for tests.

'Oh, God, when?'

'As soon as possible,' he told me. 'I don't like the look of it.'

The night before I was due to go into the London Clinic, Scott and I were sitting up in bed, resting against the pillows, holding hands and talking. We were both thinking about the 'C' word, but neither of us mentioned it. I knew exactly what was going through Scott's mind; it was written all over his face and I could hear it in his voice. 'I went away from this lady I loved and came back into her life and asked her to be my wife and now, just when we are happy and planning a future together, she is going to be taken away from me.'

I tried to put on a brave face, but I was pretty sure that they'd have to open me up to see what was wrong, and goodness knew what they were going to find. 'I'm OK at the moment, darling,' I said. 'But I don't know how I'll be tomorrow if it's not good news.'

In spite of my high pain threshold, I was in such agony I was unable to keep down any of the various concoctions I'd been given to prepare me for the investigation. In the morning I phoned the doctor, who told me not to take any more; he would give me an enema when I got to the hospital. The next day, as I went under the anaesthetic, I heard Dr Ackle saying: 'Don't worry, Barbara, everything is going to be all right.' I didn't share his optimism, but when I came round, he was patting my cheeks and telling me, 'Barbara, it's not cancer. You're going to be OK.'

I had to stay in an extra day for more tests and they diagnosed diverticulitis, an inflammation of the lining of the intestine. It's a right bastard when it comes on, but at least it wasn't what Scott and I had dreaded, and we counted our blessings that we could still make plans for our married life.

That scare apart, it had been a fabulous year. I'd been voted best soap actress, honoured by the Variety Club, chosen as the first entrant in the BBC's *Hall of Fame*. And now I had my lovely Scott back in my life. Just when I was thinking that 1999 couldn't possibly get any better, it did. In the second post, on 12 November, I was astounded to find a letter that had been sent from 10 Downing Street. It read:

IN CONFIDENCE

Dear Madam,

The Prime Minister has asked me to inform you, in strict confidence, that he has it in mind, on the occasion of the forthcoming list of New Year Honours, to submit your name to the Queen with a recommendation that Her Majesty may be graciously pleased to approve that you be appointed a Member of the Order of the British Empire.

Before doing so, the Prime Minister would be glad to know that this would be agreeable to you. I should therefore be grateful if you would complete the enclosed form and sent it to me by return of post.

If you agree that your name should go forward and the Queen accepts the Prime Minister's recommendation, the announcement will be made in the New Year Honours List. You will receive no further communication before the List is published.

I am, Madam

Your obedient servant,

William Chapman.

I was flabbergasted. My first thoughts were for Mummy: she had adored the royal family and she would have been so proud that her Babs was going to Buckingham Palace to be honoured by the Queen.

I'm quite good at keeping secrets and there was no way I'd risk missing out on the award by telling anyone in case the press found out. I desperately wanted to tell Scott, though. I had to wait until he came home at 6.30, and even then I was a bit embarrassed about it, because deep down I didn't think I was worthy of an MBE, and I've never been one for making a big thing out of good news. So we talked about his day for a while, and then I said: 'You'll never guess what. I've got an MBE.'

'*What?*' Scott was wide-eyed, open-mouthed. 'I can't believe it! That's bloody fantastic!'

The next morning, I phoned Barry and told him, swearing him to secrecy, of course. After that, the three of us had to keep our excitement to ourselves. For the next few days, I was head over heels with joy, and one evening I found myself literally head over heels as well – with painful results. Lying on the bed reading an *EastEnders* script, I leaned backwards to get a pen off the bedside table without realising how near the edge I was and I toppled over, slicing a lump out my shin. For the next couple of weeks, my leg was so swollen I couldn't bear to wear a shoe and I had to stand behind the bar in the Vic with one high heel on and the other leg swinging.

That November, just after I'd drawn a raffle at a charity function organised by the jewellers and silversmiths Mappin and Webb, a sweet young man in his thirties tapped me on the shoulder and introduced himself as Neil Cunningham.

'Oh, I've heard of you,' I said. 'You make those wonderful frocks, don't you?'

He said: 'I'd love to make something for you one day. As a present.'

I laughed. 'You won't be able to make anything for me, sweetheart. I'm not built like a plank.'

'That's why I'd like to make something for you,' Neil told me. 'You've got such a wonderful, shapely figure.'

What a fortuitous tap on the shoulder that was to prove to be for me.

All in all, it had been an amazing year for me, and I was delighted that Terry Johnson's *Carry on Cleo, Camping, Emmanuelle and Dick* had enjoyed such success as well. Not only had the play been wonderfully reviewed, picked up several awards and completed a national tour, but there were now plans to take it to a wider audience. 'You'll never believe this, Bar,' Barry told me on the phone. 'ITV want to make a film of the play.'

I was really pleased to be asked to be an adviser on the film. Over lunch at Quo Vadis in Soho, Barry, Terry, the television producer and I talked about the possibility of me playing some kind of cameo role as well. They felt it would give the piece my tacit stamp of approval, a little extra kudos. The question was, what role exactly? I didn't want to make a fleeting appearance as another character, or simply as an extra, as others had done, but featuring as myself would be tricky – after all, I was sixty-two, and Samantha Spiro was a girl of thirty playing me at thirty-eight.

However, we wondered whether perhaps it might work in the very last scene with Kenny, after Sid's death. I've often noticed that people don't seem to think of the Carry On personalities as being any particular age – we seem to have this timeless quality to us. For example, it doesn't seem to register with Carry On fans that Sid died over twenty years ago: even now I will get into a taxi and the driver will talk to me about him as though he is still alive.

Terry and the producer thought this was a terrific idea, but I was still not really sure whether it would come off. In the end I agreed to do it on the condition that two versions of the final scene were shot, one with me and one with Sam, to be on the safe side, and assured the producer that I wouldn't be precious about it if they felt mine didn't work. To get the look I wanted I went through a lot of old pictures and chose one from one of my first photographic shoots, a photo of Ronnie and me at home having breakfast, in which my hair was loosely pinned up and off my face, a style Ronnie loved.

Several more characters were written in for the film, including Charlie Hawtrey, Joan Sims and Kenneth Connor, and it was given a new title: *Cor Blimey!* It was shown on television the following year to wide critical acclaim. Geoffrey Hutchings as Sid, Adam Godley as Kenny and Samantha playing me again received good reviews, and Terry was praised for his craft in adapting his play for the screen.

My final scene was indeed used, and when I saw it I felt it worked really well. I think my appearance as myself added an extra poignancy to the end of the film and touched a chord with the public. And the wig I wore based on that hairstyle was just right. It was a nice feeling to see myself on the screen with that look after so many years.

While everyone else was making a big deal about New Year's Eve, Scott and I had no idea what we wanted to do. In fact we couldn't wait for it to be over. Then I got a call from the BBC asking me to make the Lottery draw at the Millennium Dome. It was the perfect solution, particularly as our pal Dale Winton would be presenting the show. Maybe the three of us could see in the new millennium quietly on our own.

Leading up to Christmas, I had everything mapped out: I was winding down from *EastEnders*; my *Hall of Fame* was taking shape; I'd signed for eight more appearances on *Star For a Night*; I was going to be a waxwork dummy in Madame Tussaud's, and after Christmas in Brighton, and four days relaxing at Henlow Grange, I was going to work on my autobiography. Everything, as they say these days, was sorted.

But then I got the flu, which set off my stomach problem again, and before I knew it I seemed to be spending more time in the loo than anywhere else. How I got through Christmas dinner with Scott's parents and their friends, I don't know. Being pampered at the health farm should have been a heavenly experience, but I was bedridden for two days, and in the end Scott said: 'I can't swim in the pool, have a massage or enjoy a meal while you're ill in bed. I'd rather be at home.' So home we went, and I carried on being ill in familiar surroundings.

By New Year's Eve I was no better, but of course I couldn't pull out of the Lottery show. Actually appearing in front of the cameras wasn't the problem, it was crawling out of bed, getting into a dress and heels and putting on a face after nearly a week of lying around doing nothing but feeling sick. I thought, I'll just get to the Television Centre at White City, do my bit and turn round and go home. I was back in Marylebone tucked up in bed by 11 p.m. Scott joined me and, as the rest of the country began the exciting countdown to the new century, we were watching TV. At midnight, I insisted Scott had a glass of champagne. I would have liked to have joined him, but I knew I'd only throw up. Everyone has their own memories of how they saw in the new millennium. Now you know mine.

Scott and I were certain that we wanted to get married in 2000. What we were less sure of was what sort of wedding to have. Our friends were still all for a huge affair but, to be honest, we couldn't afford it without selling exclusive rights to a magazine, and that would involve so many restrictions that it would become a nightmare. Neither Scott nor I wanted to be told what we could or couldn't do on our special day. So we started thinking about a smaller wedding, with perhaps thirty or so guests. But then who would we invite and who would we leave out? Whatever we did, we were bound to upset a lot of people.

It all started to get me down. As well as *EastEnders*, I was having to travel to Nottingham every two weeks for *Star For a Night*, and my mind was buzzing; it was all too much. At two o'clock one morning, Scott and I woke up at the same time. He said suddenly: 'Do you really want a big-deal wedding?'

'No,' I heard myself say. 'Do you?'

'No,' he said.

'Well then, don't let's have one. Let's have a quiet one.'

And do you know, the moment we'd had that brief conversation, we both heaved a sigh of relief and went back to sleep, a huge weight off our minds. Over the next few days, we decided to go for a hush-hush affair without telling anyone but family, not even our dearest, closest friends. It was going to be difficult to pull off, but we were determined to try.

I was scheduled to have the whole of June off from *EastEnders*, so Scott and I chose the sixteenth as the big day. But then I was told that Albert Square's Italian family, the Di Marcos, were being written out of the show and schedules were being rejigged: I was going to be working in June after all.

Then we decided on April. The show's new boss, John Yorke, said he could guarantee I wouldn't be working on Saturday the eighth. I had to tell him why I needed to know, but made him promise not to tell a soul. And he didn't – thank you, John. I contacted a lady named Siobhan Craven Robbins, a former beautician who was now a wedding co-ordinator. I asked her if she could arrange the ceremony at the Dorchester Hotel, in a suite as high up as possible, so that Scott and I could look out over Hyde Park. The Dorchester was special to me because it was the first posh hotel I ever went to, and Scott was happy with the idea of getting married there. Siobhan came back within the hour, saying everything was fixed: the wedding would take place at 1.30 p.m. and she had booked us into a suite on the eighth floor. So far, so good. But as it turned out, things weren't going to be quite that simple.

Mike Reid and I had been off screen for nearly twenty episodes – a lot for major characters – but now we had a big storyline coming up – plus an extra one for Mike I knew nothing about – and there was a lot of work ahead. But I was a bit worried about Mike. Steve McFadden said to me one day at the end of January, 'Mike doesn't look too good to me, Bar. I think John Yorke should have a word with him.' It was true: he seemed stressed and was sweating a lot. I asked him if he was all right, but he passed it all off as the after-effects of the flu he had had before Christmas. The following week we had done a couple of scenes and were preparing to do a third when Carolyn Weinstein, *EastEnders'* administration manager, came on to the set to talk to the director. Then she had a word with Mike and asked him to come and speak to her in her office. Mike looked at me like a little boy and held his hands up. Neither he nor I knew what to make of it.

Evidently the *EastEnders* bosses didn't think Mike was looking very well, and had been watching our scenes closely on the monitors. He was taken to see a doctor, and when we came back from lunch we were told that Mike was being given leave from the show to recover. The next thing I heard was that Mike and his wife, Shirley, had flown to their villa in Benalmadena, in Spain.

I was sorry Mike wasn't well, but quietly pleased that our big storyline would have to be put on hold. However, if I thought it would relieve the pressure on me, I was sadly mistaken. When I was called into the office the next day, John Yorke told me that the scriptwriters had already kicked into a heavy storyline involving Mike, and we had to continue with it. 'I'm very sorry, Barbara,' he said. 'Peggy is the only link that will make the storyline work. I'm afraid it's going to mean a hell of a lot of work for you.'

He was right about that. There was masses of dialogue originally written for Mike for me to learn, and what made it more difficult was that it was all about cars and meant working with Tony Caunter, who plays Roy, with whom I'd hardly ever acted before. In addition to that I still had my own storyline, and with Sid Owen, as Ricky, having to take over some of Mike's stuff, the scripts were being written as we went along, from day to day. It was frenetic. I'd get to the studios at 7.30 a.m., film all morning, then stay in my dressing room with a sandwich at lunchtime, learning my lines for the afternoon. Most days I didn't finish until 7 p.m., and I'd be in bed by eleven at the latest with the next day's lines to learn. Usually I didn't get to sleep until 1 a.m.

For such a special show as my *Hall of Fame*, obviously I had to have a special dress so I took up Neil Cunningham's offer to make something for me. After trying several styles, I settled on a full-length purple jersey forties-style dress, which looked absolutely fabulous. With that organised, I relaxed, confident that everything was being arranged the way I would want it, and that all I had to worry about was the night itself.

But then Dale came to see me, very concerned that the programme was not going to turn out the way I expected, and suggested I went to see Richard Wolff, the producer of Planet 24, the company making the show for the BBC, to ask him what he had lined up. I was relieved to hear that Warren Beatty had agreed to do a live phone link from Los Angeles, and that Joan Collins was going to record a filmed message, but little else seemed to have been arranged.

I suggested that perhaps Martin Kemp might sing 'Mack the Knife' from *The Threepenny Opera*, Martine could do something from *Sparrows Can't Sing* and Shaun Williamson, Dean Gaffney and Sid Owen could perform a parody *of Fings Ain't Wot They Used T'Be*. It sounds like I wanted the Hall of Fame to be an *EastEnders* vehicle, but that wasn't the case: all those people had wonderful voices and I felt the viewers would enjoy seeing them entertaining me.

Richard knew I wanted the programme to include 'Take Back Your Mink', the fantastic dance routine I'd performed in *Guys and Dolls*, and we were both thrilled when Tracy Bennett from *Coronation Street* agreed to be the lead singer. But getting four girls to back her proved more difficult. Richard went for two girls from *EastEnders*, Lucy Speed and Lucy Benjamin, and two former members of the cast, Sophie Lawrence and Danniella Westbrook. Sadly, commitments at Elstree meant that the two Lucys were unavailable, so two of my great friends, Cheryl Baker and Linda Lusardi, stepped in.

But I was very worried about Danniella. It was well known that she'd had a drug problem and could be very unreliable. I felt the need to rehearse her routine might put her under pressure and that she might weaken, so when she rang me, all excited about performing for me, I said: 'You don't need to do it, darling. It would be lovely if you could just be there on the night.'

'No, no, Mum,' she told me. 'I want to do it.'

Ever since she'd played my daughter in *EastEnders*, Danniella had called me 'Mum'. I hated it, but put up with it because it seemed to make her happy. I'd always been one of Danniella's supporters. She was in *EastEnders* long before I was and I thought she was the most stunning-looking young woman and an accomplished actress as well. She left before I joined but later returned to the show. I was shocked by her erratic behaviour on the set. One minute you could be talking to her in the Vic, and the next she'd be slumped across the bar, fast asleep. Then she'd wake up and start talking nineteen to the dozen. We might be in the middle of rehearsing a scene when a breakfast would come over and Danniella would be so hungry she'd shove a load of eggs and sausages down her throat. Everybody was understanding and kind to her, but she really was a mess. I remember Mike Reid remarking to me: 'Oh, God, such a pretty face, and she's ageing before us.'

The *EastEnders* bosses gave Danniella chance after chance, but she was so unreliable, holding up filming by arriving late, or not turning up at all, that in 1995, her contract was not renewed. There was talk of giving her a third chance. When Danniella heard about it on the grapevine, she rang me, pleading: 'You'll stand by me, Mum, you'll stick up for me, won't you? I'm going to beg for this part.'

Matthew Robinson called me in and asked me what I thought about the idea of Danniella being taken on again. 'Oh, yes,' I said at once. 'Please give the girl a chance. She'll be great. And I'll be there for her.' When others in the cast heard what I'd said, they all told me I was mad (though their language was rather more emphatic than that). 'Do you really want to hang around wondering if the girl is going to bother to turn up?' they asked me. They had a point. We all work at such a pace, and under such pressure, that all you want, really, is for your colleagues to arrive on time having learned their lines.

In the end Danniella was given another chance, but when she arrived, she looked awful. It wasn't just the loss of her looks that was so shocking, it was the state of her nose. She'd been in a car accident and the septum of her nose, weakened by snorting cocaine, had crumpled, leaving her with one big nostril instead of two small separate ones. I was so concerned about her that I suggested she was given a dressing room near me so that I could keep an eye on her. Stupid, really, because if someone wants to take cocaine all they need to do is to go into the toilet and do it.

Although I have never had a strong maternal instinct, I do feel I could have been a good mother. I really do care about young people. I'm the one whose dressing-room door is always open for any youngster who has a problem he or she wants to talk through. And of course, I've always got the odd aspirin or condom. In the following months Danniella and I became close. We bought each other Christmas and birthday presents, and she would turn up unexpectedly on my doorstep for a chat. One day I said to her: 'Let's get your nose fixed for you, darling. Let's do something about it.' She seemed keen, so I arranged for us to see one of Harley Street's top plastic surgeons. 'You will come, won't you, Danniella?' I said. 'You will keep the appointment?'

Danniella didn't let me down. She turned up at the right time and we went to see this wonderful surgeon who said he could fix her nose by grafting on skin from her arm. *EastEnders* were going to give her six weeks off for the treatment, but the next thing we knew she was leaving, 'by a mutual decision', because she had a film and various other projects lined up. If that was true I was pleased for her, but I couldn't help feeling a deep sadness that she might not fulfil the promising future she had in the business.

If I needed proof that my sympathy and understanding for the young lady were misplaced, I got it during the build-up to my *Hall of Fame*. After Danniella was approached, she rang me at least six times in the space of a fortnight to say how thrilling it all was. But in the final two weeks before the show, no one seemed able to get hold of her. Danniella had been given dates for costume-fitting, singing, musical direction with the pianist and choreography, but kept none of them. I didn't know about any of this until the Monday before the show, when the costume designer told me she didn't know what to do about Danniella's costume because she hadn't turned up for a fitting or rehearsals. Cheryl, Linda and Sophie arrived for rehearsal that day, but there was no Danniella. The major rehearsal was planned for the Wednesday. Someone rang Danniella's number, and was assured by the person who answered that she'd be there.

'Don't hold your breath,' I said.

The next day, Richard Wolff called me. 'I hear you don't think Danniella will turn up.'

'No, not now,' I said. 'It's too late.'

'She has promised through whoever it is we speak to on the phone that she will definitely, *definitely*, be there tomorrow.'

I didn't know what to say to that. Given Danniella's track record, anything could happen.

Although Danniella had not been to any meetings, knew nothing of the routine, she'd said she would be able to pick it up. And since she was an accomplished singer and dancer from the eminent Sylvia Young School, she had been given the benefit of the doubt.

The call for Wednesday's rehearsal was 2 p.m. for everybody. At 1.30 p.m., someone rang the producer's office to say that Danniella was on her way. Twenty minutes later, the same person rang again, this time saying that Danniella wouldn't be able to make it because she had a cold. But she might come on Sunday, the night the *Hall of Fame* was being filmed.

When I was told that Danniella had said she 'might' come on the night I blew my stack and went to see Barry to ask if he felt it would be right for me to phone her agent, Sylvia Young. He did, so I spoke to Sylvia, who I admire greatly, and told her the whole sorry story. 'Could you possibly tell Danniella that I would rather she didn't come to my *Hall of Fame*?' I asked. Sylvia was as sad as me about what had happened and promised to speak to Danniella.

It is at times like this that you find out who your real friends are, and Debbie Magee proved that she was certainly one of them. Debbie was due to spend that March weekend in Amsterdam with her magician husband Paul Daniels, but when she got a last-minute call asking her to do my show, she cancelled the trip, got up at 7 a.m. the next day, went in for costume fittings and picked up the routine in an hour.

At the last moment the producers decided they wanted me to sing. I wasn't keen, because I wanted to relax and enjoy the show without having to worry about performing myself, but in the end I agreed to do a version of 'The Sunny Side of the Street', with alternative lyrics written by Eric Merriman to reflect my own life.

As it turned out, when I arrived on the afternoon of the show, with Neil Cunningham, who had designed and made my dress, Gary, my make-up man and my hairdresser, Matthew, I felt really good. My dressing room was full of flowers and champagne, and there I was, all dressed up and feeling a million dollars, and all I had to do apart from that one song was go out and enjoy a show being put on for me by other people. For the first time in my life I had no nerves whatsoever; I couldn't believe how cool I felt. I think it was because, apart from the few suggestions I'd made to Richard Wolff, I had no idea what was going to happen so I couldn't worry about it. 'Now remember, Bar, this is a big, big tribute to you,' Scott told me in the dressing room. 'So don't just rush down the stairs and say, "Hello, everybody!" like you usually do. Take it slowly and count to six before you speak.'

In the event the audience reaction was so amazing that I counted to ten. I had to make my entrance down a staircase, and because the steps were very deep, Richard chose two young men of the same height, for balance, to walk me down them. It was a first-ever TV appearance for them and they were so excited. When we reached the foot of the stairs and I kissed them both they were over the moon. I'd never known anything like that applause. I just stood there, with my arms stretched out, for what seemed like ages, before Dale introduced me.

The audience were seated at tables, as if in a nightclub. I looked out at them, but being so tiny, I couldn't see who was there. However, during the course of the show I picked out so many of my showbiz friends, past and present, from over the years that it was overwhelming. Eddie Woodward and Danny La Rue were there, along with my *EastEnders* colleagues – I could see Steve McFadden smiling at me from one of the front tables.

Dale asked me about *Love From Judy* and *Guys and Dolls*, and I told him that *Guys and Dolls* had been a favourite ever since I'd seen Sid James in the show. Then, after a clip from *Sparrows Can't Sing* was screened, I got the surprise of my life. For there, walking out on to the stage, was none other than Joan Littlewood. I was completely staggered. Joan lived in France and never came out for anybody – even for my *This is Your Life* she'd sent a recorded message – but here she was. I just cuddled her and told her, 'I can't believe you're here!'

''Course I'm here,' she said. ''Cos you're a star. The trouble with other stars is half of them can't act like you.'

Ripples of excitement were going round the audience – 'That's *the* Joan Littlewood!', younger actors who had never seen Joan were commenting with awe. I am always being asked by other actors, 'You knew Joan Littlewood – what was she like? Tell us about her,' and I think the fact that she turned out for my *Hall of Fame* impressed some of my *EastEnders* colleagues no end.

The tributes from all my friends were just wonderful. Eddie Woodward brought tears to my eyes when he talked about acting with me in *Many Happy Returns* all those years ago. 'You were eighteen years old, sitting on a stool, singing a song about a teddy bear. You were slightly pulchritudinous. You didn't know what you were singing; you were a tiny, voluptuous lady and we loved you.'

Not everything the producers had planned came off: Warren Beatty's promised phone call didn't happen because they couldn't get him on the day, and neither did Joan Collins' filmed tribute, but although the show was not a favourite with the critics, the public loved it, and it was an amazing accolade. As well as the award, which was presented to me by Ross Kemp, I received a *This is Your Life*-type book as a memento of the occasion.

After Debbie Magee had so kindly and professionally stepped in to replace Danniella Westbrook for my *Hall of Fame*, the next time I spoke to Paul Daniels, he said: 'You owe me one.'

'Just let me know,' I told him.

Two days later, he phoned asking me if I'd attend a charity dinner at which it was hoped to raise £1 million for a children's hospital in Bristol. I was supposed to be going to Sid Owen's farewell party, but I could hardly refuse after what Debbie had done for me. I went, of course, and it ended up costing me £5,000!

In the middle of an auction of wonderful donations, Paul jumped on to the stage to offer one of his own. He would throw open his home in Reading, lay on fireworks, perform magic and invite famous people for the highest bidder and his friends. He really built it all up and was thrilled when the bidding reached £6,500. When the auction was over, however, the one person who could not be found was the man who'd bid for Paul's prize.

Ed Stewart, the disc jockey, who had been conducting the auction with the former Cabinet minister David Mellor, apologised to everyone and said they were going to start the auction for the house party again. But by then the auction was all over, everyone's money was spent, and they knew there wasn't a hope of raising another £6,500 for Paul's generous prize. My heart went out to Paul, because he works very hard for charity. Ed asked for a new bid of £5,000, which was the amount needed for the proceeds of the dinner to reach the magic million. I looked at Scott and said: 'I've had a fantastic year. I've had the *Hall of Fame*, been awarded the MBE and we're getting married. I want to bid that.'

Scott just said: 'If it will make you feel good, do it.'

So I stuck my hand up. 'I'll bid five thousand.'

'Oh, Barbara, please,' said Ed.

'No, no, I want it, really,' I insisted. Paul looked at me with a smile.

I couldn't afford the five grand, but I just thought, oh well, I'll worry about that tomorrow.

By the last week of March, I still hadn't found a dress for the wedding, so I rushed down to Neil Cunningham in a bit of a panic. 'I know you're very busy making all the wedding gowns at the moment, Neil,' I said, 'but do you think you could make me a little peachy, powdery-type floaty dress?'

'Is this for a special day?' Neil asked.

I couldn't say it wasn't, because if it hadn't been a special occasion the dress wouldn't have been needed in such a rush. So I just replied, 'Yes, I want to look my best. But it must be ready by 6 April.'

I was relieved and delighted when Neil said he could do it. I'm sure he knew what the dress was for, but he didn't press me about it, bless him. Neither did Jimmy Choo, when I asked him to make me a pair of shoes to match the fabric I took from Neil. He just smiled and asked: 'These are very, very special shoes?'

On Thursday 6 April the gods must have been looking down on me, because I finished on *EastEnders* at lunchtime, and found out I would be free on Friday as well. This meant I could bring forward an appointment to have my nails done, leaving me all of Friday to prepare for the wedding. Not that there was much to prepare: all we really had to do was get ourselves to the Dorchester on time. Scott picked me up from Super Nail at six and we went home with a couple of steaks, opened a bottle of wine and tumbled into bed, counting down the hours until Saturday.

At 3 a.m., I sat bolt upright, jumped out of bed and screeched: 'Aaarrgh! My frock! My dress!'

I was supposed to have had a fitting at 5.30 that day, but in my excitement at getting the afternoon off I had forgotten all about it. Terrified I'd forget again later in the morning, I got a pen and paper and wrote myself a note: 'Must pick up dress. MUST PICK UP DRESS'.

I did pick it up, of course, but afterwards, when I was getting everything together, I could not find the exquisite Theo Fennel cross Richard Desmond had bought me as an engagement present, which I'd planned to wear for the wedding. Not wanting to admit that I'd lost it, I rang the store in Fulham and asked if I could borrow a pendant over the weekend as I'd left my jewellery in an hotel and had no time to collect it.

Theo's staff could not have been more charming or helpful. They insisted I took several items and I walked out, shaking, with fifty grand's worth of jewellery in my bag: pendants, earrings, necklace, you name it. 'We must get it insured, Scott,' I said on the way home. I phoned my accountant, Mark Gold, who said he would take care of things, but no sooner had we breathed easily again than another panic took over: wedding pictures. Being so secretive about the marriage meant we had to organise our own pictures, so there we were, in Dixons, just on closing time, buying a reserve camera in case Scott's didn't work. Even then we were worried that something might still go wrong, so we invested in a Polaroid camera for instant snaps, just to be on the safe side. Neither of us would have been able to bear not having a record of what promised to be such a special and magical occasion.

We got home just before seven, thinking we would get our pre-wedding jitters under control with a relaxing evening on our own, when my cleaning lady turned up. She'd been due that afternoon, but had been away and had arrived home late. Seeing the suitcases in the hall, she asked: 'Are you going away?'

'Yes,' I said.

'Oh, I'll come and clean the house on Sunday then, while you're gone.'

'Oh, no,' I said. 'We'll be back by then.'

She gave me a funny look.

When the cleaning lady left, Alison Ritchie, our costume designer on *EastEnders*, phoned asking if she could pop round with something for Gloria Hunniford's sixtieth birthday mask and costume ball, which Scott and I were due to attend on Sunday. I wanted to scream, 'I'm getting bloody married tomorrow – I don't want to see anyone,' but I agreed because I didn't want to arouse suspicion.

Less than half an hour after Alison left, the doorbell rang again. This time it was Dale Winton. Dale never turns up without ringing first, but for some reason, he did that evening.

Normally, of course, I'd have invited him in, but this time I just stood on the stairs by the front door and looked at him blankly.

'Hello. What you doing here?' I asked.

'I was just passing, Bar. I thought I'd pop in for a cup of tea.'

'Oh, sweetheart,' I said, hurriedly. 'Scott and I are just getting ready to pop down to Brighton for the weekend. Can I take a raincheck?'

I felt awful being so discourteous to my dear friend, but I just couldn't have asked him in. By this time I was such a bag of nerves that I knew that once he came through the front door and we started rabbiting, I might well be tempted to confide in him.

After Dale continued on his way, would you believe it, Claire Whitely, my make-up lady on *EE*, phoned to talk about a new look for Peggy, followed by Paul Bennett ringing for a chat. Then finally Yvonne called, wanting to read me a long fan letter which needed an urgent reply. At that point we put on the answering machine! So much for the quiet evening Scott and I had hoped for to prepare ourselves.

At bedtime, Scott suddenly got superstitious and said he was going to sleep in the spare bedroom because it was bad luck to see the bride before the big day. That fact that he'd been with me most of the day already and all evening seemed to have escaped his attention. I dropped off quickly, which is rare for me, but at 2 a.m., I was woken by Scott opening the door: I'd fallen asleep with the TV and light on and he'd come in to turn them off. His superstition went out of the window and he joined me in bed for our last night as single people. Forty-five minutes later, he went back to the spare room, then he was off to the bathroom to be sick. He came back to me, but after an hour of tossing and turning he was up again. Poor Scott. He got in and out of one bed or the other five times during that restless night, but surprisingly, in the morning we both felt great.

Everything went smoothly. Gary Cockerill, one of the best make-up artists ever – he had made me look great for my album cover, for my appearance on *Parkinson*, and, of course, for my *Hall of Fame* – arrived to make me up and trim Scott's hair. He, too, was admirably discreet: if he suspected anything, he didn't show it, and he didn't ask one prying question. At 10.45 a.m., our regular driver, John Baverstock, took Scott to the hotel with our luggage and then came back for me. When I walked into the suite, it was everything I'd hoped for: there were beautiful silhouettes of English gentlemen on the walls, stunning Chinese vases, loads of flowers and two bottles of Cristal champagne. There was also a marvellous wedding present from the management: a wooden model of the hotel entrance, revolving doors and all.

Our only guests, Rita, Ronnie and Marsha, arrived at 12.15 p.m. and we all had a glass of the champagne to calm our nerves. Then Scott and I started taking pictures, giggling excitedly like a couple of kids. There had to be two registrars present and, shortly after 1 p.m., the senior registrar, Alison Cathcart, arrived with a young lady named Sam, who had been told of the wedding only half an hour before. Apparently, there had been stiff competition for the job; four other registrars had wanted it. Sam was evidently a big Carry On fan and had all the films on video. And as luck would have it, not only did she come from Brighton, but she was a cousin of our dear friend the late Brian Hall, who had been at Rita's house for dinner when I met Scott for the first time. What a small world it is.

Alison explained the procedure, asked us to sign some forms and then took Scott's parents and Marsha to a room further along the corridor where the wedding ceremony was to take place. 'Come along in your own time and make an entrance,' she said to Scott and me.

'Don't worry about that, dear,' I told her. 'I've been making entrances all my life.'

Scott and I each had a little champagne in our glasses. 'Let's finish this before we go,' I said. We clinked glasses and declared our love for each other, then I asked: 'Are you all right?' Those four little words were enough to topple Scott over the edge. His eyes immediately filled up and he lost control of his breathing. 'Don't, don't,' I said, feeling my own tears coming. Afraid that my make-up was about to run, I tilted my head. 'Please don't start all that, Scott. You'll set me off.' We got ourselves together, just, and went into the corridor where the hotel's duty manager, Adam Salter, was waiting to escort us to the ceremony. 'Thank you so much for choosing the Dorchester for your wedding,' he said.

As we walked along the corridor the doors of all the other rooms were closed and it was deathly quiet. When we went into our wedding suite, the little gathering, including the registrars, broke into spontaneous applause. I didn't dare look at Scott, because I knew that lovely impromptu gesture was just the sort of thing that would make him go. He was all right at the start, but with every wedding vow he uttered he made the strangest sound – a cross between an hysterical laugh and a cry that came out as a grunt – and I had to put my arm round him and hold him as he started sobbing. The registrar took her time, but Scott couldn't stop the tears from falling and, before my eyes, I saw his beautiful pale grey suit beginning to look as if he'd been caught in a shower. I caught myself wondering whether the salt might leave a stain. Scott was looking at me now, the tears rolling down his cheeks, and I started to cry, too, and, of course, that started his mum and dad and Marsha sniffling behind us. Poor Scott was in such a bad way that Alison had to ask Sam to hand him some tissues. As he dabbed his eyes, he managed a grin and remarked: 'Shouldn't this be the other way round?'

When the registrar asked if anyone knew any reason why we should not be married, I felt the need to crack a joke to break the tension. I looked at our three guests and laughed: 'Now you know why we didn't want anyone else here!'

As we left the wedding suite to go back to our room, the most surprising thing happened. A little old waiter appeared in the corridor and said, in what

Scott swears was a Portuguese accent, 'Sorry, I didn't realise. Carry On lady.' Then, suddenly all the bedroom doors that had been closed before opened one after another, like in a film, and a stream of chambermaids came out with their vacuum cleaners to get a look at me and say 'Good afternoon.' It was as if someone had phoned them all at the same time to say: 'They're on their way.'

Siobhan, the wedding co-ordinator, was very sweet. Her husband, Clive, was there with her and they took some photographs of us inside the room and on the balcony against the breathtaking backdrop of Big Ben and the Millennium Wheel. The registrars joined us and we had smoked salmon and prawn sandwiches with the second bottle of champagne.

At 2.45, there was a knock on the door. It was Adam Salter. 'The press are downstairs, asking us to confirm that you've got married,' he said. We were staggered. After all those cloak-and-dagger arrangements, it had taken less than an hour for someone to leak the news.

After everybody had left, around 3.30, Scott and I stood by the window, high above Park Lane, looking over Hyde Park, and it was the most wonderful feeling. The forecast had been for cold, wet weather, but the sun had been out for us all day and the temperature was in the seventies. Standing there with the man I loved, who was now my husband, the only thought I had was that this was the happiest day of my life. And with the help of the champagne we started singing Martine McCutcheon's hit song, adapting the words for ourselves: 'This is Our Perfect Moment'.

Now that the news was out, we felt we had to let people know we were married. We didn't want to speak to the papers ourselves, so Scott phoned a friend to call the press with a few details for the Sunday papers. I got a message to Barry, who had flown to New York that morning, and then I told Dale and Paul and my cousins, who were all equally flabbergasted but also highly delighted at our happy news.

At dinner in the evening, Scott and I sat at opposite ends of a ten-foot table and were served pâté, followed by roast beef, by two waiters. When they left, we toasted each other's happiness and reminisced about all the things that had happened to us on the long journey that had brought us to this point.

I was amazed at the coverage the Sunday tabloids gave the wedding. Each one put it on the front page *and* devoted two inside pages to it, even though they had no pictures of the occasion and we had given not one interview. But it was all lovely, positive stuff, and we were thrilled.

There were photographers outside the Dorchester as we left around lunchtime the next day, and two more, from the *Mirror* and *Mail*, waiting in the mews, predictably wanting to photograph Scott carrying me over the threshold. We declined to perform for the cameras, but I must say that they were very sweet and didn't push us in any way. I'm not saying that photographers are not respectful, but usually they want a particular picture and go all out to get it. These two just kept thanking and congratulating us, which I thought was lovely.

When we got in, the messages on the answerphone were endless. You wouldn't believe the number of reporters and feature writers who wanted an exclusive story for Monday's papers. Again, we declined: we just wanted to sit back on our own and enjoy our first full day as man and wife. Given the enormous press interest, we decided it wouldn't be fair to go to Gloria Hunniford's party at the Langan Hilton in Portland Place, a ten-minute walk away, so we left a message at the hotel apologising for our absence. But it wasn't long before Gloria was on the phone saying: 'You've got to come.' And then, half an hour later, her husband, Stephen, knocked on our door and gave us a note from Gloria. 'I won't hear of you not coming,' she had written. So we decided we should go after all.

When we left the house in our mask make-up, me in a black leather number and Scott in a tuxedo, another group of photographers were there. They, too, kept thanking us for letting them take pictures, and I understood why when our taxi arrived at the Langan Hilton. As Scott opened the door, three or four burly security guards converged on the cab, forming a shield round us with huge golfing umbrellas. At first we thought it must be raining, but then I heard one of the security guards screeching at waiting photographers. It made me angry and I said to one of the guards: 'What are you doing?'

'We're protecting you,' he said. 'The party's an *OK!* exclusive. We don't want anyone getting any pictures of how you're dressed.'

'You're too late, darling,' I told him. 'We've already had pictures taken at the house.'

I heard the photographer who had been denied a photo calling: 'Please can I have a picture, Miss Windsor?'

'Where are you from, then?' I asked him.

'The *Sun*.'

'Yes, that's fine. You can have one.'

So we stood there and posed for him. He thought he'd died and gone to heaven. And so did all his mates, because we'd given them a photo opportunity, too.

The head security guard ordered his men to remove their umbrellas and, as we walked into the hotel, he said, 'May I take this opportunity to apologise for that.' I appreciated the apology, because the whole business was quite frightening, and it made Scott and I realise that we had been right to get married in the way we did. Neither of us would have coped with all those shenanigans, especially on such an important occasion for us both, and we wouldn't have wanted to have subjected our friends to them, either, no matter how tempting the money was.

It was a great evening, not least because everybody made an effort to dress up in colourful costumes. I'd seen a lot of the guests – Paul Daniels and Debbie Magee, Bobby Davro, Brian Conley and many others – at a charity bash the previous week and they all said: 'You crafty so-and-so, you didn't let on to us.'

Gloria got up to make her birthday speech, but before she started, she said: 'I'd like to ask Barbara and Scott to join me so that we can all say congratulations.' I got all little-girlish and shook my head. 'No, Gloria, it's your night,' I told her. But we got the feeling that everyone wanted to wish us all the best, so we went up and joined her as everyone applauded and cheered. I said a brief thank you, and then Scott, who normally never says boo to a goose in public, suddenly took the microphone and announced: 'I must categorically deny, in front of all you people, that these vicious rumours that Barbara is pregnant are not true.' And he wasn't drunk either, just on a high, immeasurably happy and supremely confident.

Neither of us is the type to lie in bed when there are things to do, but that Monday morning we did – and we were still there at midday. It was pure luxury. But eventually the real world intervened: I suddenly remembered the jewellery and couldn't relax until I'd taken it back. Then we went shopping in Marks and Spencer, and of course the world and his wife kept coming up, offering congratulations and saying how pleased they were for us. We felt we were being swept along on a warm wave of genuine affection, and it was the most wonderful experience.

That evening, we had a lovely surprise: Scott's brother-in-law, Laurence, who had stayed behind with his three children on our wedding day, turned up unexpectedly and took us out for a Chinese meal. I was wearing old trousers, had no face on and was sporting a rash round my neck caused by a nickel necklace I'd worn to Gloria's party. I'm allergic to nickel and wouldn't have put it on if I'd known what it was made of. I wondered whether people might think Scott had tried to strangle me on our wedding night!

Michael Greco from *EastEnders* had phoned me that day to say how pleased he was for us both, and when I arrived at the studios on Tuesday, everybody else seemed thrilled – cast and management alike – and amazed that I'd managed to keep everything secret. 'If something is important to me, I can keep it secret,' I said. And that wedding was so, so important.

Steve McFadden was the only one who claimed not to have been surprised. 'I knew you'd do it like that,' he told me.

'I bet you were surprised, really.'

'No, honestly. I knew you would.'

I believed him. Steve is very deep. He doesn't say much, but he doesn't miss a trick.

33

IN THE SUMMER OF 2000 I HEARD THAT SOME OF THE CAST OF *EASTENDERS*, INCLUDING ME, WOULD BE GOING TO SPAIN FOR THREE DAYS TO FILM A SPECIAL EPISODE. I'd never been on location with the programme before, so it was something I was looking forward to, but when the shoot was extended to two weeks and scheduled for the beginning of July it created a bit of a headache for me. For one thing I really didn't want to be away from Scott for so long, and the timing also worried me. I was due to go to Buckingham Palace on 19 July to receive my MBE, and I'd been counting on being in London for fittings with Neil Cunningham for my dress and to buy all the accessories I needed. Now it looked as though it was all going to be a mad rush, which was the last thing I wanted. But there was nothing for it but to try to juggle everything.

Six of the cast – Roberta Taylor, who played Irene, and Gavin Richards, her husband Terry, Pam St Clement, Tony Caunter, Mike Reid and I – joined the crew at Luton Airport for our early-morning flight to Alicante, along with hordes of holidaymakers, who must have thought they were dreaming when they saw a band of EastEnders trooping in. We felt like we were on holiday ourselves when, like them, we had to sit in the airport for hour upon hour because our plane was delayed.

July was not an ideal time to be filming in Alicante. The country was experiencing a heatwave unusual even for Spain, and because the location was so crowded we had to do our exterior scenes at siesta time, the hottest part of the day, in the blazing sun. Normally it is only the exterior scenes that are filmed on location, with the interiors being shot on the set back at home, but for some reason it had been decided that this shoot should include interiors as well. So when I wasn't outside, plastered in Factor 30 and dodging the paparazzi, I was crammed into a ten foot-by-ten foot bedroom in Frank and Peggy's villa – along with two cameramen, a sound man, a lighting man and all their equipment, not to mention the enormous Mike Reid, all of us wilting in temperatures in excess of 100 degrees. It was so ridiculous that Mike and I kept getting the giggles because we couldn't believe what we were doing.

In spite of the discomfort we did enjoy ourselves. Scott came out for part of the time, so he and I didn't have to be apart for the whole fortnight after all, and it gave the cast a rare chance to socialise with each other over cocktails and nice dinners when we'd finished work for the day. People have the impression that the *EastEnders* actors all know each other well, but in fact at home we all come and go at different times and work on different parts of the set, so often you see very little of the people who aren't involved in the same scenes as you. There was an element of sadness too, because this was the last *EastEnders* shoot for Roberta – Irene would be staying on in Spain when everyone else returned to Albert Square – and it also introduced the storyline which would end in Mike Reid's departure.

As soon as I got back to London I dashed off to Neil Cunningham for a first fitting for the lovely pale peach dress I'd be wearing to Buckingham Palace. Then there were hat, gloves, handbag and shoes to be organised, plus an outfit for Scott, which meant negotiating the busy summer sales in between my *EastEnders* commitments. It was all a bit fraught, especially trying to buy gloves. My hands, like my feet, are tiny and I always have difficulty finding gloves to fit. I was beginning to get quite despondent, fearing that I was going to have to meet the Queen without them, when, at the tail end of a long shopping expedition, I trudged wearily into the glove department in John Lewis in Oxford Street, and the first thing I saw was the minutest pair of lacy gloves. Not only were they exactly the colour I wanted, but they were my size. 'These have been waiting for you,' said the sales assistant, and my eyes filled up as I suddenly remembered those same words being spoken to me long ago. I was thinking about my first pair of grown-up shoes, the red ones with the little heel my mother had bought me when I was about to go off on tour with *Love From Judy*. Mummy and I had walked up and down Oxford Street looking for the right thing without success, exactly as Scott and I had just been doing, and she had been on the point of giving up when we'd tried one last shop. The sales assistant there had said: 'I've got a lovely pair that have been waiting for you, little lady.' My life, it felt, had come full circle.

It had been a close-run thing, but after collecting my dress from Neil, by the eve of the big day I was at last ready to meet the Queen looking just as Mummy would have wished: Audrey Hepburn-cum-Grace Kelly. That night Scott and I went to bed at 9.30. The butterflies in my stomach were as bad as they'd been before my first *EastEnders* shoot. It was going to be a long and exciting day: after the presentation I was due to take part in the pageant to celebrate the Queen Mother's birthday. The alarm was set for 5.30 a.m. but I was awake before it went off. Scott didn't need to start getting ready until 7.30 or 7.45, so he said he would go into the other bedroom when Gary came to make me up at 6.45. But when I got out of the bath, Scott was back in our bedroom, all bright-eyed and bushy-tailed. 'I can't sleep,' he confessed. 'I want to be part of it from the word go, to savour the whole day.'

The weather had been dreadful, but outside in the mews that morning the sun was shining. On the doorstep, alongside my regular pint of semi-skimmed, there was a bunch of flowers from Tony Curtis the milkman, and George the gardener had arrived bright and early to make sure the window boxes were looking nice for the photographers. It was that bit of the East End in me, I suppose, anxious that the face the house showed to the outside world should be immaculate.

At nine o'clock, Barry, who was attending the ceremony with us, arrived in a beautiful, new, chauffeur-driven, silver Rolls-Royce from Jack Barclay in Berkeley Square. I felt great as I posed beside it for the photographers. As we got into the car, I noticed that Scott had a big handkerchief in his pocket. 'What's that for?' I asked.

'I'm not going to embarrass myself,' he said. 'If I'm going to start blubbing when you go up to get your award, I'm going to have to wipe my eyes.'

When we arrived outside the palace at 9.55, a policeman spotted me and said: 'Oh, Barbara, how lovely to see you. Get in this lane. You'll get in quicker and won't have to queue.' But despite his good intentions we got stuck. We didn't move an inch until 10.20 and were almost the last in. I was really on edge: we had to be in the quadrangle before 10.30, and I had visions of us not making it in time.

Inside the palace, a big, elderly policeman was directing the traffic. When he saw me, he said: 'This has really made my day. This must be my best day at the palace since ... I don't know ... since I was a young policeman and Charlie Chaplin came.' Tears sprang to my eyes. And to Scott's. And to Barry's. What a wonderful thing for him to say. 'May I shake your hand, Barbara?' he went on. 'To me, you are part of the royal standard, as much as the people who live in this place. You mean so much to us people.'

A fan of mine named Keith, who is a real sweetheart and follows me all over the place, has been a steward at Buckingham Palace for many years. He was waiting for us in the quadrangle, all suited and booted. 'I've told everybody you're coming,' he said, pointing up to a window. He'd lined up all the stewards and the maids there, and they were all waving.

One of them yelled out to me: 'Are you sober?'

'Sober?' I asked, puzzled. Then I remembered that the previous night on *EastEnders* Peggy had been paralytic!

Scott and Barry went to the Ballroom, where the ceremonies were being held, and I went with all the other MBE recipients to the adjoining Picture Gallery to await our calls, MBEs on one side, OBEs on the other. A Guards band in the Musicians' Gallery overlooking the Ballroom was playing lovely tunes from musicals like *My Fair Lady*. There were 120 of us in the MBE group, all kinds of different people from various walks of life, and there was the most marvellous spirit. Everyone seemed so pleased to see me, and we all became so friendly that I took a few telephone numbers! As we waited some of the ladies asked me to show them how to curtsey. Two of them were overcome by nerves and I took them to the loo, which gave me something else to think about as well. Because I am a performer people didn't expect me to be nervous, but I was. Very.

We watched proceedings in the Ballroom on TV screens in the Picture Gallery. On the stroke of eleven, four Yeomen of the Guard marched towards two thrones in the middle of the room. Then the Queen came in, with two Gurkha orderlies, an equerry and some palace officials, including the Master of the Household, and the band struck up the National Anthem. The Queen asked everyone to be seated, and the honouring of the knights and dames began.

I was relieved to see that Shirley Bassey, soon to be Dame Shirley Bassey, was wearing royal blue. Oh, good, I thought, we're not going to clash. I looked around to see if anyone else was wearing peach. Fortunately, only one lady was, and as it turned out, she was not called for her award at the same time as me. After the knights and dames, it was the turn of the OBEs. We MBEs had to wait and wait, but with the help of the strong camaraderie in our group, I was calmer by this stage. I'd befriended Mrs Peggy Wilson, a sweet little older lady, even tinier than me, who was to be honoured for services to her community in Hartley, Kent. She was very panicky about meeting the Queen, and I kept putting my arm round her and giving her a little cuddle to reassure her.

At last the MBEs were called, ten at a time, and I was glad to find that Peggy was in front of me, which meant I could look after her. 'Will I remember this?' she asked me.

'Of course, you will, sweetheart,' I said, giving her a hug.

There was a lady from the Lord Chamberlain's office checking names. 'I don't have to ask your name, do I, Barbara?' she said to me, adding that the man who normally did this job, who was on holiday, would be disappointed at having missed meeting me. Apparently he was a huge *EastEnders* fan.

At last my name was called and I walked forward with a huge grin on my face. As I approached the Queen the band began to play 'True Love' from the Bing Crosby and Grace Kelly film *High Society*. It felt very appropriate – 'True Love' was the inscription Scott and I had had engraved on our wedding rings.

The Queen looked absolutely fantastic, so pretty, and with a lovely figure. She never stopped smiling. I'd met her before, but there had been no indication then that she knew who I was, just a hello and a how are you. This time, though, she recognised me, and seemed to give me a lot of time. I felt so proud.

'Well, my goodness me,' said the Queen. 'Services to the entertainment business for a very long time.'

'Yes, ma'am.'

'How long would that be?'

'Fifty years this Christmas,' I told her.

She seemed amazed. 'You've been making people laugh for all those years? How wonderful!'

'Yes,' I said. 'But that's easy. I'm in a business I love with a passion. May I say thank you for this, ma'am?' I fingered my precious MBE. 'This is the cherry on the cake.'

The presentation over, I returned to the Picture Gallery to collect a box for my MBE, then did a quick interview for a palace reporter before going back to the Ballroom to sit in the area designated for medal recipients. I saw Scott sitting in the front row, facing the Queen, and mouthed: 'Did you enjoy it?' He gave me a discreet thumbs-up. He told me later how hard it had been for him to keep his composure. He'd smiled to keep the tears at bay and the smile had turned into a nervous giggle. Barry was trying to hold back the tears as well, and they both ended up giggling, feeling very self-conscious in the respectful hush of the Ballroom.

When I came out after the ceremonies had finished, I found a bunch of newspaper and TV journalists wanting to interview me. I hadn't expected all that. I said my bit about how proud I was, how wonderful it all was, and as the photographers snapped away, a couple of journalists asked Scott how he felt. 'The only way I can think of it,' he said, 'is that I feel like a proud father.' It sounded odd, but it was the most accurate description he could give, he said, of his incredible pride at his lovely lady getting this award. He was absolutely glowing.

We were about to leave when Shirley Bassey came out. I was very pleased to see her: as she'd met the Queen earlier than me I'd thought she must have been and gone. 'Congratulations, Barbara,' she said. 'And congratulations on getting married, too. Look at you, all in peachy pink – you look so pretty.' Because Shirley was now a dame, I curtseyed to her. It was a totally spontaneous gesture, but of course all the photographers were delighted, and that was the picture that made all the newspapers the next day.

Leaving Shirley to have her moment with the press, Scott, Barry and I got into the Rolls-Royce. Outside the palace gates, well-wishers waved to me and called out their congratulations. I got out of the car to have a chat with them. Quite a few tourists saw the crowd and rushed forward, their cameras clicking, even though they probably didn't have a clue who I was. Barry heard someone shout: 'Is she famous?'

'Famous?' said another person at the back. 'She's royalty. She's great, Our Babs.'

Scott and I went home to get ready for the Queen Mother's pageant. All I really knew about what I had to do was that I'd be driving past her in a car and was supposed to be representing the 1990s. I decided to wear a little denim jacket and pretty dress with very high-heeled shoes. I took off my Neil Cunningham frock to change, and then we suddenly realised we hadn't eaten all day – Scott is normally the one who organises our food, but in all the excitement neither of us had given it a thought.

We looked in the fridge and all we had were eggs, so we sat there eating fried egg sandwiches, washed down with a glass of pink champagne – me minus my dress but still wearing my hat and high heels!

Barry returned to collect us and take us back to the Mall. When we arrived it was jam-packed. There had already been two bomb scares, but the police were great, and allowed us through to the caravan where the participants were preparing for the pageant. I was greeted there by Dame Thora Hird.

'Hello, I'm Barbara,' I said.

'I know who you are,' she replied. 'I think you're more famous than me.'

Also there were actresses Liz Robertson, Patricia Hodge and Wendy Craig, all dressed in costumes representing different eras of the Queen Mother's life, and other celebrities taking part, including Sir Norman Wisdom, Jerry Hall and my friend Gloria Hunniford.

As Scott and Barry went off to take their seats someone from ITV asked me if I would do an interview with Kirsty Young. So at 5 p.m. I was standing there with Kirsty, my earpiece in, listening to a voice telling me, 'Any second now, Barbara,' when we were all asked to move back, and suddenly a fleet of limousines appeared, rolling slowly down the Mall. It was the Royal Family. We showbusiness people are used to the public calling and waving to us, but today the boot was on the other foot, and it was we who were the fans, cheering excitedly as the royals came by. Little Beatrice, Prince Andrew's daughter, waved to me, and so did Princess Anne, who knew me from when I presented her with a prize after she competed in *It's a Royal Knockout* several years ago. It was lovely, and there was the most wonderful birthday atmosphere.

The limousines were followed by the Queen's Dragoon Guards, Royal Hussars, Lancers and the Queen's Regiment. They all had to stop where Kirsty and I were waiting to do our interview. Just as we were about to start, one of the horses did its business pretty spectacularly just where we were standing. The steam rose up to our faces and the smell was awful. We couldn't move because of the cameras. The guard on the horse laughed. I laughed back and said, 'I'll get you for this!'

We went on air at last. 'Barbara, congratulations on the MBE you received today at the palace,' Kirsty said.

I told her how terrific it all was and then added: 'But look what we're standing in.'

'Yes, the horses have just been by,' she acknowledged, very politely.

After the interview I was to be driven past the Queen Mother in a green Morgan convertible. When the big moment arrived, I blew her a kiss and called out: 'God bless. Happy birthday!' She is such a sweet, wonderful woman, and seeing her standing there, beside a beaming Prince Charles, I was so overcome that the tears trickled down my face. As we drove on people were screaming and waving and shouting a mixed bag of greetings: 'Barbara!', 'Peggy!' and 'Carry On!'

In all the excitement on the return leg, my driver took a wrong turn and we ended up in a cul-de-sac. Four other cars followed us and we were well and truly blocked in. There was nothing I could do but get out and run. I had to laugh. When I got back to the parade, I saw Sir Norman Wisdom, who grabbed me and put me on his float, where we sat, not going anywhere, for two hours, signing autographs and having our photograph taken. Norman is just brilliant. He loves to clown around and play games with people, and although he is over eighty he wears you out. The theme of his float was 1960s films. It was an apt one for me, and I felt comfortable there.

When the parade was over I discovered that Barry, bless him, had booked a surprise dinner at the Ivy for the three of us, his mother, Celia, his partner, Richard, and our friends Paul Bennett and John Addy. Dale phoned from Spain to congratulate us – it was such a lovely evening. Everyone in the restaurant wanted to see my MBE, so Scott made me pin it on. I was so high on the day that I couldn't drink or eat anything much, and I was also aware that I couldn't stay out too late because I had to be up at 6.30 the next morning for *EastEnders*.

At Elstree the following day everybody was thrilled about my medal. The first person to come running up to me was Wendy Richard. 'Well, what's it look like?' she asked.

'What?'

'The MBE! Where is it?'

'At home,' I told her.

'You should have worn it today, Barbara.'

They were all so happy about it that it was almost as if they had been given it themselves. And in a way they had, because *EastEnders* must have played a significant part in the decision to honour me. I've been a well-known name for many of the fifty years I've been performing, but it is the award-winning soap that has made my face known to millions of people who might never have seen my nine Carry Ons or stage shows. I'd always felt I was more than just a busty blonde with a giggle and a wiggle, and I'm proud of the achievements that have demonstrated my versatility over the years. I was so pleased that Barry Burnett was able to be with me at the palace. Who knows where I'd be today if he had not taken me on and sung my praises high and low. And for the chance to play Peggy Mitchell I have to thank the BBC and *EastEnders* from the bottom of my heart.

I'm sure that some people will think I don't deserve my MBE. I can hear them saying: 'What has she done? A few lightweight films, some trivial TV comedies, a soap?' I can see their point – having read my life story, you now know that I've never had a high opinion of myself; that behind the super-confident showbiz smile, I'm riddled with self-doubt. But I do feel I've genuinely earned the recognition that medal symbolises. Others were honoured that Wednesday for serving the public in many, many different forms, and I've been doing the same, in my own way, for half a century. And it's clear, from the love affair I've enjoyed with the Great British Public throughout those years, that they appreciate it.

My one regret is that my mother did not live to come to the palace and see me receive my award. She would never have believed that her Babs would be honoured by the Queen herself. She would have been so pleased with me for choosing the right frock, the right shoes, everything, and so, so proud.

But Scott was there, and that meant the world to me. It was fitting that this wonderful, caring man who has shared the two most fulfilling and exciting years of my life should have been a part of the biggest accolade of all. Dear Scott is proud of his 'little lady', and I'm proud to be a real-life Mrs Mitchell. We've made it through the storms out on to the sunny side of the street, and everything we've got will go into keeping us there.

All of Scott. And all of me.

Index

Blackburn, Bryan 48–9, 81, 115
Blackman, Honor 128
Blaine, Vivian 30
Blair, Cherie 377
Blair, Lionel 332
Blankety Blank 397
Blok, Anthony 187, 188, 192, 193
Bloom, Johnny 62
Bluebirds 301
Blundell, Nigel 263
Blunkett, David 393
Bogdanov, Michael 239, 241
Bonnie (dog) 230, 258
Booth, Jimmy 69, 70, 74, 78, 88, 109, 110, 111, 112
The Boy Friend 132–4, 136
Boy George 391
Boyle, Katie 157
Brace, Bruce 49, 50, 51, 52, 58
Braden, Bernard 58
Bradley, Paul 359
Bradshaw, George 191
Bragg, Melvyn 290
Brahms, Caryl 126
Brambell, Mark 238
Brambell, Wilfrid 91
Brandon, Johnny 25, 27, 28, 29–30, 36, 37–8, 42–3
Brandreth, Gyles 239
Bresslaw, Bernard 109, 112, 145, 149, 156, 162, 250, 252–3, 255
Briggs, Johnny 28
Brooks, Mel 104
Brown, Georgia 45
Brown, June 321, 365
Bruce, Judith 117
Bruce, Judy 58
Bruno, Frank 389
Bryan, Dora 143
Bunnage, Avis 98
Burnett, Al 81, 82, 253
Burnett, Barry 253, 254, 264, 266,

277, 290, 292–3, 300–1, 302, 305–6, 321, 381, 392, 400, 409, 423, 429, 431–2, 434
Burnett, Roger 369
Burrell, Paul 382
Butterworth, Peter 145
Bygraves, Max 57, 79

C

Calamity Jane 184
Calhoun, Rory 121
Callow, Simon 392, 393
Cannon, Tommy 231, 389
Carby, Fanny 100
Carman, George 357
Carne, Judy 85, 87
Caron, Leslie 102–3
Carroll, Sue 340
Carry on Emmanuelle 179–80
Carry on Laughing 166–7, 168
Carry On Again Doctor 120, 123–4
Carry On Barbara 170, 171–2, 173
Carry On Camping 120–1
Carry On Cleo, Camping, Emmanuelle and Dick 350–1, 380–1, 384–5, 409
Carry On Columbus 254–5
Carry On Dick 157–8, 159
Carry On Doctor 119
Carry On Girls 140, 143, 144
Carry On Henry 130–1
Carry On London 140, 141–2, 145–8, 150, 156, 161–3, 164, 165–6
Carry On Spying 92, 94–6
Carson, Jean 25, 27, 116, 258
Carty, Todd 220
Cathcart, Alison 421, 422
Cattan, Slim 60, 67–8
Caunter, Tony 412, 427
Challis, John 271, 332
Charles, Prince of Wales 197
Charlesworth, Peter 45–6, 50–1,